D0092775

PENGUIN BOOKS

FLESH AND SPIRIT

Steven Ozment is McLean Professor of Ancient and Modern History at Harvard University. His nine books include *The Bürgermeister's Daughter* and *The Age of Reform,* the winner of the Schaff History Prize and a finalist for the National Book Award. He lives in Newbury, Massachusetts, with his wife and family.

FLESH and SPIRIT

Private Life in Early Modern Germany

STEVEN OZMENT

PENGUIN BOOKS

PENGUIN BOOKS
Published by the Penguin Group
Penguin Putnam Inc., 375 Husdon Street,
New York, New York 10014, U.S.A.
Penguin Books Ltd, 27 Wrights Lane, London W8 5TZ, England
Penguin Books Australia Ltd, Ringwood, Victoria, Australia
Penguin Books Canada Ltd, 10 Alcorn Avenue,
Toronto, Ontario, Canada M4V 3B2
Penguin Books (N.Z.) Ltd, 182–190 Wairau Road,
Auckland 10, New Zealand

Penguin Books Ltd, Registered Offices:
Harmondsworth, Middlesex, England

First published in the United States of America by Viking Penguin,
a member of Penguin Putnam Inc. 1999
Published in Penguin Books 2001

1   3   5   7   9   10   8   6   4   2

THE LIBRARY OF CONGRESS HAS CATALOGED THE HARDCOVER EDITION AS FOLLOWS:
Ozment, Steven E.
Flesh and Spirit: private life in early modern Germany/Steven Ozment.
p.   cm.
ISBN 0-670-88392-1 (hc.)
ISBN 0 14 02.9198 9 (pbk.)
1. Nuremberg (Germany)—Social life and customs—17th century.
2. Family—Germany—Nuremberg—History—17th century.   3. Behaim family.
4. Nuremberg—(Germany)—Social conditions—17th century.   5. Courtship—
Germany—Nuremberg—History—17th century.   6. Teenagers—Germany—
Nuremberg—History—17th century.   I. Title.
DD901.N92096   1999
943'.32404'08622—dc21   99–20914

Printed in the United States of America
Set in Berkeley Book
Designed by Patrice Sheridan

ACKNOWLEDGMENTS

THE YEARS SPENT RESEARCHING AND WRITING THIS BOOK would have been even longer without the assistance and support of numerous experts, colleagues, and friends. Manuscripts, illustrations, and vital information were generously supplied by the archivists and librarians of Nürnberg's German National Museum (Drs. Frfr. Andrian-Werburg, Schoch, and Löcher), City Archive (Drs. Schmidt-Fölkersamb and Bauernfeind), and Territorial Church Archive (Dr. Frhr. von Brandenstein). During my research at the Scheurl Archiv in the Nürnberg suburbs, Dr. and Mrs. Siegfried Frhr. von Scheurl were gracious hosts. Matthias Senger; Bruce Venarde; James Hankins; and Christopher Brown, who was also an outstanding research assistant in the Harvard Libraries, assisted with difficult German and Latin translations. Ben Kaplan, Ulrich Meyer, Ronald Rittgers, Samuel Schuepbach, Gerald Strauss, and Laura Smoller read and commented on chapters in progress. Berthold Frhr. von Haller answered questions pertaining to the Scheurl family, as did Doris Finley generally. Amanda Ozment filled some bibliographical holes. Mathias Beer was the first beyond my study to read and bless a chapter.

Lynn Chu and Glen Hartley proved again to be the best of

paladins, while Viking editor Carolyn Carlson persuaded an author who saw no superfluity in his manuscript to excise two hundred pages. Such safeguarding of author and manuscript actually began earlier: Andrea Ozment knew of all these things first.

Steven Ozment
Newbury, Massachusetts

CONTENTS

ACKNOWLEDGMENTS   v

INTRODUCTION   ix

Courtship, Marriage, and Early Parenthood   *1*

1. GETTING MARRIED: The Courtship of Lucas Friedrich Behaim and Anna Maria Pfinzing   3

2. BIRTH AND EARLY CHILDHOOD: The Three Sons of Christoph Scheurl and Katharina Fütterer   53

Teenagers into Adults   *133*

3. MOTHERING: Magdalena Römer Behaim and Her Eldest Son Paul   135

4. THE PRIVATE LIFE OF A TEENAGER: Sebald Welser's Semester in Louvain   192

5. FATHERS AND SONS: The Family Chronicle of Pastor Lorenz Dürnhofer   217

CONCLUSION   260

NOTES   269

INDEX   333

INTRODUCTION

SOMETIMES WHEN I LEARN THAT A FRIEND OR AN ACQUAINtance has married, or had a first child, I make a point of welcoming the newlyweds or the new parents to the great institution of the family, which, in my professional capacity as a historian, I assure them has saved civilization in the past and may be counted on to do so again in the future. Mine, however, is not a common reaction, nor a universally held historical view of the family. Today, the mention of the family over time conjures up two popular and contradictory images, one inspiring naive admiration, the other harsh condemnation. The first envisions a large, bustling, porous household of parents, children, servants, and kin united in work and play, while the second sees a cold, impersonal household ruled by an exacting *paterfamilias* who inspires fear and trembling in its members.

Today historians sharply distinguish the preindustrial household—that is, the family as it existed by and large before the nineteenth century—from the modern household we know today.[1] The family of the past is portrayed as predominantly a work station and small manufacturing plant, with little distinction between home and workplace. Parents and children were not yet its defining core, but only one of several groups constituting a larger household, each and every member of which were treated equally as "family." And as befitted its

alleged assembly-line structure and organization, the relationships
among household members, even those most closely associated by
blood and marriage, were by modern comparison impersonal and
businesslike, not yet deeply emotional or sentimental.

It is the argument of *Flesh and Spirit* that the family of the past was
neither as wholesome as the romantics portray it, nor as cruel as the
cynics suspect. Nor were its structure and internal life as different
from those of the modern family as both sides—the one intending to
praise it, the other to damn it—also maintain. No less a fiction is the
popular stark contrast between the "traditional" and the "modern"
family. The popular division of the family into distinct preindustrial
and postindustrial types—the one hierarchical, patriarchal, unsenti-
mental, and authoritarian, the other communal, egalitarian, affectionate, and democratic—is another rhetorical round in the recurring
battle between the ancients and the moderns. It tells us little that is
factual and accurate about the evolution of the family over the last
five centuries. These one-sided contrasts and sweeping generalizations about families past and present conceal the one incontestable
feature of family life since at least the fifteenth century: its sophisti-
cation and diversity in every age and culture. Those arguing otherwise have at best exaggerated the differences between past and
present, while at worst they have virtually demonized our ancestors.
Truth be told, the more deeply the family life of the past is
probed, the more "modern" the preindustrial family is discovered to
have been and the more "traditional" the modern family appears to
be. Notwithstanding the changing socioeconomic, political, and cultural milieus that necessarily give the family a different *public* face in
every age, the family has had a remarkably stable history—its basic
structure and routine a rock in the ever-changing sea of civilization,
its private life as diverse and complex in the late fifteenth century as
in the late twentieth.

When dealing with a topic as multifaceted as family life, we are
best advised to develop our portrayals in as direct a dialogue as possible with the subjects themselves. An effort is here made to view
both the family and the larger world around it through the eyes of
individual household members, and not in terms of gross scholarly

generalizations about the polities, societies, and cultures of the past.
→A family is first and foremost the product of a family and only secondarily, although certainly no less profoundly, that of a larger polity, society, and culture. In the very first instance, a family reflects not the
state, the Church, or society at large, but a peculiar private world
that has been in existence for generations. In addition to the imperatives created by larger forces around it, a family also inherits and
generates its own powerful imperatives. Its members, who remain
unique individuals, not only interact with one another in the daily
routine of the household, but they also build bridges to other families and social institutions through courtship and marriage, parenthood and child rearing, the hiring of workers, the education and
employment of offspring, and the sending of new generations into
the world.

From this point of view, the family has been at one and the same
time an eccentric and a normative institution, both internally creative and shaped from without. What happens within its walls leaves
the most lasting of marks on those who dwell therein. It is in the
family that the individual first learns to resist, accommodate, and
amend the seemingly insuperable forces of nature and culture. [A
person's first and most formative encounters are those with nur-
turing parents and siblings, nurses, nannies, and servants, guardians
and relatives, family friends and business associates—and only
secondarily with a mammoth, conforming, official public world
beyond the door of the family house.] And that small familial world—
on the one hand, closed and still, on the other, open and rushing—
possesses a powerful force and logic of its own that are neither
derived from nor necessarily serve as feasible models for society at
large.

For all its hierarchy and patriarchy, that same family has been the
nonconformist's best friend and protector. It is the one place where
first names are not forgotten and undeserved forebearance can be
counted on. There, one does not derive status and importance by re-
flecting a peer group, or by having associations with larger external
institutions. One makes it there on one's own and by the kindness of
inmates who know one all too well.

The stories recounted here begin in the late fifteenth century, when, for the first time, the right sources became available in sufficient quantity and quality to do justice to family life in both its private and public spheres.[2] Over the sixteenth and seventeenth centuries, urban patrician and burgher families amassed a variety of personal records—from account books, diaries, and letters to diplomas and physical relics (for example, locks of hair and umbilical cords)—documents that survive today in state, local, and private archives and through which a family's story can be deeply told many centuries later.

[The attempt is made here to illumine the life cycle of the family in these early centuries, from its origins in courtship and marriage to the sending forth of a new adult generation.] Because one family could no more do justice to each phase of that cycle then than a single family could do today, our study draws on the private records of five families—three merchants, a lawyer, and a cleric—over a century and a half. Each was chosen for its ability to document as fully as possible the inner life of the urban family during at least one stage of that cycle. All five families had means and power, although not every member enjoyed or exercised such privileges equally. Nor did the social standing of these families confine them to a narrow stratum of associations or spectrum of life experience. Beyond the household, they shared a common mass culture as well as one that was special and apart. [They feted, honored, and befriended the lowly as well as the mighty, opening their houses both to those who served them and those who could command them.]

In an effort to provide a rounded story of that distant age from the perspective of these domestic hubs, each narrative also takes into account the extension of the subjects' lives into the public world around them—their careers and travels, associations and achievements, conflicts and failures—in a word, the lessons, bounty, and scars they also brought home from the outside world.

All of the featured families are Nürnbergers, citizens of what was then one of Europe's great merchant and intellectual capitals. "Without Nürnberg, no fairs," was a popular German saying in the fifteenth century when the wealthy Franconian city sparkled as the "Venice of the north." "Truly the kings of Scotland should wish to live as well as the middling burghers of Nürnberg," wrote visiting Italian Humanist Enea Silvio Piccolomini after viewing the city's grand burgher houses.[3] Founded originally as a royal military base, Nürnberg had by the twelfth century become a model trading center. There, twelve major trade routes crossed. The city's oldest surviving index of master artisans (1363) lists fifty different trades and 1,227 masters. Fourteenth-century Nürnberg possessed Germany's oldest paper mill, and in the fifteenth century, it had a printing press and coined its own money.[4]

Germany's leading educators, artists, and theologians are also to be found there, not a few of them natives. The first German poet laureate of the Holy Roman Empire, twenty-eight-year-old Vienna-trained German Humanist Conrad Celtis (1459–1508), was crowned on the city's citadel by Emperor Frederick III. Celtis's equally famous friend, city physician Hartmann Schedel (1440–1514), a world traveler and collector of antiquities, created what some consider to be the crowning achievement of Nürnberg Humanism, the *World Chronicle* of 1490, an attempt both to tell and illustrate the history of humankind from its beginnings to the present. Although often derivative and inexact, Schedel's work gave Europeans their fullest representations of the known world's cities and peoples.[5] Another native son, Wilibald Pirckheimer (1470–1530), famously led the second generation of German Humanists. In 1525, Martin Luther—together with his protégé Philip Melanchthon (1497–1560), grandnephew of Germany's leading Christian Hebraist (Johannes Reuchlin) and the author of the first Lutheran creeds—dined at the great table in Pirckheimer's patrician mansion opposite the famous "Beautiful Fountain" that still dominates Nürnberg's Market Square. It was Pirckheimer's fierce satire of Luther's great opponent Johannes Eck that moved the powerful Ingolstadt theologian to attach Pirckheimer's name to the papal bull that proclaimed Luther a heretic (June 15, 1520).[6]

In the first half of the sixteenth century, Nürnberg stood at the center of both Germany's artistic renaissance and its religious reform. Home to Germany's greatest painter Albrecht Dürer (1471–1528) and the famous shoemaker/poet Hans Sachs (1494–1576), it was the first city officially to adopt the Reformation (1525) while continuing to be a frequent site of imperial diets (legislative assemblies of the estates of the Holy Roman Empire). When Melanchthon visited newly reformed Nürnberg, he praised the city as another Athens[7] and lent his expertise to the creation of a Humanistic gymnasium, or secondary school, whose studies were based on the classics.[8] There, he also feasted on a main course of pig's head, rump roast, trout, chicken, capon, pike, boar, and partridge with a select group of civic and religious leaders at a banquet hosted by the city's lead lawyer and diplomat, Christoph Scheurl.[9]

Initially, Nürnberg's trade and wealth were little affected by the discovery of America and the opening of new Far Eastern trade routes. By the second half of the century, however, its sparkle had dimmed as Atlantic seaboard trade grew at the expense of that in the southern and eastern Mediterranean, where Nürnberg was better positioned geographically to profit. Waning pride in craftsmanship and moral laxity were widely reported with the shrinkage of the city's wealth. In addition to increases in public drunkenness, lewdness, and violent assaults, local glaziers were said to pass off Bohemian glass for good Venetian at the latter's price, while city carpenters deceptively glued painted paper onto worm-eaten woodwork. On the other hand, Englishman William Smith, a resident in the city for almost a quarter century, could praise Nürnbergers to Lord Burghley in London near the century's end. In an official report to the crown, he described the city as impeccably ordered and its inhabitants honest—a place where no dung hills stood on the streets, or "urine or others" were thrown out of house windows and doors before 10 P.M., and should any man lose his purse, ring, or bracelet he might confidently expect to have it returned to him in short order.[10]

The family in these early centuries was already an integrated household centered around parents and children. Within its walls maids, servants, apprentices, laborers, wet nurses, and needy relations lived, or regularly visited. The core or nuclear family at the center of the household was then as varied in structure and composition as it is today. There were the original and continuous, blended, and single-parent families—examples of each take center stage in different chapters of our study. The original and continuous family consisted of two parents, both of whom were spared an early death and lived together for a long period, if not a lifetime. In the blended family, at least one partner was in a second marriage and, if not already a parent, likely a stepparent as he or she also looked forward to becoming a parent again[As for single parents, widowers with children almost always remarried quickly. One example in our study was thrice married and the father of eighteen, while a second counted twenty-three children by two wives.]Widows with children, on the other hand, often preferred to remain such, rearing surviving offspring with the assistance of paternal and maternal relatives, who were appointed to act as official guardians by the husbands before the latters' deaths. As subsequent correspondence with their children makes clear, those widowed mothers reared them with no lack of competence and authority.[11]

[The families who are the subjects of this book were mostly well-to-do, and in every instance played an influential role in either local political or religious life.]This study, however, is about the ordinary lives of these extraordinary people. While their public activities in the larger world are also addressed and a full story told of each, the focus remains on those segments of a family's life that reveal, both for itself and for the times[the inner life of the family.]

We first meet an engaged couple, Lucas Friedrich Behaim and Anna Maria Pfinzing (chapter 1), whose courtship has been preserved both in letters the bridegroom wrote to his bride and in correspondence he had with a colorful cast of characters, some of whom assisted the marriage plans, while others impeded or tormented them. The couple's exchange of secret vows, a puzzling conflict between the father of the groom and prominent members of the family of the bride, and behind-the-scenes conniving and diplomacy by the matriarchs of both camps reveal the surprising complexity of early modern courtship.

A second couple (chapter 2), Christoph and Katharina Scheurl, were childless through ten failed pregnancies, spread over thirteen years of marriage, before the birth of a live, surviving son. By contemporary measure, they were quite old (he fifty-one, she forty-one) when they became parents. In a century when serial pregnancy and too many children seem to have been the rule, new light is cast on conception, childbearing, and child rearing when the parents involved turn out to be barren, driven to extreme measures to gain offspring, and aware that, due to their age, their time with them will be abbreviated. The happy result of these sad circumstances for the modern historian is a surviving family archive containing perhaps the most detailed first-hand account of parent–infant/child relations in the sixteenth century.

Our third story (chapter 3) follows the efforts of a widowed mother—faced with the rearing of eight dependent children—to discipline and humanize a thoroughly spoiled yet charming eldest son. Paul Behaim was Magdalena Römer Behaim's third child, who, at seventeen, departed home for Italy to finish his preparation for a political and mercantile career, on the success of which the entire family depended for its future livelihood. Before returning home at twenty, Paul spent two and a half years and an unconscionable amount of scarce family income pursuing his studies and the pleasures of Italian cities. Turning him back north proved a long and difficult task. The confrontation with his mother and two older sisters, who were far kinder to him than the Italians, forced him to take his first, reluctant and grudging, steps into adulthood.

By contrast, Sebald Welser's passage (chapter 4) was bold and confidently pursued. A wealthy Lutheran who kept the works of his religion's namesake on his bed stand, he turned twenty while living in deeply Catholic Louvain, where he had gone to finish his legal studies. He arrived there at an epochal turning point in the political and religious struggle of the Belgian and Dutch provinces to oust the long-standing Spanish army of occupation. Tethered neither to a mother nor to guardians, and not at all strapped for money, he could study or explore as he pleased. The danger and excitement of the times were clearly animating, for he was soon caught up in the political resistance, an activity of which the founder of his faith would by this time have approved. Yet he also boldly experimented, to all appearances freely and earnestly, with local Catholic religious culture in ways that would have rolled Martin Luther over in his grave.

How did the passage from one's teens to adulthood fare when a prominent father directly orchestrated and scrutinized it? Lorenz

Dürnhofer (chapter 5) was for twenty years the pastor of Nürnberg's St. Giles's Church and a leader of the embattled minority liberal wing of the conservative post-1560s Lutheran world. Twice married, he was the father of twenty-three children, on two of whom he especially doted: the first surviving son of each marriage. The eldest, his namesake, proved to be a willful failure at everything he tried, except his father's patience. The younger followed docilely and successfully in his father's footsteps, as did also the second daughter from the first marriage. Before his father's death, however, the first—failed—son also made a success of his life, finding the right occupation and making the marriage he wanted. The grandchildren of the marriage became a joy to their grandfather in his last years, and one of them bore his grandfather's and father's name (Lorenz). However, as happens in dysfunctional relationships even after their repair, that name was given to the boy in such a way that it would always call attention to the wounds Pastor Dürnhofer and his eldest son had inflicted—the former by high expectations, the latter by poor achievement—on one another over the years.

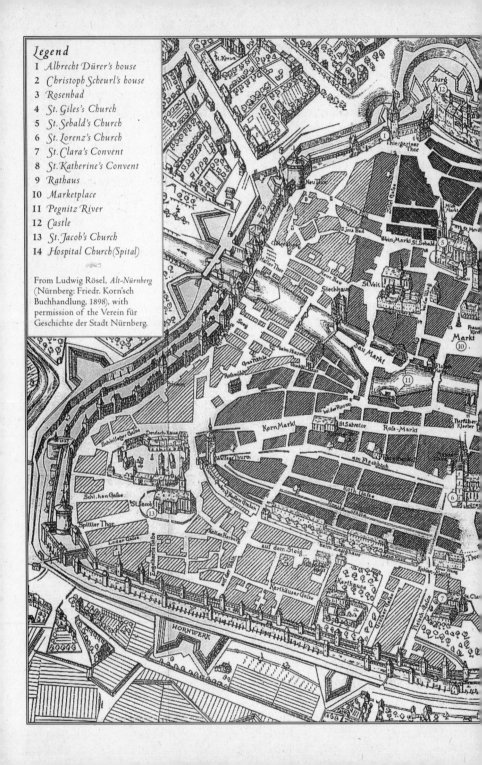

Legend

1 Albrecht Dürer's house
2 Christoph Scheurl's house
3 Rosenbad
4 St. Giles's Church
5 St. Sebald's Church
6 St. Lorenz's Church
7 St. Clara's Convent
8 St. Katherine's Convent
9 Rathaus
10 Marketplace
11 Pegnitz River
12 Castle
13 St. Jacob's Church
14 Hospital Church (Spital)

From Ludwig Rösel, *Alt-Nürnberg*
(Nürnberg: Friedr. Korn'sch
Buchhandlung, 1898), with
permission of the Verein für
Geschichte der Stadt Nürnberg.

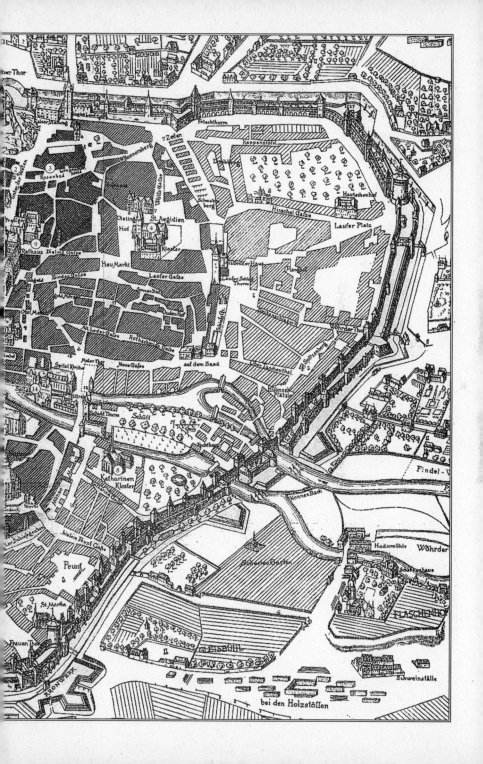

PART ONE

Courtship, Marriage, and Early Parenthood

1

GETTING MARRIED

The Courtship of Lucas Friedrich
Behaim and Anna Maria Pfinzing

IN JUNE 1612, LUCAS FRIEDRICH BEHAIM (1587–1648), AT TWENTY-five, returned to his hometown of Nürnberg after four years of intermittent "bachelor journeying." This customary period of travel and study in foreign lands capped the formal education of young Germans. In addition to broadening their knowledge and skills, and allowing them to make promising contacts for the future, the bachelor journey was also a last hurrah for unfettered youth, who thereafter settled into adulthood and a professional life. Lucas was the only surviving child of wealthy wholesale merchant and Tyrolean copper mine developer Paul Behaim II (1557–1621)[1] and Ursula Sitzinger (d. 1591), the first of his father's three wives.[2] In May 1612, Lucas and two well-to-do peers had completed a whirlwind tour of the Near East, Italy, and France—ten adventurous months abroad that brought down the final curtain on what had been for each a charmed childhood and youth.

Now educated and widely traveled, Lucas returned to a Nürnberg that was no longer the great trading and manufacturing center it had been in the sixteenth century. Located on the Pegnitz River not far from the Main (north and west) and the Danube (south), the thickly walled imperial city controlled twenty-five square miles of surrounding countryside and was a major crossroads for European

Hans Sebald Behaim

¶ Zart frewlein aller eren werd
Solch grosse schön/züchtig geberd
Von frawen leib nie ward geboren
Des halb hab ich euch auß erkoren
Zu eim bülen in trew vnd eren
Ewig mein freud mit euch zu meren
Vnd ist mein bit/mich jungen man
In solcher maß auch lieb zu han.

¶ Junckherr ich kan euch nichts zu sagen
Doch wil ich euch auch nichts abschlagen
Wann ich mein selbs nit mechtig bin
Wil auch nicht folgen eigem sin
Sonder wie dann billich sol sein
Rath haben mit den freunden mein
Eygner sin/vnd handeln vnbedacht
hat offt groß rew vnd schaden bracht.

trade going in all directions, especially to and from Italy and the Mediterranean. The Behaims had been successful merchants since the thirteenth century, carting their wares north and south, and they owned lucrative copper mines in the Tyrol as well. Trade created great wealth not only for them but for many others as well, and that wealth was still visible at the turn of the century. In 1568, 416 burghers, or 6–8 percent of households, possessed taxable wealth in excess of 5,000 gulden, and 240 of those exceeded 10,000. For the year 1549, Lucas's grandfather, Paul Behaim I (1519–1568), recorded household expenses of 2,365 gulden, which included two maids, a servant, a cook, and a very conspicuous first marriage, alone costing 570 gulden.[3]

A Nürnberg Couple Wooing

Tender Miss, to whom every honor is due,
Beauty so great and bearing so chaste
Was never before born of woman's body.
For this reason, I have chosen
To court you faithfully and honorably,
And eternally to increase my joy by being with you.
I pray that you also hold me,
Young man that I am, equally dear.

Young lord, although I can promise you nothing,
I also do not want to deny you anything.
Because I am not my own master,
I will not follow my own mind,
But rather, as it is right to do,
Take counsel with my family.
For careless thought and action
Has often brought great regret and misfortune.

Hans Sebald Behaim, "A Nürnberg Couple Wooing," in *Max Geisberg: The German Single-Leaf Woodcut: 1500–1550*, Vol. I, rev. and ed. Walter L. Strauss (New York: Hacker Art Books Inc., 1974), p. 226. (By permission of Abaris Books.)

More than half of the city's households were inhabited by artisans representing 277 different crafts and trades, which produced everything from playing cards to tobacco products. At the top of the artisan wage scale, journeymen in the cloth trade, working a 13-hour day, might earn 100 gulden a year. The city physician and schoolmaster received basic salaries of 50 or 60 gulden along with free housing within the city, while lawyers for the city council commanded between 300 and 500. Comparatively high minimum property requirements for the purchase of citizenship (50 gulden for a linen worker, 200 for dyers and butchers) kept the very poor outside the walls. In 1561, 12 percent of households, including that of Lucas's father, were headed by widows.[4]

At the other end of Nürnberg's socioeconomic spectrum was Sebastian Welser, fabled merchant grandfather of Sebald (chapter 5) and the city's richest man in the sixteenth century, leaving propertied wealth of 140,000 gulden at his death in 1567. That legacy pales, however, when set against that of Nürnberg's absolute richest man in these centuries, merchant Bartholomäus Viatis (1538–1624), whose career attests to the social mobility available to the city's most diligent and lucky. An émigré Venetian, Viatis apprenticed with a Nürnberg merchant for seven years, beginning at age thirteen, and after spending four more in Lyon, he secured a base for his own long-distance trade by marrying a Nürnberg merchant's widow, going on to accumulate a fortune of 1,125,341 gulden by his death in 1624.[5]

Money was also to be very much on Lucas's mind in the months ahead, as he fell in love and took the solemn first steps toward marriage and the creation of a new family of his own. The mother he had lost at four had left him an inheritance that, together with his father's wealth, might have guaranteed him independence for life under ordinary circumstances. However, his mother's early death (April 15, 1591) after eight years of marriage brought an immediate legal challenge of his father's custody of that inheritance by her brother (Lucas Sitzinger, Jr.), who continued to contest it during the years his nephew was entering his majority (1601–1608).[6] Because Ursula Sitzinger had died young and four-year-old Lucas was the only surviving child, her brother evidently believed, tenuously at law, that a portion of the maternal inheritance should revert back to her family.[7] Annoying as this must have been for both father and son, the uncle's enterprise, or greed, was not to be the greatest obstacle to Lucas's access to resources normally due one in his position. The greater threat rather came from his father's own highly prolific subsequent marriages.

A scant three months after Ursula Sitzinger's death (July 1591), Paul Behaim married Rosina Paumgartner (d. 1610), who warmly embraced her four-year-old stepson as if he were her very own, which is exactly how Lucas always thought of her. She embraced his father even more warmly, bearing eight half siblings—three brothers and five sisters—by the time of her death. Although none

of those siblings had any claim to Lucas's maternal inheritance, the
demands of so large a second family caused his father to disburse
that legacy to him only slowly and niggardly, charging against it expenditures he would otherwise have paid himself. By law, fathers
managed their sons' maternal and family inheritances, theoretically
having "use" of both until their death. Lucas would be twenty-seven
before he gained sole control of one-half of what his mother had
left him.[8]

His father's third marriage to Maria Baier (d. 1641) in 1611
brought still more grasping half siblings into Lucas's life, five in total,
with three surviving into adulthood, beginning with Stephan Carl in
1612. If, in his teens and twenties, Lucas was "big brother" to the
children of his father's second family, he became in his thirties and
forties a surrogate father to those of his father's third, acting as their
official guardian throughout their minor years after his father's death
in 1621 left him the male head of household.[9]

The End of Youth

Such matters were, of course, far from his mind when Lucas returned home to Nürnberg in June 1612. By then, he had actually
been away from home for the greater part of fifteen years, beginning
in 1597, when, at ten, he had taken residence in nearby Altdorf to
begin his formal schooling. There he would spend the next ten years
(1597–1607) in the recently founded (1578) gymnasium and the
academy that quickly developed around it.[10] In addition to a basic
arts curriculum, which included the study, in Latin, of philosophy,
ethics, law, politics, history, and the classics, Lucas devoted himself
to music, becoming by his graduation an expert musician and in his
later years a major patron of the school's music program. As Altdorf
was only a short wagon ride away from Nürnberg, Lucas continued
to maintain close contact with his family throughout these formative
years, routinely sending his laundry home each week to his stepmother, who promptly returned it, usually with a treat.[11]

In the summer of 1608, Lucas, at twenty-one, departed Bavaria for the first time, destined for the universities of Poitiers and Angés, where he studied French and immersed himself in the local culture.[12] The death of his stepmother in April 1610 after the delivery of her tenth child, forced a premature return home to assist his father in the busy Behaim household. It was a summons Lucas obeyed reluctantly, not arriving until December, to be greeted by perhaps five of his eight half siblings: Susanna, 10, Apollonia, 7, and newborn Magdalena, for sure, and very likely also Rosina, 14, and Maria, 12, although the latter were old enough to enter domestic service outside the home.

Happily for Lucas, the interruption of his journeying would be shorter than he expected. That was due to his father's fast-developing relationship with widow Maria Baier, a relative of his second wife,[13] who became Lucas's new stepmother in April 1611. Her marriage to his father made it possible for him to resume his wandering, now in Italy, after only a five-month hiatus. By August, he and his companions—Nürnbergers Rudolf von Bünau and Tobias Adam—were in Venice, where they hastily grabbed three suddenly open places on an English ship bound for Constantinople. News of plague there, received at sea, forced the ship to change its destination, however, turning a journey already undertaken on impulse and without parental permission into the adventure of a lifetime. Sailing via Crete and Cyprus to Tripoli and Jaffa, the three reached Jerusalem by late 1611.[14]

Upon their return to Venice in February 1612, they learned of the death of Emperor Rudolf II and the imminent election and crowning of a new emperor—always a spectacle, and one the three did not want to miss. The reign of the Jesuit-trained Rudolf (1576–1612) had been remarkable for its failure to maintain the tenuous peace between Catholics and Protestants that had existed in the empire since the landmark religious peace of Augsburg (1555), which had allowed the ruler of a land to determine its religious creed (*cuius regio, eius religio:* his realm, his religion). A melancholy man who suffered bouts of insanity as he aged, Rudolf neglected his political responsibilities in favor of patronizing a vibrant court culture in Prague, where he spent the last decade of his life in seclusion.

However, it would have taken a King Solomon to keep the two sides at peace in the later decades of the sixteenth century. For, contrary to earlier agreements, which forbade high Catholic clergy who converted to Protestanism from taking their bishoprics and dioceses with them, precisely that had happened.[15] Rudolf's father, Emperor Maximilian II (1564–1576), had addressed this problem more effectively than his son by quietly encouraging compromise and cooperation between princes of different religious confessions caught in such difficult situations. Rudolf, on the other hand, sought to revive, after decades of neglect, the so-called ecclesiastical reservation protecting Catholic property, going so far as to convert forcibly the Protestant cities of Aachen and Donauwörth back into the Catholic fold. By the turn of the century, neither the parties directly affected nor the national Protestant leaders could tolerate such actions.[16] Lutheran Nürnberg became engaged in this long-running dispute on the Protestant side, joining the militant Protestant Union in 1609, the year after its founding under the leadership of the Calvinist Elector Palatine.

With the election in 1612 of new Emperor Mathias (r.1612–1619)—the childless Rudolf's hated younger brother, whom he tried to bar from the succession—there was hope that a peaceful settlement of religious differences might occur. Although also a devout Catholic, Mathias favored negotiation with the Protestant estates. However, the aging Mathias, who was fifty-five when Germany's seven electoral princes voted him emperor, also became preoccupied with court life and proved himself incapable of mediating between the two now deeply divided sides. At his death seven years later (1619), the childless emperor would be succeeded by his cousin Archduke Ferdinand, an ominous change of direction, for he had forcibly restored Catholicism within his own lands.[17]

In the months before Lucas arrived home, that gloomy prospect had not been foreseen. In November 1611, the electoral princes of the empire convened in Nürnberg to discuss matters of succession and religious peace in light of Emperor Rudolf's rapidly failing health. The royal delegates spent a week in the city, during which they alternated meetings with banqueting, hunts, and jousts, in the midst of which they declared Mathias the new Roman king and, as such, successor to the imperial throne. With each elector bringing along his own household, the city teemed with thousands of visitors and horses, among them a great number of nonelectoral princes, prelates, dukes, lords, and foreign diplomats who took part in the negotiations. To contemporaries, it must have seemed that the entire Holy Roman Empire had descended upon Nürnberg for one last hurrah before the conflict that would become the holocaust of the Thirty Years War (1618–1648).[18]

Learning in Venice of Rudolf's death and the imminent election of a new emperor, Lucas and his friends—all Lutherans—hoped to return home in time to join the Nürnberg delegation to Frankfurt am Main for the new emperor's crowning. Although they believed that event still to be many months away, it now became a powerful inducement for the three to set a sure, if circuitous, course for home. Lucas immediately wrote his father to confirm their plans to attend the coronation. Meanwhile, he and his companions, determined to see as much of the world as they could before their bachelor days ended, set out for Lyons, where they arrived in May, still hoping to dash through Paris, Amsterdam, and even London before turning homeward. However, learning in Lyons that the election and crowning of the new emperor would likely occur before the end of the month, they departed immediately for Nürnberg.

As it turned out, Mathias was officially elected on June 13 and ceremonially crowned two weeks later in Frankfurt am Main, with Lucas and his friends comfortably in attendance. Among the events surrounding the coronation was the knighting of young patricians, among them Lucas himself, an honor he memorialized seven years later in a small painting commissioned to stand with six others as decorations on an organ he had specially made.[19] While en route from Bohemia to Frankfurt, the future emperor and his wife, accompanied by a royal train of 135 coaches, 636 horses, and 1,500 attendants, stopped over in Nürnberg, where they lodged on May 15 with the Imhof brothers on Egidienberg. The royal party also made a grand entry into the city on its return trip to Bohemia after the crowning. Nürnbergers greeted Emperor Mathias with bells and cannons, surely a pleasing sight for this ruler who would come to be known for his love of spectacles.[20]

While these days were a new beginning for the emperor, they were the end of youth for Lucas and his friends. Having had their years of bachelor travel and play, males of their age (Lucas was now twenty-six) and social class were expected at last to marry and settle down. While many appear to have looked forward to that day, few wanted to have it arrive before they had wrung every possible adventure and pleasure out of unfettered youth. While that may have been as true of Lucas as it was of his peers, it is an issue he did not, unfortunately, directly address. His half-brother Georg (1593–1615), their father's third son, did so at length, however, and very instructively for the times.

At twenty, Georg had tasted military life while on two imperial missions, the first as a page to a regent and the second as a stall master. He shared the contemporary male consensus that military exploits and a good marriage were the only sure paths to honor and wealth,[21] and while intending to pursue both wholeheartedly, he wanted first to exhaust his youth in the quest for glory and honor. However, as no significant military campaigns lay on the horizon in 1614, he begged his father to allow him to spend the last years of his youth as his brother Lucas had done, traveling freely in Italy, France, or the Netherlands.

Unfortunately for Georg, his father was then facing large expenditures on the youthful marriages of his eldest daughters,[22] and for that reason, he instead sent Georg to apprentice in the family mines in Kitzbühl, where he would learn the family business from mining the ore to keeping the books. If that news was not disappointment enough for an aspiring cavalier, the further announcement of his father's intentions to arrange a marriage for him within that very year was received by the son as a virtual death knell.

Facing the premature end of his youth, yet convinced that he could "accomplish more with a pistol and a dagger than with a quill,"[23] Georg begged anew his father's leave to travel, and since his elder brother Paul, then twenty-one and also at this time being fitted (more willingly) for a marriage, had recently been rejected by the candidate he and his father were pursuing, Georg proposed that Paul be given "the maiden from Werdau," whom his father was evidently pressing on Georg.

I am happy to cede [that opportunity] to [Paul], because I am
planning with Father's help to see some glorious military actions,
or to journey to Jerusalem and other places [before I marry]. Only
after I have done these things do I wish to follow Father's advice
and devote myself to the school of the cross and put on the
wretched legscrews [of marriage]. . . . I do not want the bloom of
my youth to decay and pass without such adventures, but to
spend it adding more glory and honor to our esteemed and ven-
erable family.[24]

In the endeavor to have his own way, Georg enlisted Lucas's support, albeit to no avail. After writing five more pleading letters to his
father from Kitzbühl without a response, he did as his father and Lucas had done before him: He struck out for Venice and the Holy
Land without prior permission. Writing from Innsbruck en route, he
audaciously asked his father "most obediently" to forgive him if, in
the absence of a response to his letters, he had been wrong to pre-
sume that he had tacitly been given the go-ahead.[25] He also apologized in advance for the costs both knew his willful action would
incur, even instructing his father to charge any expenses he did not
wish to pay himself against his (Georg's) maternal inheritance. Georg
so advised his father not only because he had disobediently struck
out on his own, but also because he had the supreme confidence of
youth that in due course a successful military venture, or a marriage
to a wealthy woman, would make him financially independent of
his father.[26]

As a man who admired strength and independence in his sons,
Paul Behaim may not have been as displeased by his son's rebellion
as Georg feared. Unfortunately for both, the young man's resolution
would never be fully tested, nor its aftermath known. After arriving in Constantinople three months later, he soon fell ill and died at
the palace of the English ambassador. His father noted his passing
solemnly in the margin of the last letter Georg had written him, jot-
ting without further comment, or evident expression of grief: "Died
on June 15, at twenty-two, in Constantinople."[27]

Private Vows

Having traveled through Italy, France, and even to Jerusalem and beheld the crowning of a new emperor, Lucas was as worldly-wise as a youth his age (twenty-six) might then be. As he settled back into his Nürnberg home in the summer of 1612, he probably did not suspect that his greatest adventure still lay ahead of him, and in his own backyard. Within months, he had fallen deeply in love with twenty-one-year-old Anna Maria Pfinzing (1591–1654), the youngest of five surviving children from the marriage of her long-deceased parents Paul Pfinzing (1554–1599) and Sabina Lindner (d. 1594). Her family was one of the city's oldest and most respected, with ties to the Holy Roman Emperor himself (Anna Maria's great-uncle Melchior (1481–1535) had been Emperor Maximilian I's secretary). A widely traveled merchant and influential councilman, Paul Pfinzing had also been the area's leading cartographer and the author of a famous atlas of Nürnberg and its environs, fruits of his service as warden of the regional imperial forest.[28] Both he and his wife died prematurely at forty-five (she in 1594, he in 1599), leaving Anna Maria an orphan at eight. She and her four minor siblings[29] from her father's first marriage were apparently all raised by her maternal grandmother and mother's namesake, Sabina Lindner. Anna Maria was still living with her in her house on Wolf Street when Lucas came courting in the summer of 1612.

The surviving Lindner children were equal heirs to the family inheritance, which came from three sources: the annual rents and interest of the family estate in Henfenfeld, a village east of Nürnberg; a continuing mercantile business run on the children's behalf by their guardians, maternal uncle Gabriel Lindner and paternal uncle Georg Pfinzing (1568–1631); and household silver and other movables more immediately at their possession.[30] Assessed purely in terms of the dowry Anna Maria could bring to a marriage with Lucas, she was not the most outstanding candidate in a city of many wealthy patricians and burghers. However, material considerations appear not to have been Lucas's main concern in selecting Anna

Maria as his life's mate. Such considerations may actually have carried greater weight for Anna Maria, whose passion for her fiancé, at least in the first months of the relationship, would require Lucas's constant fanning.

Certainly, the material side of the union held the full attention of his father, who was moved by his own prodigious family expenses to place his sons and daughters early in the best available matches. There is the suggestion that he had pursued at least one other match for Lucas.[31] And for unrelated personal reasons, soon to be revealed, Paul Behaim also had his own tumultuous history with prominent members of Anna Maria's family,[32] an unhappy past that would haunt the couple throughout the marriage negotiations.

Although Lucas and Anna Maria had known each other since childhood, there are no indications of any prior romance before his return from his bachelor journeys. Nor is the fact that they exchanged private vows a year before their public ones—for the age, prima facie evidence of deep emotional involvement by at least one party[33]—any reliable evidence that they consummated those secret vows before their wedding day.

On the other hand, Lucas's correspondence with his male friends strongly suggests that he had not been chaste during his travels,[34] and so likely brought to the relationship a degree of sexual experience Anna Maria appears to have lacked. Contemporaries certainly suspected that private vows were a pretext for sexual intimacy. Within Lucas's circle of young adult males, at least one peer viewed Anna Maria's willingness to enter a secret marriage as her consent to the wildest sexual pleasure the two could imagine.[35] However, if Lucas's description of the relationship after their secret engagement is any measure of its intimacy, Anna Maria, often to her fiancé's great frustration, remained disturbingly unimpassioned and scrupulously chaste throughout the courtship. And given the close scrutiny a courtship at their social level received from concerned parents, siblings, and friends—not to mention the possible punitive consequences for couples caught in premarital sex in late medieval Nürnberg (symbolic shaming during the wedding ceremony, fines, even imprisonment)[36]—it would have been exceedingly foolish for a soon-to-be married patrician's daughter to have taken such a risk.

Whereas in small village society, premarital sex between known, betrothed couples and nuptials in the early months of visible pregnancy were readily acceptable steps in a proper marriage, among
the urban upper classes, greater discretion and discipline were expected, and scandalous lapses in propriety could make a wedding
day as much one of infamy as of celebration.

Due to circumstances beyond their control, the wedding did not
occur as soon as it might, and certainly not as quickly as the bride
and bridegroom desired. Lucas had long been scheduled to spend
six months apprenticing at the mines in Kitzbühl in the Tyrol, there
to learn firsthand the rudiments of the family's copper mining business, which he would one day oversee in his father's place.[37] It was
on the foundations of mining and metallurgy that many a successful
patrician family in big cities like Nürnberg built mercantile and financial firms that endured for generations, and the Behaims were
among those successful families. Lucas had earlier had a foretaste
of the mines, having, in December 1607 at age twenty, spent several
weeks in Kitzbühl as an observer.[38]

When he and Anna Maria parted in early November 1612, not
only had no public vows been exchanged between them, the formal
marriage negotiations between the two families were just getting
underway. Given the rumors of their private vows, which were then
beginning to circulate among their irreverent peers, the couple's true
relationship soon became a subject of intense speculation and gossip
within their social circle, something that both frightened Lucas and
added new excitement to the relationship.

First Letter

On November 19, two days before he departed for the Kitzbühl
mines, Lucas and his bride-to-be had their first formal meal together
in the home of his maternal aunt, Maria Sitzinger (d. 1637), wife of
Wolf Löffelholz (1563–1617), then bürgermeister and soon to rise to
the city's ruling Council of Seven (Septemvir).[39] Nine days earlier

(November 10), Lucas's father, having learned of their private vows, had given his consent to the marriage.[40] En route to Kitzbühl, while stopping over in Munich, Lucas wrote his first letter to Anna Maria, and his first from Kitzbühl was written on the day he arrived (December 1) there. All of his letters to her have survived in drafts preserved in his copy book. On the other hand, none of hers to him remain—neither any drafts she may have made, nor the polished versions he mentions receiving and evidently kept for a time.

From a few surviving later letters of hers, it appears that this loss may not be a great one, as she was not "the born love-letter writer" he was, her letters being by comparison "conventional and impersonal."[41] From his frequent pleadings with her to write more expressively and from the heart, that judgment seems to be one Lucas may have shared. On the other hand, when a chastened and self-effacing Anna Maria dismissed her letters to him as "inferior, slight, and silly," he was quick to reprimand her for a description "against all truth and fairness."[42]

Having traded the comforts of Nürnberg for the primitive conditions of a mining camp, Lucas now spent his evenings around a campfire with grubby miners. Bored and filled with longing, he sought strength and consolation in religion, work, and especially writing letters to Anna Maria. His desire for information about the marriage negotiations remained ravenous, as did his need to know if their relationship continued to be grist for the city's rumor mills. Above all, he wanted to anticipate any objections to their marriage, or possible obstacles placed in its path by family members possibly unhappy with it. Yet, as vital as these issues were, another preoccupied him more when he wrote his first letter from Kitzbühl: the need for repeated and emphatic confirmation that she was thinking about and yearning for him as often and intensely as he for her.

Precious, virtuous, kindest, beloved, trusted Maiden Bride! My submissive greeting from a heart lovingly disposed to you, and with it my sincere, true love and unfailing loyalty in joy and in suffering lifelong.

I would like to believe that you have safely received my

modest, but well-intentioned letter of November 24, written
from Munich, and that you have read it with heartfelt longing,
comforted by joy. To the present hour, our good and almighty
God has accompanied me . . . permitting me to arrive with my
party in Kitzbühl not only well and hardy, but fortunate and
happy as well, having endured no hardship or accident along the
way. In this, I must also praise [His] great kindness toward you,
for you are the beloved half of my own body and my highest and
dearest good. . . .

Otherwise, I am greatly pleased by my life and work here.
This is largely because I detect that my associates like me a lot.
The supervisor[43] and the miners have promised to teach me
everything they know, and they say they mean that sincerely. I
remain optimistic that, God helping, my trip here will prove
gainful and rewarding.

As I will henceforth be going back and forth to the mountain,
which is only a short hour's ride away, and preoccupied with
other duties as well, my hope is that all this activity will make
your unhappy absence all the more bearable for me, and the time
spent away from you, which, to be truthful, already seems very
long, will become all the shorter. But apart from your company, I
have, praise God, no other unfulfilled need or desire. Still, I will
endure your absence all the better and more patiently, if I am
assured of your heartfelt love and know that your longing to be
with me is as ardent as mine to be with you.

Of course, the situation itself forces me to be patient. However,
seeing that [this separation] has been ordained by God, and that I
am now at my life's work, I can freely choose patience. The only
thing that could possibly strengthen and increase my endurance
is a short, friendly letter from you. That would console my
deepest sadness and, so to speak, make alive again in me what is
now dead. Dear love, I look entirely to you to grant me this, my
heart's desire, but to do so at your own good opportunity.

Dear Maiden Bride, as soon as there are developments there

18FLESH AND SPIRIT

18

that concern us, please report them immediately. If the situation seems to be deteriorating, I can then write to my Aunt Wolf Löffelholz, whose intervention may improve it. And, dear love, would you also tell me frankly, whether in my absence you and I have become the subject of much gossip, or whether, God be praised, our engagement[44] remains undiscovered. Also, let me know if your siblings and in-laws are [still] teasing you relentlessly, especially little Mürr.[45] Knowing, however, what you now do, you will be able to endure such teasing patiently, mindful that what they falsely accused you of before is now true. . . .[46]

Dear love, when you write again, please do not be the least bit shy, no matter how your letter is written and presented. Write to me instead with confidence, and write only what your good heart, faithful to me, moves you to feel and to say. I know that neither of us has ever written such things to anyone else before, as can plainly be seen in my letter as well. Since we are now betrothed and confidants, and, as I hope and trust, our letters will be coming into no one else's hands but our own, we have nothing to fear in this correspondence from one another.

My dear, thousand-fold beloved, I beg you above all else to commend me in your ardent prayers to almighty God and to your own dear love and loyalty, and to continue doing so until, God willing, we are happily and joyously reunited. I will do the same for you, as I continue to serve and repay you and yours with a willing heart for as long as God grants me the grace to do so. . . .

FROM KITZBÜHL, DECEMBER 1, 1612[47]

Although Lucas no more believed that another man could win Anna Maria's heart than another woman could take his from her, he fretted over his lack of certitude in the matter knowing that "God alone rules and guides all hearts." Consumed by the belief that their love and fidelity to one another could remain only as strong as their devotion to God, he searched for sure signs of both, which became the subject of his next letter. God, he believed, had recently answered a heartfelt request for assurance of his own worthiness and salvation made the previous year while he was a pilgrim in Jerusalem at the site of Christ's crucifixion.[48] That sign, he now confided, had been conveyed to him through the happy, approving reception he was enjoying in Kitzbühl.

With this letter, he also sent a copy of the private prayer he recited daily at breakfast and dinner along with two standard Lutheran ones, one of which was for strength against the temptations of the flesh.[49] With this prayer, he intended to reassure Anna Maria of her place and God's in his life, should she have doubts about either. For that distant age, a devout person's private prayer may be taken as the equivalent of a modern medical or psychiatric record in confirming a person's state of mind. That he also asked her to send him her daily prayer suggests that he was anxious to circumvent her "maidenly modesty" and gain access to her innermost feelings and thoughts about him as well.

A Coarse and Shameless Request

Lucas had still another, even bolder, favor to ask of Anna Maria, this one a less contrived and opaque revelation of his desire. He worried, however, that she would think it a frivolous waste of her time and entirely inappropriate for one "still so very shy and scrupulous."[50] His desire, however, was undeniably real, and in light of their secret engagement, he believed his request to be morally within bounds. So even though he thought it a "coarse and shameless" thing to ask, he rationalized in the end that, properly perceived, it redounded more to her praise and honor than to anything she might reasonably take offense at.

Dear Maiden Bride, in my solitude, I contemplate your good and
faithful heart intently and I am comforted by it alone. I rejoice in
it with my whole heart, and yes, I kill most of my leisure in such

pleasant thoughts of you. I must tell you, however, that such
contemplation [of your inner person] has caused the image of
your glorious, beautiful physical form[51] to vanish completely
from my mind, so that I cannot now remember or visualize it
in the least, which leaves me deeply distressed and saddened.
Therefore, I ask you very kindly, my darling, to send me a
portrait of your beautiful physical form, so that I might, from
time to time [by looking at it], know true consolation and
singular joy when such sad thoughts arise. Then, for my joy and
consolation, I may have both your external countenance and,
praise God, the inner face of your heart always before my eyes.[52]

Assuming she was agreeable, Lucas wanted to entrust her brother
Paul, who was then traveling regularly between Nürnberg and the
mines and acting as their messenger, with the name of an artist who
had once painted his own portrait and who might now be commissioned to paint hers. Despite his protestations, the request, as Anna
Maria surely recognized, was one neither a fiancé nor a fiancée could
lightly refuse.

Fraternally vigilant on behalf of his sister's reputation, brother
Paul was at this time keeping a close eye on the pair. A few months
after writing his shameless request (April 1613), Lucas learned from
his future brother-in-law that Anna Maria's eldest sister Katharina[53]
had come upon and read one of his letters to Anna Maria while visiting their grandmother's house. According to Paul's report, Katharina
fortunately found "only pure spirituality" in the letter, and thus had
no reason to "cudgel [Lucas] from behind" by reporting lewd comments and possible lewd behavior on his part to Pastor Johannes
Schröder at St. Lorenz's Church.[54]

Carnality, however, was also what Lucas then felt and feared.
Chastely lusting for Anna Maria, yet forbidden by conscience and
social convention from viewing it shamelessly as such, he worried
that his request for a portrait of her "glorious physical form" would
be construed as only carnal. Paul Pfinzing certainly understood such
things, and as his otherwise consistent support of his sister's wishes

suggests, his letter to Lucas may best be viewed as a fraternal "heads up" rather than any preemptory strike at the planned marriage.[55]

Teasing

On December 27, almost two months after his departure from Nürnberg, Lucas received Anna's first letter, dated December 8, responding to his of November 24 and December 1. It found him surer than ever that God was signaling "rich blessings" for them both, this time extrapolated from the good jobs the Behaim family graciously provided equally grateful miners. "Providence," he assured Anna Maria, "always favors undertakings that support and feed the poor over those that squeeze and oppress the common man."[56]

With every consolation, a new worry seemed to come for Lucas, and this time it was the discovery and publication of their private vows in Nürnberg. To impress upon her what he believed to be their imminent "notoriety," he shared a gossipy letter from cousin Conrad Baier, posted two months earlier from England and recently received in Kitzbühl. In it, Conrad reported juicy rumors about them ("I can easily imagine that the excitement [of the relationship] has left you near exhaustion"), and asked if he might expect a wedding invitation soon, which left Lucas exclaiming to Anna Maria:

> You can readily deduce . . . that we are now deemed to be man and wife in England as well as here at home, and to be such first and foremost [only] in the eyes of Almighty God and all His holy angels![57]

Cousin Conrad's teasing was nothing, however, compared to that of cousin Albrecht, who had himself recently (October 20, 1612) married Juliana Tucher, an event Lucas attended as a bachelor escort[58] on the eve of his departure for Kitzbühl. Three months later, in mid-January, a lovelorn Lucas wrote to Albrecht, now experienced in lovemaking, to complain about his solitary state in Kitzbühl and to confirm, apparently for the first time, the truth of the rumors of his private vows with Anna Maria. "Nobody but everybody knows," Albrecht—who had done his share of gossiping—assured Lucas in answer to his request for the latest Nürnberg rumors.[59]

Lucas evidently had also shared, as only young male adults can, the physical frustrations of being separated from his beloved, a subject Albrecht now mercilessly teased him about in his reply. Conveying his own enthusiasm for the carnal delights of marriage, Albrecht presented his faraway cousin with a provocative proposition.

I have learned from your letter of the wonderful agreement[60] that allows you now to blow fire out of your sweet little Anna's ass, something I would also dearly like to do to her myself, if only my own dear maiden would give me permission. Were she to do so, I think it could not better be done than by inserting my self-extended reed into her from the front and then blowing bravely into it, whereupon the coals and excess heat generated in her hind quarters would sail forth. If this plan of mine pleases you, perhaps you could write to my maiden [Juliana] and ask her if I may be allowed to try it. For were I to proceed without her foreknowledge, the soup would surely turn sour and kind words become dear. I am also pleased to learn that your penis is loyally standing by you, giving you your first wakeup call each day. I shall make this happy news known to Anna Maria on Sunday, *Capis Casari,* when I console her and counsel fond patience [during your absence].[61]

The Father of the Groom

At the time he read these words, Lucas had been separated from Anna Maria for three full months, and, as his letters to her plainly indicate, assurance of her love and fidelity continued to obsess him.

If such teasing left him more appalled than amused, he did not dwell on it for long, because he and Anna Maria now faced a more pressing problem: the failure of the two families to unite around the marriage. Since late December, Lucas had complained that neither his father nor Anna Maria's relatives had taken the initiative to "congratulate" one another on the creation of the new family and proceed with the wedding plans.[62]

Several factors were at play here. Negotiations with Anna Maria's grandmother and guardians were more complicated than negotiations with her parents would have been. Also, Lucas's prominent father had initially considered other matches for his son, and thus may have hesitated to extend his hand too quickly to Anna Maria's relatives on his son's desires alone. However, whatever exploring the senior Behaim may have done ended abruptly upon his discovery of their secret vows.

The more persuasive explanation of the continuing divide between the Behaims and the Pfinzings may actually lie in some thinly concealed personal history. In March 1609, Paul Behaim became the guardian of the four stepchildren of Anna Maria's eldest sister, Katharina Pfinzing (1585–1637)—this in fulfillment of the last wishes of the latter's deceased husband Jakob Imhof (1572–1609). Those children were actually Paul Behaim's blood nieces and nephew, for, before Jakob's marriage to Katharina Pfinzing in 1605, Paul's younger sister Maria (1565–1600) had been his wife and the mother of his four children.[63] In Nürnberg, it was commonplace for elder male relatives to assume such responsibilities, especially one in Paul's exalted position, hence his guardianship of his three nieces and nephew. In that position, however, he had conflicts with Katharina, their stepmother, over the children's care, and, according to Lucas, occasionally treated her "harshly." On some of those occasions, Lucas claimed to have taken Katharina's side against his father. He also praised his sister-in-law as one who always treated him favorably, even against his expectations, which was something he confessed he could not always say about his father: "God knows, I have such trust in her, more than in my father."[64]

Against this background, the Pfinzings likely had a grudge against Paul Behaim because of his treatment of Katharina after becoming guardian of her stepchildren, and those bad feelings now threatened not only the speedy completion of the marriage plans, but the newly-weds' postnuptial arrangements as well. That was because Lucas had been counting on either Grandmother Lindner or his sister-in-law Katharina—the latter now freshly married to Sebastian Imhof (November 1612), a distant cousin of her first husband—for assistance during the first year of his own marriage. Lucas hoped that one or the other would provide him and Anna Maria room and board as they were getting on their feet. He did not want Katharina and her family now to take their revenge on his father by denying him and Anna Maria that much needed courtesy—or, worse still, by stringing out the marriage negotiations interminably.[65]

By late January 1613, the marriage plans seemed to have fallen even deeper into limbo due to Paul Behaim's continuing lack of co-operation and now apparent hostility. According to Anna Maria, not only had the "slander and belittling of malicious gossip" continued in the streets, but her future father-in-law had now also become overtly unfriendly. Lucas attempted to buck her up by insisting that none of the unpleasantries she reported should be taken personally, particularly the negative behavior of his father, which Lucas knew to be directed not at her but at other members of her family.[66] He also wanted to believe that such behavior on his father's part was in part contrived—a way, to his father's mind, of keeping his son's private vows and marriage plans under wraps until Lucas returned home and the couple's formal engagement could properly occur and be honorably announced. Certainly, Paul Behaim would not have wanted Nürnberg's disciplinary Committee of Ten to know that the children of two such prominent families had willfully entered a clandestine marriage of their own. From this point of view, Lucas enter-tained the possibility that his father's behavior was intended to diminish suspicion and gossip and thereby protect the reputations of both families by keeping the public perception of the marriage within expected moral and social boundaries.

However, a much deeper personal reason for Paul Behaim's snub-bing of at least two members of Anna Maria's family also existed. Since returning to Nürnberg in May 1612 from his bachelor jour-neys, Lucas had observed that his father never had a kind word to say for Anna Maria's paternal uncle and legal guardian, Georg Pfinzing (1568–1631), nor for her sister Katharina. There is reason to suspect that the senior Behaim's alienation from both had its beginnings in separate conflicts with each: with Katharina in his capacity (after 1609) as guardian of his Imhof nieces and nephew, and with Georg Pfinzing in the latter's capacity as Katharina's guardian. However, in 1610, well before Katharina became the stepmother of his nieces and nephew, Paul Behaim had an unhappy personal relationship with her that was known within both families. According to Lucas, in 1610, after his father had become a widower for the second time, Katharina had let him "fall through the basket"[67]—that is, she had apparently rejected his overtures of marriage. Between April 1610, when his second wife Rosina Paumgartner died, and April 1611, when he married Maria Magdalena Baier, Paul Behaim had privately courted Katharina. The two had been widowed within a year of each other, Katharina's husband dying in March 1609 and Rosina Behaim a year later.[68] As Katharina's guardian, Georg Pfinzing would have played a key role in any discussion of a new marriage and likely conveyed the bad news to an unsuccessful suitor. Whatever the exact circumstances may have been, the evidence suggests that Lucas's father had been wounded by Katharina's rejection.

Against this background, Paul Behaim's persistent awkwardness toward Anna Maria's family becomes clearer. The forthcoming marriage of his son to a woman whose sister had recently rejected his own hand in marriage could only have revived memories he preferred to forget, while the prospect of discussing marriage plans with Georg Pfinzing again, now on his son's behalf, could not have been a pleasant one. On the other hand, there is also something believable in Lucas's argument that his father did not want to fan harmful speculation and gossip about the secret life of his son and future daughter-in-law by being too often at Pfinzing doors before a formal betrothal had occurred.

With the notable exceptions of her uncle and sister, Lucas believed that his father was truly fond of Anna Maria's family. In a January 1513 letter to Lucas, he reported sympathetically both the rapidly failing health of Katharina's sickly husband, Sebastian Imhof,[69] then only in their second month of marriage, and the birth of an heir to Anna Maria's sister Helena—prima facie evidence, Lucas maintained, of his father's esteem for her family.[70] That the report of Sebastian Imhof's grave illness might also have been tinged with *Schadenfreude* appears not to have crossed Lucas's mind.

There were other favorable omens in the senior Behaim's recent correspondence, particularly as regarded the deepening relationship between father and son. Lucas detected that his father liked him more and more: "he now writes to me constantly and in so friendly a manner that I perceive only approval and good will." And for the claimed first time, his father had sent him a New Year's gift.[71] None of this would be happening, Lucas believed, if he truly harbored any serious misgivings about his fiancée's family or their marriage. On the other hand, he instructed Anna Maria to apologize on his behalf to any member of her family who had been upset or offended by something his father had said or done.

Lust and Piety

In December 1612, Anna Maria was living in the home of her pregnant sister Helena (1590–1660), the wife of Johann Hieronymus Mürr, whom she had married three years earlier (September 1609).[72] Anna Maria had actually been there since September, assisting her sister with housework and other chores as they awaited the delivery of Helena's first child. The thought of her being there under such conditions delighted Lucas, who believed it to be not only a laudable sororal service, but, looking ahead to the future, excellent preparation as well for the time when Anna Maria would deliver their first child. She could now learn from her sister, the midwife assisting her, and the childbed attendant "all kinds of useful, advantageous, and necessary things" about childbirth and child care, he wrote enthusiastically.

In late December, Lucas wanted Anna Maria to take the initiative in moving their marriage plans forward. He believed that could best be done by joining forces with Grandmother Lindner, sister

Katharina, and his aunt Löffelholz—the two families' most powerful women—with an eye to setting a date certain for their formal engagement (*Zusagung*), preferably on the second or third day after his return home from the mines.[73] Since the leading male authorities in the two families (his father and her uncle) continued to threaten the marriage's progress, their best hope lay with this more amenable sorority.

Ten days after writing this letter (on January 9), while at the foundry in Kössen, Lucas received an "exceedingly friendly" reply from Anna Maria, delivered to him at 7 o'clock in the morning as he lay idly in bed thinking of her and "hoping with many heartfelt, passionate sighs" that her dawning day in Nürnberg was proving to be as blissful as his in Kitzbühl. It filled him with pride and joy to learn from her letter that she and her friends almost never met without drinking a toast in his honor. Such remembrance of him made him all the more mindful that God had blessed him with a maiden who was not only "beautiful, god-fearing, understanding, and richly endowed with every virtue," but who also loved him more than any other beyond any justifying merit or hope of his own.[74]

From the start, lust and piety had jockeyed for position in Lucas's mind and letters. The most the conventions of the age allowed him was their discreet placement in tandem, the former energizing, the latter disciplining his passion for his bride. However, inspired now by her latest letter, and wishing again to say more than convention condoned, he found a way out by couching the language of romance in that of contemporary Lutheran religion, which also held a large place in his heart. By modeling their love for one another on that of God's for humanity, he could say more than he should—a great deal more. As his passion for God and for Anna Maria had become so completely intertwined in his own mind, he did not view such modeling as a contrivance, and may even have been unaware that he was doing it. By now, it had become second nature for him to describe the experience that gave his own personal life its greatest pleasure and meaning in terms of the experience that his faith taught him gave all life its truest pleasure and meaning. In both instances, that experience was being loved freely and unjudgmentally by someone deemed to be of infinitely greater worth than oneself. With regard both to Anna Maria and to God, he also subscribed to the Lutheran truism that such love could not be earned by deeds nor adequately conveyed by words. Sensing, however, Anna Maria's growing willingness to reveal her own heart more candidly than ever before, he begged her to join him in trying to fathom the unfathomable and express the inexpressible.

> [When writing,] follow logically your own good heart and high intelligence in contemplating and pondering the love, joy, and consolation that the heart of a man as devout, honest, and true as I must now feel, when, among countless other good deeds, God, by His ordained and Christian means, has blessed that heart with a maiden as beautiful, shapely, healthy, upright, and dark-complexioned as you. In doing so, He has fulfilled that heart's every wish and desire with a person, who is not only adorned most gloriously with every physical asset any heart could want, but endowed as well with true piety and understanding, purity and self-discipline, meekness and humility, domesticity and all the other feminine virtues that could be wished for. And most consoling of all, that same maiden sincerely loves her God-given fiancé and promised bridegroom, and embraces him in such trust and kindness that it becomes difficult, near impossible, to behold so true and heartfelt a love, much less to describe or express it in words.[75]

Such awareness of God's and Anna Maria's unmerited love left Lucas fearful as well as awestruck. As with God's love, he now found himself dreading the possible withdrawal of Anna Maria's before the two of them could be united for eternity in a "chaste marriage bed."[76] As it turned out, these self-doubts and feelings of unworthiness had a completely mundane and fortunately ephemeral source: his request for her portrait. By mid-January 1613, he looked back on that audacious act as an irreparable blunder, thinking it had demeaned his love for her, especially in the experienced eye of her grandmother, whom he could not afford to alienate at this point. Learning that Grandmother Lindner had indeed "frowned" on his request for a likeness of her granddaughter's "glorious physical form," he took the only safe and honest course of action left him: He agreed with her completely. Praising her "very proper caution" as a welcomed admonishment of his "exceptionally poor judgment," he assured them both that he had never wanted the portrait for any "frivolous reason or pastime." Already he had sought out her brother Paul and apologized to him for ever having suggested that his sister have her portrait made for him. At the same time, he begged forgiveness as well for having speculated "rashly" on her future pregnancy; such "roguery," he wanted both Anna Maria and her grandmother to believe, bore no "mischievous or vulgar intent," but had only been another sincere expression of his heartfelt devotion to his bride.[77]

Good News

When Anna Maria wrote again, it was with news of Grandmother Lindner's consent to their living with her after their marriage. Joyed, Lucas envisioned leading "a quiet and comfortable life with [Frau Lindner] in her late but still good years, and doing so with the kind of devotion it is fitting for children to show to parents."[78]

The other good news, all the more surprising as its likelihood had been discounted, was Anna Maria's decision to grant his request for a portrait. Elated, Lucas swore to her that no eyes but his would ever view it.[79] He also gave sister-in-law Katharina some credit for it, suspecting she had supported Anna Maria's decision against their grandmother's objections. Nonetheless, he feared this sweet victory could prove pyrrhic, since Grandmother Lindner, having opposed the portrait from the start, might now, in defeat, be all the more ill-disposed toward him. More than ever, he would now have to rely on his bride's diplomacy to keep him in her grandmother's good graces.[80]

Although it would not matter in the end, Lucas did not do all that he might to secure that diplomacy. At this time he had received an

invitation to visit barely known relatives by marriage in the Tyrolean
mining town of Pühlersee. The purpose of the visit, he frankly told
Anna Maria, was to meet a suitor, or, as he teasingly put it, "to give
to me, as to that wolf, still another wife." The suitor in question
was Helena Sitzinger, a distant cousin on his mother's side of the
family.[81] As the relatives knew nothing about his secret marriage to
Anna Maria, any impropriety attaching to the invitation came strictly
from Lucas. Lucas, however, assured Anna Maria that he would resist any temptation that might lie in wait for him in Pühlersee.

> Please, dearest, do not be jealous; I will conduct myself in the
> most chaste and proper fashion, once there. And should that girl
> wish to be too friendly, I shall tell her straightaway that she has
> come too late, that my hide is promised and sold to you, most
> faithful love.[82]

Again, only his saving charm prevented such teasing from ending
as a taunt. He was at the time at the foundry in Kössen, where the
metal masters instructed him in the art of assaying ore for smelting.
Segueing from metallurgy into romance, he wished that he also had
a master to teach him "how to assay a maiden,"[83] hastening to add:

> But in this, my Master [God] has directed me to you, as it is
> His opinion that no one else will instruct me more loyally and
> diligently. . . . And I remain most happy and willing to learn.[84]

The Relics of Love

On January 26, Lucas received Anna Maria's letter of January 18,
which arrived with the promised portrait and, to his further surprise
and delight, a bodily part that he might actually carry about on his
person. He responded:[85]

I hardly know how . . . to describe the joy and refreshment
[your gifts] bring me in my unfortunate and increasing state of
boredom. Not only do I now have your lovely, beautiful portrait
constantly before my eyes; there is also a lock of your hair, an
actual, tangible piece of your beautiful, glorious body to console
me endlessly. With heartfelt sighs, I kiss it many thousand times
each day.[86]

A month later, he was still attesting the recuperative powers of
these personal gifts.

After God and your lovely, friendly letters, your beautiful,
pleasing portrait remains my singular consolation, which,
together with [the lock of] your golden hair, I kiss many times
with heartfelt longing during the monotonous passage of each
day.[87]

He concealed the lock of her hair in his hatband, where it remained out of sight and protected, yet always accessible.[88] A thin-
haired and apparently prematurely balding man, Lucas joked that
she could easily imagine how little of his hair would be left were he
now to reciprocate in kind. His fantasy at the moment was that her
golden hair magically ring and decorate his bald pate.[89] To his further delight, Anna Maria had also sent along a copy of her daily
prayer, which portrayed him to her Maker as an "understanding and
God-fearing fellow."[90]
The only reciprocal gift in kind that Lucas could have sent from
Kössen was a lock of his beard, which Anna Maria had endearingly
braided shortly before their separation. Unfortunately, he was prevented from doing so by a vow he had made in the spring of 1612
while en route home from France, when, for some unexplained reason, he swore to God that only the hand of his fiancée would be allowed to cut it.[91]
Despite the extremes to which Lucas might go to express his
loneliness and yearning for Anna Maria, his outbursts give every

appearance of having been sincere. For all his newfound comradery, apprenticing at the mines was arduous and dirty work. Palpable are his descriptions of making peace with the monotonous daily journey back and forth to the mine shaft, its foul odors, the tedious drilling, the hit-and-miss efforts to locate ore-bearing rock, and the unappealing diet of meat (scrags, mincemeat, and boiled meat) and noodles (lard, steamed, cut, and egg). During Passion Week in early April 1613, as he anticipated his planned reunion with Anna Maria in May, the emotional toll of the separation on him was such that his associates recommended that he take the medicinal herb *Annelein* ("precious Anna"), the powers of which his physician there confirmed. Rich in iodine, *Annelein* was the popular remedy in mining towns for goiter, an ailment for whose signs (swelling of the neck) Lucas regularly examined himself. He escaped that affliction, he believed, by avoiding the water in Kitzbühl "as if it were the Devil." However, he apparently took *Annelein*—which in his case could not have been more appropriately named—as a remedy for lovesickness as well, writing to his sister-in-law Katharina that he planned to travel to Annaberg (250 miles to the northeast) after his return home, ostensibly to gather his own supply at the source.[92]

Managing Relatives

Lucas was meanwhile taking a tougher line with his father by reminding him of the finality of the marriage and the union of the two families. He concluded his most recent letter to him with a greeting from both his Behaim and Pfinzing relatives, a way of identifying himself equally with both. In response to this "testing," Paul Behaim concluded his next letter to Lucas with an equally warm greeting, also made on behalf of both families. Reassured and emboldened, Lucas now for the first time wrote to his father not just in his own name, but conjointly with that of "my most trusted Anna Maria."[93]

Lucas approached his father so confidently because he believed they had reached a new plateau in their relationship. He had completed his formal education, was rapidly gaining the practical skills needed to work in the family's mining business and support a household, and a date for his public engagement was now within sight—all indices of adulthood and independence, which his father was at last fully acknowledging. For Lucas, the surest sign of this successful passage was a letter in which his father addressed him as "my especially dear son," words he claimed never to have heard from him before, confirming the previous intimations of paternal favor and acceptance of the marriage.[94]

Lucas now declared any further unfriendliness toward the Pfinzings on his father's part to be simply feigned, his way of "refusing to confirm other people's rumors and heighten suspicions" before the engagement became official.[95] He also blamed any past resistance to the union on his aunts and uncles,[96] who, like his Sitzinger cousins, apparently had other prospects in mind for their eldest nephew.

That the marriage plans were nonetheless progressing was indicated by Paul Behaim's visit to the home of Katherina Imhof. There he met with Grandmother Lindner, who asked his opinion of the match and requested information about Lucas's economic prospects. In his report of the meeting to Lucas, his father indicated that both subjects were discussed "as fully as each required" and that Frau Lindner liked what she heard.[97]

As far as Lucas was concerned, the unhappy episodes were now water under the bridge. While real enough, his father's "distant and rude behavior" had never been from the heart, and Anna Maria was now his "dearest daughter-in-law" and Frau Lindner his "entirely dear in-law."[98] As soon as the engagement became official, Lucas expected his father "to love us [all] openly, as we cannot trust him now to do, and to show [the Pfinzings] the kindness he now denies them."[99]

By such words, Lucas also intended to keep Frau Lindner favorably disposed toward his planned entry into her household. To that end, he instructed Anna Maria to assure her grandmother that he would in all things "heed her will like an obedient child."

She should in no way fear that I shall inconvenience her. For although I am refined enough to want to eat good food, I am

also . . . one who can make do with soup and porridge. . . . And
should the annual blessing of God . . . descend upon us and the
house become too small, the foundling home and the city
hospice will always be open to us.[100]

Lucas had shuddered at the thought of losing Frau Lindner's hos-
pitality because he and Anna Maria had no comfortable alternative,
and he was not yet in any financial position to establish an independent household of his own. His father had pledged to assist the
newlyweds, but only within the "small means" his own large and
still growing family permitted.[101] As the eldest son, Lucas was destined to inherit the family house and, had the senior Behaim's own
family responsibilities at the time not been so onerous, Lucas and
Anna Maria would likely have joined him in that house after their
marriage—the bad feelings of his father toward two Pfinzings notwithstanding. However, only twenty-two months had passed since
Paul Behaim moved a third wife into his house, and she had since
delivered her first and his thirteenth child. In February 1613, at
least five of Lucas's nine surviving half siblings still lived at home.[102]
Lucas shared all these worries with his aunt Maria Löffelholz,
through whose intervention he hoped to secure for himself as much
Behaim family wealth as possible. Because of the demands of his siblings, whom he describes as "growing daily and [thus] having to be
given more," his great fear was that the interest from his maternal inheritance, on which he then apparently supported himself, might be
withheld or diminished by his father's ever-growing household expenses. He wanted his father's guarantee of a fixed income, along
with a firm pledge to pay the cost of the wedding, so that he and
Anna Maria might start out strong and safely plan ahead.[103]
That his maternal aunt Löffelholz was the diplomat to turn to in
this matter is suggested by her handling of a final request from Lucas: "If you see a beautiful bridal belt for sale at a good price in the
main store or elsewhere," Lucas instructed, "please have Father buy
it."[104] A month later, in mid-March, his father wrote to confirm that
he had indeed inquired after a bridal belt, but remained pessimistic
about finding one "in the new style everyone wants these days."[105]
Although Lucas continued to remind Anna Maria that their final

success depended on God's intervening on their behalf "in uncount-
able ways,"[106] what he had in mind actually could be counted. This
became clear when he shared his wish list with Aunt Löffelholz, his
more predictable deus ex machina. Having successfully enlisted her
assistance in mellowing his father, might she now persuade Frau
Lindner, who had consented to provide the bridal pair with a year's
lodging, to throw in a year of free board as well? Lucas suggested
that she might feel obliged to do so on several grounds: first, in lieu
of a dowry, which, although standing *in loco matris/patris,* she would
not personally be providing;[107] then, in view of her old age and poor
health, which required her to rely on trustworthy family members
for assistance, which Lucas would join Anna Maria in continuing to
provide; and finally, in light of Anna Maria's record of having done
"more and better" for her grandmother than any of her other grandchildren. Lest Frau Lindner receive the impression that too much
was being asked of her, Lucas stressed to his aunt, as he intended for
her to impress in turn upon Anna Maria's grandmother, his readi-
ness to make do with "whatever lodging and board she deems
appropriate, just as long as I may sleep every night with my dear
Anna."[108]

How to Fail at Marriage

Lucas's association of personal faith and morally principled living
with success in courtship and marriage was not just theologically
correct for the age. He also believed a terrifying example of the consequences of doing otherwise stood directly before their eyes: the
tragic courtship and marriage of sister-in-law Katharina and her second husband Sebastian Imhof (1589–1612), who had married in
November 1612.[109] Lucas had carefully followed the couple's misfortune, which began with Sebastian's failing health in the months
before the marriage, holding it up to Anna Maria as a prime example
of "how far away God's blessing and grace remain from married couples who do not pray to him for His help and assistance." He based

that judgment on a suspicion that Katharina had not properly or often enough sought God out during her courtship and marriage, and the fact that Sebastian had known not an hour's peace since his wedding day seemed prima facie evidence that he, too, had neglected faith and morals.[110]

Lucas at this time also corresponded with cousin Albrecht Behaim about his brother-in-law's failing health. Albrecht had his own explanation for Sebastian's plight and what all assumed to he his imminent death (he actually lingered until September). Writing from Nürnberg on January 29, the day a stricken Sebastian received communion at bedside, Albrecht shared with Lucas his belief that Sebastian had been afflicted by a witch, and in the worst possible way a man could be.

> There is only one suspected cause of his illness here: the theft of his *membrum virile* by a witch. That loss now afflicts him vehemently and causes him, awestruck, constantly to pass unbelievable quantities of urine.[111]

Both Lucas and Albrecht believed in the devil, and as the one was a newlywed and the other soon to become one, each understandably may have trembled at the thought of impotence, whatever its source. Albrecht's disrespect for Sebastian's condition, however, also suggests that the wound earlier inflicted on Behaim pride by Paul Behaim's unsuccessful courtship of Katharina had not completely healed. For Lucas's part also, only God's abandonment of a couple could explain so terrible a fate, which moved him to urge Anna Maria:

> If [we] turn to God now . . . He will stand by us always with His Holy Spirit and dear angels and deny the wretched Devil and his accursed instruments [witches] any power over us.[112]

Blowup

After sending Lucas her portrait, a lock of hair, and daily prayer in mid-January, Anna Maria fell silent for over a month, and as the days and weeks passed in Kitzbühl without a letter (she would not write again until late February), the first true storm clouds gathered over the relationship. A letter from her brother Paul, received on February 15, conveyed her apology for not writing, citing pressing business. Lucas, however, believed that only physical impairment could explain such indiligence. To encourage candor, he shared with her the details of a recent illness of his own ("severe inflammation of the head, teeth, and neck") that had lingered for two weeks, but had not prevented his regular correspondence. When February ended with still no word, Lucas chided her for "desertion" and pointedly cut his letter short on the grounds that he had no news from her to respond to.[113]

Finally, on March 3, Anna Maria's letter of February 29 arrived, for which Lucas claimed to have been waiting since February 9, the last reasonably punctual date on which he believed she might have responded to his of February 1. That letter made it clear that preparations for Lent, not any serious illness, had kept Anna Maria from writing. A more dire excuse had been expected, and by this time was required. Should she, he chided again, ever in the future find herself beset with so many important and necessary chores, might she not take a quarter hour to report her well-being to him in "two or three words," which would then be to him "as dear and consoling as a long, polished, full page written at great effort and inconvenience?"[114]

The announcement that the first diet of the empire under newly elected Emperor Mathias (r. 1612–1619) would occur in Regensburg in late July and early August gave Lucas an opportunity to rattle Anna Maria's heart as she had done his by her inconstant writing. Although he was planning to attend the diet even before their blowup—the event provided a rare opportunity to meet influential people—the subject need not have been brought up in his letter of March 5.[115] Attending would mean another separation from Anna Maria not long after their planned reunion in Nürnberg, something his previous letters suggested he would sooner die than do. In other words, he appears to have wanted her to ponder—four or five months before the fact—how she would feel were he to leave town after their wedding, or possibly during the weeks of its celebration, remote as that possibility may then have seemed.

The Magic Circle of Love

Within a week, Lucas, as promised, provided Anna Maria an example of responsible spousal notification, accompanied, however, by what appears to have been a retaliatory withholding of information. A conspiracy of circumstances occasioned him to write on March 12 the shortest surviving letter of the correspondence: twenty-five lines, including boilerplate. Although declaring himself overwhelmed by "all kinds of chores that could not be postponed," and lacking a recent letter from her requiring a prompt and long response, he nonetheless wanted, while on the run,

> . . . kindly to report that I am, praise God, completely well off and remain as always devoted and true to you in my heart. Please be mine, as I am and will remain yours.[116]

He hastened to assure her that the letter's brevity did not mean there was nothing then to write to her about. There were "all kind of things," even disturbing news from Uncle Löffelholz, which he was sparing her until a more fitting time. He did want her to know his plans to be home by Whitsuntide, and he requested a report on the discussions then underway between Grandmother Lindner and Aunt Löffelholz to determine how soon their "salvation" (formal engagement and wedding) might begin.[117] Although three adult males (Paul Behaim, maternal Uncle Gabriel Lindner, and paternal Uncle Georg Pfinzing) were the legal principals in these undertakings, it was the two older women working behind the scenes at the request of the bride and groom who would make the marriage happen. No bad blood existed between Maria Löffelholz and Sabina Lindner, who always kept the interests of the bride and groom foremost in mind.

In addition, Anna Maria's siblings had to be assembled, for the law required a hearing with them before any part of the family inheritance could be apportioned to her. Exploiting Aunt Löffelholz's ambassadorial skills, Lucas hoped to move his father to set a date certain for their formal engagement. As the wife of a bürgermeister and member of the city's executive council ("the Seven"), she traversed the city with knowledge and influence, and as her home had been an empty nest since the marriage of her only child, a daughter, in 1609,[118] she had plenty of time to play the diplomat on Lucas and Anna Maria's behalf.

The months of March and April were actually to be very good ones for the relationship, which had suffered in the weeks preceding, especially after Lucas's angry letter of March 5. When he wrote again to Anna Maria on March 19, he did so in the afterglow of having read her "very consoling and Christian letter" of March 6, whose "growing, heartfelt, true love for one as unworthy as I" left him "wonderfully speechless." He now claimed to believe what he thought he never could or should: that her love for him was every bit as great as his for her.[119] Explaining that her sister Helena's delivery and recovery, which Anna Maria attended from start to finish, had preoccupied her totally, she also apologized for not having written sooner. For Lucas, the forthrightness of the apology already rendered it unnecessary. He now declared her free, as he hoped she also thought him to be, henceforth to write only when the opportunity was there and never just to please him.[120] Anna Maria most likely understood that promise to mean that she would no longer be subjected to recriminations should she again fail to reply to him within what he deemed to be the proper response time for one in good health and as madly in love as he.

Still, her letter had not exorcised all of his unhappiness. Commenting on the joy she had expressed over the recent recovery of his health, he also praised God for keeping her well,

... even though your long silence ... caused as great a fright
about your health in me as my illness caused in you.[121]

Closure with Grandmother Lindner

Despite a series of meetings with Frau Lindner, Paul Behaim
never succeeded in clarifying the terms of the newlyweds' room and
board in her house after the marriage. By mid-March, he could report only her promise of "reasonable board"[122] for a year or two, and
definitely not free. Aunt Löffelholz, who also pursued the subject,
managed to obtain somewhat more precise information, after a
meeting on April 11.

[While] I could not get a firm promise from [Frau Lindner] to
provide you board-free lodging for a year ... I perceived that she
would be happy to let you live with your bride in her house for
around 200 gulden. She did not now want to make a final decision and has postponed any further discussion of the matter until
your homecoming. In doing so, she excuses herself by saying that
she is an old woman prepared to die at any hour, and who knows
whether she will live so long. ...

However, you will surely have heard by now from your father
that the city council has promised him the dwelling on Fortress
Street,[123] which we gather will become available soon. So after the
first year, your father can provide you with a good lodging, and I
do not doubt that he will do so. My advice to you is not to worry
too much, for doing so may give you a headache, which in turn
may cause your hair to fall out. Also, the discomfort [of living in
makeshift lodging] will bring you respect, as it has done in the Tyrol, where you also have had to rough it.

Otherwise, your Frau Grandmother-in-law has responded to
my persistent and urgent pleading by agreeing to let you sleep
every night with dear Anna.[124]

On at least two further occasions, Paul Behaim attempted to reach an accord with Frau Lindner on the cost of room and board. At a meeting at the Löffelholzes' on April 15, she again refused to settle the matter before Lucas returned, although Wolf Löffelholz gathered from the conversation that she would demand fifty gulden for the first year, between 100 and 200 for the second, and 200 for a third. Paul Behaim believed the couple would have to resign themselves to paying whatever she asked, even 300 gulden, and especially if God gave them children immediately.[125] This was because Lucas could not support his own household, and his father was unable, or unwilling, at this time to help him live beyond his means.

On April 24, the senior Behaim wrote again to inform his son that Uncle Wolf's projections on room and board had been optimistic. His hope now was to keep the first year's expenses under 100 gulden, while anticipating between 150 and 200 in the second.[126] For Nürnberg's journeymen, whose average annual salary in 1597 was sixty gulden, room and board at those levels was living well. However, compared to the wealth of their parents' circle, Lucas and Anna Maria were slumming, as Aunt Löffelholz also indicated. Just what the payment for room and board finally turned out to be is unclear. However, their stay with Frau Lindner would not extend beyond a year (July 1614).[127]

Loose Cannons

In addition to pinning Frau Lindner down on such practical matters, the marriage preparations also hinged on a final accord with Anna Maria's guardians. Pointing out that "no one wanted to bell the cat" (a reference to Georg Pfinzing), Paul Behaim advised Lucas to enlist the help of new brothers-in-law Paul Pfinzing and Hieronymus Mürr (Helena's husband) and sister-in-law Katharina in approaching the fearsome uncle. At the same time, he expressed his own determination "not to allow anything to begin or proceed" until everyone was assured of "fair treatment" by him, an evident allusion to the settling of Anna Maria's dowry. Paul Behaim also advised his son to exploit Uncle Wolf's diplomatic services in settling matters with Frau Lindner and her son Gabriel, Anna Maria's other guardian.[128]

Lucas, of course, had always feared his father's ability to obstruct the marriage. Still in mid-April, he shared that concern with Anna Maria, pointing again to Paul Behaim's studied avoidance of her uncle. Earlier (April 1), he reported[129] that his father would not let the wedding go forward until Anna Maria had a final agreement with her uncle on what the dowry would be. However, by April 12, Paul Behaim had surprisingly notified Lucas through his Kitzbühl agent that he would "let the matter with Georg Pfinzing wait until after the wedding." That, however, was the most impossible scenario of all if the marriage was to occur. A binding agreement on its financial terms, as his father surely knew, was indispensable, and such whimsy left Lucas wondering whether "the inconstant April weather" had affected his father's mind. It appears that Paul Behaim had been so successful in avoiding the Pfinzings that he was unaware that Anna Maria had already reached a satisfactory agreement with her guardians and siblings on her dowry—a paternal and maternal inheritance of 800 gulden—which Lucas would reciprocate with a bride's gift of 1,000 gulden, a tidy nest egg for the newlyweds. Lucas now suggested that Grandmother Lindner or sister Katharina take his oblivious father aside and bring him up to date on the marriage plans at the first opportunity.[130]

Homecoming and Marriage

A typical patrician or burgher marriage in late medieval Nürnberg began formally with the signing of an agreement by the principals' fathers or legal guardians privately at one or the other's home, or at city hall. In the following week, a formal betrothal ceremony occurred in the home of the bride, during which she and the groom exchanged vows in the presence of their families and a notary. A dramatic handshake and pledge[131] sealed those vows and ratified the parental contract. The final large event—a procession to and from church to receive the blessing of a priest—was also the most dramatic, yet anticlimactic as far as the reality and legality of a marriage were concerned.[132]

Behind and between these well-defined scenes, as in our story, the bride and the bridegroom, assisted by a large supporting cast of relatives, friends, and go-betweens, were engaged in a real-life drama. By at least the fifteenth century, the bridal pair as a rule were acquainted before their betrothal, and physical attraction and emotional compatibility had a place alongside social standing and wealth as criteria in the selection of a spouse. With parents wanting their offspring to be happy, and recognizing that happiness served the material goals of a marriage, prospective brides and bridegrooms not only sought their heart's desire, they played a prominent role as well in the planning and development of the marriage.[133]

Sometimes, however, as in our story, a couple fell in love on their own and exchanged private vows before making their engagement or marriage known to family members or friends. According to the Church, such solemn promises, if sincerely and expressly made, created a true marriage in the eyes of God, particularly if a couple had also consummated them.[134] During the late Middle Ages, numerous "clandestine marriages" ended up in court, as it was not unusual for one party (almost always the male) to deny having made any marriage vows when soberly confronted by the prospect of a lifelong union with an undesired mate with whom he or she had been sexually active. To discourage such litigation and safeguard reputations, authorities in church and state, cheered on by parents, attempted, largely in vain, to establish a clear public record requirement for a proper and licit marriage. Those efforts notwithstanding, the ability of determined youths to pursue their desires privately was no more completely thwarted in late medieval Europe than it is today, despite greater opportunities then for parental and societal steering.[135]

After a couple had been publicly betrothed, Nürnberg's marriage ordinance allowed a family celebration at home, originally limited to twelve invited guests and a notary, each of whom was permitted to consume a single glass of table wine. Over the years, that celebration grew in number, embellishment, and coarseness. By the sixteenth century, an engagement party included a meal, a dance, and a night serenade by city pipers and musicians playing string instruments, zithers, bells, and cymbals. The legal refreshments also expanded from a glass of wine to elaborate confections, sweet wine trifles, and the ever-present *Lebkuchen*. Those able to pay for the additional services and security might also rent out the city hall for a more elaborate, catered affair.[136]

For propriety's and chastity's sake, family and friends chaperoned the bride and bridegroom around the clock in the weeks between the engagement and their appearance at church. The marriage ordinance of 1533 instructed couples to let the clergy know their plans a "good time" ahead—this to allow the wedding day to be announced several times in church well in advance of its occurrence on one of the twenty-three recognized feast days, and preferably on as many as three such days, when larger numbers of worshippers attended services. This gave anyone with a sound reason to protest the union the opportunity to do so. Such "banns" were actually a process of discovery, during which people in a position to know were given an opportunity to expose any legal or moral obstacles to a proposed marriage. Such an objection might be raised on the grounds of a prior, private commitment by one or the other party, something an old, wounded boyfriend or girlfriend might reveal. An objection could also result from the discovery of an unrecognized or a concealed kinship between a prospective bride and bridegroom— legal impediments that became far fewer in post-1525 Protestant Nürnberg.

On the wedding day, it was customary among noble and patrician bridegrooms to ride out fully arrayed to meet guests arriving from other towns when the latter crossed the city's boundary. By mid-century, the extravagance of that practice had become such that the city council took steps to regulate it. After 1556, a family risked a twenty-gulden fine if they invited more than twenty foreign guests, rode out to greet them on satin saddles with hunting horns blaring, or hired professional trumpeters to perform such honors.[137]

The wedding day began in Nürnberg with a procession either to St. Lorenz's or St. Sebald's, the two churches in the city where the marriage ceremony could be legally conducted. In the early sixteenth century, the city's sumptuary laws permitted parties of no more than twenty-four to proceed to and from the church. Well-to-do families exceeded that limit with impunity, save when they ignored the ban on candelabras, which posed a fire hazard to buildings en route. By midcentury, the rowdiness of these processions led to a ban on drums and fifes as well and a determined attempt to keep the number of participants under thirty-five.

Dressed in his best, the bridegroom fetched his bride, also dressed in hers, at her home and led her to church, she walking behind him between two honorary escorts from the processional party. In winter, sand was strewn along their path, while in summer, grasses and flowers carpeted the way. But neither before nor after the Reformation were weddings officiated during the six holy weeks of Lent and the four of Advent.[138]

The priest met and blessed the couple at the church door,[139] after which the wedding party entered the church where the wedding was celebrated at the conclusion of the worship service. The service ended with the couple's procession from the church back to the home of either the bride or the bridegroom.[140]

Meant to be a joyous occasion, the wedding could be transformed into one of shaming if premarital sexual relations between the principals were known to have occurred prior to the ceremony. For this reason, the bridal pair was held by all concerned to the strictest chastity, or the appearance thereof, in the weeks before the wedding. When premarital sexual intimacy was discovered—revealed perhaps by a bride's obvious pregnancy—the couple's "indiscipline" became a subject of the service. In the second half of the sixteenth century, a known nonvirginal bride wore a veil and her bridegroom a straw crown, and they were permitted only one lone table of guests at their wedding banquet and forbidden to dance or engage in any other demonstrative celebration. If that were not damper enough, the bridegroom might spend two weeks in the tower and his bride two in the stocks, depending on the magnitude of the scandal and the charity of the prosecutors. When "indiscipline" was discovered only after the wedding, the same penalties applied, only with an additional ten-gulden fine.[141] Given the rumors circulating about their secret vows, Lucas and Anna Maria may have contemplated such risks and worried about such penalties.

In addition to such conscience building and social control, the magistrates and the clergy also exploited weddings as opportunities to increase citizen investment in public institutions. A string of fees accompanied the process of certifying and celebrating a marriage, in addition to which the services of city officials and employees—notaries and priests, supervisors and stewards, pipers and police, and the man- and maid-servants who cleaned up in its wake—also had to be paid. During the weeks between the signing of the marriage contract and the wedding at church, officials solicited the families of the bride and groom for contributions to the city's foundling home, infirmary, and homeless shelters.[142]

Celebratory meals preceded and followed the church procession, and government attempted to regulate them as well. As many as thirty-two guests might legally attend the morning meal and forty the evening banquet, although extensions could be negotiated or bought. The city fought a losing battle to keep the fare modest on such occasions. Early in the century, numerous "exotic" entrées (partridges, hazel hens, pheasants, peacocks, capons, turkeys, ptarmigan, stags, roe, fish, and "spicy side-dishes"[143]) were strictly forbidden. By midcentury (1565), rare game and rich confections remained illegal; however, other substantial dishes might now grace a table, along with some plain species of fish (gudgeon and perch), hazel hens, and partridges.[144]

A wedding dance capped the long day, again with limits on number, duration, and fare (only fruit and table wine could legally be served). During the sixteenth century, reports of wild leaping and erotic swaying on the dance floor prompted regulations to enforce modesty. One expressly forbidden dance was popularly called "What has she got, what can she do."[145] In the aftermath of a wedding, there were also smaller celebrations[146] that allowed family and relatives to honor the newlyweds in quieter and more intimate ways.

By May 1613, Lucas and Anna Maria's wedding appeared to be in sight. His stay at Kitzbühl was coming to an end, and the arrange-ments they had worked so hard to make now seemed to be firmly in place. Only an act of God could now interrupt their well-laid plans—which it did on the eve of Lucas's departure for home. He had barely begun his last surviving letter to Anna Maria from Kitzbühl (May 1613) before ending it abruptly. Responding to hers of April 8, he was just at the point of apologizing for yet another tactless remark, when he stopped in mid sentence:

> Would you make the best of my shameless and all too naive
> recent letter—treat it as having been written more in jest and my
> usual, albeit at the time nonsensical, teasing manner, and by no
> means ill-intended . . .[147]

What had ended the letter so suddenly was the arrival of one from his father, dated April 24, bearing the sad news of his uncle Friedrich Behaim's unexpected death in Gräfenberg, at age forty-nine, from a suffocating catarrh. As his father explained, the body was scheduled to arrive in Nürnberg on the following day and to be interred on the day after. For Lucas, the news was doubly sad: He had lost his dear uncle,[148] and his marriage plans would now have to be postponed. In his father's estimation, the customary period of mourning prevented a festive wedding for at least four, possibly six, months, thus pushing their wedding day into the fall.[149]

On May 7, Paul Behaim dispatched a horse and money to Kitzbühl for Lucas's journey home. A week later he wrote again to ask that he enter the city "as discreetly as possible," discouraging any plans his friends might have to ride out and meet him as he crossed the city's boundary, which would be inappropriate during the official period of mourning.[150] A month later, the unexpected death of his eighteen-year-old half brother Martin (1595–1613), a castle page in Vienna, further dampened the wedding plans.[151]

Lucas arrived home on May 25, and a full month passed (until June 28) before Uncles Wolf Löffelholz and Christoph Behaim (1562–1624) met with Georg Pfinzing in city hall to formalize the courtship (Werbung) and put the planned marriage on the public record for the first time.[152] A week later, Georg Pfinzing feted Lucas at his home in nearby Mögeldorf, northeast of Nürnberg. On September 1, Paul Behaim and Georg Pfinzing signed the marriage contract, with Anna Maria's uncle Martin Pfinzing (1560–1619) and Lucas's uncle Christoph standing as the official witnesses.[153] Eight days later, on September 9, Lucas and Anna Maria exchanged public vows (Handschlag) in the home of Georg Pfinzing while members of both families looked on.

On October 4, after a grand family procession to St. Lorenz's, the church wedding occurred. In attendance were numerous guests, among them prominent councilmen, all of whom were treated to a musical extravaganza.[154] The standard wedding service began with the priest asking Lucas and Anna Maria their names and whether they wanted to be one another's wedded spouse. Then followed seemingly every pregnant biblical passage on the estate of marriage: "It is not good that man should be alone [etc.]" (Gen. 2:18–24); "A man shall leave his father and mother and be joined to his wife" (Matt. 19:3–9); "Husbands love your wives, as Christ loved the Church" (Eph. 5:25–29); "Wives be subject to your husbands" (Eph. 5:22); "To the woman, God said . . . in pain you shall bring forth children" (Gen. 3:16); "To Adam He said . . . in toil you shall eat [of the ground] all the days of your life" (Gen. 3:17); "Male and female He created them [and commanded them to] be fruitful and multiply" (Gen. 1:27–28); "He who finds a wife finds a good thing and obtains favor from the Lord" (Prov. 18:22).

Rings and vows were then exchanged as each pledged their trust to the other, the service ending with prayers and blessings for all!

This is a great mystery. . . . Let each one of you love his wife as himself, and let the wife see that she respects her husband [Eph. 5:32–33]. . . . Your wife will be like a fruitful vine within your house; your children will be like olive shoots around your table. . . . May you see your children's children [Ps. 128:1–6].[155]

On October 10, a last festive event capped the weeks of the marriage, with two tables of guests attending a private celebration at

Paul Behaim's home into the wee hours of the morning, concluding three hours before dawn.[156]

Over the previous month and still arriving after were congratulations and regrets from favorite kin and comrades. Cousin Albrecht had earlier sent two wagonloads of hunter's catch from Gräfenberg on September 6, with an apology for the seasonal paucity of fowl and the complete lack of white fish.[157] Never one to miss an opportunity to embroider and tease, he addressed the letter to Lucas as "Knight of Jerusalem and Castle Captain of Nürnberg,"[158] the one an apparent allusion to Lucas's recent knighting, the other an apparent term of endearment among his peers, connected perhaps with the proximity of his father's house to the city's castle. Also, on September 6, writing from France in the French he was then mastering, Paul Pfinzing extended congratulations and regrets. Although he would miss the ceremony and celebrations, he begged his new brother-in-law to extend his courtesy to an unidentified brunette known to them both, and to kiss her hands and dance a round with her in his name, should she attend the wedding dance.[159] Lucas also received a letter from his ill-fated half brother Georg, who wrote belatedly from Regensburg on October 13, where he had just arrived exhausted en route to Austria, having been forced to make the greater part of the journey by foot after his horse had gone lame. Ordered to be in Linz by the fifteenth for the emperor's arrival, he, too, was unable to join the family celebrations in Nürnberg.[160]

The new year brought the newlyweds improved family harmony and financial fortune. On January 18, Paul Behaim awarded his new daughter-in-law fifty gulden for a golden headpiece, apparently a belated New Year's gift.[161] On February 9, Lucas received his "one-seventh" paternal inheritance to do with as he pleased.[162] As Paul Behaim then had ten living children—Lucas from his first marriage, eight from his second, and two-year-old Stephan Carl from his recent third—the portion appears to have been more than an equal-share of the paternal inheritance as it then stood, padded perhaps to reflect a greater portion of joint family income dating from his father's first marriage, and also recognizing Lucas's stature as the first-born male. Ten days later (February 20), Lucas also took sole-control of one-half of the maternal inheritance,[163] evidently both

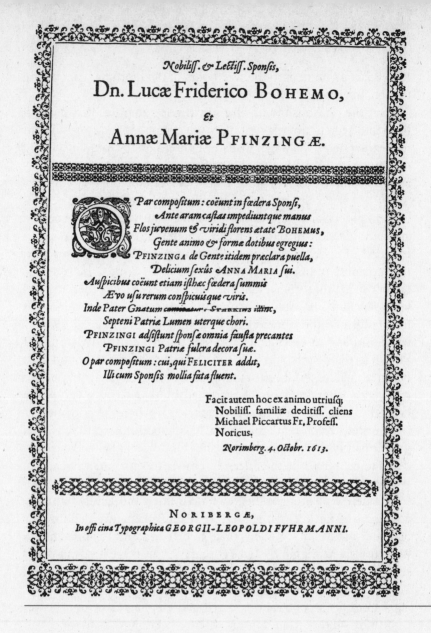

Nobiliff. & Lectiff. Sponsis,

Dn. Lucæ Friderico Bohemo,

Et

Annæ Mariæ Pfinzingæ.

Par compositum: coëunt in fœdera Sponsi,
Ante aram castas impediuntque manus
Flos juvenum & viridi florens ætate Bohemus,
Gente animo & formæ dotibus egregius:
Pfinzinga de Gente itidem præclara puella,
Delicium sexûs Anna Maria sui.
Auspicibus coëunt etiam isthæc fœdera summis
Ævo usu rerum conspicuisque viris.
Inde Pater Gnatum commestur · Stakkiws illinc,
Septeni Patriæ Lumen uterque chori.
Pfinzingi adsistunt sponsæ omnia fausta precantes
Pfinzingi Patriæ fulcra decora suæ.
O par compositum: cui, qui Feliciter addit,
Illi cum Sponsis mollia fata fluent.

Facit autem hoc ex animo utriusq;
Nobiliff. familiæ deditiff. cliens
Michael Piccartus Fr. Profeff.
Noricus,

Norimberg. 4. Octobr. 1613.

Noribergæ,
In offi cina Typographica Georgii-Leopoldi Fvhrmanni.

principal and interest, which consisted of working mines in the Tyrol and Steiermark left him by his mother.[164] As Lucas surely regretted, his father retained legal lifetime use of the fruits of the maternal inheritance, and evidently continued to draw income from the half he kept until his death in 1621, after which it all became Lucas's.

Wedding Announcement

To the Most Noble & Most Excellent Couple
Herr Lucas Friedrich Behaim
and
Anna Maria Pfinzing

O well-matched pair! The couple unite in vows
  And join chaste hands before the altar:
BEHAIM, in the flower of youth, flourishing in the vigor of his age,
  Outstanding in his family, mind, and appearance.
And from the PFINZING race, a noble girl,
  ANNA MARIA, the delight of her sex.
These vows are attended by the happiest auspices,
  By men known for their age and experience.
On either side, the son is accompanied by his father and Starrus,[1]
  Each the light of the sevenfold chorus of his fatherland
The PFINZINGS stand by the bride, praying for every good fortune,
  The PFINZINGS, the glorious pillars of their fatherland.
O well-matched pair! May he who adds his blessing to them
  Enjoy with the couple a happy fate!

Composed from the heart
By the most devoted client
Of both most noble families,
Michael Piccart, Professor at Nürnberg.
Nürnberg, 4 October, 1614

At Nürnberg
From the Printing Shop of Georg Leopold Furhmann

---

[1] The Latinized name of Lucas's other escort (unidentifiable).
(From Germanisches Nationalmuseum, Behaim Archiv, Fasz. 184.)

By the end of April, Lucas was employed in the city judiciary. On August 1, 1614, he and Anna Maria moved out of Grandmother Lindner's house and into the refurbished one on Fortress Street, earlier arranged for them by his father.[165] Paul Behaim visited them there for the last time on November 12, 1621,[166] by which time there were three grandchildren for him to enjoy: five-year-old Anna, four-year-old Georg, and six-month-old Johann. In June 1622, six months after his father's death, Lucas, at thirty-five, moved his young family into the Behaim family house,[167] where he had grown up and would now become the patriarch. In that role, he was father to his three children (a fourth and last, Susanna, joined them in 1622) and big brother and guardian to his four minor half siblings from his father's second and third marriages.[168] There, in the family house, he and Anna Maria lived together for another twenty-six years before Lucas's death in 1648, which was followed by hers six years later.[169]

2

BIRTH AND EARLY
CHILDHOOD

*The Three Sons of Christoph Scheurl
and Katharina Fütterer*

By the will of the Lord God, to whom alone praise and honor is
due in all things, my dear wife Katharina, who had calculated the
delivery no sooner than *Urbani* [May 25], gave birth to an early
son on the Friday after *Misericordia Domini,* April 19 [1532] at
three and a quarter hours sunrise, or 8:15 A.M. by the tower
clock. . . . The Frau Doctor had some pains at 1:30 A.M., yet la-
bored only a short time with the birth, which was not without
with much pain and wailing. The birth occurred in the back house
across from the *Rosenbad* in the room where we usually dine.[1]

Thus did the renowned Nürnberg jurist and diplomat Dr. Christoph Scheurl II (1481–1542), at age fifty-one, record in his daily account book the birth of his first surviving child, Georg. The birth
occurred in a detached structure at the back of the house maintained as a separate dwelling and facing one of the city's public baths
(*Rosenbad*), beyond which lay the neighborhood (*Judengasse*) in
which the city's Jews had lived until 1499. After two centuries of
sporadic persecution, the visible Jewish community lost its syna-
gogue and dispersed in that year, leaving only a few individual families behind and under constant pressure to convert to Christianity.[2]

Wife Katharina, born Fütterer (1491–1543), was the daughter of local merchant Ulrich Fütterer (1449–1524), who traded primarily and very successfully with Milan.[3] Her mother, Ursula Behaim (1473–1529), was the sister of famed explorer and cartographer Martin Behaim II (1459–1507), creator of the oldest surviving globe of the earth (the "earth apple"), and distant cousin of Paul and Lucas Friedrich Behaim. It was Martin Behaim's rudimentary map of the world that had guided Columbus to America.[4] The "Frau Doctor," as Christoph respectfully called his wife (she shared his title by marriage), was forty-one at the time of the birth.

Celebratory portrayal of the Scheurl and Tucher coats of arms.

The dedication to Dr. Christoph Scheurl reads: "Here shine brightly the Scheurl and Tucher coats-of-arms, which you, Dr. Scheurl, have inherited from your two parents"—a reference to the marriage of Helena Tucher (1462–1516) and Christoph's father in 1480. The Scheurl crest (left) displays a *Panteltier*, a legendary perfect animal, the offspring of a lion and a dragon. At the peak of the Tucher coat-of-arms stands a Moor's torso, a practice popular among Franconian families, including Albrecht Dürer's. The figure is actually St. Maurice, a white Christian soldier, beheaded in the third century for refusing to permit the Roman legion he commanded to worship the Roman gods. Because his name was also that for black ink (*Mauro*) and for Moor (*Maur*), medieval artists progressively painted him black. For Tucher merchants trading in Italy and the Near East, he was a perfect talisman. This rare manuscript recently appeared in a full-page ad in the *Wall Street Journal*, January 17, 1997, used by IBM to illustrate its new patented digital watermark.

From Eugen Schöler, *Fränkische Wappen erzählen Geschichte und Geschichten* (Newstadt a.d. Aisch, (1992), pp. 13, 94–95; Otto Titan von Hefner, ed., *J. Siebmachers grosses und algemeines Wappenbuch* (Nürnberg, 1856), II/1, p. 110, Tafel 134; Jean Devisse and Michel Mollat, *The Image of the Black in Western Art*, vol. 2 (Cambridge, Mass., (1970), pp. 215–218. (By permission of Stiftung Luthergedenkstätten in Sachsen-Anhalt, Lutherhalle/Melanchthonhaus Wittenberg.)

For the parents, the boy was a godsend for whom they had waited a seeming eternity, twelve years, in fact, having previously endured ten unsuccessful pregnancies.[5] Not only were they both in middle age when their first surviving child was born, they had also married quite late by contemporary practice. In Nürnberg at the time, women at first marriage were normally in their early to middle twenties and men in their middle to late twenties. On their wedding day (August 29, 1519) Christoph was thirty-eight and Katharina twenty-eight.

At the time of the marriage, Christoph lived alone in the sprawling family house in the lane under the city's fortress (Castle Street in modern Nürnberg),[6] just a few houses down from Michael Wolge-muth (ca. 1434–1519), Albrecht Dürer's teacher, on the opposite side of the street. Until 1509, Dürer (1490–1534/35 or 1538) himself had lived only a few blocks away, directly across from Christoph's close friend, Johannes Neudörfer (1497–1563), the city's script and math master, and tutor to the children of the city's elite. Christoph had been "orphaned" earlier in the year (January 29) when his father died of natural causes while visiting the family mines in Schlagen-wald in Bohemia, Christoph's mother having predeceased him three years earlier (1515).[7] Christoph's only sibling, younger brother Al-brecht (1482–1531), was away in Saxony at this time, having been posted to the ducal mint in Annaberg in 1518 and showing no signs of returning soon.[8]

Reform and Reformation

In addition to the isolation of the cavernous family house, bereft of parents, siblings, and a spouse, Christoph had, by 1519, to con-tend increasingly with the changing religious and political world surrounding it. Religious change had been brewing in Nürnberg since the late fifteenth century, when the city's magistrates initiated their own reforms of city cloisters and churches with the support of reform-minded clergy and laity.[9] As he now watched emerging Humanist and evangelical critics ridicule the Church's theologians as "obscure men," denounce its clergy as immoral, and dismiss key doctrines and popular religious practices (papal supremacy, clerical celibacy, monasteries and nunneries, veneration of saints and relics, indulgences, pilgrimages, and at least four of the seven sacraments) as unbiblical and mercenary,[10] Christoph could not have mistaken the difficulties that lay ahead for the city in the dawning new Protes-tant age.

Christoph had actually joined those sowing the seeds of reform in the years after becoming chief counsel (Ratskonsulent) to the Nürn-berg city council in April 1512. In 1516, he became a member of the new *Sodalitas Staupitziana,* a group of reform-minded clergy and laity that met regularly for Bible study and discussion of the controversial theological issues then seizing Germany. The sodality had been founded in 1516 by Johannes von Staupitz (ca. 1468–1524), the vicar general of the Augustinian Observants and Martin Luther's mentor and confidant since the pair's days together in the Erfurt monastery (Staupitz brought the young Augustinian Luther to Wittenberg). Staupitz and Christoph already knew each other from their student days in law school in Bologna (1498–1506), and Staupitz had later helped him land his first position, in Wittenberg, after those studies ended. Like many reform-minded Catholics at the time, both men hated the "tyranny" of the papacy and shared Luther's desire for biblical reforms.[11]

Christoph, however, wanted no part of Luther's challenge of church authority once the revolutionary direction of his teaching became clear. Having initially thought well of Luther's reforms, he would end up seeking the company of Luther's strongest critics. To his distress, the number of those critics steadily dwindled in Nürnberg after 1517. Building on the *Sodalitas Staupitziana,* long-standing local anticlericalism, the arrival of evangelical preachers, and a flood of Lutheran and Erasmian pamphlets exposing traditional doctrine and piety, Lutheranism steadily triumphed in the city. Nürnberg's *Ratskonsulent,* along with many other patrician and burgher families still loyal to the old Church, found themselves having to live with both criticism and new policies offensive to their private beliefs. However, since the ultimate outcome of these developments remained unsure in the 1520s, a certain caution and diplomacy in public behavior became the price of peace and peace of mind for many principled people.[12] One result was a long period in which Nürnberg's new Protestants and old Catholics mixed freely in public spaces, which, except for a few convents and imperial residences, were officially Lutheran, while in their private spaces, many continued as far as possible to hold and practice traditional beliefs.

Although neither Christoph Scheurl nor Martin Luther knew it at the time, their different paths through the century's greatest conflict were already signaled on the day in 1517 when Luther posted his famous *95 Theses* on the door of Castle Church in Wittenberg. On that day, Christoph, 300 kilometers away in Nürnberg, coincidently wrote letters to two Wittenberg canons in which he requested their assistance in arranging Masses in Wittenberg for his own and his recently deceased mother's soul. One of those canons was Otto Beckmann (1476–1556), a professor of rhetoric at the university and Christoph's closest friend during his earlier years at Wittenberg (1507–1512). Although still close to Luther and Melanchthon in 1517, Beckmann, like Christoph, would continue to cling to traditional beliefs after the triumph of Lutheranism. He became the prior of St. Giles's cloister in Münster and later represented the bishop of Osnabruck at the Diet of Augsburg (1530), where the definitive statement of Lutheran beliefs, the *Augsburg Confession*, was presented to the emperor.[13]

Wittenberg at this time was home to the largest relic collection in northern Europe, containing over nineteen thousand pieces—a mountain of indulgence sufficient to release sinful souls from countless years of suffering in purgatory—and housed ironically in a building adjacent to Castle Church, on whose doors Luther nailed his famous theses. The Masses requested by Christoph for himself and his mother were to be celebrated in the name of that great treasury of divine merit.[14]

Within weeks of the appearance of Luther's theses, Christoph had a copy in hand, which he duplicated and sent to select friends and officials, among them Dr. Johannes Eck (1486–1543). At the same time, he corresponded favorably about them with Luther. In doing so, he did not intend to endorse the new Wittenberg theology, much less the coming iconoclasm of the early Reformation, neither of which were apparent to the public in the fall of 1517. At this point, Christoph remained friendly to both sides, possibly hoping to play a mediating role, something Luther's future defender, the elector of Saxony, an admirer of Nürnberg's skillful *Ratskonsulent,* would in fact soon be urging him to do, as the princes themselves sought a peace-saving compromise.

Despite the pragmatic tolerance and spiritual mixing in effect beneath the harsher laws and public stance of officials in this period of religious transition, Christoph's confessional agility cannot be described as completely sincere. His loyalty to tradition, as his contemporaries knew, was deep and unyielding, and it soon brought him the withering criticism of Nürnberg's most famous Humanist, Wilibald Pirckheimer (1470–1530). In a savage satire of Johannes Eck, entitled "Eck Hewed" (*Eccius dedolatus*), Pirckheimer portrayed Christoph as the wily Dominican's Nürnberg spy. The wounds of that attack could only have contributed to Christoph's gradual retreat from local public life. Not only did he marry in 1519, he also increased his diplomatic missions abroad during the early 1520s.[15]

Such maneuvers, of course, could not go on forever. By the mid–1520s, evangelical preachers had captured a majority of the clergy, townspeople, and members of the city council. Between 1523 and 1524, the triumph of Lutheran doctrine was becoming visible in changes in church liturgy. Fearing the deep popular support for religious reform, and aware that it, too, would gain broad new desired powers over the city's ecclesiastical and religious life by such changes, the council convened an orderly religious colloquy to debate the issues. The debate, held in March 1525, went on for two weeks, during which each side had its say at length before the council declared the city, as it had intended to do from the start, officially Lutheran. That the monks invited to defend Catholic teaching and practice required a daily police escort to and from their convents indicates how inevitable that decision had become. Ever cautious, the council described the debate to the outside world as "a Christian, brotherly, and friendly discussion in all kindness." Long a center of the Holy Roman Empire, Nürnberg now became a citadel of the new German Lutheran world as well.

By virtue of his official position, Christoph not only sat as one of the presiding officers (*praeses*) during these proceedings but was also tapped by the council to give the keynote address on its behalf. That duty required him to read the following instructions, which could not have come easily to the lips of the Catholic *Ratskonsulent*.

> In this colloquy, [the two sides must] put aside popes, councils, Church fathers, tradition, holiness, statutes, decretals, customs, old usages, and the like [that is] everything that is not grounded solely on the clear Word of God, the pure Gospel, and the biblical

Scriptures, for the latter are the only currency accepted in this marketplace.[16]

The weeks after the debate saw the abolition of the Mass, the veneration of saints, and many traditional feast days, along with the introduction of Humanist educational reforms into the schools and the ascendancy of secular authority over the Church. Christoph was far from alone in his disappointment with some of those religious changes; an estimated one-third of Nürnberg city council members continued to hold Catholic beliefs as well.[17] In 1528, Christoph joined with his old critic Pirckheimer—who, despite his earlier attacks on clerical tyranny and abuse, was also no Lutheran—to protest the removal of the Mass and auricular confession from the city's churches, indelible marks of the Reformation's triumph. Junior bürgermeister Christoph Fürer (1479–1537), Christoph's maternal uncle by marriage, resigned his council position over such changes in traditional practice.[18]

Marriage

While Christoph had likely had female companions during his long years of bachelorhood—the age was far less continent than its modern reputation alleges[19]—he did not yet have a true life partner. And whatever his ultimate motives, when he married, Christoph escaped his solitude, gained the progeny he desired, and lessened his unhappiness with the changing religious and political world. Together, he and Katharina built their own mighty fortress around a traditional way of life both still found congenial, while at the same time accommodating the newly emergent Protestant majority.

As the eldest of ten children, of whom only four survived beyond birth and early childhood, including her twin sister, Katharina Fütterer had grown up with much pain and responsibility. Like Christoph, she also had important contacts with traditional Nürnberg society through her family. Her brother Gabriel (1493–1527) married (serially) daughters from three of the city's most prominent families (Paumgartner, Haller, and Muffel), while her sister Magdalena was a nun in Pillenreut cloister.

Thinking back on his wedding day in 1519, Christoph recalled his bride of twenty-eight as "pale, thin, lanky, very well-formed, quite bosomy, large-bodied, and completely beautiful." That she was conscious lifelong of her looks is suggested by his further report of her fear of growing old. When approaching fifty, she began to say she was forty-six and would let no one tell her otherwise. Throughout her life she was, according to her husband, as "healthy as a fish," never stricken with a serious illness, not even so much as a toothache. As for her inner qualities, Christoph described her as neither intellectual nor overly religious, a serene, God-fearing, and compliant person, whose first priority was always her children.[20]

On their wedding day (August 29), the Scheurls and the Fütterers, both wealthy Catholic families, treated their relatives and neighbors to a true spectacle. The formal proceedings had begun three weeks earlier, at 7 A.M. on August 6, when Christoph and his future father-in-law met at the Rathaus in the presence of the city's chief financial officer, Christoph's uncle Anton Tucher, and junior bürgermeister and cousin Caspar Nützel to formalize the marriage agreement (*Abrede*) earlier worked out in private between the two families at home.[21] Prior to this event, the nuns of St. Katharina's cloister had been enlisted as go-betweens and arranged the prior negotiations between Christoph and Katharina's parents.[22] After the signing, Christoph went with three of the officials present to congratulate the bride and to give her a diamond ring set with three small rubies.[23] A week later (August 13), the couple celebrated a Mass in honor of the Virgin, during which the city's pipers joined the church organ in a musical tribute.

On August 22, the pair notarized the marriage contract by publicly exchanging marriage vows (*Lautmerung*)[24] in the city council's chambers, after which Katharina wore her ring publicly for the first time. Officially, this was the crowning event in a nearly month-long marriage process presided over again by Uncle Anton. In the evening, seventy guests were invited to join the families in celebration. Two days later (August 24), the bride was feted at home in the

Scheurl house (*Heimladung*), and the newlyweds were congratulated at a small dinner party that included her parents and brother Gabriel, Christoph's maternal aunt and uncle—Helena and Hieronymus Ebner—who stood in for his parents (he describes them as "mother" and "father" Ebner), and a few other select relatives. The evening ended with still another dance, this one catering to the younger crowd, to which "almost all [of the city's] noblewomen and maidens" were invited.[25]

Finally, on August 29, the couple appeared publicly at church (*Hochzeit, Kirchgang*), an event that drew the largest crowd yet, as both notable foreign and local guests, including a sizable number of the city's leading officials, physicians, and "honorable burghers," gathered to witness the formal publication of the marriage.[26] Among the scores of guests stood the city's leading Humanist, Pirckheimer, and its greatest artist, Dürer. Also attending were the city's imperial mayor (Hans von Obernitz) and two prominent Dominicans destined to become Martin Luther's leading critics as the religious conflict heated up in the 1520s: Dr. Johannes Eck from nearby Ingolstadt, who was already on the attack, and Nürnberger Johannes Cochlaeus (1497–1552), soon to write the first Catholic exposé of the great reformer's life and teachings.[27] Eck presented Katharina with a bridal crown, while Cochlaeus gave her a carnelian rosary.[28]

Eck had debated Luther in Leipzig just two months earlier (June 28, 1519) and arrived in Nürnberg flush with success and boasting loudly of his triumph over the upstart Wittenberger. This did not sit well with the city's Humanists, who were then sympathetic to Luther's reforms and soon repaid the Dominican's rudeness with a round of their famous satire.[29] Eck would have his revenge as well, however. As papal nuncio, he helped draft and publicize the papal bulls *Exsurge Domine* and *Decet Pontificem Romanum* (1520) that anathematized Luther's teaching, and to which were attached the names of Pirckheimer and Nürnberg's city secretary, Lazarus Spengler, a well-known and—unlike Pirckheimer—consistent supporter of Luther, who had written the first major defense of his teaching by a Nürnberg layman.[30]

Traditional Piety and Education

That long-bachelored and devoutly Catholic Christoph Scheurl found himself both married and the legal counsel of Germany's leading Protestant city is a commentary on both the times and the man. If marriage and family solaced him in hard times, so too did his traditional religious faith. Even by Nürnberg patrician standards, Christoph's Catholic piety ran unusually deep. As a boy, he had been taken regularly to church by his devout father, and later in life vividly recalled attending Sunday and daily worship services at the parish church, claiming never to have missed a sermon. Before their deaths, both his mother (d. June 1516) and his father (d. January 1519) endowed a thousand Masses in their memory.[31]

During his childhood, he had numerous aunts and cousins in city and area cloisters, two of whom—maternal aunts Apollonia (1460–1533) and Barbara (1452–1518) Tucher—were prioresses, Apollonia at St. Clara's (after 1494) and Barbara the first prioress of nearby Engelthal. Well educated, Apollonia translated the Nürnberg cloister's chronicle from Latin into German in 1500. After her death in 1518, Barbara was buried in her cloister's arcade, which allowed her to remain almost as prominent a presence in death as she had been in life.[32]

Christoph visited the two of them often and loved them both. In his fifties, after they had grown quite old, his contact with them still awakened the fondest boyhood memories. A gift of *Lebkuchen* (honeycakes) from Aunt Apollonia on New Year's Eve 1532 reminded him of his aunts' very different recipes for these delightful pastries. Apollonia's were thin and delicate (as a boy, Christoph had called them *flinderlingen,* "sparkling gold leaves"), whereas Aunt Barbara's were thick and heavy, although tasting every bit as good.[33] Christoph's maternal first cousin once removed, Sixt Tucher (1459–1507), the prior of St. Lorenz's Church until 1505, joined the aunts in taking a special interest in Christoph during his youth. After Christoph and his brother Albrecht, at fifteen and fourteen, moved to Heidelberg to begin their formal education, cousin Sixt kept in touch and advised him.[34]

Christoph's prominent aunts and cousins were not the only nuns and clergy in his boyhood world. When he was nine, Dominican priests resided in the Scheurl house, and his father had seriously contemplated entering the city's Dominican cloister in 1503, after debtors (prominent among them the emperor Maximilian) defaulted on large loans he had made to them and a concurrent political defeat in the city council left him on the brink of financial ruin.[35] Imperial Catholic royalty also visited in Christoph's boyhood home, their comings and goings particularly memorable because the family moved to the attached back rooms when they came.[36] On two such occasions in happier times—in 1489 and again in 1491—Emperor Maximilian was his father's guest, the second time taking part in the wedding of Christoph's uncle Stephen Tucher.[37]

Like his father, Christoph would also later entertain a clerical calling—however, not in reaction to a financial crisis in midlife. Having been a sickly child, he was turned early toward the priesthood, a career his mother, who had great ambitions for her firstborn, later redirected toward jurisprudence and the university. The future she envisioned for him may have been modeled after that of cousin Sixt, who had earned bachelor's and dual (civil and canon) law degrees at the Universities of Heidelberg and Padua before returning to Nürnberg and assuming the post of prior of St. Lorenz's.[38] A law degree also opened the option of a civil career, for which Christoph's outgoing nature already gave him a head start. Early in life, his professed motto was an axiom every premodern parent, sensitive to their progeny's safety and success, endeavored to inculcate in their children: "Never ever offend anyone."[39]

That Christoph's childhood piety influenced his adult ambitions is documented during his eight years of protracted legal study and travel in Italy (1498–1506) during his late teens and early twenties. There, he first learned of his father's financial troubles, and, reacting emotionally as a loyal son, he vowed to make a pilgrimage to the shrine of the Virgin in Loreto. Undertaken in 1500, its purpose soon became lost, along with the timely completion of his legal education, amid the irresistible sights and spectacles of Renaissance Italy. Drawn inexorably from Loreto to Naples and Rome, he virtually resigned his legal studies, wandering about Italy for the next four years and delaying his degree until December 26, 1506.

The year 1500 was a jubilee year in Rome, which meant rare benefits for pilgrims—among them full indulgence for all outstanding penances to anyone taking a fifteen-day guided tour of the graves of the Apostles. Christoph took advantage of the city's advertised "specials" and joined in many other spiritual celebrations and austerities as well. With other law students, he received Church orders. In a world still profoundly influenced by the Roman Church, ordination broadened vocational opportunities as well as endowed the bearer with the privileges and protection of the Church. Christoph took only lower orders,[40] however, becoming a deacon rather than a priest, which allowed him to retain his lay status and later to marry.

For ambitious young men, ordination was also a prerequisite for academic and administrative positions in universities and other institutions affiliated with or deeply influenced by the Church. Without it, Christoph would not have been eligible to become a student syndic at the University of Bologna in 1505, nor later to assume the rectorship of the University of Wittenberg (1507). The Church also encouraged such early ordination as a disciplinary measure, for it brought university students more firmly under its control and moral influence. Because higher education at this time remained heavily clerical and the study of civil law continued to be tightly bound with that of canon or Church law, not a few students, Christoph and cousin Sixt Tucher among them, maximized their career options by taking a degree in both laws.[41]

From Wittenberg to Nürnberg

In light of his later unhappiness with the Reformation, it is ironic that Christoph's career should begin at the University of Wittenberg, where he was professor of law from 1507 to 1512 and also briefly served as rector.[42] Among his colleagues was young Martin Luther himself, then an obscure Augustinian monk in his midtwenties who regularly visited the city from his cloister in Erfurt to teach Aristotelian philosophy (1508) in the newly founded (1502) Saxon university of Elector Frederick the Wise, his future patron and protector. In the year Christoph left Wittenberg (1512) to return to Nürnberg, Luther received his doctorate in theology there and launched his epochal career.

Had Christoph been able to take his newly acquired legal skills wherever he pleased in 1507, it would not have been to Wittenberg. He coveted the post of prior at St. Lorenz's Church in Nürnberg, previously held by cousin Sixt. That position, however, had recently (1505) been awarded to Anton Kress (1478–1513), another cousin by marriage,[43] and no other comparable position was then available to him in Nürnberg. His father and cousin Anton Tucher (1458–1524), a high-ranking councilman,[44] early targeted Wittenberg as the next best opportunity.

During these years, the relationship between father and son was not a happy one. By 1504, Christoph senior's financial troubles threatened to end his son's wanderings in Italy. The strain was made apparent by the father's accusations of his son's buying clothes beyond his needs, while Christoph's mother complained to relatives about the sacrifices the parents were making to keep him in books.[45] Despite this breakdown of family harmony, all joined in the effort to keep Christoph's Italian education alive and his future bright. Cousin Sixt helped him secure loans, while his mother sent him a ring to pawn. In 1505, his father approached Elector Frederick the Wise at the imperial diet in Cologne and came away with a promise that he would consider Christoph for a post at the University in Wittenberg in Saxony. The new university had been created primarily for the training of civil servants in the craft of civil and Roman law, Christoph's speciality.[46]

Christoph made his own enterprising contribution to the Saxon job hunt. Having been chosen in 1504 by the German delegation of students in Bologna to serve as one of the university's four student syndics, or representatives—like a modern university, Renaissance Bologna also had representative student government—it became

Christoph's responsibility to give the official student oration when a Saxon assumed the rectorship in the university. Copies of his celebration of Saxony quickly found their way to key people in both Wittenberg and Nürnberg. True to his word to his father, Elector Frederick met with Christoph during a visit to Italy in 1506 and offered him a position in Wittenberg at the respectable starting salary of 140 gulden per annum.[47]

That Wittenberg was to be only a stepping stone back to Nürnberg, or possibly a position at the imperial court, is suggested by Christoph's continuing cultivation of his contacts within the patrician and imperial circles of his hometown. In addition to lobbying the ruler of Saxony, Christoph published a medley of religious writings and prayers by church fathers dedicated to Charitas Pirckheimer (1466–1532),[48] the powerful patrician abbess of Nürnberg's St. Clara's cloister and sister of Humanist Wilibald, among whose circle Christoph wanted to be numbered.

Having praised Wittenberg as "a marbled city" upon learning of his appointment there, Christoph arrived in the spring of 1507 to discover what he now observed to be an "unimportant country-town," one even Martin Luther, who loved it more, described as "the edge of civilization."[49] The new professor's salary also did not live up to what had been promised, having shrunk 42 percent by his arrival (from 140 to 80 gulden). In addition, his colleagues immediately elected him rector of the faculty of twelve, an unexpected and challenging start. Strict in his governance—he fined students half a gulden for carrying weapons and carousing at local inns—Christoph proved to be a successful administrator and was reportedly liked by the students.

He made an important friend in Lucas Cranach (1472–1553), already famous for his altars and portraits and destined in the 1520s and 1530s to immortalize the Saxon reformers in individual and group portraits, while assisting the Reformation as well with comparatively crude propaganda.[50] It was, however, Cranach's peerless renditions of traditional religious scenes that made Christoph his great admirer. In what would become Christoph's best known oration, delivered on the occasion of a Wittenberg doctoral promotion in November 1508, he praised Cranach as Saxony's supreme artist, sec-

Christoph Scheurl, by Lucas Cranach, 1509. (By permission of Dr. S. Frhr. von Scheurl, Scheurl-Bibliothek, Nürnberg.) In the inscription on the left, Cranach praises his own talent: "Traveler, if you know Scheurl, tell me who is more Scheurl, he himself or this portrait of him."

ond only to Dürer among German artists, a compliment Cranach re-paid him the following year (1509) by painting Christoph's portrait.[51]

Despite such friendships, a secure position in the university, and the opportunity to increase his much-liked diplomatic missions on behalf of the city and the Saxon princes, Christoph continued to long for Nürnberg. By 1509, he had been away for fourteen years—since 1496, when he first began his university education in Heidelberg in his midteens. Also, the active life of a lawyer and diplomat had become far more appealing to him than the contemplative life of a jurist and a teacher. Perceiving their young professor's restlessness, the Saxon princes urged him to enter their service, take a Saxon wife, and settle permanently in Saxony. Although an outsider, and already burned by the Saxons in the matter of his salary, Christoph gives every appearance of having been sincerely torn between remaining in Saxony, where his options were several and sure, and returning to Nürnberg, where his prospects remained vague. Now in his late twenties, he had also begun to ponder the pros and cons of bachelorhood, although there is no surviving evidence of any serious romance at this time.

Earlier (1506), when he had weighed a legal career in Wittenberg against a lower clerical or religious one in Nürnberg, he sought the advice of the famous Neapolitan astrologer Lucas Gauricus (1478–1558).[52] Finding himself again at a crossroads, he turned to two German astrologers—Conrad Tockler (d. 1530), professor of medicine in Leipzig and a transplanted Nürnberger (hence his popular name Noricus),[53] and Nürnberger Georg Leimbach—each of whom cast his horoscope. And, adding political advice to astrological, Christoph wrote to the prior of St. Lorenz's, cousin Anton Kress, who urged him not to serve a Saxon prince, whereas at least one of his astrologers advised him to settle in Saxony.

If such contradictory counsel from well-positioned kin and stars was not confusing enough, Nürnberg forced a decision when, in 1510, he was offered the position of city counsel. Although a year and a half would pass before he finally made up his mind, by the spring of 1512, Christoph had returned to Nürnberg for good, henceforth to be the city's lead lawyer, a sometime judge in the city judiciary, and frequent foreign diplomat at a much-improved combined salary of 240 gulden per annum.[54] These positions not only promised to showcase his legal and diplomatic skills, they also allowed him to indulge his love of travel. The result was a blending of power and pleasure, vocation and avocation, as Christoph found

himself negotiating on the city's behalf with heads of state as far
north as Berlin and Breslau and as far south as Barcelona.

Fertility

    Although Christoph wed for all the expected personal, social,
and cultural reasons, the marriage was also a response to changing
times. As becomes clear from the full record of his family life, he
gained from his marriage a satisfying communal life, which the new
Lutheran confession and politics of Nürnberg could no longer provide a couple with the Scheurls' traditional sentiments. In marriage
lay the hope of a more immediate and reliable self-fulfillment within
a new community more respectful of his beliefs and amenable to
his will.
    Christoph would not declare himself to be completely happy,
however, until the marriage transformed itself into a family by the
successful birth of Georg in 1532. As much as he may have loved
Katharina and marriage, Christoph loved his sons and family more,
the pleasures of being a parent proving to transcend those of a mere
spouse. For both parents, the boy's arrival was a miracle. Acknowledging Katharina to be a "good, savvy childbearer," and admiring
her for enduring more misfortune in childbearing than any other
mother in the city, Christoph hastened to point out that God, not
she, controlled her pregnancies.[55]
    After twelve years of trying, they had had only four miscarriages
and the nonviable premature births of three daughters and three
sons to show for their efforts. The miscarriages occurred during the
first three years of marriage, at eight, twelve (twice), and thirteen
weeks of gestation. Then, on March 15, 1522, "an eighteen-week
dead, or barely alive [recognizable] boy" was spontaneously aborted
three hours before daybreak. As the Church permitted in such instances, the child was verbally baptized, apparently by the mother,
and named ("Christoph") on the spot, a so-called "emergency bap-

tism."[56] Later, Christoph confided that his heartbreak at the loss of his first son and namesake ended only after he "became accustomed to the annual misfortune," by which he meant the steady succession of premature births that followed: Helena, who arrived nine weeks early (October 27, 1524) and lived only four hours; Ursula, nine weeks early (October 27, 1525) and five hours; Katharina, seven weeks early (September 25, 1526) and nine hours; Albrecht, eight weeks early (December 25, 1527) and thirty-two hours; and Hieronymus (March 19, 1533), nine weeks early and ninety-six hours. After Albrecht's birth, the father described himself as "never having been richer in his life," since no child of his had lived so long. However, by Hieronymus's death, he was beyond remorse: "by now," he wrote of himself in the third person, "the father was accustomed to have a child arrive about eight weeks premature [and die]."[57]

That each of the premature children was baptized and properly named, whereas each miscarriage was merely noted as such, may reflect a contemporary belief, articulated by one contemporary expert (Eucharius Rösslin), that human life did not begin in the womb before the fetus's "inspiration" or reception of a soul, which was said to occur in the third month. Prior to this time, only formless matter was believed to exist in the womb.[58] Since the Scheurls had unnamed miscarriages at twelve and thirteen weeks, such premature births in the first trimester appear not to have been recognized as true human beings, even though the announcement of a pregnancy in the second month created awareness of a new presence in both the mother and the household. Definite human form and recognizable gender appear to have been the criteria for baptizing and naming a nonviable premature child.

In the Scheurls' world, sterility was the great curse of a marriage, and miscarriage and premature birth only more perverse forms of it.[59] The standard wedding gifts of swaddling (diapers), cradles, and bathing bowls document the equation of marriage with pregnancy and family. If the pain and debilitation of serial pregnancies could encourage a contraceptive mentality in decade-old marriages,[60] such thoughts remained far from the minds of newlyweds and couples who did not yet have their full complement of offspring. Infertile women, often with their husbands at their sides, made pilgrimages to shrines rumored to assist conception. In urban households, a pregnancy was an event to celebrate; upon its announcement, newly pregnant wives might expect a gift from their husbands, a reduction of their household chores, and encouragement from all sides to take better care of themselves.[61]

The gender of the child also became an immediate topic of conversation within the household, as both parents and servants made guesses from telltale signs of maternal behavior. One late-sixteenth-century (male) gynecological authority cited cravings for coal, fruit and vegetable peelings, chalk, glue, axle grease, and live fish as good indications of a baby girl, apparently tracing such cravings to a tickling of the mother's womb by the (illogically) presumed longer growing hair on a female fetus.[62] On festive occasions, toasts were made to "little Hans in the cellar" and "little Gretchen in the oven," as the new life in the womb immediately became a member of the household. In royal and noble families, a pregnant wife might find herself toasted with a special silver service, constructed to allow the figure of a small child to emerge from a hollow space when the wine was poured.[63]

Being childless in a society that equated marriage with family, devout couples like the Scheurls could only view their condition as the curse of God. Their faith, however, also presented them with examples of biblical women whose wombs God also mysteriously closed for long periods of time, only then to allow them to become mothers several times over. Comparing Katharina's situation to that of Hannah in the Bible (1 Sam. 1), Christoph credited the arrival of their long-awaited "Samuel" (Georg) to their repeated prayers to the God of Israel.[64]

While not doubting God's hand in Georg's birth any more than her husband, Katharina also believed that medical intervention had been the chosen means. Christoph had apparently brooded publicly over their inability to become parents, and while on a business trip to Forchheim two years before Georg's birth (1530), acquaintances there, upon hearing his sad story, remembered a similarly afflicted local woman who had discovered a medical remedy. Directed to her,

Christoph learned that she had successfully ended her unhappy string of miscarriages by bleeding herself during pregnancy.[65]

In the sixteenth century, bleeding at least once a year was a widely practiced prophylaxis,[66] and health-conscious family members reminded one another of their bleeding dates, which contemporary calendars helpfully correlated with the most auspicious days of the year in accordance with one's zodiacal sign. However, as a general health measure for pregnant women and fetuses, bleeding during pregnancy was condemned by contemporary medical authorities, particularly if done during the first and third trimesters, when it was known to weaken both mother and child and likely to induce a miscarriage.[67]

After Christoph returned to Nürnberg and reported the experience of the woman in Forchheim, Katharina bled herself well into her next pregnancy, doing so at least as late as the sixth month.[68] That she, like the woman in Forchheim, delivered healthy children after such perilous experimentation suggests that the God of Israel may have been more gracious to them both than either ever realized. In fact, Katharina appears to have experimented with bleeding during pregnancy in earlier years, so that the news from Forchheim may have been less a discovery for her than the restoration of her faith in a remedy only tentatively explored earlier.

That possibility emerges from Christoph's description of the reaction within the household to her first premature birth in March 1522, after four miscarriages in the previous two years. At the time of its occurrence, Duke Georg of Saxony[69] and his staff were in Nürnberg on business, and the duke was a guest in the Scheurl house. Many years later, Christoph recalled that members of the duke's party had blamed the boy's death on the bleeding, saying that in Meissen such a practice was viewed as unusual, if not harmful. Katharina reportedly rebutted the charge, blaming the early birth and death of eighteen-week-old Christoph on her excessive anger at a suspected maid the night before—a point of view Christoph theoretically shared, as evidenced when he retrospectively explained the early birth of his ninth and last child (in 1535) as perhaps caused by preceding anger on the mother's part.[70] As an emotion particularly upsetting to the body's humors, anger was believed to threaten the life of a fetus, as it did the health of adults.

Georg's Birth

In the year of Georg's birth (1532), Nürnberg's midwife corps comprised both higher- and lower-class women, with patrician administrators overseeing a professional staff of twenty-one. In addition, there were auxiliary tradeswomen specially trained and licensed by the city to dispense medication during labor. And in the homes of the well-to-do, clinically experienced male surgeons waited in the wings, ready to render emergency assistance should the midwives require it. The upper-class overseers worked gratis, while the midwives received an apparent floating fee for service from the new parents, and the obstetrical "anesthesiologists" were paid a salary of twelve gulden per annum. All three groups took an annual oath of office before the city council.[71]

In the Scheurl household, a midwife attended the labor and conducted the delivery with the assistance of experienced female relatives and friends. On the morning of Georg's birth, Christoph, while not a direct witness to the birth, was no distant spectator either. Unlike fathers elsewhere, Nürnberg fathers appear not to have been encouraged or required to be directly on scene when their wives delivered. However, Christoph points out grousingly that he was run out of the back house by the midwife and her assistants when the time came to arrange the room for the delivery,[72] having been with Katharina up to that point. Thereafter, he remained close enough to hear her cries, which he describes.

As the first one to inform him of the birth, cook Ursula, who evidently passed the word from the midwife, later received the traditional "good news money" (*Botenbrot*). Appropriately, the message made a greater impression on Christoph than did the messenger. Six weeks later (June 3), he listed in his account book the purchase of white cloth for petticoats for "my two maids who won the

Botenbrot"—an entry later crossed out during one of his many emen-
dations of that source as he belatedly recalled that it had been Ursula
alone who had informed him of his son's arrival.[73]

Five women attended Katharina's labor and delivery: a midwife
named Anna,[74] the widows Margaretha Tucher (d. 1557),[75] Ursula
Tetzel (d. 1545),[76] and Magdalena Mugenhofer[77]—and, joining
them later, Katharina Imhof (d. 1553), Ursula Tetzel's sister-in-law.[78]
The four women assisting the midwife had varying degrees of maternal experience, with Katharina Imhof the mother of sixteen children
while Margaretha Tucher had remained childless.[79]

Ursula Tetzel's presence is a commentary on the priority of blood
and friendship over religion. A devout convert to Lutheranism, she
joined with Helena Ebner, Christoph's stand-in mother at his marriage,[80] and Frau Caspar Nützel in a highly public, litigious removal
of their reluctant daughters from St. Clara's cloister as spring turned
to summer in 1525. Ideally, new Protestant regimes dissolved monasteries and convents as unbiblical and economically burdensome
institutions. Early in the year, the city council had appointed an
evangelical preacher and confessor at St. Clara's, and ordered the sisters to replace their nuns' habits with civilian clothes in preparation
for their return to secular life. Absolutely defiant, Abbess Charitas
Pirckheimer emboldened her flock to ignore the council's directives.
As the cloister's official supervisor *(Pfleger)*, Caspar Nützel, himself a
partisan in the conflict, conducted the negotiations between the parents and the abbess[81]—bitter exchanges, to which Christoph's aunt
Apollonia, as St. Clara's prioress, was also surely party.

After several months of noncompliance, the Tetzels, Ebners, and
Nützels appeared at the cloister on June 14 with a wagon and proceeded to remove their daughters forcibly from it. The reluctant
daughters physically resisted, Katharina Ebner arriving home with
a bloodied face, after having been struck in the mouth by her
mother. While all three "liberated" daughters apparently later married, the brawl won the cloister the sympathy of onlookers and
strengthened the abbess's hand in future negotiations over its fate.

Because of such experiences, Church authorities in Nürnberg and
elsewhere in the Protestant world ruled that one or more separate
cloisters might remain open for monks and nuns who sincerely

wanted to remain in the religious life and had nowhere else to go, if pensioned off. At the same time, these cloisters were forbidden from admitting any new candidates. St. Clara's became such a cloister, remaining open until 1590, when the last sister died. During the intervening decades, its inmates reportedly received visits from the Franciscan confessor of the Clares in Bamberg, who, traveling in civilian clothes to conceal his habit, appeared several times a year to hear the sisters' confessions surreptitiously and to celebrate the traditional Mass.[82]

According to Christoph's description of his son's birth, Katharina's labor was short—under seven hours from first contraction to delivery. If the attendants followed the advice of Eucharius Rösslin,[83] the newborn was bathed immediately in warm water and its nose carefully cleaned. Milk or a fragrant blossom sap (elder or peach) may have been added to the water for the first bathing, along with a fresh egg (a symbol of fertility). Fathers sometimes slipped a silver coin into the bathing bowl, both as a bonus for the midwife and a token of their pledge to provide for the child through life. Rösslin and his counterpart at the end of the century, Johannes Coler, recommended bathing infants after naps with warm water two or three times a day, taking care not to scald the child or to get water in its ears. A rubdown with nut or other oils was recommended as protection for the skin. Attendants were further instructed "gently to swaddle" the washed and oiled newborn, and place it on the mother's left side, over her heart.[84]

Fathers, not always willingly, remained on the periphery of these events, as both men and women looked on labor and delivery as women's matters. Some fathers attempted to seize the day by planting a commemorative "birth tree," usually fruit—apple for boys, pear or nut for girls. If the human "twig" failed to grow in the direction it was bent, a father might then vent his anger by chopping down the birth tree.[85]

Once the newborn was safely delivered, housemaids took the good news from door to door, while written announcements were sent to out-of-towners. In faraway Schaffhausen, a so-called "joy maid" ran through the streets with a bouquet on her bosom to announce the birth of a girl; if a boy, she carried an additional, larger bouquet in her hand.[86] The increased plumage expressed both a value judgment and a distinction, attesting the age's preference for male offspring, which appears to have been fully shared across gender lines, particularly with respect to the firstborn. That bias reflected the brighter economic prospects of males in contemporary society, and with it the increased well-being of all dependent family members. For this reason, an elder son might expect deference and sacrifice from his siblings as well, who associated their security with his success.[87]

This was a bias Christoph fully shared. When he recalled Katharina's six short-lived births in a letter to Otto Beckmann, he described the unfortunate offspring as "three females and the same number of the better sex."[88] In Christoph's case, that sentiment may have been strengthened by the fact that he had no sisters or daughters in his life.

In the Wake of Birth

There had been little time for Christoph to savor the two most important events in his life to date. Two weeks after his marriage to Katharina, he had departed Nürnberg on a diplomatic mission to Barcelona seven hundred miles away. Even sooner after the birth of Georg, on May Day, 1532, he found himself at the imperial diet in Regensburg, sixty miles southeast of Nürnberg, negotiating on the latter's behalf.[89] However, before departing, he joined the hallowed ceremonies that inducted his son into contemporary society, as family and friends gathered to greet the new arrival and to pledge their assistance in his civic and religious growth.

The first such event was the sacrament of baptism. The traditional service was a multiple exorcism, intended to free newborns from the eternal consequences (damnation) of the corporate sin of Adam and Eve, and to prepare them, as they grew into adulthood, to resist the temptations of the devil, whose docile servants original sin also disposed them to be. Unbaptized children were deemed defenseless before their baptism, and devout parents counted the death of an unbaptized child among their greatest fears, some believing that such children thereafter became the devil's and remained reprobate souls through all eternity. Stillborns were sometimes rubbed vigorously by anxious parents until a spark of life was perceived, or imagined, and a baptism, "while alive," quickly performed.[90]

The traditional service of baptism began with the priest blowing gently under the eyes of the newborn and commanding the devil: "Flee from this child, unclean spirit, and make room for the Holy Spirit." The child then received the mark of the cross on its forehead and chest and a pinch of consecrated salt in its mouth, this time accompanied by the words: "Take the salt of [divine] wisdom, and may it atone for you in eternity." Thereafter, the priest imitated Christ's healing of a deaf-mute (Mark 7:33–34) and a blind man (John 9:6) by dabbing a mixture of his own sputum and dirt in the child's nose and ears, while pronouncing a double command, the first for the child, the second for the devil: "[Dear child] receive the sweetness [of God]. . . ; devil, flee, for the judgment of God is near." The priest then anointed the child's chest and shoulders with olive oil and placed a consecrated mixture of olive oil and balsam—the holy chrism—on the crown of its head. The final acts of the service belonged to the godparent, who took the naked, baptized child from the priest and clothed it in the traditional white shirt or gown (the *Wester, Alba,* or *Westerhemd*)—symbols of purity and acceptance into the body Christian—which the godparent provided for the occasion. The godparent then named the child, often after the godparent. The service concluded with the placement of a candle in the combined hands of the child and parent(s), who were exhorted to "receive the ardent and blameless Light [of God]."[91]

For the sake of "weak consciences," Martin Luther was prepared to allow Lutheran congregations to keep the traditional "human" additions, so long as pastors made it clear that the sole biblical element in the service was water (not chrism) and the only saving baptism and exorcism were those mediated by an individual's faith.[92] The

Nürnberg church ordinances of 1528 and 1533, under which Georg's baptism was administered, were more restrictive. The first kept the traditional service intact, save for the "unnecessary . . . superstitious . . . inappropriate, and unchristian" holy oil, salt, spittle, and dirt, while the larger and definitive 1533 ordinance called for the removal of all human elements except water and the *Wester*.[93]

In Georg's case, the baptism did not occur at church but at home in the delivery room on the day of his birth. That was both well within the Church's expectations and expressive of his parents' understandable anxiety, given their reproductive history. The clergy preferred that baptism be at church, because far more people would then share in the event and a more substantial lay-clerical intercession on the child's behalf could be made. Expectant parents were instructed by Nürnberg's clergy to adopt the following procedure in baptizing a newborn: If in their and the midwife's judgment, the child was healthy and strong, its baptism should occur in church on the next feast day, of which there were twenty-four during the year; however, if the child was visibly marginal and in imminent danger of dying, then it was to be baptized on the spot by the midwife, who, in Nürnberg, as elsewhere, received instruction from the clergy so that she could properly pronounce the formula of baptism.[94]

Georg was neither in extremis, nor baptized by a midwife. Rather, a priest came to the house later in the day, evidently at the request of the parents to placate their fears.[95] As in the Scheurls' case, which was complicated by their continuing Catholic sympathies, baptism at home appears to have been the layman's, if not the Church's, preference for much of the century. In 1625, a new city ordinance ordered that children, as a rule, be baptized at church and that home baptism become the exception—the latter apparently to be the rule only for illegitimate children, at least after 1663. In so ruling, the council and the Church appear to have misjudged the reaction, because thereafter the number of church baptisms fell off dramatically.

In addition to the preference for early baptism at home, another apparent reason for this lay reaction was the public nuisances baptismal processions had become. Families from all social classes used the occasion of a wedding or a baptism to assemble large, rowdy crowds of relatives and friends. Just as raucous wedding processions required constant scrutiny and discipline, so, too, did noisy baptismal processions, and blowing trumpets from towers and parading through the streets with candelabra were outlawed in 1647. By century's end, the baptismal service had returned to the home.[96]

In addition to the members of both households, seventeen women were present at Georg's baptism, nine from Christoph's side of the family and eight from Katharina's, most of them widows, and several in their last years of life. Mead, wine, and bread were served both before and after the ceremony.

Prominent among those present were Christoph's widowed sister-in-law and her six children—a son (Albrecht) and five daughters ranging in age from one to nine. These children had recently become their uncle's responsibility after the kidnapping and brutal murder of their father and Christoph's only sibling, Albrecht (1482–1531). While returning home from the family mine in Joachimsthal in October 1530, the latter had been waylaid by brigands near Eger, the crossing point from Bohemia into Germany. His captors delivered him into the hands of an infamous renegade knight, Thomas Absberg, who feuded throughout the 1520s with the Swabian League, a confederation of princes, cities, and knights responsible for law and order in upper Germany, and as quick to punish noble outlaws as rebellious peasants. Pleased to have such a promising pawn, Absberg held Albrecht for ransom for nine months before executing him in June 1531, apparently in retaliation for the Swabian League's execution of some of his men. When the League later caught up with Absberg and executed him, Albrecht's ring, prominently bearing the Scheurl coat of arms, was found on his corpse. Removing it from his hand, the executioners sent it with other evidence confirming Absberg's death to King Ferdinand in Prague, who returned it to Christoph in Nürnberg through their mutual friend, Cardinal Christoph Glöss of Trent.[97]

Although the bonds of blood were reason enough for Christoph to assume responsibility for his nephew and nieces, he may have felt a special obligation to do so in light of the advice he had given his sister-in-law after his brother's capture. Knowing her husband to be ill, Anna Scheurl had wanted to ransom him immediately, regardless of the cost, and she turned to Christoph for assistance. Christoph, however, counseled her not to hurry the matter, since doing so, he believed, would only encourage his abductors to keep their victim and raise the ransom. Protesting her willingness to surrender everything she had for her "dearly beloved husband," she pleaded with her brother-in-law not to let concern for money cost Albrecht his life.[98]

Whether swift compliance with Absberg's, demands would have spared Albrecht Scheurl is unknown. Given the habits of outlaws at the time, Christoph's assessment of the situation was reasonable and his advice sound. However, the tragic result, particularly after his sister-in-law's protest and pleading, could only have heightened Christoph's devotion to his deceased brother's family.

On the night of Georg's birth, two other special guests resided in the Scheurl house: Duke Georg of Saxony's chancellor, Simon Pistoris, J.D. (1489–1562), who in the course of his own life fathered twenty-three children by three wives,[99] and his brother-in-law, Wolf Widmann, the bürgermeister of Leipzig. Pistoris had apparently been sent in advance to stand in as godfather for Duke Georg, Christoph's long-time friend and baby Georg's official godfather.

As both an honor and a responsibility, godparentage signified a lifetime commitment to the moral and material well-being of a godchild, and the godparent, as in this case, was almost always of the same or higher social rank than the parents, and could also be more than one person. In 1600, the entire city of Nürnberg, in the persons of two council members, stood as godfather to the son of Baron Hans Adam of Wolfstein.[100] Stand-in or surrogate godparents, like Pistoris, were not uncommon in patrician and burgher families. A busy godparent in a faraway place could hardly anticipate the day of a godchild's birth, especially when dealing with a mother who calculated terms and delivered as erratically as Katharina. Pastor Lorenz Dürnhofer (1532–1594) had three godparents for at least two of his children, and stand-ins like Pistoris were also treated as true, if secondary godparents (baby Georg took Duke Georg's name, not Pistoris's).[101]

That Georg Scheurl's godfather was one of Germany's most pow-

erful and devout Catholic princes was not without consequence
in 1532 Nürnberg, where, since 1525, the Protestant sermon and
liturgy had progressively displaced or modified the Mass and other
traditional practices, including the sacrament of baptism. For the
sizable number of Nürnbergers continuing to hold Catholic beliefs,
it was still possible to confess one's sins, receive Communion, and
baptize and confirm one's children according to the old rites, but
only by traveling to churches outside the city's jurisdiction. In the
late 1520s, a small number of Nürnberg patricians joined together
to support the services of an Italian priest in nearby Buchenbach bei
Erlangen within the Catholic bishopric of Bamberg, and other options for Catholic services also existed within easy traveling distance
of the city.[102]

Although the new Lutheran rites of baptism and dedication
seemingly differed only slightly from traditional practice, in an age
when a great many people counted on religion for their security in
both this life and the next, the concept of a "modest" sacramental or
an "insignificant" liturgical change was an oxymoron. Whatever
other difficulties there may have been, Georg's godfather and namesake, Duke Georg of Saxony, actually refused to be personally present at his godson's baptism because of a single deletion from the
traditional rite. An electoral state since 1356 (that is, one of the
seven lands that could cast a vote for the Holy Roman Emperor),
Saxony had been partitioned in 1485, one part remaining an electoral state, the other becoming the powerful dukedom now ruled
by Duke Georg. Unlike in electoral Saxony, where the also devoutly
Catholic Frederick the Wise (d. 1525) had become Martin Luther's
protector, and his sons and successors the great reformer's devoted
followers as well, ducal Saxony was now the center of German opposition to the Reformation, with Duke Georg personally organiz-
ing and funding the propaganda campaign against Luther.[103] His
personal presence in Nürnberg would have sent a certain political
message as well.

On Whitsaturday before Georg's birth and baptism, Duke Georg
had written directly to Christoph to explain his "inability to ratify
the godfathership" in person, and to assure him that his absence
was against his own wishes and not indicative of any disrespect

or disfavor. He singled out the Lutheran removal of the chrism (*chrisma*)—the holy anointing oil of the Catholic rite—as the obstacle that prevented his coming.[104] By this, the duke did not mean that Nürnberg authorities were in any way threatening or obstructing him. Although a Lutheran stronghold, the city continued to welcome numerous Catholic lords and merchants from Catholic lands, who were there by long-standing right or on business, not the least of whom were its own political overlords, Emperor Charles V and Roman King (emperor-elect) Ferdinand I. Visiting Catholic dignitaries did, however, use such occasions to lobby the magistrates on behalf of the surviving monasteries and cloisters, which Catholics both inside and outside the city hoped might someday become the citadels of a resurgent Catholicism there. While there, they could also receive the traditional sacraments at the Commandery of the Teutonic Knights across from St. Jakob's Church.[105] Like the city's several still-open nunneries—the Dominican (closed in 1546), Franciscan, Cistercian, St. Clara's, and St. Katharina's (the last to close, in 1596)—the Commandery continued to conduct traditional services for its inmates. Although a new Lutheran Mass, performed by Lutheran priests and confessors, was imposed on the nunneries after 1525, it remained strongly contested in the 1520s and 1530s, as the occasional arrest of prominent citizens caught surreptitiously attending Catholic services in the city indicates.[106]

Duke Georg's letter to Christoph reflected his unwillingness, both as a matter of conscience and as a protest against heresy, to be party to the new Lutheran rite. That Christoph had no expressed qualms about his son's receiving that rite reflected less his personal acceptance of Protestantism than it did a pragmatic peace the Scheurls, with others, had made with the new Lutheran regime.

A scant month after Georg's baptism, between May 13 and 15, a Catholic ruler even more famous than the duke of Saxony paid his respects at the crib of Georg Scheurl: Cardinal Albrecht of Brandenburg (1490–1545), the archbishop of Mainz and an electoral prince. The cardinal had been the church official most directly connected with Luther's rise to prominence, for it was he who authorized the sale of the St. Peter's Indulgence, against which Luther wrote his 95 *Theses* after the indulgence-hawker Johannes Tetzel began selling it on the borders of electoral Saxony. Before departing the Scheurl household for Regensburg in the early morning hours of May 15, the cardinal presented the new parents with princely gifts: a gold-plated, ball-shaped wine service for the father and a high-grained, gold-thread chain bracelet for the mother. Christoph, who always took note of such things, put the latter's worth at sixteen gulden. To Christoph's recently widowed sister-in-law Anna, then residing in the Scheurl household with her six children and still in mourning, the cardinal extended his sympathy in the amount of ten gold gulden. Nor were the servants of the two households then celebrating Georg's birth forgotten by "this truly generous electoral prince and lord," who left eight gulden behind to divide among themselves as they saw fit.[107]

Christoph's many diplomatic missions to the courts of Catholic princes in the 1510s and 1520s had won him their respect, and he continued to count Emperor Charles V and King Ferdinand among his clients and lords. At the other end of the political and religious spectrum, Christoph also retained the esteem of Luther's protectors, Elector John of Saxony (r. 1525–1532) and his son and successor, John Frederick (r. 1532–1547), a pillar of the Lutheran Schmalkaldic League that formed against the emperor and the pope in the 1530s. Like Elector Frederick the Wise before them, these Lutheran princes also counted Christoph among their most trusted advisers.[108]

That Christoph could wear more than one confessional hat simultaneously attests to both the transitional nature of the times and his own ability to separate his public and private lives. Particularly in the 1520s, it was still unclear how the confessional wars would end—whether Lutheranism would maintain itself as the city's sole legal religion, or whether the old Church would regain its former dominance—or whether some informal middle way might be found. The one thing that was clear, however, was that Catholics would maintain a presence in the city, and that residents on both sides of the confessional divide had the resources to weather whatever changes occurred in church and state. Families like the Scheurls proceeded quietly and confidently with their accustomed private

lives, having in their own familial and social networks a religious
and cultural identity that was stronger and more determined than
any perceived official bigotry and public conformity.

White Bath

After baptism, the next major event in the life of a newborn was
the so-called white bath (Westerbad), which customarily occurred on
the third day after birth. On this occasion, the special white gown,
swaddling, and sometimes accompanying cap in which a newborn
was clothed at baptism, were ceremonially removed. The child was
thus "bathed out of the Wester" and dressed in what would henceforth become its daily wear.[109] In Georg's case, Katharina's childbed
attendant, Margareta, performed the honors.[110] Like baptism, the
"white bath" reminded family, friends, and household of their collec-
tive responsibility for the newborn's rearing. Nürnbergers held the
event at home until the seventeenth century, after which it moved
progressively into the churches, where, however, it did not remain
long. Contrary to the city's strict sumptuary laws regulating numbers of participants and the event's splendor, celebrating families
marched so rowdily to and from church that the white bath also fell
into public disfavor and returned again to the confines of the home
by century's end.[111]

Although a secondary event theologically and religiously, the
white bath appears to have been even more festive, perhaps because,
unlike baptism, which preferably occurred on the day of the birth, a
crowd from outside the immediate household and family could be
assembled. When Paul Behaim II was baptized on December 10,
1549, his father served his guests thirty-six pints of mead, forty-
eight pastries, ten pints of new wine and seven of (superior) dark
red Rivoli, in addition to which there were pastries, Lebkuchen, and
dates. Three days later at the boy's Westerbad, two tables of guests—
the men seated on the upper floor of the house, the women on the

ere served seventeen boiled and salted fish, a rabbit, two
s, twenty-four geese, two ducks, two doves, bacon, two
ns, white bread, fruit, seven pints of Feldliner (new) wine, and
equal number of the previous year's production.[112]

In comparison to his baptism, Georg's white bath was a strikingly
lesser affair and remarkably subdued, perhaps because, in light of
past experience, Christoph expected him to die. The two births preceding his had been premature sons, who lived thirty-two and six
hours respectively, and the Scheurls had never known a child to survive. When Georg was "joyfully bathed out of the baptismal gown"[113]
on Sunday, April 21, the only guests mentioned, apart from his temporarily residential nephew and nieces, were Margaretha Tucher and
her three stepgrandsons. The latter had evidently been assembled
as playmates for nephew Albrecht, then seven, and his five sisters, all of whom shared mead, wine, and bread with the family and
household.[114]

In earlier times and still elsewhere in Catholic lands, the white
bath awaited the new mother's public reentry into church and society, which did not occur until six weeks after the birth and then de-
finitively marked the end of her lying-in. Six weeks was also the
length of time the new mother waited before resuming sexual relations (today, the postpartum visit to the physician occurs in the sixth
week, the last obstetrical visit of a pregnancy). In an apparent nod to
this practice, Katharina, on May 28, six weeks after Georg's birth,
ceremonially cooked and served an omelette to the household, and
Christoph sent their neighbors and laborers gifts of pork, venison,
and other wild game, along with lard cake, wine, and, for a select
few, expensive Westphalian ham[115]—all evidently intended to proclaim Katharina's complete recovery and return to full-time household administration.

Anna Erhart

While delivery and baptism/naming were the defining moments of a child's birth—the first establishing physical fact, the latter a legal record—the biological and religious sides of the story were only two scenes in a much larger drama. From the preparation for the mother's lying-in to the release of the wet nurse a year or so later, having a baby in sixteenth-century patrician and burgher society, especially a firstborn, was a major event, even a spectacle. Christoph's first expenditure was neither on a midwife (delivery) nor on a priest (baptism), but on twenty-one yards of fine blue and gold Bruges satin.[116] Seventeen and a half yards of that satin were given to the nuns in the Dominican cloister to sew into bedcovers for Katharina's lying-in, while the remaining three and a half yards became a six-stripe canopy adorning the newborn's cradle—a new, full-framed, finished wooden model, adorned with plain white and spongy yellow linen linings, topped with a silk coverlet.[117]

Additional personnel were specifically brought into the house for the birth and its aftermath: a notary, manservants, two maids, a bed attendant for Katharina, and a wet nurse for Georg. Signed on April 27, the wet nurse began her duties on May 1, twelve days after the birth. In Christoph's absence—the Diet of Regensburg called him away after the white bath—Margaretha Tucher interviewed several candidates before hiring a widow, Anna Erhart (born Hofmann), whose husband, a roofer, had recently fallen to his death.[118] The choice clearly pleased the father, who described Anna upon his return as "a fine, modest woman, just right for the job," and whose hire had put his mind at ease.[119] That Anna was all that a parent might then wish for in a wet nurse is indicated by Christoph's awarding her an extra gulden on the boy's quarter birthday (July 19), doing so, he praised, "because she attends him so faithfully, getting up in the night with him, and not letting him cry for long."[120] In addition to her room and board, Anna was paid an annual salary of eight gulden in quarterly installments, plus an extra gulden, or a more expensive gift, at New Year's and other meritorious awards.

Judging from her dominant management role throughout the birth and its aftermath, Margaretha Tucher appears also to be the anonymous godmother mentioned by Christoph in the account book. Helena Ebner, his stand-in "mother" at his wedding, might also have taken that role, but she was by this time deceased. As an active, wealthy, and childless widow, Margaretha had a presumed need for a godson and the manifest ability to guide and indulge him.

If Anna Erhart's integration into the household put Christoph's mind at ease, it likely relieved hers as well. In the great majority of Nürnberg's burgher and patrician households, mothers nursed their own infants, and in those households where they did not, the parents as a rule brought the wet nurse into their home rather than place a newborn in hers.[121] The absence of any mention of children of Anna's own, together with the fact that she lived four years with the Scheurls, suggest that she had lost not only a husband, but also a newborn or nursing infant of her own on the eve of joining the Scheurl household. From the beginning, Anna Erhart "nursed in" and tended Georg around the clock, and after his weaning (mid-October 1533) she became his full-time nanny,[122] remaining on Christoph's payroll until 1536.

On the same day that Christoph paid Anna Erhart her first quarterly salary (August 10), he also paid a milkmaid half a gulden for three months' prior daily delivery of fresh milk, starting at a pint a day (*seidlein*) and rising to a quart (*mas*).[123] That milk was surely intended for Anna Erhart to keep her strong and her own milk supply plentiful. The Scheurls would have known the risks of feeding raw bovine milk to a newborn[124] and, barring an emergency, would not have done so until the boy's health had been well established.

According to a later, retrospective entry in the family chronicle, Katharina had wanted to nurse Georg herself, as she had planned to do with all of her previous, failed children. However, her milk supply proved immediately to be inadequate to the boy's need.[125] So while Anna Erhart's first quarterly payment covered the period between May 10 and August 10,[126] she had in fact been urgently needed in the nursery from the very beginning. Most likely, she began supplementing Katharina's meager feedings immediately upon her arrival in the household (May 1), if not already from the day of her hire (April 27) on a visiting, per diem basis. Examples of birth mothers nursing their infants for as few as four weeks and as long as seven months before turning them over to a wet nurse have been documented in the city.[127]

Although the Scheurls did not begin weaning their children in earnest until they were a year old, beer and wine also became a supplement to breast milk at least as early as four months.[128] Once an infant had safely passed the vulnerable first months of life in good health, the parents evidently believed that the alternation of human milk with bovine milk, beer, and/or wine was the best way to provide it safe and plentiful nourishment, while advancing it steadily toward weaning at age one.

Being both older and first-time parents, the Scheurls understandably wanted to create new pregnancies as soon and as often as possible, which Anna Erhart's arrival in the household also allowed them to do. Unlike the many fertile and successful mothers in Nürnberg who weaned their children as late as possible to take advantage of the contraceptive effect of prolonged lactation,[129] Katharina had no desire to delay a new pregnancy by any means, God and nature having taken that need from her by closing her womb for so many years and then diminishing her milk supply when she successfully delivered.

Gifts, Prayers, and the Stars

In the weeks and months following Georg's birth, the parents had many helping hands to repay, and there were large numbers of relatives and friends who wanted to meet the newborn and congratulate the parents. Festive gift-giving began on the day of birth, the start of a seemingly endless stream during Georg's boyhood that rose and ebbed on numerous fixed and serendipitous occasions. From St. Clara's cloister, Great-aunt Apollonia, whose fertility had never been tested, sent Katharina fifteen fresh eggs in celebration of hers, while

Margaretha Tucher, in an apparent fit of piety and presumption, presented the new mother with a painting of the Magi bearing gifts to
the infant Jesus on His birthday.[130]

On St. Georg's Day (April 23), the newborn's name day, Christoph dispatched a quarter keg of expensive wine to five prayer-
ful friends and relatives, two of whom—Charitas Pirckheimer,
abbess of St. Clara's, and Aunt Apollonia, the cloister's longest living
resident—were particularly well positioned to intercede with the
saint on little Georg's behalf. All five reported back that the saint
was prepared to be "kind."[131] On the boy's two-month birthday
(June 19), baby Georg, his father guiding his tiny hand, wrote his
great-aunt Apollonia a long letter, in which he emphatically thanked
her sorority for assisting his growth and development with their
prayers. That letter adduced numerous quotations from Scripture
and was accompanied by a generous supply of grain for the cloister.[132] That Georg's two-month birthday was celebrated in this way
suggests that his father continued to vacillate between fear of his
early death and hope for a long life. Although this letter could have
meant nothing to baby Georg at the time, it was both a solicitation
of continuing prayers and the boy's introduction to family and
friends to whom he would owe lifelong allegiance and gratitude.

Nor were helpful staff forgotten in these early weeks. Gifts of
money or clothing went out to Ursula the cook, junior maid Endlein
Krafft, Anna Erhart, and Katharina's bed attendant, Margareta.[133] By
Christoph's estimate, a hundred noblewomen "enjoyed themselves
with us and our son" during Katharina's recovery, depositing over
two gulden in small change in the cradle as a gift to the mother, who
later bought a fine black apron with it.[134] Having been dubbed a
"golden boy" by local prognosticator Sebastian Wagner,[135] Georg received a half dozen gold-colored articles of clothing (including a
gilded shirt, fur wrap, pinafore, and handkerchief) from household
staff and patrician relatives alike.[136]

There was also mineral gold and silver for the boy. Between June
and December, Georg received seven shares in Saxon and Bohemian
mines from his father's business associates.[137] By December, the
eight-month-old was receiving such "booty" from those shares that
his father boasted of his "having become a miner."[138] There were

also gifts more appropriate to the boy's age: the glorious *Lebkuchen* of Aunt Apollonia, a rattle from Martha Tucher in Pillenreut cloister, and a black pony from his uncle Seifried Pfinzing.[139]

Georg also proved to be golden in terms of his health. Only cramps (*fraislich*) plagued him during his first eight months, which his great-aunt Juliana Spengler treated by mixing powdered Lindenbark into his porridge, while Aunt Katharina Kress hung a protective charm around his neck (a piece of elkhoff encased in gold and silver).[140] His first free-sitting tub bath occurred on November 20, at seven months, a special event in the household for which a master leather maker made a bathing cap and a cooper a new, boy-size tub.[141]

The boy's attendants regularly inspected his body for irregularities. During his bathing on the fifth day after his birth (April 24), his skin was discovered to be so yellow that it had discolored his swaddling. A visitor in the household recalled having heard that yellow skin was a sign of long life, an explanation pleasing to the father.[142] While a modern reader may suspect jaundice, the more plausible explanation probably lies neither in prophecy nor disease. On or after the day of his birth, Georg had likely been rubbed with nut or another oil, early use of which contemporary physicians recommended as a protection for the skin, and that had most likely discolored his skin and swaddling.

The maids also found Georg's forehead to be "quite wide for his little head," another claimed indication of long life. Invoking the Vulgate's rendering of Genesis 30:22–25, and comparing Katharina to Rachel, Christoph believed that even more might be read into this sign: the promise of a second son.

> Then God remembered Rachel, and hearkened to her and opened her womb. And she conceived and bore a son, and said, "God has taken away my reproach." She called his name Joseph, saying, "May the Lord add to me another son."[143]

The household servants urged Christoph not to cut Georg's hair until he was a year old and to save the first year's growth. Infant hair was widely believed to preserve and invoke the memory of the newborn as nothing else, and Christoph believed it might "help one in other ways"[144] as well—an allusion to the magical properties people generally imputed to shags of baby hair and umbilical cords, the two relics of birth popularly regarded as lucky charms.

For surer information about his son's future prospects, Christoph turned to the astrologers, the "scientists" of the age.[145] A Catholic so devout that he prayed the canonical hours and observed the Church's Lenten and quarter fasts,[146] Christoph was not totally credulous about such prophecy. He could urge that one not "yield to or put great faith in" astrologers yet at the same time acknowledge his own "special liking" for them, having found their predictions to be true as often as they are false. As a student in Bologna, he had visited a Jewish palm reader in Mirandola, near Modena (1505), who predicted he would have a good life, succeed with princes and lords, attain worldly honor, have two surviving sons (one of whom would be "an exceptionally great man"),[147] and die rich, if only he remained diligent in his studies. His good fortune was to commence at age forty (post-1521) and last until his death at seventy-five. Looking back on such prophecies, Christoph believed most had come true. Diligence at his studies had brought him a good life, honor, and riches, and his good fortune had arguably begun after his marriage to Katharina in 1519, when he was thirty-eight.

During Georg's first two months, Christoph consulted his favorite astrologers: Lucas Gauricus, future bishop of Naples, who had advised him during his student years, and local prognosticator Sebastian Wagner. Guaricus did not confirm the maids' intuition that Georg's life would be long, although in all other respects, he told Christoph exactly what he wanted to hear: the boy would be "fair and attractive like his father," rich in land and property, and "should he live, have two wives and many children of both genders." Wagner's horoscope was equally flattering, suggesting the boy's possession of the best qualities of his father and grandfather.[148]

Poor Relations

When, in mid-October 1532, Georg, at six months, began to crawl and pull himself up, Christoph brought seven-year-old Anna Scheurl, the daughter of poor relations in Dilligen (a hundred kilometers to the southwest on the Donau River), into his house to watch and rock the boy.[149] With her came her five-year-old brother Mathias, both delivered to the Scheurl house by their father, Lienhart Scheurl. The decision to do so was a service to both families. Lienhart Scheurl was an indentured servant, but his son had been released from servitude and into Christoph's custody by the bishop of Augsburg, possibly through Christoph's intervention. Upon their arrival, Mathias, "a poor, scabby boy," was placed in the household of Christoph's barber-surgeon, apparently for rehabilitation and basic training. About nine months later, after plague struck Nürnberg in midsummer, 1533, Christoph sent the boy to live with a buckle maker for a few months, apparently outside the city, before finally taking him permanently into his own household, which occurred no later than January 1534.[150]

In explaining these actions, Christoph quoted the Greek dramatist Menander on the duty of the rich to help the poor, especially poor relations. Anna Scheurl remained in the household as Georg's big sister until her death around New Year's, 1535, after which her seven-year-old sister Ketter (Katharina) was delivered by her mother to join Mathias, now "Georg's dear servant," in the Scheurl household.[151]

While Christoph's acceptance of nephew Albrecht and cousins Anna, Mathias, and Ketter into his household was an act of familial duty and charity, he also had an ulterior motive: He wanted Georg to begin his childhood in the company of welcoming, supportive children who would also begin preparing him for life outside the home. That his Dilligen cousins were his social inferiors also served that purpose. Describing Georg, Anna, and Mathias one day at table, Christoph referred to Mathias as "junker" Georg's "servant" and to Anna as his "maid."[152] On another occasion (October 1533), while watching Mathias, then six, and Georg, one and a half, ride their stick horses around the house, it pleased Christoph "not a little" to see Mathias "waiting on [Georg] as a servant on his lord."[153] The father surely saw in such behavior an appropriate foreshadowing of the different social positions into which the two boys were predestined in their adult lives.[154] However, his reaction seems less a self-confirming social judgment than simple delight and amusement at the older boy's fond solicitation of the more fragile, less adept toddler; in the first instance, it is Georg's "love" for Mathias that is stressed.

Georg was approaching seven months of age when he ventured into the public arena for the first time. On St. Martin's Day (November 11, 1532), he and his parents, clad in their finest attire, attended a dedication service at St. Sebald's Church. During the ceremony, Christoph ratified a solemn parental vow to raise his son in the ways and commandments of God. The day happened also to be Christoph's birthday, the beginning of his fifty-second year of life, and, he noted emphatically in his account book, "the year in which Master Lucas Gauricus has predicted another son for me."[155]

Hieronymus

His faith confirmed and his outlook on life brightened by the birth of a first son, Christoph looked expectantly to the arrival of a second in the new year, promised him, he believed, both by the biblical story of Rachel, who had a second son after God had finally opened her womb with a first, and by one of Italy's greatest prognosticators. By this time, he also had in hand the prophecy of his young Wittenberg-educated nephew, Erasmus Ebner (1511–1577), later destined for the city's diplomatic corps, who assured him that, God willing, Katharina would "definitely carry a son into the new year."[156] That Katharina was pregnant again is first mentioned in the account book when Christoph reports a visit to the phlebotomist on January 16, 1533, soon after which the child in her womb was said to have become "quite animated."[157] By her own calculation, Katharina was then in her sixth month of pregnancy, having conceived, she believed, on August 1. She expected the birth in May and hoped it might occur on Walpurgis (May 1), exactly nine months from the date of conception and the beginning of spring, to her mind apparently an auspicious day to welcome a newborn. Given the fact that all of her previous pregnancies had ended prematurely, and her only successful one (Georg) had barely gone eight months, that hope was at the very least optimistic.

As it turned out, the new pregnancy just exceeded thirty weeks, counting from August 1, when it ended on March 19 with the birth of a son, Hieronymus. Christoph gave witness both to his faith and his credulity by recording the event in the following startling manner: "[After Katharina's bloodletting in January] God richly blessed me with my dear son *Georg* on the following *April 19*"[italics added]— with lines then drawn through "Georg" and "April," and "Hieronymus" written over Georg and "March" over April.[158] This was no slip of the pen, but Christoph's dramatic way of recording for posterity his belief in the fulfillment of prophecy in Hieronymus's birth.

The boy arrived between 2:45 and 3:00 A.M., an hour his father also recorded in the most fastidious manner both for future astrological calculations and to celebrate the live birth of a second son.

My son Hieronymus was born on Wednesday . . . March 19, as the day began to be thirteen hours long and the night eleven hours long. The birth occurred as the quarter struck past eight [hours into night], that is, two and three-quarter hours after midnight, which was two and three-quarter hours before daybreak, or 2:45 A.M.[159]

Labor and delivery lasted only two and a half hours, all of which Christoph missed, learning of the birth while still in his bed. Despite the early arrival, the boy was in good condition "with [finger and toe] nails and all his parts appearing fully developed," and endowed as well with a more than average head of black hair.[160] However, as the weather was "ominously windy, rainy, and nasty," and the new-

Silver medallions of the Scheurls, by medallion maker Matthes Gebel (1533). From Arthur Suhle, *Die Deutsche Renaissancer-Medaille* (Leipzig: Verlag E.A. Seemann, (1950), p. 53, Tafel 22. (By permission of Verlag E.A. Seemann.)

born "somewhat exhausted" by the delivery, Christoph, heeding the warning signs, summoned the steward to come immediately from St. Sebald's Church.[161] The boy was baptized before breakfast, the Sacrament administered on a table at the foot of the birthing bed in the "back room" across from the Dominican cloister.[162] Christoph's "good friend and fellow citizen" Anthony Vento was then in Nürnberg and stood as the boy's godfather, bestowing on him after his baptism the name of Christoph's uncle Hieronymus, a deceased Breslau merchant and councilman.[163] "Thus did I have two sons," the elated father wrote,

> neither of whom was yet forty-eight weeks old, one small and one tiny, and never in my entire life had I been richer than I was on this day [March 19, 1533], praise be to God.[164]

On the third day after birth (March 21), Hieronymus's baptismal clothes were ceremonially removed in the presence of family and relatives. This white bath was an even more subdued affair than his brother's, evidently because the parents, observing his fraility, recognized the slim chances of his survival. The only guests mentioned

from outside the household were Christoph's widowed aunt Magdalena Mugenhofer, who had earlier assisted at Georg's birth, and
her sisters Anna and Christa, who later received gifts of money and
five hundred sewing needles for having assisted during delivery
and recovery. On March 23, Christoph sent a gulden to St. Clara's to
buy mead and bread for the sisters—again in gratitude for the
prayers Aunt Apollonia had made on the unborn child's behalf prior
to her own death on January 15.[165] Knowing that only God could
fulfill a prophecy, Christoph attributed Hieronymus's successful
birth directly to those prayers.

The gift giving was this time also subdued. The godfather awarded
the mother an equal measure of brown and rose satin and one of
plain gray camel hair; Cardinal Albrecht sent thirteen kegs of Rhine
wine from Mainz; and the wife of Dr. Gregory Kreutzer, Christoph's
colleague in the city judiciary and city advocate after 1530, delivered two chickens to the house.[166]

Despite Gauricus's prophecy of a son "blessed with good fortune,"
Hieronymus died as those gifts were being received. On March 22,
severe cramps and convulsions, suggesting an abdominal obstruction, tormented him, and by the time of his death the following day,
his right side had turned "black from his little foot up."[167] He died at
2:45 A.M., also the hour of his birth so carefully memorialized by his
father four days before.

Having soberly faced the odds against ever becoming a parent,
Christoph, at fifty-one, had found himself the father of two sons
within the space of a year, only then to have that miracle collapse as
it was occurring. The grieving father confronted his loss with both
the hope his faith still held out and the favor his broken heart now
demanded of God.

[Hieronymus] lived exactly four days, and never was I richer than
when I was with these two sons of mine. I have thus had a griev-
ous rejoicing, as my happiness was turned so quickly to sadness.
This happened, however, by the will of my Lord God, whom it
has pleased to do this, and whose will I should justly and joyfully
accept. So let there be praise, honor, and thanksgiving to Him; He

gave the son, and He has taken him back.[168] He remains a powerful Lord, who can still readily compensate my loss[169] and make
me happy again, which I now sincerely ask Him to do by granting
my son Georg a long life.[170]

Although Christoph could not know it at this time, there would
be a gracious divine settling of accounts. Not only would he have
the pleasure of Georg's lifelong company, but there was to be still another "second" son in his life. And although the father would not
live to see it, Georg's life span would exceed the biblical threescore
and ten by six months, and the first surviving son would also die,
poetically, on November 11, 1602, his father's birthday.

Georg at One

Hieronymus's death only intensified the parents' devotion to the
one son they still had. One impressive indication of that attention is
the annual record Christoph kept of Georg's growth, behavior, and
activities between ages one and ten.[171] Each year on his birthday,
Christoph described the salient features of the boy's development,
doing so with exceptional fidelity and detail during the first six. The
result is a rare clinical account of sixteenth-century childhood. The
first and fullest entry describes the boy at one year.

This Sunday, April 19, my dear son Georg is one year old. So far,
he is hearty, and apart from an episode of colic has remained
healthy. Presently, only his teeth, of which there are five and a half
(the upper front two being great shovels) have caused him to run
a temperature. [The milk of] his wet nurse has agreed with him
throughout the year, and his physical growth and development
have been good. He has a large, strong head, likes to laugh, and
is a happy, high-spirited child. He can say "ka, ka,"[172] extend his

little hand to Father, and point to birds in the bird house on the window. He also likes to go out into the open air. When he sees Father washing his hands, he must wash his too and splash about in the sink. He also takes after his father in liking horses.

There are about ten warts on his body, which our neighbor Weidner says is a sign of long life, as is also the soft spot that can still be felt on his head and is the size of a gulden.[173] He is a fast eater and drinker. By no means will he sit or otherwise remain still in his chair, but he bends over double, as he struggles against it. Otherwise he does not whine, nor is he willful. He freely allows the nurse to suckle him and points out the chair to her [when he is hungry]. He loves her very much, as she does him. And he goes happily to Father and loves him too. Moreover, he is Father's every joy, delight, and treasure. May the Lord God long grant them both [father and son] His grace, so that the two of them may walk together in His commandments and love and rely on Him alone in all things. . . .

Father will say to him: "Georg, be a bad one,"[174] and he then wrinkles up his nose and sneers. If Father coughs, he coughs too; and he can sit only beside Father. He can understand and duplicate an action [once it has been shown him].[175] In sum, Georg Scheurl, by his bearing, gestures, and role playing, presents himself at one year as a pluckly, resolute child.[176] He is learning to use his hands now and really likes to go through books, letters, and papers; he throws up his arms and shrieks with joy.[177]

On June 22, 1533, a Sunday, Georg made his first trip out of Nürnberg, traveling by wagon with his mother, Anna Erhart, and cousins and playmates Albrecht and Eberhart[178] to visit Aunt Magdalena Fütterer in Pillenreut cloister, where Christoph and his Italian business associate Anthony Vento later joined them.[179] Although unknown to them all at the time, this well-planned, leisurely family outing was to be a warm-up for a hasty, fearful flight from the city two months later, when plague breached the walls.

Already in mid-July, with plague threatening and the prognosticating Erasmus Ebner pessimistic about Georg's chances of survival, Christoph again summoned all the supernatural help he could for his son. In Gnadenberg cloister, Aunt Juliana Tucher received a gulden to retain her prayers on the boy's behalf (July 12). Three days later, on the half-year memorial of Aunt Apollonia's death, Georg was sent to stay with the nuns of St. Clara's, there "to be blessed in the temple of God, dedicated to the Lord God, and to ask God [through the nuns] for His grace, so that he might be raised and grow up in His ways and commandments"—a measure deemed necessary after Ebner's forecast of "much misfortune and evil" in the boy's future.[180]

As the dying began in the city, sister-in-law Anna fled east to Amberg with Albrecht and her five daughters. Invoking Psalm 71 ("My hope is in the Lord God"), Christoph kept his family in Nürnberg, strictly quarantined within the house, evidently remaining in the city because the council was slow to declare an official plague, and his duties as counsel prevented him from departing at will. The confinement greatly annoyed him, despite efforts to pass the time with his books.

When thirty a day began to die around them, the time had come to move the family out of the city. Christoph requested the city council's permission to visit Breslau and assist with a family litigation there,[181] pledging to conduct the city's diplomatic business at strategic stops en route and during his return. The request was apparently made on August 21 and initiated what he calls the ten most trying days of his life. On August 23, the council granted a five-week leave, commencing on the day of his departure. By August 30, Katharina, traveling with twenty-five gulden in hand to cover expenses, had moved her shrunken household, now including Georg, Anna Erhart, cook Margareta, and wards Anna and Mathias Scheurl, into the home of Pastor Johann Frank in Henfenfelt, which lay due east of Nürnberg on the Pegnitz and along the family's route to their destination in Amberg.

They departed the city none too soon. On the twenty-ninth, Christoph's servant (Mathias Perger) became stricken in Nürnberg and had to be isolated in the Scheurl garden by the Zoo Gate, where assistance was arranged for him. Entrusting his house and personal matters to Hans Meuschel—the city's famed trombone and trumpet maker and onetime adviser to the papal orchestra in Rome—and dear friend Johannes Neudörfer, Christoph set out to join the family on August 31, a day the plague claimed fifty-four lives.[182]

Arriving in Henfenfeld the following day to discover Anna Erhart, cook Margareta, Anna, and Mathias gone—apparently a lack of sufficient accommodations at Pastor Frank's house had forced them to separate and go on ahead—Christoph continued on to Amberg with Katharina and Georg, sleeping en route in the bush on September 2. Arriving on the third and reassembling his household, Christoph remained in Amberg only long enough to help the family settle into their new accommodations, departing on the same day with a merchants' convoy for Breslau.[183]

Traveling via Bamberg, Christoph visited the cottages of Nürnberg merchants and kin near Arnstadt,[184] and made additional stops in Weimar, Leipzig, and Dresden before finally reaching Breslau. During his three and a half weeks there, he was the bishop's guest. On the return trip, he made ten stops, meeting with Duke Georg in Dresden, numerous old friends in Wittenberg, and Cardinal Albrecht in Halle. He also checked on his and Georg's mines in Annaberg and Joachimthal, where Count Hieronymus Schlick (1494–1550), an early developer of the mines, and Georg Neusesser (d. 1547), Christoph's friend and middleman there and also a very devout Lutheran, entertained him.[185] There was a stopover in the mining town of Schlackenwald as well, where Christoph's father was buried.[186]

After an almost two-and-a-half-month separation, the family's reunion in Amberg on St. Martin's Eve (November 11) was joyous. During his father's absence, Georg had turned one and a half (October 19) and was weaned without any difficulty. It greatly pleased his father that he recognized him immediately and would not be taken from his side. "He can now walk, run, dance, and ride," Christoph noted; "however, he will ride no black stick [horse], only a peeled, white one."[187] To his father's disappointment, however, the happy, laughing boy was still not talking, a developmental problem that would increasingly concern the parents.[188]

Father and his male friends always looked for signs that the boy was growing into their world, and judging from the gifts they now gave him, they clearly believed that could not happen fast enough. Uncle Seifried Pfinzing, who had given him a pony at eleven months, now presented him with an engraved dagger in a silk sheath at fourteen.[189] Having become a miner at nine months, when his shares began paying handsome dividends, Georg now received ore specimens and red-gold pieces of hardened silver from his father's "brotherly friend" Georg Neusesser. Silver portraits of the counts Stephan and Lorenz Schlick, who had originally developed the Joachimthal mines, and one of Bavaria's King Ludwig and Queen Maria, Joachimthal's rulers since 1528, also arrived.[190]

Although sensitive to the fact that his son was a toddler, Christoph also attempted to make him feel important beyond his years and comprehension. In the final week before the family's return to Nürnberg from Amberg, Christoph, already in Nürnberg, sent the one-and-a-half-year-old a long, open, fur-lined mantle, accompanied by instructions to nephew Albrecht and Johannes Neudörfer, who apparently transported the gift, to put it on the boy and bless him with a long, Latin prayer Christoph had freshly written for the occasion. "May the Lord gird you in righteousness [Eph. 6:14], so that you may keep all his commandments perfectly," read the most pregnant line. Only an enclosed pouch of sugar indicated that the recipient of such sublime attention was a child who could not yet even talk.[191] Nine months later, the father reported that the boy's mine shares were worth a whopping 7,500 gulden, wealth so great for one so young that it moved the father, who wanted both to inspire his son to riches and teach him not to love them, to write another Scripture-based Latin exhortation to righteousness, which he evidently assumed the boy would one day read and heed.

> Observe diligently, O Georgiole, dearest son, that God's saints fear the Lord, because those who fear Him are denied nothing (Psalm 33) [and] those who seek the Lord will have every good thing (Matt. 11). So seek Him, my Georgiole, and you will live and prosper. May our most kind and merciful Lord Jesus Christ give

you this. Solicitude is the mother of riches, but if riches abound, do not put your heart in them. Rather use them to honor your Creator and to help the poor.[192]

Georg at Two

On December 9, the family was reunited in their greatly missed Nürnberg home, ending a more than three-month absence.[193] Against the background of the previous harrowing months of plague and separation, it seemed appropriate enough to begin the new year by sending gifts of money, wine, and cheese to the sisters of Gnadenberg, Pillenreut, and St. Clara's. Between January and July, Christoph did so on four occasions in the hope of fulfilling what he called "always my greatest desire, request, and plea to God . . . that my dear son receive God's grace and grow and walk in His commandments.[194]

Gifts both exotic and ordinary continued to flow to Georg, strengthening the bonds within the family's private world: a pair of gold-colored Nördlinger shoes; a black velvet Spanish beret; Milanese silk arlas in the family colors, out of which a miniature heraldic coat was made; brass fittings for his horse's bridle, chest strap, and saddle; and a silver portrait of godfather Simon Pistoris.[195] A few days after Georg's second birthday, Christoph purchased a new bed, equipped with a railing and an eiderdown quilt. That the boy had outgrown his bed was a special occasion for the father, who made a point of tucking him into the new one on the first night he slept in it. As was his custom with an especially important event, Christoph drew a decorative box around this diary entry.[196]

In addition to his sound physical development, Georg also passed his second year of life without any catastrophic falls or collisions—after disease, a toddler's direst threat, since contemporary medical treatment of deep wounds and broken bones was poor. That Georg was an active two-year-old is evident from his father's description of a running, jumping child, who liked to whirl the Murascha[197] (a vigorous dance), and whose greatest delight continued to be "riding and horses,"[198] presumably now both real and stick, the former in the lap of his father or another adult. Christoph's only misgiving about the boy's development at this stage was a persisting inability to say any words beyond "mamma" and "dada," even though he continued to understand everything he was told.[199]

At two and a half (October 1534), Georg was considered to have passed the critical years of infancy and his prospects for the future henceforth to be brighter. On November 2, his father acknowledged that safe passage by rewriting his will to make him his primary heir and nephew Albrecht a secondary legatee.[200] As the eldest male in a new generation of Scheurls, Albrecht had up to this point been Christoph's direct male heir. At the same time, Christoph designated four male guardians to assist Katharina in managing the family estate on the boys' behalf in the event of his death.[201] That this alteration did not threaten young Albrecht's future prospects is suggested by Georg Neusesser's earlier investment (April 23) with the counts of Schlick—Neusesser's well-connected royal lords and Bohemian mining magnates—of 4,000 gulden on Albrecht's behalf and 1,000 on Georg's.[202]

In addition to Georg and Albrecht, Christoph invested no less responsibly in the futures of his wards Anna and Mathias. In February, when they were eight and six, respectively, he sent them both to school, placing Anna with a tutor (Caspar Schmidt) so that she might learn to read, write, and receive moral instruction, while enrolling Mathias in St. Giles's[203]—educational opportunities neither child would have received had they grown up in Dilligen rather than in Christoph's household. Christoph also gave their parents 500 gulden from his and his brother's mining profits, which, however, the Lienhart Scheurls reportedly did not invest wisely and realized little increase from.[204]

Georg at Three

When Christoph wrote his annual report on Georg's third birth-day, the first item mentioned was again the toddler's having survived another year without a catastrophic collision or fall.[205] The second observation, however, was a novel one: the boy's strong attachment to his mother, something Christoph seems to have been a bit jealous of, because he found it necessary quickly to point out the boy's equal love of Father, henceforth to be a recurring theme. A stronger mater-nal bond was encouraged both by a mother's nursing (although Katharina's had been very brief) and by contemporary child-rearing practice, which placed far greater responsibility for child care on the mother in the early years of childhood. Fathers were expected to be indulgent and not to take firm control of their children until they reached six or seven, by which time a child was deemed to be capa-ble of responding to a regular discipline and advantageously intro-duced to the workaday world outside the home—predominantly that of the father.[206]

Beyond his parents, three-year-old Georg was passionately at-tached to the color red, both in his clothes and in wine, which he now regularly drank. Fish, crayfish, and calf brains had now become his favorite foods. Again, he is described as always happy, never whining, and boundlessly in love with horses, riding, and travel, to which a new pastime had been added: taking baths.[207] On the other hand, his vocabulary had increased by only three words—"aia" (cousin Albrecht), "tin" (plate), and "wine"—according to his father, a "very remarkable" lack of progress, although his mind remained quick, and he continued to understand everything he was told.[208]

His only true distress at three was a reported fear of being spanked when he misbehaved, something his father, however, did not consider altogether bad. "Georg sometimes thinks he can run away from father and the rod,"[209] he wrote in his diary; "may the good Lord God be praised and give him the grace to be raised in His ways," by which Christoph surely meant to say: May the boy take his punishment like a man and learn from it, so that he does not have to be spanked. Parents generally at this time considered verbal threats and corporal punishment—which had no relationship in their minds to terror and brutality—to be appropriate measures for dealing with willful disobedience and chronic wrongdoing. That Georg ran away by age three was good news for the parents—an indication that he was now able to understand right and wrong, cause and effect, and control his behavior accordingly.[210]

Intensification of the boy's religious upbringing, was another part of his maturation, and this meant increased contact with his spiritual mothers in the cloisters. On a Sunday in July, the entire household—now consisting of Christoph, Georg, Katharina, Aunt Helena Kress,[211] Helena's unidentified trustee (*Pfleger*), Anna Erhart, Albrecht junior, Mathias, and Ketter—spent an entire day at Pillenreut, singing, worshipping, and praying with the nuns from early Mass to evening prayer in a special celebration arranged for Georg.[212]

Christoph III

Georg soon had a rival for his father's attention. On August 3, 1535, brother Christoph III, namesake of his father and grandfather, joined the household. He is described as the "ninth child," his father still taking care to keep the six prematurely born children who preceded Georg and Hieronymus within the family. Born at noon, the new Scheurl sibling was baptized at vespers, with script master Johannes Neudörfer standing in for his absent official godfather, Georg Neusesser, away at the mines of Joachimthal. Earlier in the new year (January 6), Christoph had sent Neusesser a supply of wine and two-plus gulden for various carting services—apparently goods and personnel he had transported to and from the mines on the Scheurls' behalf. On that same day in January, Georg also sent a letter to his father's "dear and true friend" Neusesser, accompanied by the more distinctive New Year's gifts of a bright-green shaded, spiraled reading lamp, six white candles, and a box of licorice powder, to which a four-candle table lamp for Frau Neusesser was added.[213]

Christoph, too, had been absent at the hour of his son's birth. The good news reached him through cook Margareta's husband, who searched him out among the guests celebrating Anton Tucher's marriage to Felicity Imhof in the great house of the bride's uncle Andreas. As Margareta had sent her husband to find him, she was awarded the "good news prize" of gold-colored linen for a petticoat.[214]

Although he came tardy to the birth, Christoph rose quickly to the occasion. On both the boy's birthday and that following, generous supplies of fine wheat flour and mead were sent to Pillenreut, St. Clara's, St. Katharina's, and the Franciscan cloister, as the father again mobilized prayers on a new son's behalf. Later, the nuns of Pillenreut devoted a day (August 30) to special services on the newborn's behalf.[215]

On the occasion of the white bath (August 6), there were gifts of money for the midwife and her assistants, and she later joined eight other women, among them sister-in-law Anna, to celebrate the event—a mixing of family and servants, upper and lower classes, that was commonplace on joyous occasions in the Scheurl household. "We ate rather good melons and were happy and gay, praising and glorifying God," Christoph wrote of it.[216]

The birth of a new son was also, however, a painful reminder of the last time he had two sons. On August 7, he noted that Christoph III was now "older than four days," by which he meant to say that he had lived longer than Hieronymus, who had died on the fourth day of life. That made this the longest period in Christoph's life when he had two living sons, a milestone that allowed him to repeat again the very same words he had said after Hieronymus's birth: "Never in my life had I been richer than on this day." In the father's mind, this new pinnacle rose with every day the two boys lived.

As he had previously done at Hieronymus's birth, Christoph attempted to make his new son's birthday (August 3) a date that would live famously in posterity. On this best of days, he reported the "good news for my newborn son and the whole of Christendom" of Emperor Charles V's defeat of the army of Heyreddin Barbarossa

(d. 1546), the Algerian leader of the Ottoman Turks and commander of the Turkish Mediterranean fleet. Elevating the birth of his
son to the stage of world history, Christoph described a "splendid
unfolding" of recent events in the family diary: the fall of Goletta
(July 14), the surrender of the castle and town of Tunis (July 21),
and the birth of Christoph Scheurl III (August 3)![217] A month later
(September 11), the boy's first horoscope, freshly cast by Italian astrologer Constantine Bonomen, was attached to the letter his father
had received informing him of the emperor's victory in Tunis,[218] the
two documents henceforth preserved as one among the family
records.

As a godfather's gift, Georg Neusesser sent the new mother and
son a gold medallion engraved with the images of Moses and the
Good Samaritan, symbols of the Old and New Testaments. Christoph
called it the beginning of the boy's "future treasure," both in a spiritual and a material sense, citing the Apocryphal Ecclesiasticus 29:14:
"Put your treasure in the commandments of the Most High, and it
will return more to you than gold."[219] As with infant Georg when he
became a "miner," Christoph wanted his new son to have every
worldly success, yet to remain untainted by it.

Relatives and friends kindly did not forget the feelings of a first
child upon the arrival of a second. In September, Uncle Erasmus
Fütterer (1505–1552), himself a fourth child who could remember
the days of sibling rivalry, sent Georg a red Milanese camel hair beret
adorned with a striking ostrich feather. With that cap also came a
cured ham, a smoked tongue, and six and a half pounds of parme-
san cheese for the recovering household. Lienhart Scheurl, father of
Anna, Mathias, and Ketter, added a sack each of eating and drinking
(or mead) pears to the postbirth larder.[220]

The Son One Did Not Have

The old saw about getting in the second child the child one did not have in the first proved all too true for the Scheurls. Despite the many initial auspicious signs, Christoph III proved not to be the healthy babe his brother had been. Between October and December, he fell prey to all the child killers of the age. "The blisters" (apparently smallpox)[221] struck in mid-October, followed soon by the intestinal blockage and convulsive cramping (*das fraislich*) that had taken Hieronymus's life—only this time treated successfully with an herbal remedy prepared by a clever milkmaid. For three sleepless nights, St. Anthony's fire (*das versegnt, rot, erysipelas*), a streptococcal infection, inflamed the boy's skin. Then, to Christoph's "terror," his son and his residential cousins came down with measles (*flecken*) in mid-December.[222]

Whereas Georg was slow to speak and continued to have difficulty learning words, baby Christoph had an eating disorder—an uncontrollable impulse to overeat. Observing the boy at five months, his father expressed surprise that his growth and development had remained normal, given his insatiable appetite. Not only did he continue to eat after he was full, he did so to "overflowing," leaving his father perplexed and resigned.

> It is good to oblige him in this, for as soon as he is hungry, he becomes very short-tempered and screams, and he continues to disturb everyone's peace until he has been fed all he wants.[223]

Such behavior caused his wet nurse, Katharina von Staffelstein,[224] to be "very rushed" with him, but otherwise good to him. Many reportedly saw in the boy's aggressive nature that of his grandfather, an active, athletic man renowned in his prime for his dancing and leaping ability, but also high-strung, rash, and sarcastic to the point that it hurt his business, as potential customers were reluctant to deal with him.[225]

A typical sixteenth-century father in wanting to anticipate his children's future performance, Christoph was always on the look-out for clues to their basal dispositions and aptitudes. Predictably, he consulted an astrologer in the weeks after Christoph III's birth, this time Sebastian Wagner, who brought back both good news and bad. On the one hand, the stars said he would grow to be a frank and crafty adult, capable of governing his own affairs, while on the other, he was destined to be larger and less active than his brother, and slow to say a kind word[226]—not the outgoing diplomat his father was.

Christoph III remained, however, a child his father could love. Observing him in December at four months, stricken with measles, he wrote admiringly of his son's indifference to the affliction.

> He is now a bad little boy, yet he is dear to Father. He is beginning to babble. When he drinks wine and beer, or eats sugar candy, he seems to have a fishbone in his throat, for he becomes hoarse and coughs. This happens more and more frequently now. . . . At the moment, he has the measles, as do all my brother's children and his general age group. Stricken on December 13, he has lain in his room for twelve days. He does not, however, let it bother him much.[227]

Given this long string of illnesses, it is not surprising to find among the boy's New Year's gifts an encased wolf's tooth[228]—an amulet sent by an unidentified woman (Frau Kaiper), perhaps at the father's request, to be worn around the boy's neck. It arrived none too soon, for Georg was striken with measles on January 13, and his six-month-old brother was ill again two weeks later.[229]

Creating a Proper Nursery

Given Christoph's penchant for social engineering, Georg's growing up and the arrival of a second son made the presence of still
more children in the Scheurl household desirable. So on August 23,
1535, Christoph took in Georg von Rotenhan (1531–1565), the son
of Count Hans von Rotenhan (d. 1559) of Rentweinsdorf,[230] a village northwest of Nürnberg not far from the Scheurl compound in
Fischbach. The boy is described as having been "six years and eight
days old" upon arrival and was to be in the household without conditions for an indefinite period of time, during which Christoph
pledged "to educate and teach him good manners and virtues."[231]

The boy's arrival was partly a favor to his recently deceased uncle,
the knight, Humanist, and imperial counsel Sebastian von Rotenhan
(d. 1532). He and Christoph had been friends from youth, having
studied together in Bologna, and, in later years, they shared a common allegiance to the Church after the Lutheran challenge.[232]

As with his charity to his nephew, nieces, and Dilligen cousins,
Christoph viewed the reception of Georg von Rotenhan as both a
self-evident duty and an opportunity to expand still further Georg
Scheurl's social world; his presence would allow the boys to grow up
in noble company as well.[233] Indeed, the addition of the six-year-old
"royal" now completed three-year-old Georg's social circle of companions and playmates, complementing eight-year-old Mathias (his
"servant") and nine-year-old first cousin Albrecht (his patrician
peer). Christoph had long dubbed Georg "junker" and had recently
taken to applying that title to his brother as well. Against this background of high paternal ambition and social engineering, it is unfortunate that Christoph could not at this time have foreseen the
future, for five years later, in 1540, in recognition of his service to
the empire, King Ferdinand would elevate him, his sons, and his
nephew and nieces to the nobility by awarding them four additional
ancestors to the family tree and crest.[234]

There was a further filling out of Georg's social world in November 1535 with the arrival in the household of the twelve-year-
old son of Georg Neusesser, Christoph III's godfather. This was a

more straightforward apprenticeship arrangement, in which Christoph pledged to "raise, teach, discipline, respect, and show fatherly kindness" to the youth[235] as he prepared him for entry into higher education and the mining business of his father.

As with Georg von Rotenhan, more than a favor for a friend was here involved. To place a youth ready for training under the care and instruction of a trusted and well-connected person was a major goal of contemporary parents, and Christoph could hardly have accepted his new ward without having a possible future reciprocal arrangement for his own sons in the back of his mind. Later correspondence between Georg Scheurl and Georg Neusesser, Jr.,[236] suggests that the latter played the role of big brother in the former's childhood world.

While a devoted master to all his wards, both kin and friend and high and low, Christoph's treatment of Ketter Scheurl suggests that he did not suffer indefinitely children who wasted their opportunities. For four years, Ketter had been trained to do every conceivable household chore,[237] yet, according to Christoph, she had in those years learned "neither the fear of God, prayer, reading, or spinning." In 1539, at eleven, she was sent to work as a domestic servant in a neighbor's house, thereby ending both her stay with Christoph and any greater career enhancement at his hand.[238]

The Retirement of the Nurses

Since May 1532, Anna Erhart had been constantly at Georg's side, first as his nurse, then as his nanny. With the approach of his fourth birthday (April 1536), her responsibilities had been reduced as he was increasingly being placed in the hands of males. The time for Anna to depart the household had come. Christoph let her go in early September 1536 with generous severance of almost a year's salary, by which time she had, in his words, "faithfully mothered and raised" Georg for four and a quarter years.[239]

Christoph III's wet nurse, Katharina von Staffelstein, departed on the same day, having been a part of the household since August 5, 1535. Like Anna Erhart, she was widowed before her hire,[240] while unlike Anna, she also had a child of her own, who was apparently already weaned when she began suckling Christoph III in August and thus could be left with family or friends. No mention is made of the child until Katharina von Staffelstein's departure. Since Georg and Christoph had known their "nurse mothers" virtually from birth, the separation was stressful for the entire household: "There was much crying," Christoph acknowledged in the account book.[241] Although gone from the household, the nurses continued to be an intimate part of the Scheurls' circle of friends.

Unmentioned in Christoph's records up to this point is another pressing reason for their retirement: Each had imminent plans to marry, which they did within a week of one another. November 6 was Katharina von Staffelstein's wedding day, and two weeks before (October 24) Christoph presided over her exchange of vows (*verlobung*) with carpenter Peter Weishamer, also in his employ, in the Scheurl garden by the Zoo Gate.[242] After a morning wedding, a celebratory meal was held in the home of Wolf Krell, possibly the bride's guardian, with four and a half tables of "good people and friends, both male and female" attending, prominently among them Christoph, Katharina, and other patricians.[243] A midday dance followed at an inn, during which four-year-old "junker Georg" had the first dance with the bride.[244]

Anna Erhart's wedding to master currycomb maker Mathias Dhener occurred on St. Martin's Day (November 11), also Christoph's fifty-fifth birthday. A wedding party of fifty men and women departed the Scheurl house for the early church service, at which Christoph and patrician Bartel Haller stood as the bride's foster fathers (*vetter*) in the place of her presumably deceased parents. A noon meal was served at the White Crown Inn to three tables of guests, including several of Christoph's well-to-do friends. In the evening, he hosted a dinner at home for "Anna Currycomb-Maker," as he henceforth called Georg's former nurse and nanny. Afterward, a dance was held in the Scheurl house—which the former Katharina von Staffelstein and her new husband attended—evidently a combined celebration of the two weddings and Christoph's birthday. The newlyweds and a few other guests remained in the Scheurl house for two nights before departing on November 13.[245]

When Anna Erhart later became a new mother (March 23, 1538), Christoph stood as godfather and namesake to her son. In August 1539, a toddling Christoph Currycomb-Maker received a yellow arlas coat from his godfather.[246] Anna also became the subject of the last entry in Christoph's account book (November 1541), when he recorded his arrangement for her to receive about two gulden "so that she might pay the rent."[247] He later (June 1539) stood as godfather and namesake of the first child of Peter and Katharina Weishamer and continued to show that new family charity as well.[248]

The Boys at Five and Two

In Christoph's annual report on the changes in Georg's development and behavior at age five (April 19), it is the boy's spiritual and intellectual growth that particularly stands out. The prediction of Lucas Gauricus that he would be *verbosus* was being fulfilled, yet he still could not pronounce his "r's," and another year would pass before he could properly say "father."[249] He now liked to pray, and at table before meals, he could recite in Latin the *Benedicite* or blessing, the Lord's Prayer, the Hail Mary, the Apostles' Creed, the Ten Commandments, the Golden Rule, and other such Christian guidelines, which he had committed to memory. On the other hand, he remained a normal, playful, materialistic five-year-old. Horses and amusements continued to preoccupy him, he still delighted in wearing golden shirts and silk clothing, and his exceptional fondness of wine remained such.[250]

It is a commentary on Georg's avid riding that he was at this time given a figurine of a horse,[251] apparently an amulet to be worn around his neck to protect him against a fall. It may have been at this time that he also began to urge his father to convert the back rooms and the back house, along with the large rooms of the main house, into "plain horse stalls, with nothing but a lot of horses in them."252

When Georg turned five, Father appeared to be gaining in the friendly competition with Mother for both boys' affection. Georg is said "to begin to love Father more" now, and Father's doting was keeping pace as well.

> Three years ago [when Christoph III was born], Father in his old age received the greatest compensation and joy of all, and he looks [today] on his two sons as his greatest treasure, esteeming them more highly than a princedom. That is why he calls Georg a "count Palatine" and "Duke Georg of Fischbach". . . . I praise, honor, and thank my Lord God [for them], and implore Him . . . that I shall raise my dear sons to walk in His divine commandments and ways [which] would now be my greatest joy on earth.253

Four months later, on Christoph III's second birthday (August 2), it was the boy's good health and physical development that most impressed his father. His vocabulary, however, remained limited ("da" and "ma"), exactly as his brother's had been at age two.254 Of greater concern was his continuing to drink nothing but milk. Whereas Georg's breast milk had been supplemented with wine and beer at four months, efforts to include them in Christoph III's diet only left him coughing and hoarse. Otherwise, he was a delight.

> He is a beautiful, happy, sweet boy, who loves Father very much, and falls on him with wide-open mouth and kisses him. He is dearly loved by Father in return. Less exuberantly, he very much loves Mother too, and he has great affection for horses. There are also indications that he likes to pray.255

Christoph and his two sons in the last years of his life. The Scheurl coat of arms is in the foreground—like father and sons, prostrate before the crucifix. Possibly a drawing from the Cranach workshop. (By permission of Germanisches Nationalmuseum, Graphische Sammlung, NTL. Mp. 21140.)

As besotted with affection for his sons as Christoph was, he could also view them soberly, something perhaps helped by his own fraternal experience. Only a year separated him from his brother Albrecht, with whom he had quarreled incessantly during boyhood, a rivalry for which both were severely punished by their father.[256] That Georg and Christoph III, at five and two, could also ruin a grown-up's day was tacitly acknowledged by their father when, on a festival Sunday in May, he sent the two of them off to Sister Katharina Pirckheimer at St. Clara's. She had entertained them before and had recently sent them pears for the Lenten season. Commenting on the event, Christoph compared the visit of his "two dear sons" to sending her "a sour milk."[257]

In November, Georg also attended the ceremonial "crowning" of his widowed aunt Juliana Tucher Spengler (d. 1540) as she joined the sisters in the cloister for her last remaining years—something not unusual for devout and lonely widows. Sending the boys off to visit their cloistered aunts and cousins on such occasions, like making them join their parents at table when guests were formally entertained at home,[258] was again part and parcel of their early socialization.

Shaking Off Childhood

Among the boys' New Year's gifts for 1538 was an unexpected silver medallion from godfather Georg Neusesser. He had earlier sent Christoph III a golden medallion displaying Moses and the Good Samaritan—models for their mature moral behavior. The new medallion bore a practical message that looked ahead to their adolescent years. On one side stood a winged justice on a pedestal with sword and scales surrounded by the inscription: "Keeping the law is the true test." On the obverse side was a portrayal of Samson killing a lion, with the words: "Women's wiles outdo [one]; live strong."[259]

The sexual temptations of adolescence still lay far off for the boys, so "women's wiles" in the sense intended by the medallion did not yet threaten them. However, the year it arrived (1538) was one in which deceit and seduction had found their way into the Scheurl house in an unprecedented fashion that did not escape the boys' notice. For over three years, since September 1534, a young preceptor (Michael Schmidt) had tutored children in the Scheurls' social circle, including Georg, Christoph III, and their Dilligen cousins. According to Christoph, he came and went freely in the house and was treated as family. That made all the more bitter the discovery on September 16 that Schmidt had impregnated not only Christoph's junior maid Ursula, but Frau Külin's maid in Dilligen as well. Christoph immediately paid the guilty parties their salaries, extending Ursula's to November 1, before "driving all whores and knaves out before nightfall,"[260] henceforth to live with family or friends.

Also unusual in the Scheurl household in 1538 was Christoph's writing his annual reports on the boys in January and February rather than on their birthdays. He profiled Georg on January 9, three and a half months before his sixth birthday, and Christoph on February 3, his three-and-a-half-year birthday.

The sixth birthday was a very big one for a child in the sixteenth century, especially for boys, as it marked the point at which preparation for life outside the home began in earnest. At six or seven the division of the sexes occurred, as boys then traded in the unisex smock all children wore for male trousers.[261] Christoph sensed a quantum leap in Georg's physical development, intelligence, and love of his father—a perceived transformation that apparently made the other days of the year as special, or no more so, than his birthday.

My dear son Georg Scheurl will by the grace of God be six years old on April 19. He is now growing so fast that he has become completely ungainly, his face something of an oval. He likes to learn, delights in it. He is now learning the *Donat* [the Latin grammar of Donatus] and can already cite it from memory. He says grace at the table, but keeps his hands clasped so that he is not looked on as a child. . . .[262]

Although he still cannot pronounce "r" . . . or speak perfectly, he chatters away. He knows where everything he puts between his

teeth comes from. . . .[263] Crabs, [calf] brains, and berries are his
favorite foods. He likes to drink both red and new wine and takes
good, deep draughts. . . . He goes about [the house] in leaps. He
now holds Father dearer than Mother and brother Christoph.[264]

Christoph III also showed significant growth and development,
although his father still saw only the toddler in him.

By the grace of God, my dear son Christoph Scheurl becomes
three and a half years old on February 3. He swills about a quart
of good, warm, creamed-over cow's milk daily. . . . To date, he
has drunk nothing but milk, which suits him well.[265] He learned
to run on the Wednesday before *Laetare,* and while he under-
stands everything he is told, he still cannot say anything except
"dada," "mama," "no," and "yes.". . . His hair is blonder than his
brother's. He clings constantly to Mother and has a powerful love
for Father, whom he hugs, caresses, snuggles with, and treats
sweetly. He waits for Father to leave his study and go to supper.
Then, he tries to take away Father's spoon and knife. He is easy to
raise, has not yet had a [catastrophic] fall, and does not whine or
scream. He is healthy as a fish: corpulent, growing well, strong
and stout . . . rosy-faced, and has good color. He is also highly intelligent and has two extraordinarily beautiful black eyes. [The
two boys] love one another very much, and Father loves them
both very much in return, finding all his joy, compensation, and
riches in these two sons, whom the good, merciful Lord God has
graciously given him in his old age.[266]

Two new ventures made clear that Georg was departing the world
of his brother and entering that of his father. The first was his
first fencing lesson. On July 14, fencing master Lamprecht dined at
the Scheurl house and afterward held a "fencing school" for patrician youth at the New Gate. There, Georg fenced with his eight-
year-old playmate Daniel Tucher, winning applause from onlookers
and a laurel wreath from Master Lamprecht—"and not as a sign of

disfavor,"[267] in the understated praise of his proud father. In mid-September, the entire fencing school visited the Scheurl house—thirty boys, seated at two tables, served buttermilk, wedge-shaped pastries, wine, and bread after the exercise, while drummers entertained them.[268] Dressed for success in what must have been the contemporary six-year-old's "power suit," Georg wore a brilliant hormuzine doublet and brown pants with yellow silk linings, and again fought well enough to receive a laurel wreath.[269]

Georg's other new venture occurred two weeks earlier, on a Sunday, when he rode his horse unaccompanied for the first time to the cloisters of Pillenreut and Kornberg, southeast of the city, there to visit the sisters. Uncle Erasmus Fütterer escorted him home on the same day, making sure that he arrived before the city gate had closed for the night.[270] That journey, like fencing school and Latin school, which Georg was to attend in September, signaled his first large steps out of the nursery and into the world of his father.

Farewell to Children and Wards

Christoph's account of the boys' lives over the last three years of his own (1539–1542) is sporadic and deadpan, his eyes trained mostly on signs of waning childhood and true maturation. Only the most perfunctory notice is taken of their eighth and fifth birthdays in 1539.

Today, April 19, at three and a quarter hours sunrise [8:15 A.M.] my dear son Georg Scheurl has, by God's grace, turned eight. . . .
Today, August 3, at noon, my dear son Christoph has turned five.[271]

The occasional fond anecdote still appears, but the earlier irrepressible paragraphs, in which a father marvels self-indulgently at infancy and early childhood, are gone. Diminished capacity probably accounts for some of the diminished commentary. In November 1539, Christoph turned fifty-eight, and in the months thereafter his health deteriorated. In June 1540, recurring pain in his left side led to his being bled three times from his liver, which his barber-surgeon tapped into through the vein in his right arm—a therapy Anna Scheurl's fine wines and Magdalena Neudörfer's stewed fruit (an original concoction topped with buttered almonds, cloves, and a rich wine sauce) helped him recover from and forget.[272]

Such treats may in turn have contributed to the gout that began to afflict him regularly in these same years. In April and May 1541, he was housebound with a swollen right foot that would not heal. The new ailment brought both the physician and the barber-surgeon to the house, the former to treat him with "little pills that produce ten stools a day," the latter to bleed him again, this time by getting at his foot by way of the vein in his right hand.[273]

Illness, however, may have played a lesser role in reducing Christoph's annual commentary on his children than did the latters' own maturation. For sixteenth-century parents, departing childhood was an unambiguous good, and by age six, the boys were moving rapidly in the direction their parents desired, flat out toward adolescence and adulthood. By seven, Georg had become an able horseman, an achievement his father acknowledged by allowing him to give nephew Albrecht and cousin Christoph Zingel "safe conduct" when the pair departed Nürnberg in April 1539 for distant Ingostadt. Georg accompanied them all the way to the city's territorial boundary. Later in the year (September), Georg gave safe passage to the visiting Mathias von Rotenhan and his guardian, escorting them into the countryside and onto the road back to Rentweinsdorf.[274] Earlier in the year, Georg also made his first solo boat trip,[275] presumably along the Pegnitz.

It was another sign of Georg's growing up that Father had his portrait painted for the new year, a framed likeness costing six gulden.[276] In October 1540, the court tailor in Neuenmarkt (Jacob Tegler) cut and sewed Georg's first formal attire: a black hormuzine doublet with liver-colored pleated pants and a matching jacket trimmed in velvet and adorned with the family coat of arms, a gift direct from the livery and shop of Count Palatine Frederick. Although it may be difficult to envision so stately a youth with a bloody nose, the last information conveyed about him for the year (1539) was a report of a nasty accident at school on November 23. Attempting to walk across a cracked bench after Latin class, he fell through it and broke the bridge of his nose, an injury treated by barber-surgeon Peter, who was invited to dinner on the evening of the accident for that very purpose.[277]

During the last two years of his father's life, Georg reached two further milestones. At the celebration of the marriage of Hans Ammen and Helena Taig (October 1541), the now nine-year-old danced with a girl his age, apparently at his own initiative and for the first time. The lucky partner was Margaret Betterman's daughter, the only maiden at the table.[278] More important, he wrote his first independent letter in early 1542, a New Year's greeting from himself and brother Christoph to Georg Neusesser, Jr., the son of Christoph III's godfather,[279] a relationship that made young Neusesser also Georg's and Christoph III's "brother."

Georg's ability to write an independent letter filled his father with pride, for it was still another sign that the twig was growing—intellectually, socially, and morally—in the direction it had been bent. A second such letter accompanied two baskets of figs, which a thoughtful Georg sent on to his three aunts in Pillenreut cloister,[280] a recycling of an original gift from Uncle Lorenz Tucher.

Georg's tenth birthday (April 1542), and the last his father would know, was a subdued affair, as were all of the birthdays after the sixth. The only guests mentioned at the evening celebration were six-year-old Michael Behaim, Jr., accompanied by his father, and Aunt Anna Scheurl and her four daughters, who contributed a hazel hen.[281] A far happier scene of youth appeared in the diary's penultimate entry (May 18, 1542), the last mention of Georg in his father's hand. There Christoph noted his son at play with five peers—two old friends (Christoph Pühler and Michael Behaim) and three others who appear to have been new ones (Engelbrecht Tehl and cousins Carl [age 14] and Moritz [age 12] Fürer).[282]

Even fewer are the substantive entries describing Christoph III

A portrayal of upper-class boys at ten and twenty. At ten, they are said to be full of play and most accident-prone, while at twenty, they are full of themselves and have only half good sense. From Walter L. Strauss, ed., *Max Geisberg: The German Single-Leaf Woodcut, 1550–1600*, vol. III, (rev.) (New York: Hacker Art Books, 1975), p. 1041; cf. ibid. vol. 1, p. 30. (By permission of Abaris Books.)

between ages four and seven. The boys are described on New Year's Day 1540, dressed in their new "liver-colored, hooded coats with velvet borders"—gifts from Aunt Anna Scheurl, which particularly delighted Christoph III, as it was his first formal wear.[283] Thereafter, he wore the coat only on holidays, or when taken to church.[284] In the minds of his parents, the greater milestone was reached five months later, when he at last drank a glass of wine. Having reconciled themselves to a milk-addicted child, the parents believed the breakthrough promised a healthier son. Christoph described the event as a spontaneous, happy accident.

> Saturday, May 29, my dear son Christoph ate a bratwurst from a [glass of] wine and then proceeded also to drink the wine [in which it had been standing]. To this day, he had never drunk so much as beer, only milk. He will, God willing, be five on August 3. Today, he makes his father, mother, and brother Georg very happy. As soon as he had drunk the wine, he drank [another] to his health out of the gilded silver cup his godfather, Georg Neusesser, had given him.[285]

The boy's habit of "overfeeding" did not, however, end so suddenly, as he himself acknowledged many years later as an adult, when he annotated a passage in his father's account book. In 1538, Christoph had reported a Mirandolan palm reader's prediction many years earlier that he (Christoph) would have two sons, one of whom would become "an exceptionally great man." "[That palm reader] spoke truly when he predicted a great son," Christoph III now wrote self-effacingly in the margin beside his father's entry, "[great] that is in size."[286] That the boy's size still worried his father in the last years of his life is suggested by the only other pertinent anecdote about him preserved in the diary. It describes a marriage ceremony in mid-December 1540 attended by Christoph with his son in tow. At its conclusion, the newlyweds invited the guests to "share a piece of meat" with them. Hearing the invitation, the then five-year-old wondered aloud why the guests were not being offered more to eat than just a piece of meat.[287]

Christoph also called nephew Albrecht and his five nieces (four after 1538) his "dear son and daughters." In Albrecht's case, he may have received a bit of help from another obligated party in his rearing and education. Before his death in 1528, Albrecht Dürer had

☆ ☆ ☆ ☆ ☆ **TIME ZONE** ☆ ☆ ☆ ☆ ☆

DATE _____ SEP 0 5 2001

LOCATION _____

1 YEAR WATCH WARRANTY

Your Quartz Watch is warranted for a period of 1 year from the date of purchase against defects in material or workmanship EXCLUDING BATTERY, CRYSTAL, WATCH BAND OR IF WATCH WAS TAMPERED WITH OR WATER DAMAGE.

Should your watch need servicing send it directly to our Service Dept. with your warranty and original sales slip. It will be repaired or replaced at our option, with the same or similar model. Enclose $4.95 to cover postage, insurance and handling charges. New batteries are available for an extra $2.50, otherwise battery will not be changed.

Watches received without proper Warranty or Sales Slip will be subject to regular repair charges. Similar charges will be applicable to watches abused or tampered with. An estimate will be sent before we proceed with repairs.

| TIME ZONE , P.O. BOX #16506 |
| BEAR CREEK SURREY, B.C. V3W 2P5 |

THIS IS A MAIL IN WARRANTY
NO WALK IN SERVICE

WATCHES SENT BACK WITHOUT HANDLING CHARGES
WILL NOT BE REPAIRED AND RETURNED

NAME _____

ADDRESS _____

CITY_____ TEL: _____

PROV._____ POSTAL CODE _____

NO REFUND, EXCHANGES ONLY WITH
IN 7 DAYS WITH THIS WARRANTY SLIP
☆ ☆ ☆ ☆ ☆ ☆ ☆ ☆ ☆ ☆ ☆ ☆ ☆ ☆ ☆ ☆

Any Complaint or Wholesale Franchise Enquiry
Please Fax: (604) 502-8101 • email: watches@sonnietrading.com

been the boy's godfather and namesake.[288] Although the Dürers attended Christoph and Katharina's wedding in 1519, judging from Christoph's records alone, the relationship between the Scheurls and the Dürers appears to have been based on the famous artist's contacts with Christoph's brother Albrecht. After Dürer's death, Christoph's only indication that Dürer relatives had any contact with their godson was a gift of "three art books in the Dürer style" from the artist's sister-in-law and major beneficiary of Agnes Frey Dürer's will (Katharina Zinner), sent to Christoph in January 1540, seven years after young Albrecht had become a member of the Scheurl household.[289]

Whatever his relationships outside his uncle's household, Albrecht Scheurl, Jr., never lacked supporters and admirers within it. When he returned for a visit in late summer 1541, he had grown so much in the intervening fourteen months that Christoph claimed that neither he nor his mother immediately recognized him. That was clearly not the case with his first cousins, who alternated sleeping with their "big brother" on the first two nights he was home.[290]

Good Clares

The world Christoph and Katharina created around their children was Catholic, kind, and happy. Nürnberg's status as both a major imperial and Lutheran city gave them advantages few other German metropolises arguably could. In what other contemporary Protestant city might Christoph have listed casually among his dinner guests, as he did on Ascension Day 1540, "our confessor (*peichtvatter), Petz*"?[291] In the last years of their lives, the Scheurls watched as an international ecumenical movement, led by liberal thinkers on both sides of the confessional divide, failed miserably, with majority conservatives in both camps deriding such efforts as crypto-Lutheranism or covert Catholicism. The Scheurls nonetheless enjoyed their bonds with both worlds and entertained dignitaries from each.

They continued to visit the local cloisters and to raise their boys to be "good Clares,"[292] that is, men as pleasing to God as they believed the sisters of St. Clara's to be. When, in March 1539, Christoph received word of Johannes Eck's impending death in Ingolstadt, he had six-year-old Georg write a letter to the old enemy of Luther, which was accompanied by a large trout and twenty white fish from a recent catch.[293] In 1540, Emperor Charles V sent Christoph a fine self-portrait that so transformed his study that the latter thereafter became known as the "Emperor's Room."[294] Charles's secretary, Nicolas Perrenot, lord of Granvella and father of the future cardinal Antoine Perrenot (he later become King Philip II's minister and nemesis of the Netherlands' Protestants during the 1560s), lodged with Christoph for four days in February 1541. Even the aging warhorse Cardinal Albrecht of Mainz (d. 1545), instigator of the indulgence controversy of 1517, made a last appearance bearing his usual assortment of extravagant gifts.[295]

The most surprising guest from the heated world of religious politics was one Christoph did not personally invite: Landgrave Philip of Hesse, who, with the elector of Saxony, shared the leadership of the German Lutheran world. In the city on business, the landgrave entered the Scheurl house on March 23 for a two-day stay at the request of the city council. Christoph reports dining with him twice and their getting to know one another well. The prince and his party were also said to love the house, which the royal gifts upon departure also suggest: a garnet ring for Katharina and twenty gold batzen for sister-in-law Anna, while Christoph was promised a goblet with the landgrave's royal seal.[296]

From Christoph III's later description of his father's religious sensibilities, it is clear that the civility of the meeting was a commentary on his father's professionalism and the pragmatism of the age.

He liked to meet and make friends with many great junkers and foreigners, whose gratitude, power, and favor he gained by his writing, the news he delivered to them, and the genealogical information he could provide. He was a good friend to emperors, kings, and Austrians, to priests and to the Church, also a good Tucher, nobleman, and patrician, [however] a bad Lutheran.

As he writes of himself: "I hated that evil church as one that blasphemes, reproaches, and damns, while pronouncing itself righteous."[297]

Benevolence

In his various roles as father, godfather, guardian, master, and teacher, Christoph treated those under his authority—his own children; his nephews, nieces, and cousins; his wards, servants, and apprentices—with tolerance and charity by the standards of the age. In his adult years, Christoph III remembered his father as having been far more patient with him and Georg than Christoph could recall the boys' grandfather ever having been with him and his brother. Whereas the latters' rivalry and wrongdoing frequently brought them hard blows from the senior Scheurl, particularly when he caught them in a lie,[298] Christoph III, who lost his father at age seven, remembered him as a much kinder and gentler man.

[Father] loved his sons so much that he let the youngest [Christoph III] ride on his shoulders, and he bit his tongue [when the youngest misbehaved], successfully overcoming [that son's] disagreeableness, aggression, and constant annoyance by patience.[299]

Georg, on the other hand, may have had memories of Father less pleasant than those of his brother, who wrote here only for himself and in what was, after all, the official family chronicle. Being both the eldest son and having lived with his father through the important male transitional years between seven and ten, Georg had known a stricter regimen than his younger brother. Already at three, by his father's account, he lived in fear of being spanked and attempted to flee when the rod was raised. Fear and discipline held a respected place in child rearing at this time, but his father's doting on and indulgence of both boys are even more amply documented. Integrated into the household from infancy, the boys had been included in and often made the centerpieces of family celebrations and outings, reports of which may have been their father's truest revelations of the family's private life.

Christoph believed his religion demanded annual, indiscriminate benevolence in addition to other charitable contributions. On the occasion of his fiftieth birthday, he and Katharina arranged to devote one-thousandth of their total estimated worth, based on both fixed and movable assets, to the buying of coats for the anonymous poor.[300] Among other charitable endowments was an annual grain supply for the poor (established in 1536 in memory of his parents in nearby Gundelsingen, the original Scheurl settlement); an annual stipend for a needy Nürnberg student (1537); and three-plus gulden quarterly for the worthy poor, which his barber-surgeon dispensed.[301]

Whenever workers, servants, relatives, and friends, for want either of resources or parents of their own, sought Christoph's assistance in forming their own unions and households, he gives every appearance of having rendered it. In addition to kindnesses to the boys' wet nurses, cook Margareta celebrated her marriage to scribe Georg Schmidt in the Scheurl house in October 1535.[302] Five years later (June 1540), Christoph conducted the marriage of his sister-in-law's cook (Katharina Kreft) and master carpenter (Caspar Rosdorfer) in his home as well, again picking up the expenses.[303] In his last years, he was the foster father (vetter, Pflegevater) of both an orphaned bride and an orphaned groom. At the marriage of Felicitas Pfanmüsin in January 1540, he shared that paternal responsibility with another, having six months earlier (August 1539) taken Felicitas and cousin Anna Tucher into his household, agreeing to prepare and assist the two women in finding the right mates,[304] much as he prepared and placed male apprentices in appropriate positions— only doing so here without any stipend or compensation—as a favor to needy kin and friends. At the October 1541 wedding of orphaned cook Elspeth Hofmann and her orphaned bridegroom (carpenter Blasius Hubschman), Christoph and Katharina shared the role of foster parents with another well-do-to couple, celebrating the humble union in the Scheurl house with a socially mixed guest list.[305]

These friendly contacts with distant kin and nonkin, and be-

tween higher and lower social groups, extended the original parental bonds into new generations and the larger society beyond the
household. A final example is the relationship between Christoph
and Georg Götz, whom he describes as his loyal "overseer" (*Schicht-
meister*) and "godfather." The title of overseer suggests that Götz may
have been another who looked after Christoph's mine interests. (In
his last will and testament, Christoph left him a share of his holdings in a Bohemian mine.[306]) The title of godfather was honorific,
acknowledging the spiritual kinship Götz gained with Christoph
when, in August 1536, Christoph stood as godfather to his newborn
son. Four years later (July 1540), Georg and Christoph III sent the
Götzes a gift (unidentified) in recognition of his years of faithful service to their father and in celebration of his wife's delivery of a child.
On the same day, cousin Albrecht joined the two boys in sending the
Götzes a silver goblet engraved with the Scheurl and Fütterer coats
of arms. Ten months later (May 1541), godson Christoph Götz, now
almost five, sent each of the Scheurl boys a three-pint tankard engraved with the Scheurl's new, enhanced coat of arms.[307] Thus did
Christoph's and Georg Götz's godfathership evolve to envelop the
new generations in the friendship of the older.

It was especially on the occasion of private dinner parties, outings
to the countryside or to another's home, and celebrations marking
family or household milestones in all of the above locations that
Christoph declared himself to be unambiguously happy. Describing
himself at leisure in a familial world largely of his own making, surrounded by family and guests of his own choosing, he frequently
ended his account with the words: "We were happy and gay"; "we
were merry and content"; "we lived well and enjoyed ourselves"; "we
danced sprightly and were joyful"; "I danced with both my sons."[308]

On such occasions, he liked to mix and mingle different social
and age groups, much as he had done earlier in the boys' nursery. To
the marriage of cook Katherina Kreft and carpenter Caspar Rosdorfer he invited his best friend (Johannes Neudörfer), the family of
Peter von Watt (well-to-do Pirckheimer relatives), and his eldest
niece, Anna Scheurl.[309] On a summer outing to Fischbach in mid-
July 1539 to visit his sister-in-law, the traveling party divided itself
harmoniously into apparently favored upper-class riders and depen-

dent lower-class walkers. Georg rode his horse, while the widow of Andreas Tucher[310] and Frau Helena Taig (the aunt of another of Christoph's godsons, Melchior Taig, Jr.) joined Christoph, Katharina, and Christoph III in the wagon. Comprising the corps of walkers alongside were Christoph's live-in ward Felicity Pfanmüsin, junior maid Elsbeth,[311] cook Katharina Kreft, and Kechela Schmidt, an apparent relation or possibly child of scribe Georg Schmidt and his wife, Margareta.[312]

The joy of such gatherings is suggested in one of Christoph's few, modestly expansive descriptions of what awaited them at journey's end. On a day in August 1539, the family visited the garden house of widow Ursula Gandelfinger on the Spitzenberg in the eastern part of the city, where the following menu, briefly glossed by Christoph, was served after hors d'oeuvres.

Trout and carp (an enormous carp); a roasted piglet; fowl and such; a meal of crabs; a cream; hazelnut; about eight large melons; red and white wine. We lived like princes![313]

Christoph died in June 1542, and Katharina followed him seven months later (February 1543). At her death, she resided in the back house where she had given birth to her two sons, the main house having been surrendered to the then visiting Elector Palatine Frederick III. Christoph III's godfather Georg Neusesser, cousin Jobst Tetzel, and Balthasar Dörrer became the official guardians of ten-year-old Georg and seven-year-old Christoph III.[314] A successful merchant, Dörrer (1509–1586) served in the city judiciary, where he held numerous high positions, including that of bürgermeister.

In 1554, Georg, now twenty-two and apparently employed in the city judiciary, married Dörrer's eldest daughter Sybilla (1531–1586), with whom he would live for thirty-two years without offspring before becoming a widower for another sixteen. Brother Christoph also pursued a legal career in the city judiciary, where he served most notably as the emperor's representative in capital cases.[315] The only other "professional" accomplishment cited in his brief genealogy is a third-place ribbon in a private joust in 1561.

Christoph III's better documented domestic life is another story. In 1560, he married Sabina Geuder (1537–1610), and, unlike the marriages of his father and his brother, theirs was prolific well beyond contemporary odds. They had eleven children, nine of whom outlived their father and eight their mother, and six of whom married into the city's most prominent patrician families: Haller, Tucher, Stromer, Hölzschuher, Löffelholz, and Dietherr. The 1593 union between Christoph III's eldest son (Hans Christoph) and Johann Jacob Haller's second daughter (Katharina) would become the link connecting the Scheurls of the sixteenth century with those of the late twentieth,[316] who today live modestly in the city's suburbs and are the guardians of many of the documents used in this study.

PART TWO

Teenagers into Adults

3

MOTHERING

Magdalena Römer Behaim and
Her Eldest Son Paul

O N A LATE WINTER DAY IN 1575, THREE YOUTHS IN THEIR late teens, all from prominent families related by marriage and each destined to play an important role in their city's politics, departed Nürnberg for the German House in Venice. A combined lodging, storage facility, and marketplace, the German House was the gateway to Italy both for German merchants buying and selling there and for apprentices and students headed for its workshops and universities. The merchants had done business in Venice for centuries and even had their own chapel there, decorated with a Dürer painting celebrating the Rosary.[1] For well-to-do patrician and burgher youths, such travel and study abroad was a final rite of passage, the journeys to and sojourns in foreign lands the capstone of their education and the threshold of adulthood.

At seventeen, Paul Behaim II (1557–1621) was the youngest of the three and destined to hold great political power in the city.[2] His late father, Paul I (1519–1568), had risen from modest beginnings to become, at twenty-nine (1548), a full partner in the Imhof Trading Company, a Nürnberg-based firm trafficking in spices, paper, furs, linen, barchent (a cloth made of cotton and linen), copper, and silver, with major posts in Saragossa and Venice. From that position, he was four times elected the city's bürgermeister. One of the company's three principal owners, Andreas Imhof (1491–1579), was Paul I's maternal uncle,[3] so he had blood as well as diligence to thank for his ascent within Nürnberg's mercantile and political world, as would also be the case with Paul II.

At nineteen, Carl Imhof (1555–1619) was the oldest and wealthiest of the three wayfaring youths. Like the Scheurls, his family also retained their Catholic beliefs after Nürnberg had become an officially Lutheran city, and Carl would later hold major posts in Catholic lands, serving successively at the imperial court in Regensburg, as Emperor Rudolf II's war commissioner in Siebenburgen, and as a member of the appellate court in the royal kingdom of Bohemia. His very powerful father, Wilibald (1519–1580), who also served royalty, was a renowned collector of German antiquities, the grandson of Nürnberg's famous Humanist Wilibald Pirckheimer, and a godchild of Albrecht Dürer.[4]

Finally, there was Jobst Friedrich Tetzel (d. 1612), the third youth in the party. He would also follow in the footsteps of his well-to-do father, later becoming a member of the city council and serving as one of its chief financial officers.[5]

In the setting of an international university (Padua), the three boys studied the language and explored the culture of Italy as they pursued degrees in Roman law. Their sisters, with whom they regularly corresponded, did not wander in foreign lands. In contrast to their brothers—and also to lower-class female peers in the trades, who also wandered to gain vocational skills or to find employment[6]—the educational goals of young upper-class women were not as ambitious, their youth devoted to the acquisition of homemaking skills in preparation for marriage.[7] On the other hand, a few upper-class women might receive a classical literary education at home rivaling even that of their professionally trained brothers and husbands. Some such women became accomplished enough to win the praise of famous Humanists, as happened with Nürnberg abbess Charitas Pirckheimer, sister of Wilibald, whose mastery of the liberal arts Desiderius Erasmus compared to that of Thomas More's daughters.[8] As a rule, however, woman's world in these centuries remained vocationally and geographically more circumscribed than man's, although no less intensely and imaginatively cultivated.[9]

Portrayal of upper-class girls at ages ten and twenty. At ten, girls are said to
be like gentle quails, but only if one does not spare the rod. Sexually mature by twenty and ready for marriage, they are like doves, their heads pop-
ping up and surveying a world full of temptations (the fiddle player),
against which they must be vigilant. From Walter L. Strauss, ed., *Max Geisberg: The German Single-Leaf Woodcut, 1550–1600*, vol. III. (rev.) (New York:
Hacker Art Books, 1975), p. 1036; Ibid., p. 31. (By permission of Abaris
Books.)

The Eldest Son

    Paul Behaim II had already studied humanities and law at the
University of Leipzig (1572–75)[10] before gaining his mother's permission to move to Italy, there to spend another three years in legal
studies and travel. To be abroad for so long was a privilege (Albrecht
Dürer's "bachelor's journey" had lasted four),[11] but in Paul's case so
many years of study and travel also threatened to erode the family's
wealth. Because of his father's premature death in 1568 at age forty-
nine, Paul's family did not have the resources of those of his traveling companions. The senior Behaim had left behind a widow and
eight children, four boys (including Paul) and four girls, born at
one- to two-year intervals over thirteen years of marriage. Paul's
mother, the former Magdalena Römer (d. 1581), had been his father's second wife.[12]
    As a widow, Magdalena Römer Behaim had two things working in
her favor: She lived in an age when single motherhood was commonplace, and she was the maternal granddaughter of Jacob Welser (1468–1544),[13] the former chief of the Nürnberg branch of the
famous Welser mercantile and banking empire. Still, with eight dependent minor children requiring her care and support, even a well-
connected patrician widow, living in a society prepared to assist her,
could not escape a serious challenge to her standard of living.
    In 1575, all eight children were still alive and well, and each was
at least as needy as the eldest brother. Three of the four oldest were
female (Paul was the third child), and for that reason, their futures
were not as promising and secure as his without successful marriages. The eldest, Magdalena (1555–1642), was now twenty, and
the youngest, Georg (1567–1593), was eight, and not one of them
was in a position to contribute one pfennig of new income to the
household. The resources of a family of such size and appetite had
been modest enough at their father's death in 1568, and they had
dwindled steadily since. As Magdalena put it in 1582, the family was
"living off a string," plucking away at a livelihood that only de-
creased and was never added to.[14]

Of all the consumers, none was more insatiable and threatening to family comfort than Paul, who arrived in Venice in the spring of 1575 with creditors still looking for him in Leipzig. The continuation of his education at the more expensive Italian university posed both new sacrifices for his family and a moral challenge for him. How mindful of family and capable of self-restraint might a seventeen-year-old, loose in Renaissance Italy, be expected to be?

The family would have preferred for Paul to become a provider without any further delay. But at seventeen, he was not yet ready, and there were good reasons to grant his wish to wander in Italy. Even in German Protestant lands, where the practice of partible or more equal inheritance among siblings remained strong, being the eldest son still entitled one to special treatment. Younger siblings in these lands might expect a more equitable share of property and income than children in lands where strict primogeniture held sway (such as England).[15] Still, the eldest son received the lion's share of parental attention, educational opportunity, and ancestral property (as a rule, he succeeded to his parents' place in the family house)— all of which was intended to allow the family estate to continue intact under his subsequent leadership. In actual practice, partible inheritance appears to have encouraged as much rebellion as conformity in eldest sons, and as much passive acceptance as resentment among younger siblings.[16]

Younger family members understood the reasons for favoring the eldest, and they trusted such sacrifice to redound to the benefit of all by enabling the family to maintain its position of strength for another generation. To keep internal resentment and conflict at a minimum, the eldest son had by law to compensate younger siblings for the greater ancestral property he inherited. In lands practicing partible inheritance, this appears to have been done by cash payments or annuities calculated to do him the least harm—for example, made on the basis of the original purchase price of a property in question rather than its current market value.[17]

A major reason that Paul's request to wander in Italy could be granted was the willingness of his elder sisters Magdalena and Sabina to allow him to draw down the paternal inheritance to meet his new expenses. At twenty and nineteen, respectively, they were approaching a favorable marriage age and very conscious of the integrity of their dowries. In doing so, they took the reasonable gamble that what helped their brother strengthen his position in the world would also help them move about in it more easily as well. No doubt they were influenced in that decision by their mother and guardians Wilibald Imhof and Jobst Tetzel, the fathers of Paul's traveling companions and Behaim relatives by marriage. They, too, would have viewed investment in the eldest son as a prudent family decision, one that promised to better equip Paul for a legal and political career, while at the same time enlarging family contacts throughout the Italian mercantile world.

If the stakes thereby increased for the family, they were also raised for Paul, who now more than ever became the subject of heightened family interest and scrutiny. Much was given to an eldest son in the traditional family, but much was also expected of him.

Money

When the three youths departed for Italy on a late February day, they had no sure destination beyond Venice. Once situated there, they planned to visit several major cities until the right mix of schooling and accommodations was found. In Venice, they went directly to the German House, where temporary lodging and the camaraderie of their countrymen awaited them, along with the latest information about conditions and opportunities in other locales.

During their first year in Italy, the three were in the care of a German preceptor, Gabriel Gienger, a relative of Jobst Friedrich's[18] by marriage and an experienced Italian traveler. The families paid his expenses in exchange for his services as tutor and guide. It was he who introduced the three to the Italian language and culture, managed most of their money, and oversaw their activities. Through an advance arrangement with the Imhof trading house in Venice, the boys drew monthly stipends in Italian crowns, which Gienger collected and disbursed to cover the costs of lodging and board for the four of them. The arrangement greatly displeased Paul, who claimed to be far more restrained in his appetites than were his companions, although each contributed equally to the group's common expenses. Each also had relatively free access to cash for his own personal needs and pleasures, which Paul, again, insisted his companions, being less disciplined and frugal than he, also abused.

On April 23, almost two months after his departure, Frau Behaim received her first letter from Paul announcing his safe arrival and immediate plans.

1. Paul to Mother[19]
Dear mother . . . On April 20, I and my three traveling
companions and comrades arrived in Venice well and hearty and
rented a room in the German House. We have taken off a few
days to see the city and plan to depart by sea for Ferrara on
April 24. There, at your suggestion, we want to check out the
town and the program of study. If Ferrara proves not to favor us,
we could try another place, Bologna or wherever.

As for a horse, things went very well—better than for Gabriel
Gienger and Carl Imhof. As I write this letter, I am actually on
the verge of a bargain. As for money and living expenses, you will
shortly receive an accounting from Gienger, in which you will
see that 100 gulden has not been enough. . . . Venice, 23 April,
1575.

Y[OUR] L[OVING] S[ON], PAUL BEHAIM

Prevented from sailing south by weeks of heavy rain, the four set out for Ferrara on horseback, only to discover en route in Padua that the flooding of the Po had cut off access to Ferrera by land as well. Happily, Padua promised to meet their educational and domestic requirements even better than Ferrara. So they committed themselves to at least half a year there. Selling their horses, they purchased new clothes befitting the Italian academic world they were about to enter, and set about furnishing a small rented house. At the same time, Paul and Gienger ominously succumbed to an irresistible indulgence.

2. Paul to Mother[20]

Dear Mother . . . By the grace of the Almighty, I and my comrades arrived well and hearty in Padua on 2 May. For several days, we have been held up here because of rain and flooding, which has everywhere destroyed the embankments. In the end, we felt advised to stay here . . . and accustom ourselves to the Italian climate and mores. There is no chance whatsoever now of getting to Ferrara anyway because of the flooding. The Po is so swollen that one can no longer travel a day away from Ferrara, nor is it safe to be on the water. There is also [price] inflation; word has it that Ferrara is now more expensive than Padua has ever been. In addition, Ferrara has no program of study [studium], either by Italian or German [scholars]. So all things considered, our preceptor thought it best to spend half a year here . . .

I unburdened myself of my horse for twenty crowns, or thirty gulden, and have kept one crown of that for my own refreshment,[21] entering only nineteen, or twenty-eight-and-a-half gulden, into the account book. . . . Carl Imhof paid thirty-four gulden for his horse and has let it go here for twenty-eight-and-a-half, while Gienger's cost thirty-five in Nürnberg and was sold here for . . . thirty. Both of them had to stable their horses here for a week as well. I have used the money from the sale to have the simplest coarse green clothing made for myself—a jacket with modest trim, pleatless trousers (like those Gienger wears at home), and a hooded coat with a knapsack made from a cloth called "rasch."[22] Lest you think things are cheap here, all this has cost me approximately seventeen or eighteen crowns, even though it was as plain and simple as could be. I could not have been more amazed when I saw [that bill] than you will be when I send it to you [translated into German] heller and pfennig.

We four have rented a small house in Padua without any furnishings, for which we pay ten crowns for half a year. It is in the outermost part of the city, so that no [student] society[23] or any German can [bother] us. We have an old maid, to whom we give money and tell daily what to buy and cook for us. The other things we need—benches, books, chairs, and tables—we have leased from a Jew in Padua, whom we pay a monthly fee.

Gienger and I have also invested in a piece of heaven,[24] that is, a small organ. It belongs to an organist in Padua whom we pay one crown for a half-year's use. . . .

When you answer this letter, please let me know the status of the debt [I left] in Leipzig. I cannot marvel enough at the faithlessness of David Richter [there], who was almost closer to me than my own brother; I [believe I] had no better friend. . . .[25]

Y L A[ND] G[RATEFUL] S, PAUL BEHAIM

By the second half of the sixteenth century, the port cities of Antwerp and Lisbon had replaced Venice and Genoa as the centers of international trade. That shift of maritime activity from the Mediterranean to the Atlantic did not, however, lessen the importance of Italian cities to Mediterranean trade nor their attractiveness to northern Europeans. Particularly in terms of tourism and university study, Italy continued to be the place most northern Europeans wanted to visit. Italian cities were also Europe's most expensive, and in time of natural disaster, such as the floods Paul decribes, prices soared.

Settling into Padua in late spring, Paul and his colleagues soon discovered the inadequacy of their resources, which was all the more shocking since each had long grown accustomed to spending what he pleased. Already en route from Germany to Venice, money had proven tight, and after two months in Italy, bickering over it began to divide the group. Although Paul portrayed himself as the most abstemious of the four, his mother's incredulity grew as the receipts piled up, and she began early to question his discretionary spending. Judging the world by the cheaper Nürnberg markets, she and his elder sisters, who wrote to him about such matters with one

voice, did not believe all of his expenditures to be reasonable. Whereas his mother thought a seventeen-year-old could get by on less,
Paul protested that what she perceived to be more was, by Italian
standards, actually less. It did not bode well for their relationship
when, barely two months into Italy, he proposed that he forgo an accounting of individual expenses for the first year and simply be
given open-ended credit at the Imhof trading house in Venice.

3. Paul to Mother[26]

Dear Mother . . . I have learned . . . from your last letter [June 2,
1575] that you are not completely satisfied with the coarse green
suit I had made.[27] Let me say, first, that this was done not by my
choice, but at your command. Already before we left Nürnberg
(as you must still remember), you, Jobst Tetzel, and Wilibald
Imhof agreed unanimously among yourselves that we should
wear only clothing made from coarse green and from neither a
grander nor a lesser fabric, saying that a better fabric was not
appropriate for us young men, nor any other as strong and neat
in appearance. So when [Carl and Jobst Friedrich] bought
somewhat fancier . . . I alone remembered and respected
what had been said. . . . In buying my clothes, I have very
conscientiously followed, as always, your counsel.

You now write that I should have gotten a linen fabric.
However, the only linen fabric used here to make clothing is one
called "rasch," which costs two crowns, or three gulden, per eln
[65 centimeters], and linen cloths are also not in style here. . . .
In my humble opinion, one should not live by German habits
and customs in Italy. So having thought it over and consulted
experienced people here, I have not dressed myself shabbily, but
in a neat and durable fabric in the Italian manner.

It will astonish you even more to learn that it is the custom
here (indeed, it is all one knows) to wear only simple stockings
knitted from thread and detached from the pants,[28] which,
moreover, cost more than two gulden. . . . Otherwise, one can get

linen stockings made of buckram [a coarse linen], which the
artisans wear. One just must live according to local custom.

Were I to buy something from the Jews, as it is customary here
to do, they would certainly give it to me for less, but then it
would not last more than a third as long. You should have no
doubt whatsoever that in this case I have as little desire to spend
money as you. When I think what it is still going to cost me to
live here, my hair stands on end. The first weeks have been
frightening enough, and a lot of money has already been
withdrawn [from Venice], most of it going to our common
household expenses and individual needs, an accounting of
which we intend to send you every six months.

However, since this year we must include the expenses of
our preceptor in with our own,[29] I think we should postpone [an
accounting of individual expenses] until [Gienger is no longer
with us and] we can address them properly. There is truly
nothing I can do now to prevent the frequent withdrawals of
money from Venice. God willing, I will continue to be the
smallest item in the account book. I just want you to know that
I will be happy to see how you [and Jobst Tetzel and Wilibald
Imhof] settle accounts among yourselves, given the fact that the
one here consumes more than the other.

In addition to all of this, I must also tell you that the
gentlemen there [Jobst Tetzel and Wilibald Imhof] have led us
to understand that they are sending us elsewhere when winter
comes. I mention this because that is going to double our
expenses. Although we have barely established ourselves here
with great sums of money, should we move elsewhere so soon
and our expenses double, as I think they will, it will not be good
for us in the long run. Here [in Padua] prices have peaked, and
the more we move about, the more expensive it always is. Still,
the gentlemen there have already let Gabriel Gienger know that
wherever he chooses to move with us, they will be satisfied. I
think it will be either Bologna or Siena. . . .

I wanted to write you at some length about what we are doing, and you can now make of it what you will. I have not wanted to hold anything back, as my own humble mind has perceived it. . . . Would you let me know how it stands with the payment of my bills through the Imhof agent's office, and whether they are extending you the credit [I need to cover them]. . . .

There is one last thing I must write you. Your last letter caused much trouble and confusion in Padua, because it arrived here addressed only with the words: "To Be Delivered into the Hands of My Dear Son in Padua." When the messenger bearing it read this [aloud] and showed it to others, each wanted to be his mother's dear son [and claimed the letter]! Thus, it caused much disturbance until the messenger found its rightful owner. . . . Padua, 18 June, 1575.

Y L S, PAUL BEHAIM

Taking Control

By mid summer, Paul could pledge frugality and complain about the size of his monthly stipend with the same stroke of his quill. He had not, however, entirely forgotten the larger purpose of his Italian years and their importance for his own and his family's future. Mastering Italian was the boys' first imperative, for until they were fluent and could act confidently on their own, their legal studies and cultural explorations would suffer and a preceptor remain a necessary expense.

4. To Mother[30]
Dear Mother. . . I hope you have by now received my last letter. Meanwhile, I have not yet gotten a reply from you, so I have nothing very pressing or specific to write about at this time. I just

wanted to assure you that, with the grace and help of almighty
God, I do intend to make the most of my time here and of the
large expenditures that are being made on my behalf. Not one
unnecessary heller will be spent on myself. . . .

In regard to my studies, I am now devoting most of my time to
Italian, making it my top priority. We have a language teacher
with a doctorate,[31] who comes every day to teach us for an hour,
for which each of us pays him one taler a month, and we have
several months to learn. That we do not in the meantime forget
Latin, Gabriel Gienger reads with us for an hour a day from a
book of laws called the *Institutiones Juris*.[32] I also wanted to write
you about this so that you could report it to Herr Dr. Flick,[33] and
to anyone else there who might inquire [about my studies here].

As for the news here, there is nothing to write about at this
time except the terrible heat wave . . . which has weakened and
rendered people idle. . . . Freshly slaughtered meat seldom keeps
for more than half a day. . . . One must take proper precautions
for one's health and not eat or drink a lot, or one may pay for it
in the fall.[34]

Gabriel Gienger has received a letter from Jobst Tetzel in which
he expresses the opinion that we should remain in Padua for the
winter, which pleases me for all kinds of reasons. . . . As soon as I
have some free time, I will write a Latin letter to Herr Dr. Flick.
Meanwhile, greet him for me. . . . Padua, 27 July, 1575.

Y L S, PAUL BEHAIM

The hardships and excitement of settling into Padua provided no
antidote to the boys' homesickness. On August 4, Paul wrote sister
Magdalena to complain that two of his closest Nürnberg friends,
first cousin Paul Imhof and Caspar Reh, had yet to write to him, a
five-month silence. Both were then in the process of getting married
and understandably distracted. Through Magdalena, Paul demanded
that Reh, who had recently become the pastor of a neighboring
Nürnberg village (Ezelwang), send him an invitation.[35]

Three weeks later, Paul alerted his mother to the imminent arrival
in Nürnberg of the boys' account book (*Register*), the first detailed
record of his spending over the previous six months. Anticipating
her unhappiness, he endeavored to explain why he had spent so
much, while at the same time preparing her for his spending still
more. Already he had insisted upon and gotten his way in previous
confrontations. He now feared, however, that the onrushing account
book would put an end to such bravado and indulgence.

Why was an annual stipend of 200 gulden, a sizable sum—
Martin Luther's salary in the 1520s was not much more[36]—insuffi-
cient? One reason was the comparatively inflated prices of staples in
Italy. However, the more serious budget buster, in Paul's opinion,
was the presence of Gabriel Gienger, whose support he alleges was
possibly doubling the group's expenses. If a strict budget was to be
successfully enforced, he believed the group would have to disband
and each live independently. He dramatized his fears by relating the
plight of a Nürnberg youth well known to his mother, who was then
stranded in Italy without any means of support from his family.[37]
The story of this unfortunate peer may genuinely have moved Paul,
and he could imagine himself in similar straits should his own
family withdraw their support. He shared the crisis with his mother,
however, in the hope that it would move her once again on his own
behalf.

5. To Mother[38]

Dear Mother . . . An account book (*Register*) is being sent to you
through Herr Jobst Tetzel or Herr Wilibald Imhof. It contains,
first, what I have consumed in food and drink over this half year,
which is now reported as a group expense. Then follows what I
have spent on other things for my daily needs, expenditures that
pertain only to me. You [three] there [Frau Behaim, Wilibald
Imhof, and Jobst Tetzel] will know how to divide all this up fairly
among yourselves, [remembering] that I am the one who has
spent the least, Carl Imhof the most, and Jobst Friedrich Tetzel
somewhere in-between. . . .

I do not want to withhold from you the news of Sebastian
Hölzschuher (d. 1579), Caspar Hölzschuher's [eldest] son,
who recently arrived here and has begged our assistance. He
appealed directly to . . . Gabriel Gienger, whose mother was a
Hölzschuher. Gienger gave him two gulden and we have given
him one-and-a half. We asked him if his family had given him
any money to come here. He replied: "They gave me six gulden,
but as I could not come this far on that, I joined up with
merchants in several towns along the way and helped them sell
their small wares." When we asked him where he wanted to go,
he said that he had sought work at the German House in Venice,
but there was an opening only for a waiter, so in the end he
got no work at all. He also informed us that he had been [a
merchant's apprentice] in the Stöckel firm in Nürnberg, where,
due to his inexperience,[39] he had caused the loss of about fifty
gulden. That so upset his family that they drove him away and
into poverty.

There, dear mother, you can see clearly enough what great
disgrace results for one such as Sebastian, and for an entire
family as well, when one is robbed of one's parents' support and
also may not turn to relatives. Denied and sent away by his own,
he now must be a servant of servants. This Hölzschuher first
lamented his situation to Veit Hölzschuher,[40] who refused
assistance to him from the [Hölzschuher] Foundation, one of
city's most eminent [charities]. We Nürnbergers here have shown
Sebastian far more friendship than his own family. He begged
us . . . to let him stay with us as our servant, and while we gave
his request lots of thought, it was not what we wanted to do.

From this experience, I know that after God, who has
given me you, I cannot thank you enough, for I now see and
understand for the very first time what kind of mother I have. I
deplore in myself the many times I have offended and angered
you over the last six weeks, how often the accursed devil has
succeeded in provoking me against you. I have not been worthy

to have you look on me as a son. For this reason, my trust is
now placed entirely in you never to hold such sins and offenses
against me, but to forgive and pardon me as one who has lacked
understanding and wanted to go entirely too far. You now have
my sure promise henceforth to conduct myself and to honor you
as it is fitting and proper for a son to do a mother. . . . Padua, 25
August, 1575.

Y L S, PAUL BEHAIM

The Italians

Although there was at least as much manipulation as genuine
feeling in those words, Frau Behaim soon had reason enough to
sympathize with her son. Having just assured her that large expenses were inevitable in Italy, neither of them could have anticipated that he would write again within a week to report the theft of
all of the group's ready cash and some valuables as well, a loss Paul
put at about 150 crowns.

6. *To Mother*[41]

Dear Mother . . . I must tell you with a sad heart that on
August 29, as we were eating dinner in the evening, all the cash
we had in common, which came to about 100 crowns, was
stolen, along with a small necklace with a malachite heart worth
about forty crowns, and a pair of velvet trousers with silver trim
and a pair of linen sheets, altogether worth fourteen or fifteen
crowns. Except for the money, all the stolen items belonged to
Gienger. But lest anyone think that we are to blame, or that
Gienger was guilty of any negligence, we know for a fact that
the door to the room in question had been closed and securely
locked, and that the trunk from which the items were taken
was also sealed with an Italian lock. After Gienger [whose room

it was] ascertained [these facts] early on the morning of
August 30—he had not slept there that night because he had no
sheets—we asked many lawyers for advice, and they told us that
we should lodge a complaint against those we suspected with the
podestá, the highest official in Padua, and have them arrested.

Before all others, we suspected the old woman who cooks for
us. She had a soldier friend who was always with her, to whom
she often gave portions of our meal even before the night of the
theft. As we dined that evening, she twice went to the door and
opened and closed it. Having heard many earlier conversations
between them, we could easily tell that she was letting her soldier
in and out of the house. That soldier had every opportunity to
learn from her the lay of the house and the place where our
money was kept. [We believe that once in the house] he climbed
through the window of Gienger's room, broke the lock on the
trunk containing the money and Gienger's necklace, trousers, and
sheets, and made off with them all. While he was in the house,
he also unhinged a little door facing a ditch that flows on the side
of the house, so that one would think the thief had entered there,
thus throwing suspicion off the cook.

Having recognized this, we had both the woman and the
soldier arrested and started a legal process against them. We
wanted the woman tortured so that she was made to confess and
make clear her thievery, because no one else had done it but her.
We also have many witnesses to a stolen linen sheet in the water
closet, which was completely clean and thus had not been there
long. One can also infer the woman's guilt from the fact that none
of the other trunks in the room were tampered with in the least;
only Gienger's room was robbed, and the cook knew that he
managed the money.

Since filing our suit, justice has been done us. However,
because the cook is not to undergo torture until tomorrow, we
cannot know for sure what the final outcome will be. As soon as
we can, we want to send you the *acta* or papers assembled for

our case, so you can see what is involved in a legal process here. Everyone is on our side, even the podestá of Padua himself and his advisers, all of whom assure us that we shall get our money back—and if not all of it, would to God at least half. . . . [Meanwhile] we have . . . moved into another house, as we cannot live in the old den of assassins. If almighty God now helps us out of this ghastly mess, our lives will become easier and cheerier, and the great cost of living here will also be lighter and more bearable. . . . Padua, 1 September, 1575.[42]

Y L S, PAUL BEHAIM

The boys' hopes were soon dashed. Before half a week had passed, Paul wrote again to announce the failure of Italian justice: Instead of having their money and valuables returned, as everyone had assured them would happen, they now found themselves accused of making false accusations. This unexpected turn of events resulted from the inquisitorial nature of contemporary judicial procedure. Rather than viewing an accused man or woman as innocent or guilty, courts at the time treated them circumstantially as the best source of the truth: In the absence of eyewitnesses, the accused was the person most likely to know the truth or falsity of an accusation. On that assumption, the accused was subjected to a relentless interrogation in an effort to elicit the truth he or she knew, much as a conscientious priest might treat an obdurate penitent in the confessional. However, in criminal cases, much as in contemporary witch trials, physical torture might also be applied to achieve that goal. The thinking here judged it worse for a guilty person to go free than for an innocent person to suffer. As with the victor in an ordeal, a man or woman who successfully withstood torture in a criminal trial was deemed to have been exonerated by God.[43]

That now happened with the boys' cook and her lover. With no eyewitnesses to corroborate their accusation, nor any confession from the accused, the Italian court was powerless to act against either. And once the pair had been exonerated, the boys became the villains in the court of public opinion.

7. To Mother[44]

Dear Mother . . . On the matter of the theft, I must unfortunately tell you that on September 2, the lover of our cook, who had been arrested with her, was acquitted and released, so that we may now be safe neither on the streets nor at home. On that same day, four men, apparently hired thugs, confronted Gienger and demanded that we repay the man for everything it cost him while he was in prison. I think this is just a pretext and the beginning of greater hostility and harm for us, which, with the great loss we have already incurred, will very soon drive us from Padua. . . .

Meanwhile, our cook remains in jail, and although everyone thinks she is guilty and takes her for a thief, because she still will not confess to anything, one cannot proceed against her. For this reason, I think she, like her lover, will also be acquitted and released against our knowledge and will. Please ponder our situation and do not withhold your loyal maternal advice.

With sad hearts we [also] . . . learned from Wilibald Imhof's letter to Gienger of Jobst Tetzel's . . . departure from this world. With the death of his uncle and patron, Gienger is now planning to return home at the earliest, and when he does so, I intend to take control of my own affairs. Otherwise, it may cost us too much [for me to stay here]; as things now stand, we are already marked people.[45] In the immediate future, I will act to hold down large expenditures, while elevating manners and the matters of the mind. . . . Padua, 4 September, 1575.

Y L S, PAUL BEHAIM

When Paul wrote again, he and his companions had become laughingstocks in Padua. On October 19, separate letters were written to Magdalena and Sabina and his mother, bringing them up to date on the aftermath of the lawsuit. Since his arrival in Italy, his sisters had not been the faithful correspondents he had expected them to be. Earlier (August 25) he had scolded them for not finding the time to send him a letter when their mother wrote, especially when they knew that "half a page, even one line" would suffice.[46] By mid-October, Sabina had written to assure him that it had been plague, not any illness or negligence on their part, that prevented their writing. Forced to spend most of their time indoors, they were not abreast of the news and gossip Paul so longed to hear and relied on them to supply. He wrote now, however, not to scold them, but to vent his spleen at Italian justice, aware that he would nowhere find more sympathetic ears.

8. To Magdalena and Sabina[47]

Fraternal love and loyalty, dear sisters Madel [Magdalena] and Sabina. . . . From your letters, I gather that you are having both good times and bad, that grain and wine are plentiful, but that there is much dying as well, especially among young men and women, who are now going to become rare.

Doubtless, mother has told you about the misfortune that befell me and my companions here. The incident was difficult enough to bear, but now the Italians only make fun of us and mock our lawsuit, so that we cannot find an honest man who can help us in this matter. I believe one cannot find a more deceitful people in the world than the Italians, who are more godless and uncivilized than pagans. Just look at what happened after we had our cook and her lover arrested! I do not know what drink the Devil gave them so that they managed to say nothing after being tortured three times. . . .

Time and God will advise us whether we should remain in Padua. . . . Padua, 19 October, 1575.

Y L B[ROTHER], PAUL BEHAIM

A Maternal Challenge

The theft of 150 gulden was also no small matter for Frau Behaim, who now had to make up Paul's part. Money had always been a major topic of their letters, but given Paul's increasingly clear determination to carry on as before—his emphatic denials notwithstanding—it now became the most unpleasant one as well. Although not an uncharitable woman, Frau Behaim strongly disapproved of Paul's support of Sebastian Hölzschuher at a time when he himself was spending and losing hundreds of gulden. In his own defense, Paul protested that once his housemates had contributed, he could not honorably refuse to do so, and he reminded his mother that "one who is wretched and despised in his youth can often later become honorable once he reaches his majority and is finally a man, so that one cannot know what almighty God yet has in store for this wretched Hölzschuher."[48]

Paul now faced the personal and financial disaster of the Paduan experiment. Not only were the townspeople "laughing in [their] faces and enjoying it," the boys' lawyer was advising them to be kind to the less fortunate cook and her partner in crime. But having been mugged so thoroughly, Paul lusted only for vengeance, and left his mother another chilling reminder of what they were up against.

9. To Mother[49]

Dear Mother. . . . I cannot withhold from you that on the very day I am writing this letter, [Nürnberger] Georg Fütterer[50] has gone to sleep in God. . . . Three weeks ago, he was Carl Imhof's evening guest and arrived [at our flat] drunk. We pleaded with him to stay the night, but he left late to go home, and en route three armed men fell upon him, wounding him in many places, most seriously on his forehead, where they inflicted a finger-length gash . . . that cut all the way to his brain. At first it did not appear to have hurt him so much. However, a high fever soon ensured, during which he vomited large amounts of blood from his internal wounds . . . after which he was unable to swallow and started to gag. So now a week later, amid the repeated prayers to God we recited to him, he has blessedly died. Padua, 25 November, 1575

Y L S, PAUL BEHAIM

Despite such circumstances, Paul and his colleagues still wanted nothing more than to remain in Italy as long as possible. So adamant was Paul that he asked his mother "to make a virtue out of necessity and inquire if some aid might be extended [to him] by the Foundation"; that is, a charitable contribution to supplement his annual share of family funds, so that he could meet his needs in the coming months. That he was aware of the impropriety of raiding a charity for his own self-indulgence was made clear by a further request that she "please do so quietly, lest some view it as dishonorable on my part."[51]

New Rules

By December, the group was all but dissolved. Gienger would depart for good with the new year, and Jobst Friedrich and Carl were exploring moves to other Italian cities. A self-righteous Paul could at last contemplate a life alone. But although he had promised his mother greater self-discipline and savings once on his own, his acquisitions, both recent and planned, suggested that old habits would die hard.

10. To Mother[52]

Dear Mother. . . . I received your letter of November 29 in which you seem to think that Gabriel Gienger has so carelessly handled the money he takes from Venice for the group that it could easily be stolen, or idly strewn along the streets. To relieve you of such suspicion, let me say from the bottom of my heart that the money he has spent on his own personal needs is little

enough in itself (even though a bit much by my purse). Yet, even
when it is added in, the account book would not have become
so inflated had Tetzel not been digging so deeply into it during
these months. . . .

Looking ahead to winter, I have bought a camel's hair coat
lined with fox fur for four crowns, which, depending on my
circumstances later, I can resell at a good price. Otherwise, I
would have to pay the Jew ten *batzen* [sixteen pfennig] a month
just for the loan of such a coat. . . .

For this reason, I also intend to buy the Latin edition of the
Corpus Civile outright. It consists of five books I am always in
need of, for they contain all the law one needs to know in court[53]
and are the books from which one must learn all law. . . . In a
year and a half, at most two, I would pay the Jew as much to
lease these books as it will cost me now to buy them outright.
The total cost of all the books may come to ten or eleven crowns,
which I would otherwise pay the Jew to borrow them over two
years. For the aforementioned five books of the *Corpus Civile*,
one must give the Jew seven *batzen* a month, and for the other,
smaller ones two *batzen* each.[54] I leave the decision [to buy or to
borrow] to you. Should you have a compelling reason for me to
borrow, I will heed it. . . . Padua, 14 December, 1575.

                                        Y L S, PAUL BEHAIM

While Paul and his companions viewed the prices charged by
Jews on their rentals as exorbitant and frequently complain about it,
no anti-Jewish religious rhetoric, much less any anti-Semetic racial
slurs, ever accompany the descriptions of Jewish lenders. This seems
surprising at a time when Italian Jews were the objects of a new
wave of Church persecution. In 1553, the pope pronounced the
Talmud sacrilegious and blasphemous and placed it on the *Index of
Forbidden Books*, where Erasmus's Greek and Latin editions of the
New Testament (which contradicted in places the Vulgate) then also
appeared. In 1555, the papal bull *Cum Nimis Absurdum* mandated
Jewish ghettos, modeled on that of Venice, in all papal territories.

Fourteen years later, Pope Pius V's bull *Hebraeorum Gens* expelled all Jews from the papal states, with the exception of Ancona.[55] A possible explanation of the absence of anti-Jewish sentiment in Paul's confessionally mixed group (Carl Imhof's beliefs were Roman Catholic, Paul's and Jobst Friedrich's solidly Lutheran) is that Christian lenders were by this time exploiting their clients no less.[56]

Déjà Vu

With the new year 1576, the group dissolved. Jobst Tetzel had already gone, and Gienger would depart for France within days. Although Carl Imhof remained in Padua, he was now also living alone. As Paul, at eighteen, anticipated becoming sole manager of his money and his life, he saw a new day dawning. Perhaps it was a sign of this new freedom and the anxiety accompanying it that his first request of his mother in the new year was a copy of Martin Luther's songbook[57] and another of his prayer books "as soon as possible." That request was ominously followed on January 13 by a projection of his new expenses, which he placed at two gulden a month for room, bed, and furnishings, and around nine for food and drink. He wanted her to know this right away because he expected she would find his previous quarterly expenditures (October 1575–January 12, 1576), then in the mail, to be "rather much," and think him "again [to be] buying furs, musical instruments, and the like."[58] He did not believe a recently purchased instrument to be such an extravagance, since he thought he could sell it later at a profit.

When he wrote again three weeks later, he was settled into his new lodgings, now accompanied by a German companion from his Leipzig days. His mother by this time had in hand the record of his expenditures, which did indeed weigh heavily on her mind, confirming her doubts about his ability ever to change. Attempting to cap this discussion, he cheerily presented his mistakes as a salutary warning to his brothers when they later undertook their own

bachelor journeys, which was not the gloss his mother put on his
spending.

11. To Mother[59]

Dear Mother. . . . As I wrote to you earlier, I moved into
my new dwelling on January 12, where I share a table with a
nobleman, Otto von Starschedel[60] . . . who has moved in . . .
with me. As we had been together in Leipzig . . . and his conduct
and studies are such that people can only praise him, I had
reason to join up with him [again]. Of course, I hope I conduct
myself toward him in such a way that he will also have no
complaints whatsoever about me. . . .

I hope you have by now received my last letter [of January 13]
along with the account book. Therein, I could not have explained
my expenditures more exactly. . . . My only thought now is the
obscene amount of money[61] that has been spent so quickly. I
would not advise any of my brothers to come here with a
preceptor, or in the company of so many others. Why is one sent
around to the German universities anyway, if not to get to know
people and to learn self control?[62] Truly, that discipline is best
that one imposes on oneself. . . . 2 February, 1576

Y L S, PAUL BEHAIM

Anxious about both of their futures, Frau Behaim had asked Paul
to send her his best guess on his basic expenses for the coming year.
The calculation—195 gulden—was significantly more than she had
expected and showed none of the restraint of his earlier protestations. Thrown quickly on the defensive by his mother's criticism,
Paul feared she might transfer him back to a somewhat cheaper German university for the completion of his studies, something he
warned her would lessen the value of his education and future
prospects for very little savings.[63]

In her responses to his recent letters, Frau Behaim had left no
doubt in her son's mind that his stay in Italy would be neither as

open-ended nor as leisurely as he desired. While he never gave up on his ability to persuade her otherwise, he did resolve to visit quickly as many of Italy's great cities as possible in whatever time did remain, eventually landing in Rome. If such aggressive tourism did not cost any more than staying put in Padua, as he dared to claim, it did require far easier access to cash on the road. As his sight-seeing ambitions unfolded before her eyes, Frau Behaim could only have seen red—both in anger and in ink.

12. To Mother[64]

Dear Mother. . . . I am letting you know that we are now in the third month [of the new year], and I will need my thirty crowns for the next quarter. Since almost a year has passed since I had a new suit of clothes, I will soon be needing that as well. So this time I will take forty crowns [instead of thirty] from Isaac Greck[65] in Venice, for if the new clothes are to be made from camel's hair, they will cost nine or ten crowns. Just now, I can find no better or more durable material here for myself than camel's hair. . . .

I now have a great desire to strike out, to go first to Bologna and then . . . to tour Siena and Rome, where my expenses will be no greater than they would be here. Should I have only a short time left in Italy, as I understand your letter to say, and not have the opportunity to see more than one other city, I would be ashamed to say that I had been here at all. I would also count it not the smallest disgrace to have to end [prematurely] the pursuit of my studies and good manners, which has always been my first priority.

The single obstacle to my going to Bologna seems to be access to money there. I would like to be able to get money on the spot and not have to wait for it to be sent to me from the Imhof office in Venice. Not only will shipping it be difficult enough, there is also the danger that it may not reach me. I know of no better way to arrange [readier access to money] on my behalf than for you to appeal to Stephan Braun[66] in Nürnberg, as he has his son and an

agent in Bologna, whom he could instruct in advance to deposit
money for me there after my arrival. . . . Braun worked out such
an arrangement for Sebald Welser[67] when . . . [he] came to
Bologna. I will await your counsel here at the earliest possible
time. . . . Padua, 2 March, 1576

Y L S, PAUL BEHAIM

Time Out

The battle between mother and son over new spending rules
could not immediately ensue, because another thief now burst into
Paul's life, one that threatened to take everything from him, and
against whom neither he nor his mother had any effective defense.
By April, one of the century's deadliest plagues encroached on the
region around Padua, news of which reached Paul's family by the
merchant grapevine weeks before they heard a word about it from
him.[68] In mid-May, he wrote the first of a steady stream of vivid letters describing the new crisis in Venetia.

13. To Mother[69]
Dear Mother. . . . I understand from your letter what you think
about the move I am contemplating [to Bologna], and my
thoughts about it have always been the same as yours. I have let
you know my plans in a somewhat more timely fashion for the
following reason. Here, it is the custom for a prince or a lord,
as soon as he learns that plague is threatening another city, say,
Padua, to order and proclaim throughout his realm that no one
from that city be allowed to enter or take refuge in his land, or
to have any contact with his subjects there, on penalty of death.
Should, God forbid, such pestilence establish itself in Padua—
and it could easily be brought here by the Venetians—there is no

doubt that the duke of Ferrara and the pope, to whom Bologna
belongs, would proclaim Padua a city of pestilence throughout
their lands, and I would then be stuck here. Any lands I could
then enter would either already be plague-stricken, or I would be
turned away because I came from Padua.

Now that you know what is happening, I am sure you would
approve my departing Padua at the first signs of pestilence,
before the princes seal their borders, and there is still a chance to
make it to Bologna. Such would be impossible were I to ask your
permission only after the plague arrived, and try to wait out your
reply here. Then it would be much too late, and I would be
trapped here. . . Padua, 17 May, 1576.

Y L S, PAUL BEHAIM

When Paul next wrote, the plague's march toward the city had
quickened. Whether or not it would breach the walls, he was weary
of Padua and wanted to be gone. Living on his own for five months
had not met his expectations. He now missed his old companions,
of whom he had grown fonder in their absence. Prolonging his stay
in Padua now threatened to deprive him not only of his life, but
of something almost as important to an eighteen-year-old Nürnberg
patrician: a proper Italian experience. "Should I not go anywhere
else," he lamented, "I will depart [Italy] the same goose I was when I
arrived."[70]

The steady stream of Venetian refugees into Padua left no doubt of
the plague's imminence. Paul had, however, waited too late to escape
south; with greater resolve than Padua, Ferrara and Bologna had already banned travelers from the north. The choices now seemed to
be to return to Germany or to stick it out in Venetia. For one willing
to pursue any other alternative, a third loomed: Verona, a safe, literal
middle ground between Germany and Padua, where brother Christoph and cousin Christoph Imhof then lived. Reasoning that he
might have spent a month or two in Verona anyway (the summers
there were cooler and more conducive to study), Paul made a new
plan—to wait out the plague in Verona until the journey to Bologna
could be safely made.[71]

Unfortunately, plague enveloped Padua by the second week of July, cutting the route to Verona as well. Why, after all the advance warning and planning, had Paul not fled sooner? Clearly, plague had stolen a march on the city in late June, isolating it suddenly on all sides, so that by the time he was ready to depart, strict quarantine rules hobbled the healthiest of travelers. In such an emergency, it became no small challenge for a foreign youth, even one as clever and well connected as Paul, to arrange safe transit and accommodations elsewhere.

14. To Mother[72]

Dear Mother. . . . I must tell you that plague has spread . . . five miles south from Venice and is now well-established among us, so I now must look for another place to go. Since I cannot go to Ferrara or Bologna, I am inclined simply to follow the [fleeing] masses, although some good acquaintances of mine here have recommended among other good places on the route to Germany one called Koniglohn[73] where there should be adequate provisions and good air. I am prepared to stay there until my options improve.

Two hundred people are now dying every day in Venice, some in the hospital, while others drop . . . on the streets. In Padua, the death toll is still small by comparison, perhaps fifty a day. My departure [north] with several Augsburgers is now set for the eighteenth of the month. . . . I had wanted to spend the summer . . . in Verona, but I have been otherwise advised, since the plague has made travel there impossible as well. . . .

I took the watch [you sent via Christoph Imhof] to a skilled goldsmith and asked what he would charge to solder the cover over the numbers. He said that it would also have to be gilded again and that he could not do it for less than two gulden. So I am continuing to use it with the cover broken. I would rather have seen it fixed there [in Nürnberg].

Know also that I have already carefully drafted the Latin letter I shall write to Herr Dr. Flick;[74] however, due to the preparations

for my departure, I have not been able to copy it. So I am saving
it until I write you another time. A week ago, I again received my
three month stipend from Isaac Greck in Venice, which amount
you will know to forward to him after he sends you the
receipt. . . . Padua, 12 July, 1576.

Y L S, PAUL BEHAIM

When Paul wrote again, it was from the village of Monte Ortone
southwest of Padua.[75] He had since been stricken by plague, although not mortally. In this new circumstance, unprecedented in his
young life, his fear of being without means and at the mercy of the
physicians became as great as that of plague and death.

15. To Mother[76]

Dear Mother. . . . I am letting you know why I have not written
for so long. Six weeks ago, plague devastated Venice, with five
to six hundred dying daily, and a month ago, a great pestilence
erupted among the people of Padua, leaving sixty or seventy
dead each day, a lot for Padua. It continues in fits and starts from
one city to another, and many physicians have said they fear it
could envelop the whole of Italy. Travel has also been made very
difficult. If someone from Venice wants to enter another territory,
he must first be quarantined[77] for forty days, until it can be seen
if he has brought the plague with him. No one can go to Bologna
or Siena; and the only way one can reach Verona is to travel
north to Germany and come back down. I am not, however,
counting much on Verona, since the air there is almost always
bad. Depending, however, on how bad it is, I would then wait
out the plague in a German city, say, Innsbruck or some other,
and await further instructions there from you—or just stay put
for a month or two until things are a little better in Verona or
Padua.

I must also tell you that when plague appeared in Padua, I . . .
moved with two others[78] . . . to a village nine Italian miles away
[Monte Ortone], where we lived for two weeks in complete

comfort and good health. Then, two other noblemen we knew
in Padua arrived and wanted to share our table. Unable to deny
them, we let them join us. Three days later, while dining, one
of them fell ill with plague and died three or four days later. No
one, however, wanted to drag his body to the grave and bury
him. So his companion, a Saxon nobleman, had to put him in a
coffin, cart him alone to another village an Italian mile away, and
bury him there along with the cart.

As soon as we saw that it was plague, we three moved into
an isolated house in a field with a bedstead without any bedding
and had to content ourselves with straw. The cold chilled our
stomachs and we all were soon stricken with a high fever. Just
an hour before, I had written to you. I ran a fever every day, but
there was little medicine to be gotten for it from Padua, and what
a good friend did manage to bring, I had to pay double for,
which I did with much gratitude.

The food I eat is now always boiled three or four days in
advance, so that one has only to warm it a little before putting
it on the table, as it keeps well. I drink boiled barley water. Oh,
how often have I thought about you and your tender care! Were
I out of this shack, I would pay as much for a pint of beer as one
pays there [in Nürnberg] for malmsey. But since one cannot get
beer here, one must leave it to God.

Finally, I must tell you that the traffic between Venice and
Padua diminishes daily, as the terrible plague rages in both
cities. A catastrophe can suddenly befall one at any time, and
to be caught without plenty of cash is to count oneself more
dead than alive. So I have sent a letter to Greck in Venice by
way of a good friend requesting still another thirty crowns,
which, if I have them in cash, I think I can stretch them as far
as ten.

What I now fear most is the physicians,[79] who in these
circumstances know all too well how to empty one's pocket. Also,
should I want to travel to Germany, one is allowed to take only
what one can carry on one's person. . . . So, if I take a couple of

shirts with me, fold two pairs of trousers together, stick a coat
under them, and add a few books, everything else . . . will have
to stay behind. . . . Written in Monte Ortone [August 1576].

Y W[ILLING] S ALWAYS, PAUL BEHAIM

Frau Behaim did not hear from Paul again until early December.
For four unbroken months, he lay ill and incommunicado in Monte
Ortone, on two occasions reportedly near death. Acting only on her
hopes, his mother continued to write to him; however, only one of
her letters reached him, and then belatedly. Thinking he had gone
on to Koniglohn for good, she had sent her letters there rather than
to Padua, whence they might have been forwarded to him in Monte
Ortone.

In late November, Paul, still weak and feeble, returned to a relatively plague-free Padua, where he discovered his mother's letter of
September 18, the last she had sent to him there. Although not yet
physically recovered, he was now coping with a plague of another
kind: the financial ravages of his healers.

16. To Mother[80]

Dear Mother. . . . I have received only your letter of September
18, and that plenty late. In it, you speak of other letters you sent
to me in Koniglohn. You do not, however, say through whom I
was supposed to receive them. Please let me know as soon as
possible where they can be found, and I will [try to fetch and]
answer them. Had I gotten them earlier, I would not have been
able to do so because the fever that struck on August 24 broke
only two weeks ago. During these months, I have been feeble and
unable to read or to write. When I can do so, I will write you all
about the illness and pain I endured during those months. Twice,
my two companions took me for dead and washed me down
with vinegar as I lay unconscious. I am now nothing but skin
and bones and remain exhausted, the greater part of my day
still spent in bed. When I am up, I can barely move about as I
normally do.

I have learned that the other Greck has left [Venice] and
turned his entire business over to Herr David Otto.[81] So please
tell me what procedure I should now follow when I need
money. Apart from a surgeon and my medicine, I had to pay
the physician a crown in cash every time he visited me, as he
had to ride about four Italian miles to reach me at the solitary
farmhouse in [Monte Ortone]. As he often did so two or three
times a week, I am now broke.

Because the dying has subsided in Padua and Venice, I
returned to Padua on November 25 and think I will remain here
this winter. . . . Padua, 6 December, 1576.

                                        Y L S, PAUL BEHAIM

Between God and the Physicians

Before Paul could send his mother the promised details of his illness, an unhappy Frau Behaim, apparently convinced that he was
willfully lingering in Italy at the risk of his life, had already written
to scold him for disobeying her repeated instructions to depart
Padua at the first sign of plague. Although his stranding was not
completely his fault, he appears at the time to have dreaded the ter-
mination of his wandering in Italy more than the possibility of having
his life cut short by plague.

The sudden discovery of his mortality had, however, made an impression on him. A devout Lutheran, he ruefully portrayed his brush
with death as part of the larger drama of divine punishment and human penance, which he claimed to have survived with renewed faith
in God. However, the experience had not brought him any closer to
the principled self-denial his mother so long hoped to see.

17. To Mother[82]
Dear Mother. . . . I . . . learned from your latest letter . . . how
anxious and worried you have been on my behalf. It has all been

in vain, since neither of us could receive the other's letters and
know the other's will. I do not remember in the slightest, nor can
I find in your letters of four months ago, any clear command that
I come home if the plague intensified [around Padua]. And to
have done so at the time would have been very much against my
will, although it might have happened, had our Lord God not
struck me down with such a long illness so soon after I left Padua
[for Monte Ortone]. Thereafter, when people saw me from afar,
they fled or turned their faces away, lest they inhale my
poisonous vapors.[83]

In sum, almighty God has seized upon and punished me . . .
here in Italy, so that I might know His anger at sin and avoid it in
the future. Still, His mercy toward me has been even greater, for
He has preserved whole and untouched in me the one thing
needed for my soul's salvation, His divine Word, which this land
abuses. . . .

Presently, I can neither rejoice much over health, nor complain
much about illness . . . I have continued to have either chronic
diarrhea (to put it mildly), or catarrh and a deep cough, so I
cannot keep any food down and have so far been unable to
regain my strength . . . Padua, 3 January, 1577.

Y L S, PAUL BEHAIM

Still in mid-January of the new year, Paul could not "shout much"
about his health. Night bouts with fever continued and he again required a physician. Fearing the plague's revival, he asked his mother's
permission to leave Padua.[84] Two weeks later, he announced his full
recovery at the hands of a new physician. He would soon be able to
travel again, but where should he go and what should he do?

18. To Mother[85]

Dear Mother. . . . By the grace of God and the counsel of
physicians, I have made such strides toward regaining my former
health that I hope soon to be up and out of the house. Two weeks

ago, however, I had to send for a physician again because my
fever has never completely gone away. The reason [I now have
learned] is that its cause and source had not been eradicated. My
most recent physician has explained it clearly to me for the first
time. According to him, the liver's foul fluids can only exit the
body through the lungs. When the lungs fill up with these fluids,
they become soaked, swell, and cannot function properly. And
when that happens, the stomach cannot digest food properly, so
that food passes out of the stomach in the same form in which it
entered. The body, in turn, retains the foul fluids because the
lungs cannot process them, and those fluids cause fever and
continuing illness. Before I can get well, the swelling in my lungs
has first to be alleviated by syrups and salves, and the remaining
foul fluids purged. . . . But now that my new physician has
destroyed the source and cause of my fever, I have every hope
that it will not return soon. . . .

Regarding my departure from Padua, I have not been able to
understand exactly what you mean when you write: "Meanwhile,
if you can arrange something, you may leave when the weather
and your health allow, whether it be to come here, go to another
place to study, or sightsee,[86] which is a matter still to be advised."
I do see clearly from these words that I should leave Padua and
change climes, but to tell the truth, it is not clear where you
think I should go and whether I should await further instruction
from you here. So in your next letter, please make it clear just
what your opinion is. . . . Padua, 27 January, 1577.

                                   Y L S, PAUL BEHAIM

Progress Report

In mid-February, Paul announced plans to depart Padua for Verona after Ash Wednesday. He wanted to escape both the plague, which remained active in the region, and the inflated prices for staples like lard, veal, and table wine, which had more than doubled. Because his physician allowed him to eat only fowl, he was forced to buy scrawny chickens for six or seven *batzen* apiece. Nonetheless, he remained upbeat and looked forward to visiting Ferrara or Bologna over Easter. Should renewed plague or illness abort those plans, he would make his way home at the first opportunity.[87]

Before a month had passed, he was safe in Verona, the northern gateway to Germany, and planning to spend the summer there. He also found himself on the spot to fulfill a duty he had managed to evade since beginning his studies in Italy. During his almost two years in Padua, his mother, whose own fortunes and prospects were tied to those of her son, had several times asked him to inform Nürnberg jurist Bartholomaus Flick of the progress of his studies. Both as a disciplinary measure and to reassure the family, Flick, a family friend, relative by marriage, and city council member, had earlier agreed to oversee Paul's legal studies abroad. In March, Frau Behaim reminded Paul once again of the need for a progress report, "whether it be great or small," and this time, Dr. Flick had sent along a request of his own.

For Paul, writing such a letter was a nerve-wracking exercise. It had to be written in proper Ciceronian Latin, itself a measure of his progress, and in the knowledge that no error would escape the eagle eye of the learned jurist.[88] By his own description, his legal training to date had been rudimentary, and he confided to his mother that much of what he had learned during his first year and a half in Italy had been forgotten during the months he lay ill. So when on March 13, he wrote the long-promised letter, he blamed any shortcomings Dr. Flick might perceive on circumstances beyond his control (the rowdy Italian classroom, the poor instruction of his professors, and the terrible toll taken on all by the plague). Having procrastinated to the very end, he had hoped to take still more

time with the letter. However, having now been pressured by Dr.
Flick himself, he concluded that the greater shame lay in further
delay.[89]

19. To Dr. Flick[90]
To Herr Doctor Bartholomaus Flick. Most famous man and
cherished relative, I was [newly arrived] in Verona when I
received your letter, which, while all too short, is most pleasing
to me because of its clarity and elegance of expression. . . .
Certainly I do rejoice, partly for my sake and partly for all of you,
when I know that there [in Nürnberg] you have everything in
abundance and are rich in all things, truly possessing, as they say,
the horn of plenty, even though we here [in Verona] suffer want
and lack everything. . . .

   As I watch as this terrible plague drains away nearly all our
strength . . . I marvel at the incredibly healthy, mild air and the
true happiness granted you by the singular benevolence of the
greatest and highest God. . . .

   Before I describe for your Excellency the plan of my studies
and the progress I have made during these two years, in part in
the liberal arts and in part in legal studies, I must first lament the
present fortunes of the Academy (*gymnasium*) at Padua. Although
once most famous and celebrated among men of many nations, I
tell you now that, because of the great crimes committed there
and the recurring brutality of the plague, the sun has never shone
on a fouler, more forsaken, or more ignoble [school]. . . . The
impudence and shamelessness of Italian students has grown to
such a degree that even in the middle of classes . . . they drown
out the professor and force him to finish abruptly a lecture not
yet properly begun and leave it uncompleted. . . . I declare these
public lectures, which [actually] contain more refinement and
word-play than wholesome, useful learning, to be the greatest
harm and loss to my studies. . . .

   I have deemed it appropriate to an accounting of my studies

and to Your Excellency's most wise counsel to add to this letter,
as a sort of corollary, a recapitulation and list of the subjects I
have taken so far. [First] so that [my] exposition [of the law]
might begin with the principles of legal knowledge, from the
rudiments and cradle of laws, I read through the more familiar
of those materials in my first year, along with François Hotman's
commentary and dialectical analysis of them,[91] leaving aside
those matters which, due either to the long passage of time or
recent imperial decrees, have changed and fallen into disuse. I
also heard the public lectures of Professor Stephan Castellanus[92]
on three other subjects: bequests, degrees of kinship, and
obligations. To these, I gradually added Conrad Lagus's treatise
on civil law, a little book surely worthy of a careful reading—a
golden book.[93] These are the things I did in the first year.

I had hoped that the plan of study in the second year would
be much happier and more laudable than that of the first, both
because of the abundant future rewards [of advanced study] and
a desired opportunity that suddenly presented itself. In a gesture
of favor and goodwill to the Germans, who diligently attended
the study of law, one public lecturer, Piso Guarinus Soacia,
promised to explicate sequentially [in lecture] and privately [in
tutorial] the great Pandect volumes,[94] elaborating them with great
care and vigor, so that the study of a work distinguished for its
methodical arrangement might be brought to its desired end in a
short period of time.

Even though I knew personally of his commitment and
thoroughness in public teaching from numerous confirmations,
which many others had earlier seconded, because of my absences
[due to illness], I was forced to taste the science of that ancient
practical wisdom with, so to speak, only a touch of the lips, even
though I had already managed by one or another route to acquire
training in the *Institutes*.[95] Had that serious attack of plague and
my own alarming illness not stood in the way of the professor's
careful and shrewd explication and my own application to it as a

student, I would have mastered this science easily and quickly.
However, his teaching and my learning, joined together as if by
a single knot and link, were undone by the plague; indeed, the
professor was completely undone by it![96]

From those subjects of local and foreign law found in the titles
of the first book [of the Pandect], and the instruction in
jurisdictions begun in the first title of the second book, I made
my way to the third. After a whole year of public lectures and
private lessons, however, I still did not fully understand these
matters, so I often made them the subjects of my own practical
exercises. I elaborated the meanings of selected general and
simple propositions, and I rendered a good bit of advanced
material from Latin into Italian and then from Italian back into
Latin, using the original and true phrases of each language to the
extent that I could, all of which being an exercise in style . . .

Your Excellency now has what he has wished from me: a
written account of the order and progress of my studies. If I have
foolishly or inelegantly brought forth something that offends
the most acute judgment of Your Excellency's ears, I beg Your
Excellency courteously to ascribe it partly to the shortness of the
time available to me for the composition of the letter, and partly
to the long duration of my disease, which interrupted the course
of my studies. May the kindness and heartfelt goodwill that you
have until now shown to me and my dearest mother continue to
be true and complete. In Verona, 13 March, 1577.

[PAUL BEHAIM]

Throughout April, Paul claimed to have "waited every day" for his
mother's report of Dr. Flick's reaction.[97] Having acknowledged his
limited, although by no means disgraceful academic achievement,
and knowing his family's continuing unhappiness with his habits of
consumption, the specter of his mother's precipitously pulling the
plug on his Italian sojourn must have haunted him. However, no
such report ever came; there is no surviving letter of Flick's on the

subject, nor any indication that Frau Behaim received any assessment, oral or written, from him, or reported such to Paul.

Whatever opinions about Paul's progress may have been communicated to his mother and guardians, the family had already decided that his achievement over two years did not entitle him to any bonuses. Even his sisters, who had always stood by him, now supported a reduction of his stipend.

Confronted by this new criticism and a tighter budget, Paul dug in his heels, claiming to have lived on the level of "the coarsest peasant and the raggediest ragman"[98] in Padua, ashamed to be seen on the street by a proper gentleman, and he lectured his mother on how one got ahead in Italy:

> He who wants to learn and discover something new . . . must
> make the acquaintance of noble people, or others who lead
> honorable lives,[99] circulate among them and learn from them
> what is good and worthwhile. One does not put oneself in such
> company in tatters and rags, for these are people who are always
> tidy and neat, and they expect those they associate with to be so
> as well . . . So one must at times do a bit more and not count the
> cost. . . .[100]

Siblings and Cousins

Although Magdalena and Sabina joined the family chorus censuring their brother's spendthrift ways, their correspondence was never filled with dark suspicions or hard feelings, but rather conveyed the teasing, gossip, whining, rivalry, and affection typical of siblings in every age and culture. In the summer of 1577, Paul wrote to them in this same vein, inquiring why they had not written to him for so long: "I know you must work in the garden at this time of the year," he agreed, "but surely you have a short hour or two left left over in the week to sit together and write a few lines to me (don't laugh)."

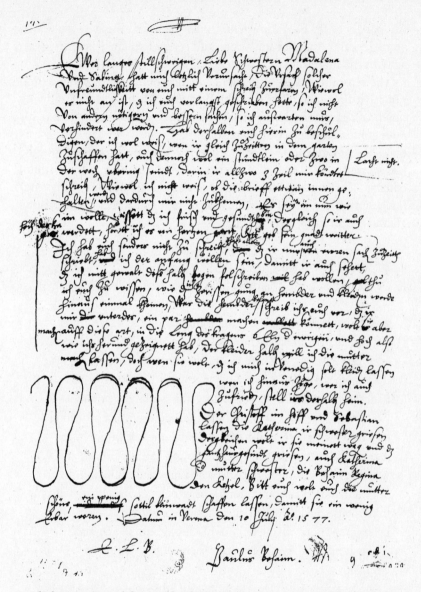

Paul's letter to Magdalena and Sabina (Verona, 10 July 1577), asking them to make two shirts for him in penance for their unfriendliness. At mid-page, a line is drawn in the left margin to indicate the required height, beneath which he sketches the desired style. (Germanisches Nationalmuseum, Behaim-Archiv Fasz. 106.)

As "penance" for their "unfriendliness," he asked them to make two shirts for him, the desired height and style of collar he sketched exactly in the margin.[101]

The reason for their long silence turned out to be one Paul could not have imagined. It had nothing to do with his cavalier drawing down of the paternal inheritance he shared with his sisters, nor his own confessed neglect of them, nor the demands of the spring garden. It was rather due to an inadvertent and unrecognized role he had played a year earlier in alienating Magdalena from their Imhof cousins, Christoph (1551–1593) and Paul (1550–1584),[102] by carelessly letting a letter of hers, in which she had criticized Christoph's character, fall into the latter's hands.

20. Magdalena to Paul[103]
Dear Brother. . . . Christoph could barely have arrived [in Padua], when he wrote to his brother [Paul] here about the letter. Paul was then angry with me for about three months, which I first noticed at a banquet at Andreas Imhof's, when he danced with everyone except me. Then, at Andreas Imhof's wedding, he also did not speak to me. I could tell then what hour had struck. Behaving like a child, he was taking a harsh revenge on me. However, later, at Andreas Imhof's homecoming party,[104] while he was dancing a second round with me, I asked him why he had earlier been so angry. He said that he had never been angry with me, but had thought that I was angry with him, and then he wished me every good thing, speaking many beautiful words from a false heart. We did, however, become friends again, after he saw that I only made light of his anger, and he was also ashamed that he should ruin our friendship by acting so childishly. . . .

Mother now says I should write to [Christoph] and ask for his forgiveness, and since he is not far from Rome, he should send me a little indulgence letter as well.[105] I did not do this, however, as I worried that I might throw it out with the scraps [should he actually send it]. . . .[106]

Please greet Christoph for me and let me know what he says.
He is still very angry at me, particularly over what he said he
read in [my] letter [to you] a year ago.[107] He also wrote to Carl
Imhof, as if to his best friend, to tell him all about it as well
(whereas when he is here he rather tells all about Carl)! We must
commend him to God, as Carl himself says. Carl [by the way] is
not here now, but in the Netherlands with Sebald Welser. . . .[108]
preparing for his [law] exams. . . . [Nürnberg] 24 July, 1577.

MAGDALENA BEHAIM

Unknown to Magdalena, her brother was himself by this time engaged in an even nastier conflict with cousin Christoph. After arriving in Italy in 1575, he had on occasion turned for advice and
assistance to his older (by six years), wealthier, and more experienced Catholic cousin. There was, however, an air of superiority
about Christoph that Paul never admired, something Magdalena
picked up on early as well. Paul, ironically, had written to his
mother about his troubles with cousin Christoph on the day after
Magdalena had written to him about hers. Portraying Christoph as
his dearest cousin one day and the foulest enemy the next, he confided in her a recent confrontation the two had in Verona that almost
cost him his life.

21. To Mother [109]

[Dear Mother]. . . . I am writing only to let you know that I have
moved back to Padua. I want you to know the reason why, so
that you do not think that I am just going idly from one place to
another. While I was still in Padua, Christoph Imhof wrote me
several letters, which I still have, in which he said he would help
me whenever he could [should I come to Verona], whether it be
a matter of money, or anything else, and he would never fail me.
After my arrival, he was at first true to those words. However,
after I borrowed about twenty-one crowns from him, he in time
renounced his friendship with me, telling me to stay out of his
affairs and never to importune him again about money, even

though he had loaned me money on only two previous
occasions. . . .

He came again one day to my house . . . and there began to
say several unkind words, pointing directly at me, so I could tell
they were meant for me. In the presence of my companions I
defended myself as best I could, in response to which he lashed
out, saying I was lying through my teeth—those were his very
words. I then asked him three or four times if he meant to call
me a liar, and every time he said yes. I then flew into a rage and
slapped him, and he, in turn, began to denounce me furiously,
saying, finally, in sum, that I was a person totally without honor.
I wanted to attack him again, but my companion asked me to let
him speak, and so I did.

He now spoke of the friendship and respect he had shown in
bringing me to Verona, and threw other such things in my face.
Whereupon, I replied with these very words: "[Son] of a mother
of whores," which is something one says here. He, however, did
not take it that way, and began to speak again, saying, "Your
sisters are the whores of your mother!" On hearing such words, I
could never contain myself, and as I happened to have a dagger
at hand, I drew it, however, only to threaten, not to harm him.
I said to him: "Do you mean to call my sisters whores?" He
answered back with kind words and then left—but only to go
out and hire some thugs to lie in wait for me on the street, and
as is the custom here, to cudgel or stab me to death, when I
appeared. Christoph was actually seen and heard speaking to
them, first, by my patron, and then by my loyal companion, who
told me that I could expect nothing good from Christoph Imhof.

Surely you would not have wanted me to save my honor and,
more importantly, your own by remaining in Verona and being
strangled to death—and this at the behest of a cousin who
arranges such crimes for four or five crowns! It is also true that
had I wanted to remain in Verona and been willing to wager eight
or ten crowns myself, I could also have hired three or four thugs

for my own protection. But, then, you and the family might never have seen me again. It just seemed more advisable to choose the lesser of two evils and betake myself to Padua without great cost, although the damage has been around six or seven crowns. That is the true and just reason for my return to Padua.

So that Christoph Imhof also may know this and have nothing to complain about, I have sent a version of this letter to him in Verona. Since I have been here, he has sent word to me through my companion there that he regrets that I took things so personally and returned to Padua. He says that I should come back to Verona, that he wants to be my dear cousin again. What hypocrisy! Having seen him behave this way on other occasions, I give nothing he says much credence. You may tell his brother that, if you wish.

I am confiding all this in you because I cannot forget that I have known nothing here but misfortune, fear, and want. First, our money was stolen from Gienger, then all last summer long I lay ill, again spending great sums of money, and now, when no misfortune is at hand, my own cousin has to waylay me, for which I hope evil enough shall befall him when he and I return home. . . . Padua, 25 July, 1577.

Y L S, PAUL BEHAIM

Regression

Far from gaining any sympathy from his mother, the brawl with cousin Christoph left Frau Behaim appalled, as she now saw Paul in full retreat from manhood. She had reason to suspect that he was using the incident as an excuse to reposition himself in Padua, the jumping-off point for his planned tour of Italy, once the road south became safe.

The new conflict between mother and son became the subject of their subsequent letters. Drawing up the contemporary teenager's heavy artillery in confrontations with parents, Paul now compared her unfavorably to a stepmother—no small insult in the sixteenth century[110]—and refused to remain in Italy on anyone's terms but his own. Still, in a fleeting moment of awakening maturity, he also confronted the end of his youthful wandering.

22. To Mother[111]

Dear Mother. . . . I received your letter dated August 7 . . . and I am aware of the chapter of the epistle and the gospel [you quote],[112] to which much might be said in reply. However, it is not fitting for me to oppose you again as I have done in the past, only thereafter to regret it.

As for the conflict with Christoph Imhof, I will only say that, were I thirty or forty years old and someone said to me what he said in the presence of a nobleman and my companion, I would do the same thing all over again, even if others thought I was acting like "a child," "a fool," and "a blockhead," as you call me. . . . I leave it to honorable and reasonable people to judge who is right and who is wrong in this matter. As for your comment that it would have been more becoming for me to have laughed and said nothing [to Christoph], I would agree with you, had he and I been arguing in private and not in the presence of other, esteemed people.

Moreover, you must know that what I did was more for you and my sisters than for myself, putting your honor before my own. . . . Yet, the thanks I have earned for it I would not have expected from a stepmother, although I leave that to others to judge. I will not mention how [initially] welcome to me this letter of yours was. Coming at the height of a three-day fever, and expecting to ease my pain by reading it, I could hardly look at it without feeling worse.

However, what will be will be; I let everything take its course. However, if a son can ever get something from a mother by asking, I have two things to ask, which if you are ever to see me

again—I mean, if you ever want to see me again—you will not
deny. First, I ask you not to write such a letter to me ever again,
wherever I may be, for you can make your point clear enough in
another way. Secondly, in regard to the budget you now present
me with, I ask you, with the concurrence of my guardians, to
command me to come home in two months,[113] as it is clear that
I have greater expenses [than it allows]. I will still have my room
and board here until then, and I am not willing to stay here on
your budget.[114]

   You may now do with me as you wish, for I have firmly
resolved that we will not become subjects of gossip over this, that
we can survive our words and make amends. Furthermore, I do
not write to you only so that you may think that I do so from a
rash and unfriendly heart, as you say [of my previous letter]. . . .
If [you think] that is not so, I still have a copy of the letter, which
I can show you, if you wish. . . . Padua, 22 August, 1577.

                                                     PAUL BEHAIM

Still smarting from his mother's letter of August 7 and the freezing
of his resources, Paul nonetheless hoped to break her will once again
by pleading righteousness, illness, and crushing medical bills. She
had touched another sore point by lecturing him on how lucky he
was to have a mother and siblings who allowed him to spend down
their inheritance as well as his own. Seizing in his anger upon the
most unfortunate of phrases, he now compared her unfavorably to
the *worst* of stepmothers and accused her of abandoning him. On
the one hand, he proposed that she liquidate his share of inheritance, presumably to enable him to do as he pleased, while on the
other, he remained adamant about quitting Italy in the fall if adequate resources were not forthcoming. Either way, he did not intend
to exit Italy without a tour of its great cities.

23. To Mother[115]

Dear Mother. . . . You do not know the extent to which you are
placing me at the mercy of others[116] [by reducing my stipend].

I have never heard of such a thing happening to anyone before,
even one who had the cruelest possible stepmother. While I
concede that I would have had somewhat less to spend, if each
[of my siblings] had taken his or her portion [of the income from
the paternal inheritance],[117] I leave it to you to consider whether
you have sufficient cause for your unhelpful letter. Although I
know it cannot be done without diminishing my honor and rank,
I would like to take that [part of the] principal[118] [that belongs
to me]. . . . I also ask you again to grant the requests of my last
letter, for I think I would spend next winter more profitably
[in Germany] than here [under present conditions]. . . . There,
I would also have the opportunity to do something new. . . .

Meanwhile, if I still might have the opportunity to tour[119]
Florence and perhaps also Rome, I do not want to miss it. The
bottom line for me: I would not like to be called, as you write,
"a goose when I flew here and a goose when I returned." Perhaps
in the next month and a half everything can be arranged so that I
might start for home before the onset of winter. . . .

Nothing more for now except the hope, pending the
opportunity, that I not be in Padua [but off sight-seeing] when I
receive your reply to this letter. . . . Padua, 29 August, 1577.

PAUL BEHAIM

As those last words indicate, the request to travel through Italy in
the fall had been a virtual demand. Opposed by his guardians on
grounds of expense and the interruption of his studies, the tour was
strongly supported by Paul's sisters, who could imagine themselves
in such an adventure and relished the idea of vicariously sharing it
through him. Pressured from both sides, Frau Behaim capitulated to
his wishes. That her consent was grudging and remained faint became evident in a letter Magdalena, the family mediator, wrote Paul
in late September, which accompanied and elaborated on a long-
delayed letter from his mother.

24. Magdalena to Paul[120]

Dear brother Paul. . . . I, too, decided to write you a letter,
especially as it can now be sent with Mother's. She had decided
not to write you so often anymore, since all the writing back
and forth about whether you should leave or stay has been so
completely annoying to her. Also, Wilibald Imhof told her that
she should not let you tour as far as Rome because you cannot do
so for under 200 crowns. That so frightened her that she wrote
you immediately to forgo any such trip. However, that was before
she received your letter [of August 29] . . . in which she learned
that you can [tour as far as Rome] at small cost. . . . When she
reported this to Wilibald Imhof, he marveled: "Amen, it cost
Jobst Tetzel 150 crowns to do so!" That may still be true, if one
sets out from Nürnberg with a servant and tours many cities,
including Rome, as Tetzel did. . . .

So you can well imagine that further consultations about [your
tour] have not been going on here due to its cost, but because
you have not provided us any more information about it at one
time than you did at another. That is why mother is now writing
to you after not having done so for so long,[121] namely, to tell you
how you should proceed [with your tour], when you have the
opportunity. She knows her letter is a gamble,[122] because she
concludes from your last that she will not find you any longer
in Padua. [What she wants you to do is] take the money you
would otherwise have spent this winter [quarter in Padua] and
sightsee. . . . So, you may now take off . . . as soon as you can,
and then start for home. We too, I and your sisters altogether,
beg you not to leave [Italy] before having seen something that
redounds to your reputation and ours too.[123]

Because so much has already been spent on you, neither of us
will concern ourselves with the twenty or thirty [extra] crowns it
will now cost you to sightsee. We expect all the money spent on
you will not have been wasted, and we trust you some day to pay
it all back to us. We do not want to be as unfraternal[124] as the

guardians and deny you an opportunity that is so much to your
benefit and profit.

I want you to know that I have read in several of your letters
to Mother about how very unhappy you are that she "abandons"
you. She does not think she has done so at all, but that
everything is happening for the best. She has so often been
made unhappy by your many letters because there seemed to be
so little progress [on your part], and at times she has just wanted
to tell you off. For this reason, it pleased her that you wrote to
Wilibald Imhof so that he can now write directly to you with
his opinion, which will certainly be that you should stay put [in
Padua at your studies] for the winter [on the stipend the
guardians have set], which in my limited view of the matter
would not be entirely to the good. [If I were you] I would seize
the opportunity to tour . . . while it can still be done before
winter settles in, and then come home. And when you arrive
home ahead of winter, you can then tell [the guardians] you have
done so to save money! There is reason to be concerned that the
guardians will give you no money [after the winter quarter] for
such a tour next spring, but make you come straight home
without seeing Rome or anything else.

I wanted to share my few thoughts with you on this matter. . . .
If this is not to your liking, you may do as you please, for you
yourself must know best how to arrange your affairs and make
your way home. We do not have much in this world to entrust
to anyone except God alone. . . . So just hope in Him, and do
whatever you do in his name and with a prayer, and He will give
you and us all every good fortune and blessing. . . .

I have not yet begun to make the shirts you wrote about, but it
will happen soon, and you will find them waiting for you when
you come. . . . 25 September, 1577.

MAGDALENA BEHAIM

The Same Goose

Apart from her grudging support of the tour, Frau Behaim's let-ter of September 24 also made it clear that the damage done by Paul's intemperate language was far from repaired. In that letter she scolded him as a foolish and ungrateful child—the harshest words she had yet written. He feared that in her anger she might leave him to the mercy of his guardians, whose desire to keep him at his books in Padua was all too clear. So again, he plied her with earnest reassur-ance, now theologically embellished, in another attempt to bridge their emotional impasse.

25. To Mother[125]

Dear Mother. . . . As for your saying that my frequent letters are wearing you out, I must admit that there have been a lot of them. . . . I[126] gather unhappily from your letter that you are totally convinced that I resent and hate you and your letters, and that the obedience, love, and loyalty a child owes a parent are completely extinguished in me, all because I . . . compared you to a stepmother.[127] For me, your [rebuke] was a very hurtful and rough surprise; I could not read it or let it pass my lips without true pain. Dear Mother, do you not think that I consider what I do and write as carefully as anyone else? Or do you perhaps take me to be more brutish and godless than a mindless animal, which has never been found to be ungrateful or unfriendly to its parents, or to those who raise it, even though it is strongly inclined [by nature] to do so? Do you think that I, who am now spending my sixth year in a foreign land, and on whom so much money has been spent, have not learned any better? If I have no reason to rebel against a mother, I should not do so. And even if there is reasonable cause, I should still admonish my siblings to show you every loyalty, love, and obedience, since without you we would all be nothing and dead. So please strike those awful thoughts about me from your mind, and have no doubt that it is neither you nor I, but the vexatious devil, who is behind them. He is the enemy of all unity and the father of all division, and he keeps trying to find a way to tempt and agitate people until he has them where he wants them, especially husbands and wives, parents and children, [and] siblings. He will make one little word the cause of dissension.

   I ask you always to see in me a son a mother can trust, and also one who will bring far more honor to his ancestors and family than shame and disgrace. Please continue to include me in your prayers to almighty God, as I do you, and to ask Him for the grace of his Word, to which He may soon summon me. [Padua, 10 October 1577]

                                        Y L S, PAUL BEHAIM

Were those last words a true intimation of mortality, or simply further play on a mother's sympathy? Given his recent brush with death, one might think the former. However, the manipulating teenager remained very much alive. Fretting aside, Paul managed to depart Padua and reach Rome in late November for a month's holiday in the region. Unfortunately, a recurrence of his bimonthly fever put him in bed for the first two weeks. When he wrote again (December 7), his health had returned, and he enjoyed a ten-day tour of the city. However, his plans to tour Naples now had to be cancelled. On December 29, he resumed his studies in Padua with "an ill and empty purse," as his guardians had forewarned he would do, the tour of Rome having cost far more than he had so self-assuredly predicted. And once more, he was explaining himself to a mother again recoiling from higher than promised bills.

   This time, however, he had a story worthy of her sympathy, if not complete credulity. To save money, he had traveled to Rome with Italians who knew both the route and the bargains along the way. Riding all day until an hour after dark, the party would arrive weary and freezing at a village inn, only to rise two or three hours before dawn and do it all over again. On the road, they often made do with berry shoots, beans cooked in rotten oil, and small, still-bloody

hunks of pork. By so roughing it, Paul hoped to counter any maternal reproach for extravagance, and claimed to have cut his expenses
to half of what they otherwise would have been had he stayed in
Padua—a potential net savings of eight or nine crowns if only his
fever had not returned and created new physician's fees in Rome.
This was not a new explanation of his financial spirals, which he appears to have acknowledged by ending on a note of lame Lutheran
humor: "The pope and his cardinals send you their greetings!"[128]

Along with his strong defense of the tour, he also uttered words
his mother had long waited to hear, as he assured her that the tour
of Rome was the climax of his wandering, that he was now prepared
to bring his studies to a proper conclusion, return home, and repay
his debt to the family.

> For as you correctly write, it is about time that I began to think
> about my own and my dependent siblings' needs and welfare,
> because everything I now know, can do, and have seen, I duly
> owe, first, to you and then to my brothers and sisters. The esteem
> I expect to gain from my studies, I could not have gotten on my
> own; you have made it all possible by your generous assistance
> and kindly exhortations. . . . In all that I now do, I am devoted to
> securing your happiness and welfare and the honor of us all. . . .
> [Padua, 16 January 1578].[129]
>
>   Y L S, PAUL BEHAIM

Hope springs eternal in a parent's heart, but Frau Behaim knew
by now that such eloquent words did not always stand the test of
time. When his next quarter's spending (January to March) far exceeded his thirty-crown allowance, it was a mother's turn to barrage
a son with questions. Did he really expect to live this way indefinitely? Had he not for six years been granted his every wish in pursuit of his education? Might he now have studied long enough to
find gainful employment?

If the son had become all too predictable to the mother, so also had the mother to the son. When he answered her ultimatum in early March 1578, his rebuttal was as artful as her criticism incisive.

26. To Mother[130]
[Dear Mother]. . . . I have read with sadness and horror the words that your death may be of more use [to the family than my education]. . . . It troubles me greatly that you should feel so burdened and oppressed on my account and yet through no fault of my own. For my own sake, I would never in my life have seen Italy, had I known that my doing so would diminish one moment of yours. . . . Measured against the time and money spent . . . I have devoted myself as much if not more than anyone else to my studies. . . . You, however, think that after two or three years of study, one can just become a doctor of imperial law and immediately get a job.[131]

I must also tell you that I have never in my life been filthier or more disheveled . . . and if your will remains inflexible and I cannot have a new suit of clothes made here, I will come home to you in rags. . . . And once home, forty gulden will not be enough to buy the books I need, since none of the books I am studying here are there. You might better appreciate this, if you sought the counsel of another [who knows]. . . . [Padua, 6 March 1578.]

Y L S, PAUL BEHAIM

Paul continued his legal studies in Padua for three more months, through March, before leaving for home in April 1578. His last two letters indicate that he departed grudgingly and, as he had also done three years earlier when he departed Leipzig, with unpaid bills. He hoped to travel home in the greatest possible comfort, not counting the cost. Frau Behaim's heart must have sunk, when she read what he most looked forward to doing upon his return: shopping for a new suit of clothes. On the other hand, it was a good sign that he planned to check on brother Christoph, then apprenticing in Augsburg, en route—an act of fraternal oversight appropriate to Paul's senior status in the family.

27. To Mother[132]

Dear Mother. . . . I understand that you and my guardians want
me to return home at the end of April and that you advise against
buying my own horse for the journey. As always, I am prepared
to obey your wishes and to undertake what you command. . . .
As for renting a horse, I have two options. For eleven or twelve
crowns, I can get a simple rental from the Augsburg carrier in
Venice for the journey from there to Augsburg. However, this
would be without feed either for the horse or myself, which I will
then be responsible for. On the other hand, I can pay the carrier
nineteen or twenty crowns for everything—horse and feed for
the both of us all the way to Augsburg. His tip for taking care of
the horse en route is up to me, so add another half crown or so.
I will inquire with others what it will cost me to bring along a
trunk.

I leave the choice between these two options to you. In my
opinion, they are virtually the same, except that innkeepers are
often deceitful and would likely take advantage of one [on his
own] in a way they perhaps would not do the carrier. The
carriers also take much better care of the horse, when they feed
it. For these reasons, as well as to avoid more work and effort
(two weeks on horseback is not fun), I think the second option
would be best. But, again, I leave the decision to you.

As for my clothes, I accede to your wishes [to have them made
in Nürnberg rather than in Venice]. However, if you want to
have clothes made there that are a bit more respectable, I think
camel hair is the only material to use. I say that knowing that the
smallest piece cannot be gotten [in Nürnberg] for less than half a
taler. . . . So I was thinking, if you also find it satisfactory, that I
would just buy an entire bolt en route in Venice, which will cost
at most around ten ducats. A bolt holds 26 to 28 eln at half a
gulden an eln by my calculation, which does not seem too much
to me. However, I leave this to you; just tell me your wishes. I
will not act until I have your definite answer.

As for the journey home itself . . . it cannot be done for less
than twenty-four or twenty-five crowns, as you can deduce from
the above calculations. I will lay over in Augsburg for at least two
days before making connections to Nürnberg. There, I will talk
with brother Christoph's master,[133] if he can be found. . . .

As for luggage, there won't be much—a few books, some
papers that I cannot imagine leaving behind, and a pair of
tattered shirts—altogether a trunk-load of twenty to twenty-five
pounds. . . . I will also be leaving my mantle behind. Meanwhile,
would you look around for a good material for a waistcoat, one
like that worn by a great many people here. Or if it pleases you, I
could have a finely tailored one made for myself there from a
piece of the leftover camel's hair. . . . 2 April, 1578.

                                          Y L S, PAUL BEHAIM

Exactly when Paul, now twenty, returned to Nürnberg is unclear. His last letter (April 16) left the departure date up in the air, as
he was then having another bout of fever and seasonally purging
"bad blood and every kind of filth." He hoped to be strong enough
to travel before May. He also had more bad financial news for
his mother: new surgeon, physician, and pharmacy bills. Also, the
trunk he had taken to Rome was too small for the journey home,
and he had shredded his riding boots there as well, so new ones
now had to be purchased. Finally, and not least, he felt obliged to
throw a farewell dinner for a couple of close associates—all of which
added another five crowns to his departure costs. And once home,
he wanted to rejoin his family and its social circle only slowly, after
first recuperating and extending for several weeks the independent,
solitary life he had left behind in Italy. "If God helps me make it
home safely," he wrote in his final letter,

what I wish above all else is to be left completely to myself and to
do as I please in the garden, to have several books with me and
to be completely free of the company of others. . . . I hope you
will readily grant me this, especially in the first two to four weeks

I am home and might not yet be outfitted with [my new] clothes, which seems to me a fair and reasonable request.[134]

Was the goose that had left her six years earlier returning home unchanged, as Frau Behaim had feared? Like the best-laid plans, the direst expectations also often go awry. By October 1578, Paul not only had completed the transition back into Nürnberg society, but was successfully clerking at the imperial court in Prague.[135] Although his mother would not live to see it (Magdalena Römer Behaim died on December 31, 1581), he would become Nürnberg's chief financial officer and its imperial mayor.[136] Until his death, at sixty-four, in December 1621, he was a major figure in the city's local, regional, and imperial politics. Married three times, he became the father of eighteen children—equal numbers of sons and daughters—nine of whom survived him. In numerous letters to and from his sons,[137] he relived his mother's parental experience—surely on occasion hearing in them echos of his own youthful protests and her maternal censures.

4

THE PRIVATE LIFE
OF A TEENAGER

Sebald Welser's Semester in Louvain

B Y MODERN COMPARISON, THE YEARS SPENT AT HOME BY CHIL-
dren and youth in the sixteenth and seventeenth centuries were
fewer, yet parental solicitude and oversight extended over a longer
period of time[1] For all social classes and careers, professional training also started earlier than it does today, yet for most young adults,
an independent, self-supporting life in a trade, as well as marriage
and a household of one's own, came later as well. However, by one's
late teens and early twenties, the new shoot had tapped most of its
resources and was fleshing itself out.

After family and household, peers and teachers, rulers and clergy
had taken their turns at bending the twig, in whose direction did it
grow? In an age often portrayed as predictable, that question was
answered with some surprising twists and turns in Sebald Welser's
(1557–1589) transition from youth to adulthood. In the spring and
summer of 1577, this devout Nürnberg Lutheran found himself, at
nineteen, on his own in Catholic Louvain, where he had moved to
finish his legal education. That same year also saw the turning point
in the political and religious conflict between the Spanish army of
occupation and the territories we know today as Belgium and the
Netherlands. These were unusual circumstances for a visitor to a
new culture, and they put Sebald's character to a test.

Sebald Welser in 1577. (By permission of Georg Frhr. von Welser.)

That test was one many of his contemporaries, and certainly the modern reader, might deem him to have failed. For although he privately scorned as superstition the popular Catholic practices he now saw everywhere, he publicly—and by every indication freely—embraced two that Martin Luther had condemned as among the vilest.

Born to money and power, but sadly not to good health and long life, Sebald was the eldest son of Nürnberg patrician Sebastian Welser (1527–1559) and an equally well-to-do mother, Maria Haller

(1534–1583), whose father Sebald (1500–1578) served as one of the city's chief financial officers. That same maternal grandfather was also young Sebald's namesake and guardian, after his father's death. On his father's side were Uncles Hans (d. 1601) and Jakob (d. 1591) Welser, who ran the Nürnberg branch of the famous Augsburg-based Welser banking and mercantile empire. Sebald was not much more than a year old when his father died prematurely at thirty-two—the same age Sebald would be at his own premature death in 1589. In the later words of his own eulogist, he had been left without "a guide for his life, protector, and pride of his youth,"[2] as fathers then were kindly described.

The widowed mother married again in 1561, once again choosing well. The new stepfather was Julius Geuder (d. 1594), a member of the city council's executive Seven and a high-ranking member of the nearby Altdorf Academy's board of governors. Fortunately for the then toddling Sebald, the marriage was his stepfather's first, and he embraced his stepson from the start as his very own.[3]

Between ages eight and fifteen, Sebald attended Latin school at St. Giles's (1565–1572) and spent the following two years at the internationally famous Humanistic gymnasium of Johann Sturm (1507–1589) in Strasbourg, then the model for the new Protestant world, both Lutheran and Calvinist.[4] By his midteens, Sebald had chosen a career in law, the most fitting for the position he expected later to hold in the family business and for his likely service in local or territorial government. In Sebald's social circle, the profession of law was hallowed. The description of it presented two decades later at his funeral oration was one he would have shared as he took his first steps toward it:

> The lawyers dispense justice and have knowledge of what is right and fair, for which reason, they are the ones closest to God and to divinity [and] deserve no less praise than those who proclaim God's word.[5]

It was in further pursuit of his legal education, already earlier begun in Strasbourg, that Sebald, at seventeen and accompanied by a tutor, traveled to Padua via Venice in September 1574. His studies there were cut short, however, by failing health that forced him to return to his parents' home in the spring of 1576 to convalesce for a year.[6] By late spring 1577, he was ready to resume his legal education, this time in the Belgian city of Louvain. On June 1, Sebald, at nineteen, set out for the university there, escorted by his prominent stepfather, his two famous uncles, and two wealthy Nürnberg peers: Wolfgang Harstörffer (1560–1624) and Carl Imhof (1555–1619), childhood friends with whom Sebald had traveled before and who would now be his classmates for a semester in Louvain.[7]

Arriving on June 17, Sebald devoted the next six months to his law books and the exploration of the region, whose history was just then becoming epochal.[8] Long beseiged by a Spanish army of occupation, the seven largely Calvinist northern provinces (roughly the modern Netherlands) and the ten largely Catholic southern provinces (roughly modern Belgium) had joined together in an unprecedented declaration of regional religious sovereignty set forth in an agreement known as the Pacification of Ghent (early November 1576). That document made possible formidable, unified resistance, against the Spanish, which expressed itself at the beginning of the new year in the Union of Brussels, (January 1577).

In the 1560s, the Spanish first began to impose a government loyal to Spain and the Roman Catholic Church on the seventeen provinces. In 1559, an executive council of regency had been set in place under Antoine Perrenot (after 1561, Cardinal Granvella) to implement those efforts. At this time, the northern provinces were both the richest and the most independent within the Spanish Hapsburg kingdom, and it was not long before two members of the council of regency—William of Nassau, Prince of Orange (1533–1584), and the Count of Egmont (1522–1560)—broke away to form an opposition.

In 1561, the Catholic Orange, as he was popularly called, took a prominent German wife, Anne of Saxony, the daughter of Lutheran Elector Maurice and granddaughter of Landgrave Philip of Hesse, who, with earlier Saxon electors had captained the original Protestant cause. In 1567, Orange declared himself a Lutheran, only to change his confession again six years later (1573) by becoming a

Calvinist, apparently betting that Calvinism would be the dominant force throughout the Netherlands.[9]

Aggressive Spanish efforts to impose Catholicism throughout the northern provinces particularly spurred Calvinist opposition within the ranks of the lesser nobility and townspeople. The Netherlands' higher nobility, who feared rebellious Calvinists as much as they disliked the tyrannous Spanish, initially remained aloof from the confrontation. However, by the late 1560s, the threat of popular rebellion against Spanish rule in the northern provinces was real enough to move King Philip II to send an army of ten thousand soldiers under the command of the duke of Alba. The result was a reign of terror, during which several thousand Protestants were killed, Egmont executed, and Orange sent fleeing to Germany.

The 1570s saw formidable resistance coalesce around Orange, whose forces steadily gained ground with the discreet help of the English. It was, however, only after unpaid Spanish mercenaries massacred seven thousand inhabitants of Antwerp—a day remembered as the "Spanish Fury" (November 4, 1576)—that the northern and southern provinces had the holocaust both needed to bridge their religious differences and unite decisively against the Spanish. Shortly after the grand unions of late November 1576 and January 1577, the retreat of the Spanish army began. It would, however, be a long, slow march, with fighting and negotiating continuing off and on into the late 1590s, while final recognition of the Netherlands' independence did not come until 1609.

A Kiss in Brussels

Sebald's long semester in Louvain is documented in a deadpan journal he kept for the year. Typical of the age, it was actually an almanac of thirty-two pages created by Nürnberg astronomer Johann Pretorius (1537–1616), to which 184 pages of writing paper were happily appended.[10] On many of those pages, Sebald briefly wrote down his observations and thoughts of the day in brief, chopped Latin and German sentences, which sometimes intermingled. With the mysterious exception of the month of December, his activities for the entire year were covered there: the first five months on the local scene in Nürnberg; the next six months (June through November) traveling, studying, and sight-seeing in the Netherlands.

While in Louvain, this young visitor from the first city of German Protestantism had frequent opportunity to observe the region's rich religious culture. To say that he was no bashful tourist in the Roman Catholic world in which he now found himself[11] would be an understatement. He immersed himself in it to a degree that, given his devout Lutheran beliefs, must startle the reader of his journal. In mid-July, four weeks after arriving, he and his companions traveled to Brussels to witness the famous procession of the Eucharist there.[12] This spectacle dated from the fourteenth century (1369) and had originally commemorated the punishment of a Jew alleged to have stolen and desecrated a host. Revived in 1529 after a plague miraculously broke, the procession had since become an annual event.[13]

The celebration in 1577 was both a political and a religious statement. At this time, Brussels was a much contested city politically and religiously, with union and Spanish forces alternately occupying it, while its religious life seesawed back and forth between Catholic and Calvinist radicals. This year's procession indicated that the Spanish held the upper hand. When Union forces controlled the city, as they soon would do in September with William of Orange's triumphant return, the Calvinists also made the most of the opportunity to display their confessional colors.[14]

At the center of the procession was a golden monstrance containing three hosts (the consecrated or transubstantiated bread of the Eucharist).[15] If Sebald followed the parade with mixed emotions at first, his feelings appear to have clarified along the way, for he did something that could not have been foreseen at the start: "I kissed the artifice,"[16] he writes. The derogatory German term he used to describe the monstrance (*gauckelwerk*) connotes drivel, twaddle, foolishness, or trickery. That he should use such a term in retrospect suggests at least ambivalence. But does that explain so great a loss of self-discipline and seeming hypocrisy in the osculatory moment? A week later, he again startles the modern reader of his journal by announcing his purchase of an indulgence at St. Michael's Church in Louvain.[17]

Had he been so emotionally unprepared for the spectacular forms of traditional piety he now encountered that he had fallen momentarily under their spell? Might he have been, like Christoph Scheurl in the 1520s and 1530s, a closet Catholic, perhaps compromised by his earlier visit to Italy? Or were these actions less the compulsive behavior of an innocent or a possible convert, and more the mockery of one who knew all too well what he was doing?

Growing Up Lutheran

Sebald's personal religious devotion is the subject of repeated commentary in the journal. At the beginning of the year, long before his departure for Louvain, he had established for himself "an order of prayer and [Bible] reading,"[18] designed to take him systematically through most of the Old Testament by year's end. He read in a steady but circuitous fashion through the books of Daniel and Ecclesiasticus and into those of Proverbs and Ecclesiastes, digressing briefly and without explanation into various New Testament letters seemingly arbitrarily chosen.[19] On eighteen occasions he records his progress, most of which occurred during the six months in the Netherlands, occasionally accompanied by outbursts of relief ("happily finished!" "completed that, thank God!"), as he reached the end of more difficult or less interesting biblical books.

He also arrived in Louvain fully armored with Lutheran prayer books. At the beginning of the year, while still at home, he had purchased a copy of the Latin edition of the prayer book of Andreas Musculus: *Prayers From the Old Orthodox Doctors, the Hymns and Songs of the Church, and the Psalms of David* (1575; 2nd. ed., 1577), to which two other devotional books were later added.[20] The diary is filled with quotations and references to these prayers, as well as peppered with invocations of divine aid, which Sebald makes as readily to accomplish a routine task as to see himself through some great chore. So frequent are such appeals that he resorts to abbreviations.[21]

The bona fides of Sebald's Lutheran devotion is further documented by his youthful philanthropy. Thanks to his paternal and grandpaternal inheritances (he received a whopping 26,329 gulden from Grandfather Sebastian Welser alone), he was a very rich man by his early twenties. In 1581, he endowed both a library and a scholarship at his alma mater, the Latin school of St. Giles's Church, and his generosity also built an auditorium for the study of law and public policy at the Altdorf Academy, still known today as the "Welserianum." At the time of his donations, he described his gifts as both an obligation of Christian charity and the best way to keep the light of the Reformation burning bright in Nürnberg,

> . . . because before all other people, the true, gracious God has caused the light of the Holy Gospel to shine pure and clear upon us Germans, to the preservation of which, nothing is more fitting than the building and maintenance of Christian schools.[22]

Like many Nürnberg patricians, Sebald also had numerous close Catholic associations. Throughout his boyhood, he was a regular visitor to the city's longest surviving Catholic cloister, St. Katharina's, because, from 1550 until his death in 1578, his maternal grandfather Sebald Haller supervised the cloister on the city council's behalf.[23] With the triumph of the Reformation, new Protestant governments banned the religious life and dissolved many but not all local cloisters, turning their vacant physical plants over to secular use, or, more often, transforming them into public hospices or educational institutions with a still strong, but now distinctly Protestant, religious aura. In large cities like Nürnberg, with its rich Catholic heritage and prominent families with centuries-old attachments to the old faith, one or more cloisters remained open permanently for those religious who could not or would not be pensioned off with their peers.[24]

St. Katharina's was such a cloister, with powerful Catholic patrons, among them the emperors Charles V and Maximilian II. Like their counterparts across the English Channel (contemporary queens Mary Tudor and Mary, Queen of Scots), the Holy Roman Emperors and other Catholic princes looked on a city's surviving nunneries and monasteries as footholds for the restoration of Catholicism in Protestant lands, to which end they pressured magistrates to safeguard them from iconoclastic Protestants, permit traditional religious services to be regularly held, and allow new recruits to enter. As a rule, Protestant cities guaranteed their safety, and might wink at traditional services for inmates while firmly resisting new recruits. As happened with St. Katharina's in 1598, such cloisters closed with the death of the last surviving nun.[25]

During the visits to St. Katharina's with his grandfather, young Sebald, much like young Christoph Scheurl in the 1480s and 1490s[26] became close friends with the sisters there and enjoyed their company. On such occasions, he would take his meals with them, once banqueting into Walpurgis Night (the eve of May Day).[27] Before going to Louvain, he donated the legal expertise he had acquired in Padua to the cloister by twice balancing their books, a service he also performed for the city's Pilgrim Hospice of the Holy Cross, another "Protestantized" old Catholic institution his grandfather administered in the interim.[28] While away in Louvain, he twice wrote to "the worthy women of St. Katharina's" and on one of those occasions he sent the prioress a pencil sketch of a great fish, "fifty-two shoes long, forty-three around," caught off Antwerp in July.[29]

Cultural Shock

Sebald's most explicit comments on his own spiritual life occurred when he confronted traditional religious practices that were not his own. Prior to his departure for the Netherlands, he had witnessed the annual Annunciation festival in the neighboring village of Dormitz, a spectacle he derides in his journal as "a few foolish people bringing offerings to St. Mary."[30] He reacted in a similar fashion when he watched the open-air performances of the Jesuits in Mainz while en route to Louvain: "On the streets of the city, the Jesuits performed their deceit with the manna and showbread of Aaron in monstrances."[31]

Notwithstanding such partisan dismissals, which never disappear from the journal, the farther Sebald penetrated into Catholic Germany and the Netherlands en route north, the more ambivalent his attitude toward the old religious culture appears to have become. Was amazement displacing criticism as he beheld the visible feast of medieval Catholic art and architecture and witnessed the great festivals of the old Church? He could not have been totally unprepared for the sights he saw, since even reformed Nürnberg had splendid churches and religious processions, and he had visited Venice and Padua for sixteen months. But unlike the rituals and institutions he had grown up with in Nürnberg, those he now beheld were not treated by the population as mere memorials or monuments to the past. They were believed to embody the sacred in the present life and to do so spectacularly—a palpable divine presence against which a teenager, even one from the first city of the Lutheran world, had few sophisticated defenses.

In Cologne, another stop along the way to Louvain, Sebald beheld the elaborately ornamented shrine of the three kings of the Orient who had visited Jesus at his birth, glimpsing their relics, with difficulty, through a narrow grate—an arrangement whose very awkwardness in viewing, perhaps by design, must have enhanced the mystery of the subjects.[32] During a tour of Cologne's Rathaus, Sebald credulously imbibed an ancient story, preserved in the white stone walls along the building's staircase, of angry priests who once tried to kill the city's bürgermeister by locking him in a room with a starved lion—an attempt that backfired when the suspicious bürgermeister killed the lion with a knife he had concealed on his person, thereafter escaping to accuse the priests and see them hung. Sebald describes the tower across from a church where the murderous priests were executed.[33] In Cologne's Dominican cloister, he viewed the glassed-in remains of Albertus Magnus, St. Thomas Aquinas's famed teacher, whose head nestled on a silk and gold-gilded pillow, a haunting presence of the brain trust of medieval Catholicism.[34]

Stopping next in Aachen, Sebald beheld for the first time some of Germany's most famous relics, among them the sword of Charlemagne, a piece of Christ's cross, the blood of St. Stephen, and the remains of numerous martyrs. The longest and most detailed diary entry during the visit describes admiringly the beauty and craftsmanship of the Celestinian cloister at Heuren.[35]

It was not only a young man's eyes that were being captivated. Sebald also found himself debating numerous religious subjects, some for the first time. He argued with Carl Imhof over whether the Dominicans, who normally wore black and white attire, wore only white in choir—a matter weighty enough for the two of them to wager a bottle of wine on the outcome.[36] Carl held Catholic beliefs and would later be arrested in Nürnberg with other citizens for surreptitiously attending Mass at a city cloister.[37] On another occasion, Sebald spent an evening discussing the imperial relics stored in Nürnberg, particularly one known as the "lance of the Lord," a spear dating back to Charlemagne that allegedly contained a nail from the cross of Christ.[38]

Some of the subjects that preoccupied the boys appear bizarre, even contrived. One night, when the topic of debate was God's love of humankind, Sebald posed the question of whether the human race could continue if either all the men or all the women in the world were killed. The agreed upon conclusion was that the extermination of men would have no effect, since there would still always be some pregnant women able to continue the species.[39] Apparently, he and his associates did believe that the sudden disappearance of womankind would spell certain disaster for the human race.

The success of the Reformation and the ongoing Protestant-Catholic conflict in the Netherlands also posed hot topics for debate. One was whether children who died unbaptized went straight to hell,[40] an ancient issue recently revived by the Protestant stress on original sin and salvation by faith alone. Belief that they did had earlier moved the Church to console concerned parents by permitting midwives to baptize premature and nonviable infants immediately upon birth, which in difficult deliveries might occur as soon as the head or a limb of an unfortunate child could be grasped in the birth canal.[41] The Reformation's closing of cloisters made that policy a topic for debate among the boys as well.[42]

For the international body of students in Louvain, these were not just academic questions, but personal and "national" ones as well. Their discussion kept students at table late into the night and could even occasion a brawl. Once when debating why Sunday rather than the Sabbath (Saturday) was a Christian holy day, Sebald found himself confronted by an angry student from Westphalia who interpreted the Bible literally. "I had my Bible on the table," Sebald writes, "and [he] was completely enraged."[43] Another argument that invited mayhem was the question of whether anyone had ever seen God the Father. Contrary to everyone else, the same Westphalian youth insisted that Moses had done so, because it was written in the Bible that Moses spoke to God face to face.[44] Despite his fundamentalism and short temper, the Westphalian youth apparently had a kinder and gentler side, because Sebald also reports having "learned knitting" from him.[45]

Sebald understood both the destructive and the edifying sides of religion. Six month earlier, while still in Nürnberg, he had visited an aging and badly injured assistant of his grandfather, a man deeply depressed by religious worry[46] and who four days before Sebald's visit had tried to jump to his death. But while obsession with religion was not a new experience for him, Sebald appears not to have encountered it previously in quite the alternating grandeur, pettiness, and danger with which it now surrounded him in Louvain and Brussels.

Agility

Sebald's fascination with the Catholic culture of the Netherlands did not, however, prevent him from expressing his misgivings about

it while there. Privately, he continued his Lutheran devotions, particularly on the anniversaries of important days in his life. He commemorated his first visit to his beloved physician, Dr. Melchior Ayrer,
by reading a Christocentric prayer from the collection of Musculus.[47] When he turned twenty (September 11), he spent the entire
day immersed in that same prayer book, recording in his diary the
first lines of each prayer he said, and he repeated those same prayers
twice in the following week.[48] He also prayed for the Protestants
he met, who lived among Catholics. Breakfasting one morning with
the duchess of Aershot's ladies-in-waiting, and learning that two
of her daughters were Protestant, he expressed his wish that God
might give them the strength to remain such.[49] (At the time, the girls'
father—the governor of Flanders—was a rival of William of Orange
and had opposed his appointment as provincial governor of Brabant.)[50] Whereas in Nürnberg, where Sebald had taken the Sacrament with his friends and attended Easter service in his finest, at the
end of his first week in Louvain, he and his companions skipped local church services and feasted the morning away at the inn where
they lodged.[51]

Again, it may seem a puzzle that so apparently devout a Lutheran
could ever have surrendered himself in seemingly so casual a fashion to a religious culture he manifestly did not share and privately
scorned. One possible explanation is suggested by his reaction to
the discovery that a strongly worded oath of allegiance to the Roman
Catholic Church was required of all matriculating students at the
university. The oath was an enhanced version of a previously perfunctory one, now so sharply worded that non-Catholics wishing to
enroll at Louvain had to do so at new levels of hypocrisy. In the hot
new religious climate, with Dutch Calvinists triumphantly on the
march, Louvain university authorities, deeply Catholic and loyal to
the king of Spain as well, had deemed the milder version lax. The
new oath required each student to "deny [Martin] Luther and all
other heretics," and to swear allegiance to the Catholic church "under the absolute authority of the pope in Rome."[52]

That requirement, at least in its new version, had taken Sebald by
surprise, and he complained about it to his stepfather and grandfather. In response, they contacted the Welsers' Antwerp agent

(Daniel Rindfleisch) entrusted with Sebald's financial and other official affairs while he was in the Netherlands. Assured by him that the oath could not be avoided, the senior Welsers nonetheless retained legal counsel in Louvain in a further futile attempt to find a way for Sebald to skirt it—a clear indication of the seriousness with which the family looked on an oath of allegiance to the pope. Unlike other German students, who refused the new oath and returned home, Sebald by all accounts complied. Two years later, he would take a similar, well-documented oath as a student at the papal university of Bologna.[53]

It was not unusual for merchants and students abroad to defer to foreign practices in the interest of their businesses and programs of study, and host governments expected foreign visitors to respect local culture and religion for the safety of all. However, merchants and students protested when pressure to conform seemed more like harassment than a matter of propriety.[54] Short of such coercion, public compliance with local practice was not deemed unreasonable by foreign students and their parents.[55] And those, like Sebald, who found themselves caught in such situations could console themselves with the knowledge that in the fortress of their hearts and minds they remained immune from the sacrileges expected of them in public.

Although Sebald was not the only Nürnberger to take the oath in 1577, such pragmatism may have been more incumbent upon a young Welser than upon other youths. Sebald's family operated a trans-European financial empire, in whose debt even the reigning king of Spain then stood.[56] So loyalty to family—a community to which he was more beholden for his life and welfare than to any church—may have dictated his compliance.

When, however, Sebald kissed the monstrance in Brussels and bought an indulgence in Louvain, he was not simply acting expediently. There was no expectation or coercion either from peers or local Catholic authorities requiring him to go as far as he did. Nor were these the acts of an enthusiastic tourist in search of a good story or souvenir to impress friends with after his return home. On both occasions, Sebald appears genuinely to have been carried away by the emotion of the moment—and such experiences were not only occurring in the spiritual realm. His bold religious behavior in

Louvain and Brussels is also reflected in his simultaneous pursuit of new intellectual and political interests. He could read with interest the writings of a Catholic moralist, yet when he visited Antwerp, he joined with citizens there to demolish a citadel the Spanish had used to besiege the city, boasting of having thrown "three shovels full" of rubble down the hill while keeping a stone from the pile as a relic of his participation. The episode so absorbed his interest that he sent a charcoal sketch of it to a friend, replete with the toppling of a statue of the duke of Alba, Spanish scourge of the Netherlands, that had long stood at the top.[57]

Such behavior arguably exposed feelings that are larger than religion and seek outlets in other actions as well. It is telling that Sebald was just as fascinated with the region's contemporary politics as he was by its traditional religious culture. He stood as much in awe of the men who led the resistance to the Spanish occupation as he did of the saints and martyrs he had seen—here, too, readily playing the idolater. In Brussels, he twice visited the homes of the counts of Egmont (d. 1568) and Mansfeld (d. 1604), local heroes of the resistance. On his second visit, he observed that ball was being played in front of Egmont's house, apparently thinking it disrespectful of the man who, nine years earlier, had been publicly executed at the height of Alva's reign of terror over the southern provinces.[58]

During their second visit to Brussels, Sebald and his companions caught sight of the prince of Orange himself, as the great leader of the resistance rode past the inn where they lodged. The next morning they followed him as he entered the city council, and when he left an hour later, at noon, Sebald continued after him, watching quietly from a distance as he entered a tavern and ate lunch. Smitten, he writes of his brief contact with "this completely good prince, one worthy of every praise." A week after the sighting, he composed an essay praising Orange's promotion to commander in chief of all the Netherlands' forces.[59]

Contemporary political symbols and debates captivated Sebald almost as much as the living heroes. He sent Grandfather Welser running accounts of the major events, along with such political relics as copies of the capitulation articles presented to the resistance leaders by the famous Austrian Don John—victor over the Turks at

Lepanto six years earlier (1571), but now the unhappy commander of the humiliated and retreating Spanish army of occupation.[60] Although he mentions them less often, Sebald also joined civic debates as quickly as he did those over religion, citing one on the question: "whether a citizen who had been coerced against his will by the state could continue to be a citizen of that state."[61]

The Temptations of the Flesh

Sebald lived in an age of conflicted emotions not only in regard to religion and politics, but also in the more elemental sphere of sexuality, which may also offer a clue to his behavior in Louvain and Brussels. No group in the sixteenth century had greater reason to be circumspect about sexual relations than urban youth in their late teens and early twenties, and not just because of their peaking sexual feelings. From experience, city governments were pessimistic about the moral strength of their young citizens and kept them under close surveillance.[62] Churches, schools, and parents assisted those efforts by attempting to instill an ethic of self-denial and restraint in new generations.

The guardians of youth especially attacked the temptations of sex, alcohol, and the theater, and while the clergy could go to great lengths to persuade twelve- to fourteen-year-olds of their dormant bestiality and the need for constant vigilance, adult badgering did not necessarily demoralize the young.[63] Beset by the adult world's well-intentioned scrutiny of their lives, Sebald's generation grew up in heightened awareness of the tension between their public and private selves, their well-drilled consciences commanding self-denial while their innermost desires begged them to let go.

Sebald appears to have been no stranger to moral temptation. While still in Nürnberg, he declined two invitations to "spinning bees"—also known as "spinning parties," "spinning rooms," and "maidens' courts" (Spinnstuben, Jungfrauenhöfe). These were informal gatherings in both private homes and public places by unmarried

youth of similar age and social standing—the sixteenth-century equivalent of "hanging out" and "partying." They provided single men and women the opportunity to meet privately and pass the time together in the apparently wholesome atmosphere of a sewing circle. Concerned parents and officials knew that such gatherings— "emotionality anchored outside the family"—were also occasions for the unfolding of sexuality and sensuality,[64] and accordingly feared them as potential "sowing" circles. In 1572, the Nürnberg city council prohibited them on just such moral grounds.

Sebald's first-mentioned invitation to such a gathering came from a male friend evidently tapped to round up the appropriate male cohort. Sebald reports the invitation being declined on his behalf, as it was known that the host "had a meeting with girls" in mind.[65] The next day he received a second invitation to another such party, which he personally declined.[66] That the first was declined for him by an unidentified third party suggests that an alert adult authority may have thwarted his own wish to go. The question is a fair one, because six weeks later he did attend a spinning bee with Carl Imhof and the two remained until midnight.[67] On two other occasions, Sebald attended dances with seemingly similar ambivalence. At one, a wedding party, he says he did not dance at all, while at the other, he claims to have danced until midnight.[68]

Despite the impression left by a Hieronymus Bosch or a François Rabelais, it was not characteristic of Sebald's contemporaries to talk openly in public about private sexual matters, even though they did so with intimates in their correspondence and presumably also in their own youthful assemblies.[69] The dangers of discovery always remained great, for one never knew when a private letter might fall into the wrong hands and a messenger accidentally or intentionally open it, or a careless recipient leave it lying around for another to discover and read. Even when spouses and lovers discussed sexual desire, pregnancy, infidelity, and venereal disease in presumably secure private communications, prudence demanded that they do so obliquely, deferring to public norms of propriety and good taste.[70]

While his own journal entries on the subject are few and harmless, Sebald does talk about sexual matters in a fashion and even jokes lamely about them. He reports, for example, the burning of

holes in the facial cheeks of "five sluts," who had illegally solicited customers on the steets of Neuenwald after the city's closing of the public house.[71] In a possibly lighter vein, he mentions an agreement between himself and another Nürnberg friend in Louvain (Sigmund Oertel), in which they promised to give one another an appropriate gift on their respective wedding days, Sebald pledging the customary seven pounds of silver coins (computed at thirty pfennig a pound), his friend promising him a woman's undergarment and a bridal crown.[72]

The journal does a better job of documenting Sebald's losing battle with alcohol, a major health and social problem at the time for young and old alike.[73] Sebald and his companions knew that too much liquor, like too much religion, could kill. He recalled the ignominious death of a debauched man found one day at noon behind a table in a Nürnberg tavern, having dropped dead unnoticed on the spot. "Here pertain the words of St. Paul, the words of Wisdom, and divine punishment," he observed.[74] If there was an eternal lesson in this story, Sebald was not yet ready to learn it. He reports numerous occasions on which he and his companions drank to excess. He remembered the night in August when his French teacher got completely drunk and demanded a vacation.[75] On another late night, in September, after much wine had been consumed, he bet his companions they could not walk upright into the great tower that dominated Louvain's fortified walls—an underestimation that cost him two additional rounds.[76] A week later, the fencing master, whom one might have expected to be a steadying influence, joined a few of them at dinner and the boys again drank "uncommonly well."[77] There was also the evening they "drank heartily" with master shoemaker Hans, in the course of which they relieved him of his knife, apparently for the safety of all.[78] Sebald confesses to having gotten "completely" or "extraordinarily" drunk on three occasions, on one of which (a visit to Heuren) becoming so intoxicated that he could not remember the next day what he had done the previous night.[79]

The final great temptation of his youth was one to which Sebald succumbed without hesitation or guilt. Here, again, he was at odds with the clergy and the magistrates, for whom contemporary theatrical productions were a morally gray area at best. In January 1577,

Nürnberg's city council ordered the play masters at St. Martha's Pilgrim Hospice Church, whose performances Sebald frequently attended, henceforth to seek official approval before performing any future plays—a rebuke aimed at their having staged allegedly "shameless and undisciplined epilogues."[80] Sebald deemed the theater a pure pleasure, and in February and March attended a play by Terence (*Adelphoi*), a biblical drama (*Ahab and Jezebel*), and an unnamed comedy, along with three pieces by Nürnberg's famous poet and playwright, Hans Sachs. Sebald himself appears to have contributed to the staging of one of the latter.[81]

Dark Linings

The journal is filled with reports of happy days with peers, for whom Sebald had real feelings. They looked forward to their times together, whether at work or at play, traveling or carousing.[82] Something of their affectionate relationships is revealed in such things as the butter cookie treats, in the shape of a lamb and stags, that Sebald gave Carl Imhof after the two had spent a day traveling around Nürnberg together before returning to Carl's garden for an evening meal.[83]

Emotions ran both ways. In Louvain, Sebald had a falling out with his other traveling companion, Wolf Harstörffer. He alludes to the incident with the comment that he did not want Harstörffer to share a candle with him any longer—that is, to be in the same room with him. Eventually the two reconciled, because six weeks later (October 31), Sebald remembered Wolf's birthday with a gift.[84]

Taken together with Sebald's privilege and success, such friendships make it easy to overlook a dark undercurrent in his temperament. Unobtrusive most of the time, it appears oppressively in the journal when he faces his fears, which seem always to have been lurking beneath the surface and threatening in even the best of times.[85] It is here that the immediate circumstances of Sebald's seemingly contradictory religious behavior in Louvain and Brussels may best be illuminated.

On a February day, when his parents were away and he was home alone, Sebald recorded two deaths. The first was that of a woman who, six weeks earlier, had fallen on ice and broken her leg while en route home after attending a birth on New Year's Eve—an accident as ironic as it was fortuitous. The second death Sebald reports was his own, which he had foreseen in a dream the night before.

> Last night I dreamed what happened to me on this day [February] 12, how I was clubbed to death. I sincerely commended myself to my Lord God, and my grandfather was very sad. I thought it would happen as I was going to bed, that I would then be bludgeoned to death.[86]

Given the times, this was no bizarre dream. Murder by bludgeoning was commonplace, and as a frequent traveler often at the mercy of strangers, Sebald had reason to fear being waylaid. Later he would record the burial of a local gun engraver savagely clubbed to death by unknown assailants on the streets of Nürnberg.[87]

His own death was not the only one foreseen in a nightmare. Five weeks later (March 21), he envisioned that of his grandfather, whose health was then failing. Early in the month, inflammation (flus) and swelling had the old man on the brink of suffocating and brought Pastor Lorenz Dürnhofer to his house, apparently in the expectation of his death. Sebald's dream occurred about a week before the old man's tongue swelled to the point that he could not speak, a development that brought the chaplain from St. Giles's to his bedside to arrange for him and Sebald's grandmother to receive the Eucharist together on the next morning in preparation for the old man's passing. "Thus, unfortunately has my dream of March 21 come true," wrote a gloomy Sebald on March 30, as he expected his grandfather's death to occur on that very day.[88]

Fortunately for them both, Sebald's dreams were poor prognosticators of actual events. Under the care of two physicians, who

administered a most effective enema, Grandfather Haller recovered
his strength within a week, and would remain among the living for
another year and a half.[89]

Recurrently throughout the year, Sebald, too, was seriously ill,
and a growing fear that he would never get well affected his outlook
on life. On August 4 in Louvain, he commemorated the anniversary
of the day he had first consulted a physician about his new illness.[90]
Already in the spring of 1576, the appearance of that illness had
forced him to return home from Padua prematurely. Before his
departure, Paul Behaim, then also in Padua, had written to his sister
in Nürnberg that Sebald was "nothing but skin and bones, long
shanks."[91] So the illness had been besieging Sebald off and on for
well over a year.

From what was he suffering? Despite frequent comments on his
condition, he provides few clues to its exact nature. His first
recorded visit to a physician in 1577 was on April 1, at which time
he produced a urine specimen for Dr. Ayrer. Italian-trained and having practiced medicine in Nürnberg since 1549, Ayrer was as experienced a healer as one might then find, a circumstance that did
not, however, guarantee a successful result. Two days after his initial
visit, Sebald returned to deliver a second specimen and to receive
medication, which he thereafter took morning and night. On the
following day (April 4), he stayed home and purged, producing five
stools by day's end, each of which Dr. Ayrer examined on the prem-
ises while the exhausted Sebald slept. The only mentioned action
taken after this careful analysis was a prescription for nose drops.[92]

Sebald visited Dr. Ayrer again later in the month, after having returned a "musk capsule" to him. This was a container for medicinal
salves or herbs which was presumably filled with a special medication and returned to Sebald.[93] Sebald remained in Ayrer's care
throughout May, purging again for four days in the middle of the
month, and paying Dr. Ayrer four gulden for his services at month's
end.[94] When Sebald departed for Louvain in June, Dr. Ayrer's reme-
dies also went with him. On the day of his arrival, he shared a
purgative with a friend (Wilibald Imhof) who reportedly had had a
"bad day."[95]

Two weeks later, a swelling of his back forced Sebald to resume his medication and left him praying for his health.[96] On that same day, he also took note of a custom still practiced at the Unversity of Louvain when doctoral students pass their degree exams: successful students went directly to the Church of St. Peter and placed a coin on the altar beneath a portrait of the Virgin,[97] the university's patron, who was believed to give them their success. Having been ill off and on for over a year, and once again taking purgatives with no resolution in sight, such intercession must have seemed for Sebald at least a vicarious consolation.

In addition to his poor physical health, he also feared a brutal death. On the day before he purchased the indulgence (July 20), he brooded over the hordes of unpaid, pillaging, plague-infested Walloons who made travel hazardous for civilians everywhere while at the same time leaving a trail of plague wherever they marauded.[98] Little wonder that by late August, he was again "praying constantly."[99]

That his fears had not been exaggerated is documented by a subsequent disaster he narrowly escaped. By November, plague was in Mecheln, twenty kilometers away, and despite Louvain's strict ban on refugees from plague areas, it engulfed the city in the new year, killing a reported 36,000.[100] Having received reports of plague in Mecheln on October 25, Sebald's stepfather had written immediately to instruct him to contact Daniel Rindfleisch in Antorff and arrange for his flight there at the first sign of plague on the outskirts of Louvain. "Mother reminds you," he added, "to take all the available precautionary medicine[101] daily, also to fumigate your room morning and night with candles and other incense, as you already know to do." A similar instruction arrived from Sebald's Uncle Hans, who wrote in the name of Grandfather Haller and Sebald's stepfather as well—apparently a duplicate warning in case one letter failed to get through.[102]

Indulgence

Two days after Sebald bought an indulgence in Louvain (July 23, 1577), another Nürnberg Lutheran, in a completely unrelated incident, also contemplated such a purchase. That person was Magdalena Behaim, the twenty-two-year-old sister of Paul Behaim, who had befriended the ailing Sebald in Padua the previous year. Under normal circumstances, the Behaims would not have discussed indulgences, much less contemplated buying one. However, as in Sebald's case, an unusual personal situation had made such an act thinkable within another devout Lutheran family. That circumstance was Magdalena's alienation from a Nürnberg Catholic cousin, then in Padua, about whom she had written some derogatory remarks in a letter to her brother Paul there, which the cousin had come upon and read.[103] In retaliation, the cousin's brother in Nürnberg had several times insulted Magdalena. Moved by her daughter's growing distress over the incident, her mother suggested that she send an apology to her cousin, and as he was then in the vicinity of Rome, that she also ask him to send her a letter of indulgence from the papal see—the latter request apparently intended to be an indication of the bona fides of her apology. Although she briefly pondered the suggestion, Magdalena did not in the end act on it, expressing a proper Lutheran disgust at the thought.

On hearing stories about devout Lutherans kissing monstrances and buying indulgences, a modern reader might conclude that the sixteenth-century family was a spiritually groping institution and the Protestant Reformation something of a failure. A better lesson to draw may be the inconsistency of human emotions, which neither parents nor priests—historically the specialists in such matters—have ever successfully resolved. The inner life is exceptionally prey to the force of circumstance and the power of the moment, and those who would subject it to unbending rules, or unbounded idealism, whether in the late sixteenth century or in the late twentieth, can only disappoint and possibly tyrannize themselves and others.

Always embattled, the inner life may never have been more so than in the spiritually turbulent sixteenth century. Then, the weapon of last resort for besieged hearts and minds was religious faith—and preferably one, like Sebald's, that was capable of unpredictable spiritual maneuvers. In that confessionally conflicted age, the vast majority of laity, Catholic and Protestant, believed that Christ had martyred Himself for their sins, so that they need not do so themselves. Therein lies still another explanation of Sebald's experimental and seemingly contradictory religious behavior: the prayers of the Lutheran Musculus on his lips in the privacy of his room, those same lips on a monstrance at a public procession in Brussels, three Lutheran prayer books at the ready on his bed stand, and an indulgence in his hand after shopping the streets of Louvain.

On a personal level, core beliefs are the bedrock to which both reckless and principled behavior return, and they remain as fixed as behavior is fickle. Sebald was no less a Lutheran for having kissed a monstrance and bought an indulgence, nor did the fact that those acts seemed to belie his Lutheran beliefs make them unpleasant or useless to him at the time. His faith could handle the contradiction; it consoled him precisely because it accommodated his need to behave as he did.

Here, to a point, the goals of religion and family may be said to coincide and be natural allies. The discipline religion imposes and the divine forgiveness it promises have their prior counterparts in the family, the first and foremost institution devoted to the discipline and forgiveness of its members—also with an eye to their survival and success in this life and the next.

Although it seems less true today, the family has historically had an advantage over other social institutions in shaping human behavior. For good or ill, we are primarily the creatures of the small families into which we are born and within whose social circles our lives receive their first deep imprints. That the young Lutheran from Nürnberg could survive the discordant religious cultures of the Netherlands and also immerse himself freely in its society and politics are not explained solely by the agility of his religious faith, which in those decades was known as well for its ability to produce proud bigots and unwilling martyrs. Before Sebald arrived in Louvain, he had been carefully tutored at home, schooled at nearby Altdorf, and studied in Strasbourg and Padua. Even then, he departed home for the first time at an older age (fifteen) than other Nürnberg youth, a circumstance for which Nürnberg's excellent primary and secondary schools may be credited.[104] As docility and obedience— patient learning—had been the first lessons of the home, a youth's first duty abroad was also accommodation: to a new household, new languages and customs, new skills and habits, and, not least, a changing, maturing self. That the world outside was a place of many languages and cultures, in which solitary lives and exclusive behavior were frowned on, had also been a major lesson of the home. Whatever contractual guarantees of fair treatment and vocational training a visiting servant, apprentice, or student might negotiate with a new master and mistress, there was never any thought that a host household should suspend or modify its own civic, religious, and cultural practices in deference to a visitor. But neither was a youthful visitor likely to encounter familial values, rules, and expectations jarringly different from those of his own household. Despite uneasy adjustments and frequent complaints, the new arrangements were never entirely a surprise,[105] because so much of what one needed to succeed abroad carried over directly from the prior experience of the home. Sebald accordingly grew boldly in his own chosen direction.

5

FATHERS AND SONS

The Family Chronicle of Pastor Lorenz Dürnhofer

THE YEAR 1586 WAS A SPECIAL ONE FOR LORENZ DÜRNHOFER (1532–1594), for almost twenty years pastor of Nürnberg's St. Giles's Church, one of Nürnberg's three main churches.[1] In that year, at age fifty-four, he witnessed four events, the combination of which would be rare in the life of any man in any age or culture. Between January and October, his eldest son and second daughter married (he on January 19 and she on May 16), his twenty-third and last child was born (October 1), and his first grandson, the eldest child of his firstborn, arrived (October 25).[2] Twice married, Lorenz fathered eleven children by his first wife and twelve by his second, most of whom did not live long enough to know either parent.[3]

Of the twenty-three children, only nine, slightly under 40 percent, survived into adulthood. As reported by Lorenz, that seems at first to be exceptional child mortality for an age when parents, on average, lost one-third of their live offspring in infancy or childhood. However, excluding the five early miscarriages or spontaneous abortions, the Dürnhofers' mortality rate approaches the norm, while twenty-three pregnancies, even over two marriages, remain high for the age.

We know about these events through the survival of a four-generation Dürnhofer family chronicle, in which Lorenz took his turn

Lorenz Dürnhofer at eighteen, by Gaspar Multz, 1550. Germanisches Nationalmuseum, Reichsstadt Nürnberg XVIII Dürnhofer 1.

as the family scribe between the story his father had told and the
one his second son, Leonhard, would write after him. A sixteenth-
century family chronicle was a highly personal, quasi-official attempt
at autobiography and family history. Lorenz's entries are terse reports
of basic facts with no literary pretensions and rare elaboration, yet
compared to his father's truncated and prematurely discontinued entries, they seem almost novellike.

Lorenz's portion covers the period from January 29, 1532, the

day of his birth, to May 17, 1594, the last entry before his death two
months later. He wrote from memory and saved family records during the later years of his life. Exactly when he began doing so is unclear. However, entries for some years are more substantial than
others and give the appearance of having been written close to the
events recorded, perhaps saved for transcription into a later, grand
composition during the last decade of his life. The main purpose
was to preserve a reliable record of family wealth and debits, successes and failures, honors and misfortunes, as the author and his
families grew and changed.

Lorenz accordingly wrote in the first and last instance as a
paterfamilias—as husband and father. After announcing his own
birth and identifying his parents and godfather, he devotes the first
entry (1532) entirely to enumerating and naming the twenty-three
children his two wives bore him over their lifetimes.[4]

Despite this large paternal shadow over the chronicle, Lorenz was
also a "father" in another sense. At age twelve he had already placed
himself on a clerical track that eventually landed him in the pulpit of
St. Giles (1567) during a new epoch of religious upheaval and division, and layered among the primary family matters in the chronicle
is Lorenz's recounting of his own long clerical career and the period's
hot ecclesiastical politics.

Ecclesiastical and religious historians describe the decades between
1560 and 1590 in Germany as the age of "Protestant Scholasticism,"
a mildly derogative term intended to draw a parallel between the
fractured Protestant world of the late sixteenth century and its Roman Catholic counterpart in preceding centuries. Whereas the latter
had seen bickering Dominican and Franciscan orders and rival Augustinian, Thomist, and Ockhamist schools contest Catholic doctrine,[5] the former watched as Lutherans and Calvinists battled both
internally and against one another for hegemony within the established Protestant world.

During his years in Nürnberg, Lorenz would become the leader of
the minority liberal wing of Lutheranism, a role that made him a
lightning rod for the majority conservative Lutherans who were beginning to impose a new orthodoxy throughout the larger Lutheran
world. The liberal wing soft-pedaled doctrines of original sin and

the bondage of the will that were popular with conservatives, and at the same time shied away from Martin Luther's teaching of a real physical presence of Christ in the Eucharist—another acid test of genuine belief for conservatives.

Like his life as a twice-married spouse and a prolific parent, Lorenz's career as a churchman in a religiously divided city and land was both unusually productive and painful. The combination in the chronicle is a rare juxtaposition of family and church history.

Death and Love

Lorenz's father, Leonhard Dürnhofer (1500–1544), settled in Nürnberg in 1520, and eleven years later, as a self-made, prospering merchant, was able to purchase the rights and privileges of citizenship. Born the following year (1532), Lorenz was only twelve when his father died prematurely at age forty-four (January 1544). Attentive to his children, the senior Dürnhofer sent his son to German school at age three and to Latin school at St. Sebald's Church at age four,[6] about as early a start on the acquisition of professional skills as a burger child might then expect.

After his father's death, Lorenz became the ward of his mother (Anna Beur) and two official guardians, merchant cousins Hans Meilendörfer and Lorenz Spengler. Expecting to prepare him for a merchant's career, they sent Lorenz to German scribe Leonhard Kamerer, where he might learn the writing and arithmetical skills needed for the merchant's trade. However, Lorenz had no liking for such work, and, wanting to extend his schooling and pursue an academic track, he made his wishes known to his guardians. Acceding to his request, they allowed him to board at the *Spital*, the city's poorhouse and infirmary, where resident Lutheran educator and dramatist Leonhard Culman gave him advanced instruction in Latin.[7]

The following year (August 1545) Lorenz's mother married a successful, widowed Nürnberg printer and bookseller, Johann Petreius, who in 1541 had stood as "father" with Christoph Scheurl at the wedding of the latter's orphaned cook and carpenter.[8] The new stepfather was a fortunate choice for Lorenz, as he fully supported his stepson's scholarly ambition. He arranged for him to spend two months with the locally famous German writing master and arithmetician Johannes Neudörfer (1479–1563),[9] who was Petreius's brother-in-law, before sending him off to Salzburg (November 1545) and the tutelage of Rector Johann Mulino (known as Stromius), with whom he studied the liberal arts and languages for the next four years.[10]

After spending the winter of 1549–1550 in Nürnberg, Lorenz's stepfather outfitted him with a new wardrobe and sent him off to Wittenberg in early March to begin training for the ministry. Bearing a letter of introduction from his well-connected stepfather, Lorenz arrived on March 10, 1550, four years after Martin Luther's death, and reported directly to Philip Melanchthon (1497–1560) on the following day. Melanchthon had been Luther's handpicked professor of Greek and the major force behind the university's restructuring of its curriculum during the early years of the Reformation. It was he who introduced the educational reforms of German Humanism into both Wittenberg and Nürnberg, whence those reforms spread throughout the German Lutheran world, influencing Catholic educators as well and earning Melanchthon the title *praeceptor Germaniae*, Germany's tutor.

Melanchthon also gave the new Lutheran faith its first systematic doctrinal formulation in a summary work entitled *Commonplaces (Loci communes)* (1521), a statement of the cardinal teachings of 1520s Lutheranism, which stressed especially the sole sufficiency of Holy Scripture in writing articles of faith. In subsequent years, that small work would grow through many editions, yet from its first draft the seeds of later internal Lutheran conflict were sown in the author's "materializing and leveling down of the ideas of Luther [and] knowing advocacy of different positions." Still, the older reformer deeply admired the younger Humanist, perhaps the only colleague who could disagree with Martin Luther with relative impunity—a fortunate circumstance, given the younger man's irenic temperament and later willingness to compromise with the opposition.[11]

It was at least flattering for the eighteen-year-old Lorenz to be welcomed by the famed *praeceptor Germaniae,* who commended him to the care of then physics professor Paul Eber (1511–1569), in whose house Lorenz found a temporary room, while taking board at the home of grammar professor Matthias Blochinger, with whom he would soon also lodge. During the 1550s, Eber taught theology and earned a doctorate in the subject (December 1559), thereafter becoming a pastor in the city's church.[12] Having been Lorenz's preceptor during these years, he would become his lifelong friend and sponsor and honor him uniquely in 1560 with the gift of his doctoral gloves and beret.[13]

Two days after his arrival (March 12), Lorenz was "deposed"[14] at the home of Melanchthon with many university professors joining in the exercise. This was a rite of passage into university study intended to test a new student's level of preparation, particularly his proficiency in Latin and knowledge of classical texts.

Sometime between March 1 and 10, 1550, while Lorenz was en route to Wittenberg, his stepfather died unexpectedly. There is no indication from Lorenz of his having attended either the funeral or the third marriage of his mother to local cloth merchant Thomas Schweitzer in the spring of the following year.[15] Accompanied by a Wittenberg roommate, he did visit the newlyweds in Nürnberg in the fall (1551), staying on with them until the end of the year.[16] During these two months, Lorenz addressed unspecified matters of pressing business,[17] apparently the disposition of the paternal inheritance and joint family property in the wake of his mother's remarriage. Whatever negotiations the three of them had at the time, there is no suggestion that they were not amicable.

After his return to Wittenberg with the new year (1552), Lorenz soon found himself smitten by feelings he appears never to have had before. The story begins on the eve of Ash Wednesday, when he attended the wedding of old schoolmate Barthel Wankel, recently appointed schoolmaster in nearby Kemberg, whose bride was the daughter of Wittenberg's provost. A few days after the event, many of the guests in attendance were stricken with a lethal brain fever (apparently a strep infection) that proved fatal for most.[18] On the day after the wedding, Lorenz set out on foot for Torgau, about thirty-five kilometers south of Wittenberg and also on the Elbe,

Paul Eber, professor of mathematics and Hebrew, and rector of Wittenberg University, 1564, at age 53. The portrait bears the dragon-winged serpent trademark of Lucas Cranach (lower left) and was from the Cranach workshop in Wittenberg, then under the direction of the artist's son, Lucas Cranach the Younger. From Walter L. Strauss, ed., *Max Geisberg: The German Single-Leaf Woodcut, 1550–1600*, vol. 1, (rev.) (New York: Hacker Art Books, 1975), p. 152. (By permission of Abaris Books.)

where he too fell ill while lodging with widow Margaretha Balsmann. Many around him despaired of his life, and he would remain
bedridden for six weeks before "God and the city physician" (Christopher Leuschner) helped him return to good health. However, during the long recuperation, he was shown "every Christian love and
friendship" by Frau Balsmann and her daughters, particularly the
youngest, Elisabeth, to whom he suddenly found himself "drawn"—
new emotions he retrospectively attributed to God's "special providence."[19] When fully recovered, he shared those feelings with Frau
Balsmann and asked her permission to marry Elisabeth. Frau Balsmann requested time to consider the offer and to consult her daughter's guardians, and, respecting her wishes, Lorenz returned to his
studies in Wittenberg, there to await a response. No surviving correspondence exists between Lorenz and Elisabeth during this interval,
nor is there any indication in the chronicle of any physical contact
between the two of them, although subsequent events suggest a relationship that had gone beyond words and eyes.

In the meantime, the same plague that felled Lorenz a few weeks
earlier had made its way to Wittenberg with the beginning of spring,
forcing the university's overlord, Duke Maurice of Saxony (r. 1541–
1553), to transfer the university temporarily to Torgau, where the air
was "fresher and healthier." Lorenz thus found himself back in Torgau, occupying his old room in the Balsmann house.[20]

By this time, he had shared his marriage plans with mentors
Melanchthon and Eber, another indication of the trust Lorenz, at
twenty, enjoyed with these famous men, both of whom were more
than twice his age (Melanchthon was fifty-five in 1552, Eber forty-
one). He must also have believed that they had his emotional life as
much at heart as that of his mind, for it was not youthful enthusiasm
alone that moved Lorenz to confide in them at this time.

Learning of the plague's encroachment on Wittenberg, Frau
Dürnhofer had recently twice ordered Lorenz to depart for home
immediately. At this time, she knew nothing of his romance and
marriage plans, neither of which, he had already anticipated, would
please her. Not only was he still in school and quite young (at
twenty, he was at the bare minimum age for a man of his rank to
marry), but equally against him was the fact that the object of his

desire was a stranger from another town about whom his mother knew absolutely nothing. So, before departing for home in obedience to her command, Lorenz had asked his mentors to recommend him to her as one who, in their opinion, was ready for marriage, apparently convinced that a good word from such luminaries would overcome any doubts his mother might have.

Melanchthon did in fact write such a letter to Anna Dürnhofer, vouching not only for Lorenz ("naturally gifted, disciplined, and honest") but for Frau Balsmann ("an honorable, godfearing widow and matron") and her daughter ("devout, chaste, and reasonable person") as well.

> Since, as God often arranges, [Elisabeth's] heart and your son's are now drawn together, I ask that you also give your consent and support. Once such a relationship has honorably begun, I would not advise a separation. . . . I hope with God's grace your son will be a praiseworthy husband. And as he marries, he must also resolve to pursue his studies earnestly. May [you as] the [guardian] mother consider all these things carefully and give your maternal love and approval.[21]

Lorenz personally carried the letter home to his mother, where it found a place with other communications from his famous teacher in the family archive. The letter did not, however, have the desired effect on Frau Dürnhofer. As Lorenz had feared, she expected him to marry someday, but not this soon, and to choose a local burgher's daughter known to her, not a stranger 250 kilometers away. "Along with the letter, I was ill-received by my mother," he tersely recalls.[22] Fortunately, his guardians came to his rescue, apparently having been more impressed by the authority of Lutheranism's leading light than was his mother—and perhaps also detecting, as Melanchthon appears to have done, a certain inevitability in Lorenz's determination to marry Elisabeth Balsmann.

Anticipating a marriage early in the new year of 1553, Lorenz, at twenty and legally in his majority, now formally relieved his mother and guardians of their responsibility as trustees of his paternal and grandmaternal inheritances. Henceforth, he would personally over-see his own holdings and manage his own financial affairs. On the heels of that act, Frau Dürnhofer relented and sent her future daughter-in-law several gifts through her son.[23] In 1551, she had, af-ter all, married again herself and was now a member of a new family, while Lorenz's only sibling, younger brother Leonhard (b. 1542), was still in his minority and living with her and had no cause to contest the apportioning of the paternal estate.[24] Such actions on Lorenz's part were public declarations of his new vocational compe-tence and presumed ability to support a family, the contemporary benchmarks of adulthood.

Returning to Torgau with his mother's consent to marry and his paternal inheritance now legally his, Lorenz gained the consent of Elisabeth's mother and guardians.[25] On January 6, 1553, a formal betrothal (handtschlag) occurred in the presence of her family and several university professors, as well as three tables full of guests and witnesses attending from Wittenberg and Torgau.[26]

Finding Work

Lorenz and Elisabeth wanted to marry immediately; however, the plague's retreat and the return of the professors and students to Wittenberg made it advisable to postpone the wedding day until a "more pleasant" time.[27] Lorenz now also felt a new urgency to finish his education and find employment before incurring a family. He re-turned to Wittenberg with the other students on January 21, and by June, upon Melanchthon's recommendation, was ready to enter the job market. He became a candidate for a beginning teaching post[28] in Hayn near Meissen, 100 kilometers southeast of Wittenberg, only to lose out to an inside candidate. Having no other options, he continued on in school, earning a master's degree in early August, graduating fourth in a class of eighteen. With that milestone reached, he was determined to go ahead with the wedding despite the lack of a job, and he returned to Nürnberg at month's end to take his inheritance fully in hand.[29]

In early October, a schoolmastership opened up in faraway Oelsnitz, sited between Zwickau and Annaberg, 185 kilometers northeast of Nürnberg. Aided again by his mentor—and this time without an inside candidate waiting in the wings—Lorenz, at twenty-one, became gainfully employed for the first time.[30]

The wedding occurred in Torgau two weeks later (October 16), with three wagonloads of professors, masters, and students making the trip down from Wittenberg, a testimony to Lorenz's popularity and the solidarity of the university. Another wagonload traveled about the same distance from the Lutheran stronghold of Leipzig in the south. To mark the occasion, Melanchthon wrote a poem celebrating Torgau, which he sent with a Hungarian gulden in place of the traditional epithalamium. Evidently, he deemed the poem a more fitting tribute to his favorite student and the city in which he had fallen in love. The exercise also gave the famous educator still another opportunity to showcase his enormous erudition for posterity. The newlyweds barely had ten days together before setting out, on October 27, for Oelsnitz, a three-day journey.[31]

The schoolmastership in Oelsnitz did not prove to be a happy experience. A growing conflict with the local bürgermeister (Wolf Michel), whom Lorenz describes as "malicious and tyrannical," made their lives miserable. Whether their mutual hostility stemmed from the bürgermeister's aggressive oversight of Lorenz's work as a novice schoolmaster, or possibly from a confrontation over the training of his children, whom Lorenz portrays as "spoiled and mischievous," is unclear. The result, however, was Lorenz's sudden resignation[32] in June 1555, after nineteen months on the job.

During their year and a half in Oelsnitz, the Dürnhofers had been sustained by many friends and supporters there, as well as by cheering visits from Torgau and Nürnberg relatives. Among the visitors in 1554 was the family of brother-in-law Hieronymus Resch, who delivered into Lorenz's and Elisabeth's tutelage and care Lorenz's younger brother Leonhard, now twelve and ready to pursue his higher education outside the stepparental home. In September 1554, that home had also lost Lorenz's widowed paternal grandmother, who had spent her last years with his mother and stepfather. This was an unusual example of a daughter-in-law (Lorenz's mother) continuing to have a close relationship with a mother-in-law, even though she was now two husbands removed from that mother-in-law's son (Lorenz's father). In gratitude for their care, Grandmother Dürnhofer had left her first daughter-in-law her entire inheritance, minus twenty-five gulden and a silver cup each for grandsons Lorenz and Leonhard.[33]

Leonhard's arrival was not the only addition to the family in Oelsnitz, nor was Lorenz's resignation its only misfortune. In February 1555, Elisabeth gave birth to their first child, a son, Georg, named after Lorenz's paternal grandfather. Three godparents stood at the birth and baptism—witnesses also to the diverse friendships Lorenz and Elisabeth had made and the breadth of their social circle. The three godparents were the city chaplain, a shoemaker, and a widowed innkeeper, who together presented the newborn with two taler and a Hungarian ducat. The boy, however, died after two days from seizures apparently brought on by a bowel obstruction.[34]

In the weeks before the couple's departure from Oelsnitz, the city council offered Lorenz the position of chaplain, which had suddenly opened after the city of Nördlingen successfully enticed Oelsnitz's chaplain to a pastorate there. The offer came at a time when Lorenz's mother and stepfather were paying a surprise visit to Oelsnitz, and was reportedly extended to him in their very presence. Lorenz, however, declined it on the grounds that he was "still too young and inexperienced" a preacher.[35] He may have suspected that the offer was neither a compliment nor a promotion, despite the esteem in which he was held by his friends and supporters. Due to his youth and inexperience, he may not have been an effective diplomat in the sensitive post of schoolmaster. If so, the offer of the chaplaincy may have been an effort to improve the match between skills and responsibilities, while placing Lorenz beyond the bürgermeister's immediate scrutiny. However that may be, Lorenz departed Oelsnitz with a positive recommendation from the city council, another document preserved in the family archive.

Pastor and Father

Arriving in Wittenberg on June 8, 1555, and finding no house readily available for occupancy, the young family moved in with Elisabeth's sister, whose husband (Sebastian Mathias) was a Wittenberger. There they remained until Michaelmas (September 29), by which time they were able to rent a house of their own for twenty-two gulden per annum. Earlier in the summer, Lorenz enrolled Leonhard, now fourteen and part of the family household, in the university.[36]

The first mention of new remunerative work did not come until late June 1556,[37] when Lorenz preached his first sermon in the neighboring village of Zaan. Thereafter, he supported the family by irregular but increasingly steady guest preaching in area churches, even though he did not become an ordained minister until May 1557. During these twelve months of largely itinerant sermonizing, he also substituted for Wittenberg's chaplain and preachers, on two occasions delivering the catechism sermon to the city's eleven- and twelve-year-olds in chief pastor Bugenhagen's place. This was a welcomed and rewarding clinical experience for Lorenz, as were also the well-paying opportunities to examine master's candidates at the university.

Another highlight of the summer of 1556 was the birth of a second child, Lorenz Jr. (August 4), this time with Melanchthon and Eber standing among the boy's three godfathers. But again, this new light was a flickering one, as the boy died three weeks later.[38]

The year 1558[39] also did not begin auspiciously, although it would be the turning point in Lorenz's career and the family's fortunes. Falling ill in February with suspected tuberculosis and soon completely incapacitated, Lorenz was given little hope by his physician, and he contemplated an early death. That he did not resign himself entirely to the grave may have owed something to the birth of a third son on March 25—this one, at last, destined to survive and live a long life. Lorenz attributed both his illness, which plagued him for two years, and eventual recovery to God's just punishment

and unmerited grace. The new son was baptized Lorenz Jr., a favored family name now passed on to him from his deceased brother.
Again, three godparents attested to Lorenz's widening social circle: a
widowed, exiled Austrian baron (Hans von Ungnad), then in Wittenberg because of his Lutheran beliefs and recently wed to Countess Magdalena von Barby, who ruled a village on the Elbe a few
hours' ride northeast of Wittenberg; a noble-born student at the university (Conrad Schiller); and the wife of a university professor of
medicine.[40]

In late September 1558, Lorenz moved his budding family into
cheaper housing (sixteen gulden per annum), and, declaring that a
change of air might revive his spirits, he departed for Leipzig and
the October fair with brother Leonhard. From there, the two continued on to Nürnberg, where Lorenz moved into his stepfather's
house until Christmas. That he had more than a change of air on
his mind in undertaking this journey is suggested by his preaching
two sermons at St. Lorenz's Church. Shortly thereafter, councilman
and church supervisor Hieronymus Paumgartner (1498–1565) approached him on behalf of the city council and offered him the next
available pastorate in one of the city's three churches—in effect, a
ladder appointment in the city's ecclesiastical establishment. Lorenz
was invited to move his family to Nürnberg in the spring (1559),
there to await, as an "Expectant,"[41] the opening of the promised position. As a pledge of the city's good faith, he was given fifty of a
promised two-hundred-gulden annual salary before returning to
Wittenberg to fetch his family.

In making the offer, Paumgartner and the council had likely been
lobbied in advance by Lorenz's famous Wittenberg teachers. Not
only were the clergy of the two cities historically close allies, Paumgartner had himself been a student of Melanchthon in the 1520s and
had known Luther as well. In later years when the old bürgermeister
was kidnapped during his return home from a diet in Speyer (May
1544) and held for ransom by a renegade knight, Luther had sent
his family a consolatory letter.[42]

Leaving behind Leonhard, who would soon continue his education, and end his life, in Padua, Lorenz returned to Wittenberg with
the new year, there to find Elisabeth slowly mending from an omi-

nous first bout with kidney stones.[43] In the week after Easter, the two of them set out for Nürnberg with their infant son, traveling via Torgau and Leipzig to Coburg, where they lay over several days with Elisabeth's sister Susanna and her husband (Wolf Heiner). There, the ailing Lorenz was bled on the advice of the city physician before continuing on to Nürnberg, where the family arrived on April 16. Again, they moved in with Lorenz's mother and stepfather, paying them two gulden a week for room and board. It would not be until June that the city made good on a promised house directly across from the parsonage of St. Lorenz's, which had previously been occupied by schoolmasters and other city preachers.[44]

Now settled in the city the family assumed would be their home forever, Lorenz's spirits brightened and his health improved. However, as the weeks and months passed and the promised pulpit did not materialize, gloom set in. After a year had elapsed without an appointment, an inactive and bored Lorenz asked the council to allow him to return to his studies in Wittenberg, promising to return immediately upon request, if and when the elusive opening finally materialized. It was an indication of the city's embarrassment that Lorenz left with a "departure gift" of two hundred gulden and a formal reassurance of the city's continuing commitment to his employment.[45]

Intraconfessional Politics

The family set out for Wittenberg on March 30, 1560, traveling via Oelsnitz, where old friends warmly received them and the city council sent them wine. In Wittenberg on April 11, they again lodged with Elisabeth's sister and brother-in-law, and on the very same day, Lorenz paid a visit to his old, dying mentor Melanchthon, now sixty-three and bedridden with kidney stones. "We talked about everything," Lorenz recalls, as he had one of the last round conversations with the great reformer and educator, who, depleted by tertian fever, died a few days later following seven violent seizures.[46]

Lorenz rented an inexpensive house (fifteen gulden per annum) previously lived in by a book peddler and resumed his theological studies. He spent the first week of May in Torgau preaching the Sunday sermon in the main church and networking among clergy and old friends there. Both annoyed and blessed by his leisure, he devoted himself particularly to the rearing and education of Lorenz Jr. In August, the two-and-a-half-year-old toddler "took his first torch to a new master"; that is, he met his first tutor, a Dane, ostensibly to begin learning the rudiments of Latin. By the time he was seven, the boy had had no fewer than sixteen private tutors, among them men with master's degrees and doctorates, as his father began methodically in these tender years to give him a headstart on the schooling required for an academic career.

Before he turned three, the pace of little Lorenz's life was quickened by the appearance of a rival for his parents' attention: a sister, Anna, who arrived in the household on December 27. As the choice of her godparents already promised—one was the wife of a local bookseller (Elisabeth Rügel), the other Pastor Paul Eber's daughter—she, too, would receive the best education a girl in her position might then expect.[47]

In mid-January of the new year (1561), Lorenz got his first deep immersion in regional church politics when, accompanied by Pastor Eber and Dr. Georg Major (1502–1574)—the latter another Wittenberg theologian and Melanchthon protégé, who would later ordain Lorenz—he visited the Torgau castle of Saxon Elector August I (r. 1553–1586). Eber and Major had been summoned there by the elector to prepare a Saxon delegation of area rulers who subscribed to the *Augsburg Confession* (1530), the definitive Lutheran creed, for a forthcoming meeting in Naumburg.[48] Of the several issues then bitterly contested among Lutheran theologians as well as between Lutherans and Calvinists, the nature of Christ's presence in the Eucharist was the most worrisome to the princes. The absence of theological accord on so central a doctrine threatened political division, much as earlier disagreements between Luther and the Swiss reformer Ulrich Zwingli had obstructed a desired Swiss-Saxon alliance in the late 1520s. With the German Lutheran world then attempting to maintain a unified front against the awakening Jesuit-led Counter

Reformation and newly aggressive German Calvinist rulers, Elector August demanded unity on this key issue.

On one side of the issue in the divided Lutheran camp were the so-called Philippists (after Philip Melanchthon), whom Eber and Major then represented and Lorenz would one day also lead. That opprobrious label was the creation of their conservative critics, the self-proclaimed defenders of the true teachings of Martin Luther, whom historians refer to as "Genesio (original/genuine)-Lutherans." Led by Matthias Flacius Illyricus (1520–1575), a Hebrew professor and skilled church politician at the University of Magdeburg in ducal Saxony,[49] they accused the Philippists, like their namesake before them, of betraying Luther's teaching on both good works and the corporal presence of Christ in the Eucharist. And Melanchthon and his followers were indeed inclined to treat a person's moral life as an acid test of true faith, while viewing the notion of a corporal presence of Christ in the Sacrament as neither biblical nor proper Protestant teaching. On both issues, the Genesio-Lutherans ridiculed the Philippists as "crypto-Calvinists"—that is, theologically in the camp of Reformed Protestantism.

Although unfairly portrayed as betraying classic Lutheranism, the liberal wing of 1560s Lutheranism did have real differences with the founder.[50] Whereas Luther had taught that faith was "active in good works" and that true Christians performed good works as naturally as healthy trees produced good fruit, he had been loath to appeal from works to salvation, or in any way to calculate a person's eternal worth in terms of moral activity or worldly success, no matter how god-pleasing he acknowledged the latter to be.[51] And no less uncompromising had been the great reformer's defense of a real corporal presence of Christ in the Eucharist. Convinced that a Lord's Supper celebrated as a "memorial" to Christ, whose presence was said to be "spiritually invoked" by the faith of believers, was both an unbiblical and spiritually inadequate consolation to devout laity, Luther had insisted that the incarnate, crucified, and risen Christ was really present "in, with, and under" the elements of bread and wine, just as the orthodox Formula of Concord (1580) would later also proclaim.[52] In so arguing, Luther stressed the unique ability of Jesus' human nature to share, miraculously, the qualities of His

divine nature, among which was ubiquity, or the ability to be everywhere in one and the same form at one and the same time.

Close though it may sound, such argument was not in fact a
weakened version of the Catholic doctrine of transubstantiation.
Here no priestly power to transform bread and wine into the body
and blood of Christ was recognized—only the miraculous "consubstantiality" of the material elements of the Sacrament and Christ's
crucified and risen body by virtue of His biblical promise to be truly
present at the celebration of the Last Supper in His name. However,
for Protestant clergy and laity wanting a more dramatic break with
tradition, such teaching seemed insufficiently reformed.

The conservatives, on the other hand, insisted that sinners and
faithful alike truly masticated the true body and blood of Christ—
the former to their damnation, the latter to their salvation. Drawing
what seemed to be a logical conclusion, Philippists and Calvinists
mockingly theorized that any rodent happening upon the unat-
tended sacramental elements must do so as well! The Formula of
Concord later dismissed such irreverent put-downs of conservative
Eucharistic teaching as "presumptuous, scoffing, and blasphemous."
Still, the founder of Lutheranism had bequeathed a real problem to
his followers, and seven Lutheran lands and fourteen cities, among
them Nürnberg, continued to resist such teaching after the Formula
of Concord made it official doctrine. Those dissenting preferred,
if prefer they must, a teaching closer to that of Reformed Protestantism, which envisioned a "real spiritual" rather than a "real physical" presence of Christ, which did not lend itself to such crude
imagery and ridicule.[53]

Already by the 1560s, Genesio-Lutheranism was everywhere in
ascendancy in German Lutheran lands and conflict between divided
Lutheran factions was threatening to break out. For Saxon Elector
August, the diplomatic challenge was at this time particularly great.
Within his lands, "Philippism" had found strongholds in the universities of Wittenberg and Leipzig, while those of ducal Saxony, where
the Genesio-Lutherans held sway, despised it. By 1567, the elector
gained new power in ducal Saxony by becoming the legal guardian
of the minor princes there—this after the emperor imprisoned their
father on charges of treason.[54] Although the elector permitted the

extension of Philippism into Thuringia in the late 1560s, it was imperative that he keep an even hand on the internal Lutheran conflict, which he was more or less able to do until the publication of the Formula of Concord. Once that official theological statement was firmly in place, and with Palatine Calvinists making significant inroads into Saxony and other German lands, the elector would have no choice but to suppress Philippism and enforce the new orthodoxy throughout Saxony.[55]

That final resolution was still two decades away, when, on March 17, 1561, at the elector's order, the theologians of the universities of Leipzig and Wittenberg, Lorenz again among them, now assembled in Dresden to work out an interim consensual statement on the Eucharist with that city's clergy. Arriving in May, Lorenz made important new friends and contacts while displaying his own talents. That he was gaining a reputation in local theological circles became clear in November, when a delegation of Siebenbürgen or Moldavian Protestants, whose beliefs stemmed from the Bohemian reformer Jan Hus, arrived in Wittenberg to compare their teaching with that of their German Lutheran allies, particularly in the contested area of Eucharistic theology. Before returning home, the Siebenbürgens asked that two Wittenbergers accompany them back to Hermannstadt, one to teach philosophy in the school there, the other to preach in the city church. Pastor Eber recommended Lorenz for the latter post and allowed him to showcase his theological and oratorical skills by preaching a sermon in the presence of the visitors. That they were favorably impressed became evident by their immediate offer of a salary of 200 Hungarian ducats (350 gulden), in addition to wood, grain, wine, meat, and other staples.[56]

First Things

Lorenz could not accept the Siebenbürgens' generous offer because of the challenge so major a move posed for Elisabeth and Lorenz Jr. Now chronically ill with kidney stones and pregnant again, Elisabeth was more depressed than ever over her health. Lorenz recalled a nightmare she had in September, in which she dreamed she was standing by a bier on which a corpse lay. When, on the following day, Lorenz Jr. fell down the cellar stairs, his father viewed the accident as a near tragic fulfillment of that terrible dream, even though the only injury sustained was "some difficulty in talking,"[57] possibly a result of the fright. The family was neither physically nor psychologically prepared for a sudden move to Hungary.

Also at this time, Lorenz could not have doubted that the odds favoring his employment in Wittenberg, or preferably Nürnberg, would only increase in the new year with his growing reputation. In March 1562,[58] another well-paying position in a faraway place was offered him by Margrave Johann of Küstrin's (r. 1535–1571) chancellor, whose lord was a Lutheran stalwart famed for his resistance to the emperor after the latter's victory over the Lutheran princes in 1547.[59] Upon hearing Lorenz preach a sermon on the raising of Lazarus, the chancellor invited him to become the margrave's court preacher at his residence in Küstrin (Kostrzyn), which lay north of Frankfurt an der Oder, over four hundred kilometers away from Nürnberg. Claiming always to have "loathed court life,"[60] Lorenz declined without excuse or regret, apparently foreseeing himself trapped there in a politically charged and morally compromised environment he would be powerless to alter.

The next month Lorenz found himself exactly where he wanted to be. In April, the Wittenberg pastors chose him to succeed the recently deceased church deacon (Johannes Stör), an appointment that now put him directly in the footsteps of Martin Luther: "I was [now] required to preach the Vesper sermon that Herr Luther preached as long as he had lived," Lorenz recalled. The position paid one hundred gulden and twenty-five bushels of grain, in addition to other perks,[61] which, taken altogether, raised his annual salary beyond two hundred gulden. The family also had a government house, into which they moved on July 3, and Lorenz was permitted to continue his studies at the university as well.

The year nonetheless ended on a bittersweet note, with the birth of second daughter Margaretha (December 28), and the sudden death on the same day of the children's nanny of five years.[62]

In addition to the income from the Wittenberg diaconate, Lorenz continued preaching in Torgau and examining master's and bachelor's candidates at the university. On one occasion in 1564, he joined in the testing of fifty-three students, for which he received thirteen gulden. For such service over the years, the faculty recognized him with a six-month deanship of the philosophy faculty in the summer of 1566.[63]

If, by 1562, Lorenz's professional career was beginning to settle, his family life was becoming more demanding. Henceforth, it would occupy an increasingly disproportionate share of the family chronicle. Lorenz Jr. suffered at five his first serious accident (July 1563), falling down the second-floor stairs and cracking his head on the door jam at the landing, a wound that required his first stitches. Also in July, after three years of private tutoring at home, he began public school. At seven (May 1565), he enrolled in Latin school, where the schoolmaster's learned brother privately tutored him.[64] Although his father was not a rich man, Lorenz Jr. could not have received a better education between ages two-and-a-half and seven. At the same time, his four-and-a-half-year-old sister, Anna, was enrolled in a girl's school run by the widowed sister of grammar professor Plochinger, with whom Lorenz had lived when he arrived in Wittenberg as an eighteen-year-old. There, Anna received instruction in reading, writing, manners, and morals.[65]

During the mid-sixties, Elisabeth's health progressively declined. Pregnant for the sixth time in September 1564, she endured the "unspeakable pain" of a kidney stone that would not pass for ten days before triggering the premature birth of a stillborn son, and almost taking her life as well.[66] Early the next year, she passed a second large stone, only then to develop still another that would not budge the year after (March 1566). Pregnant again at the time, the ordeal left another premature son dead on the birthing table shortly after his baptism, a depressing streak of medical and maternal misfortune from which Elisabeth would not recover.

> After this illness, my dear wife never again knew an hour of good health until she was in her grave, for the stone stayed in her and would by no means be expelled, apparently due to its great size.[67]

The arrival of plague on the outskirts of Wittenberg in May 1566 promised to make all such individual suffering anecdotal. By July and August, many students were fleeing with their professors to the countryside, while those who remained in the city faced a possible terrible death. Among the first to flee was Lorenz Jr.'s Latin tutor, gone already in May before the crisis was clear, leaving his tutee's instruction to a less-qualified colleague. By July, Lorenz Jr. and his sister had been yanked out of school and strictly quarantined at home. There, Elisabeth's nephew (Benedict Heyner), a Coburg native living and working in the household, tutored them both. A year later, Lorenz became the guardian of Heyner's orphaned siblings as well, traveling to Coburg to sign the legal papers and to escort the children back to their new home in Wittenberg.[68]

Despite the exodus of students and faculty in the summer of 1566, life in plague-stricken Wittenberg went on by and large as usual. The thirty-eight master's candidates still in residence continued to receive Lorenz's instruction. The graduation ceremonies and faculty banquet (*prandium Aristotelicum*) which traditionally closed the academic year occurred as usual on August 20. For the first time, the banquet was held in the great hall of the cloister that had been Martin Luther's home, a building Elector August had purchased from the reformer's heirs and refurbished before donating it to the university. The elector even sent the customary roasted stag for the occasion.[69] Nine months would pass, however, before the last remnants of plague disappeared (March 1567) and the students and professors, some of whom had been absent for almost three-quarters of a year, returned and the normal academic calendar resumed.

Despite the misfortunes of these months, Lorenz and Elisabeth had not soured on the city. Offered an escape to a pastorate and superintendency in Mersenburg, south of Halle, they chose to stay put, Lorenz again citing Elisabeth's timidity and his own unspecified reasons, among them surely his own continuing doubts that she could survive a move.[70] His worse fears about her were confirmed the following May, when she fell down the second-floor stairs while exiting the bedroom, breaking the larger toes of her right foot and bruising much of her body. Although she recovered after a difficult few days, Lorenz looked back on the incident as forshadowing her death,[71] ominous signs of which now seemed to be everywhere.

In early June, the two of them traveled to Torgau to visit Elisabeth's dying mother, only to find her dead on the day they arrived. Returning to Wittenberg after settling the estate—the lion's share of which (family house, gardens, and meadows) went to Elisabeth's brother Benedict—Elisabeth found that not only the death of her mother weighed her down. Another new pregnancy and the ever-recurring kidney stones did so as well. When in mid-July, an ill wind blew a slate loose from the roof of their house, striking daughter Margaretha in the head and requiring stitches, all of the "burdensome circumstances" under which Elisabeth had been living suddenly caved in on her.[72] Driven to her bed, she miscarried within three days, losing still another son three months into a new pregnancy.[73]

Her decline was now rapid and irreversible. Stricken with a suffocating catarrh, she "went to sleep in the Lord" on a Sunday afternoon in July after two seizures.[74] She was thirty-four. In summarizing their fourteen years together, Lorenz remembered her as a "good Christian," who had lived with him "in unity, constant love, and trust."[75] On the day after her death, he buried her in the cemetery on the outskirts of town appropriate to their social rank, where several of their deceased children also lay.

According to Lorenz, had Elisabeth wished, she could have been interred with the upper classes in the parish church cemetery in town, a privilege to which his position in the church entitled them both. Although that would have pleased him, whenever they discussed the subject, the thought of being buried there "horrified" her.[76] This was apparently not because she felt unworthy to lie with the city's noble dead, but because she wanted to be with the children she had known only in her womb and had carried only to their deaths. In fulfillment of both a wife's and a mother's wishes, Lorenz laid her to rest with their children in the appropriate, if lesser cemetery.

Burial outside of the parish church cemetery did not, however, preclude a ceremony befitting Elisabeth's esteemed position within the community. Her funeral drew a great crowd of students and burghers, who accompanied the coffin to the outskirts of town,

... a spectacle, the likes of which had not been seen since the deaths of Luther and Philip [Melanchthon]. Such was the love and honor in which she was held by the many who knew her many special, God-given virtues and talents, for which she herself often gave heartfelt thanks to God.[77]

As memorials to the wife he described as god-fearing, humble, patient, diligent, devoted, friendly, reasonable, modest, respectful, and never failing to serve others to the best of her ability, Lorenz placed an arched stone over her grave and commissioned a painting of the Visitation of Mary to be placed in the parish church in Wittenberg. Although later something of an iconoclast, Lorenz evidently did not view a tribute to Elisabeth in Wittenberg's parish church, where traditional religious images had long been tolerated as *adiaphora* (Luther himself reportedly kept a Cranach painting of the Virgin and child in his study all his life), as idolatrous.[78]

Escaping Widowerhood

Thus it was that Lorenz found himself in August 1567, at thirty-five, alone with three minor children: Lorenz Jr., now nine; Anna, six-and-a-half; and Margaretha, four-and-a-half. A scant month after Elisabeth's death, the opportunity arose again to escape to Meissen, and had Lorenz not then been in mourning for Elisabeth and in shock at the thought of managing a household without her, he might well have gone, for this time he professed a desire to do so.[79]

If ever the call from Nürnberg was to come, this was the moment Lorenz needed it most, and come it did on September 3, repeated again ten days later. Addressing Lorenz as a native son and citizen,[80] church superintendent Joachim Haller wrote on the city's behalf to make good at last on the promise made seven years earlier. The offer was a pastorate with house and stipend, and Haller urged him to return to Nürnberg with his household posthaste. After consulting Pastor Eber, Lorenz resigned his church service in Wittenberg, preached a farewell sermon to his clerical colleagues on September 21, and two weeks later bade his boarders and friends farewell.[81] Then, having paid off his creditors and collected his outstanding debts, he and the children departed Wittenberg on October 12.[82]

Arriving in Nürnberg on the twentieth, the four of them descended upon Lorenz's mother, with whom they would remain for nine months before the promised government house became available to them. However, Superintendent Haller immediately formalized Lorenz's appointment at St. Giles's at a salary of 300 gulden per annum and presented him to his colleagues in the ministry at the end of the month. On November 2, 1567, Lorenz preached his first sermon, and on December 17, Lorenz Jr., now eleven, began school at St. Sebald's.[83]

Lorenz had hardly taken up his new regimen when he was seized upon by the local Genesio-Lutherans, or "Flacians," as he preferred to call them, after Magdeburg theologian and archenemy Matthias Flacius Illyricus. Already known for its "Philippist" or "crypto-Calvinist" leanings before Lorenz's installment at St. Giles, Nürnberg had become something of a pariah in the larger, unforgiving Lutheran theological world.[84] Inasmuch as Lorenz had been a student and intimate of Melanchthon, and now occupied one of the city's two Philippist churches, he could not reasonably have expected to escape such attacks. Although never identifying his local adversaries by name, he described them generically as "mutineers" who threatened civil peace and required the constant vigilance of church and state.[85]

Given the strain of the move, around-the-clock care of three minor children, and a religious ferocity the likes of which he had not seen before, Lorenz was fortunate indeed to have the immediate assistance of his mother. Her contribution diminished rapidly, however, after she was diagnosed in March 1568 with advanced cancer in her left breast, the beginning of six painful months that ended with her death.[86] Evidently anticipating the worst, Lorenz became engaged to a Nürnbergerin in the very same month (March), even though only seven months—well short of the prudential year—had passed since Elisabeth's death.

The new bride-to-be was Katharina Lebender, and judging from Lorenz's brief entry describing the day of the betrothal and his bare comment on the engagement thereafter, the match appears initially to have been based overwhelmingly on mutual need and convenience, Katharina receiving a reasonable living and Lorenz some urgent stepmaternal assistance, not to mention the mutual conjugal comforts.

> March 19 [1568], I dined with Hans Chan[d]ler and took my second wife, namely, Miss Katharina [Lebender], the surviving daughter of the deceased Hans Lebender.[87]

Their wedding occurred on June 16, eleven months after Elisabeth's death, and as neither Lorenz nor Katharina had a living father, three males, one of whom was a relative, stood as their "fathers" at the ceremony.[88] The bridal pair lived with Lorenz's mother until July 8, when the parish house behind St. Giles's became available to them. His ailing mother likely also moved there with them and her grandchildren for her remaining two months. In February 1569, five months after Frau Dürnhofer's death (September 1568), the Dürnhofer family house was sold to a new owner.[89]

After the wedding, Katharina's name does not appear again in the chonicle for nine months, when Lorenz records, again with the greatest restraint, the birth of their first child: "On April 7 [1569], my second wife had her first child, a daughter named Katharina . . . who died on May 9."[90] When, ten months later (February 17, 1570), a second daughter was born, a warming of the couple's relationship may be indicated by Lorenz's addition of at least one kind word to a still terse recollection: "My dear wife gave birth to her second child, Maria Magdalena," who also died within a week.[91] Again, as with the first daughter, Lorenz seems to view the experience and the child as more "hers" than "his" or "theirs."

However, even if the motives of the second marriage were initially more pragmatic than those of the first had ever been, they did not prevent the second marriage from deepening over time and with familiarity. Given his new official responsibilities and professional enemies, Katharina's presence as homemaker and helpmate could only have been a godsend. In March 1568, her presence made it easier for the three children, now ranging in age from ten to four-and-a-half, to receive the attention and care required at a time when the education of each was reaching a critical stage. In the premodern family, pragmatism also had a respected place in relationships; the advancement of household order and physical well-being was also a great virtue, even a kind of self-sacrificial love.

The Eldest Son

Ever in search of the best possible instruction for his children, Lorenz moved them from tutor to tutor and from school to school. In July 1568, Anna and Margaretha were sent to math and script master Hans Strobel, there to gain the arithmetical and writing skills they would need when they entered service and eventually ran households of their own. In September 1569, eleven-year-old Lorenz Jr. was taken out of St. Sebald's, where he had been a student for almost two years, and enrolled at St. Lorenz's, where he came under the tutelage of Andreas Beham (1538–1611), recently appointed rector there. That Beham held a degree from Wittenberg and was a friend of leading Philippist Georg Major (1502–1574), who had ordained Lorenz a decade earlier (1557),[92] surely influenced Lorenz's judgment that he was then the city's best mentor.

Around the same time, Lorenz Jr.'s sisters went, in succession, to three different tutors over only nine months: Chaplain Johannes Beyl, who bequeathed them to "the indiligent Hans Heyen," after whom they came into the very capable hands of Erhard Hausslaub.[93] The instruction they received in language, manners, and morals was intended to endow each with a level of literacy and a degree of poise that might brighten their future prospects in the city's marriage market, while in the meantime increasing their usefulness to themselves, their father, and possible domestic employers.

By the summer of 1570, Lorenz had emerged as Nürnberg's premier churchman and was increasingly at the center of local and territorial church politics. In early June, he dined twice with imperial court preacher Francis Lambert, the first time at the latter's Nürnberg lodging, the second at the parsonage, where the two were joined by imperial secretary Martin Gerstmann (1527–1528). Destined soon to become the bishops of Neustadt (in Austria) and Breslau, respectively, Lambert and Gerstmann were then in Nürnberg as part of the emperor's advance party. Although Lorenz gives no hint of what they talked about, ecclesiastical politics, both Lutheran and interconfessional, were surely discussed late into the night. Between the two dinners, Emperor Maximilian II (r. 1564–1576) made a grand entrance into the city (June 7) accompanied by the German princes, all of whom lodged in the castle inside the city walls before traveling on to a diet in Speyer.[94]

By summer's end, anonymous Flacians had posted a "shameful, poisonous pamphlet" on the community bulletin board attacking Lorenz and other city clergy. So provocative was this new attack that the city council requested a response from Lorenz and his colleagues, while continuing to search in vain for "the assassins" (Lorenz's term)[95] who launched it. A year and a half later (May 1572), another anonymous defamatory pamphlet threatened the city's peace, this time prompting a 200-gulden reward for information leading to the apprehension of its author(s).[96]

Such challenges might have shaken Lorenz a great deal more had his family life not then confronted him with even greater ones. In the fall of 1570, Lorenz Jr., Anna, and Margaretha were stricken successively with measles and apparently smallpox,[97] the great child killers of the age, which, against the odds, all three survived. When deadly diseases were not stalking the children, academic failure did. That dreaded vocational crippling, which promised a future filled with need, was almost as great a fright to contemporary parents as illness, particularly when a first son was stricken by it.

In January 1571, Lorenz Jr. changed schools for the second time, now going from St. Lorenz's to St. Giles's. His father's stated reasons for the transfer were locations, St. Giles's being much closer to home, and its new schoolmaster, former cantor Caspar Nentwich, whom Lorenz respected as "a devout and diligent man."

There was, however, another, unstated reason for the transfer, which Lorenz could not at this time bring himself to state bluntly in the family chronicle: Lorenz Jr. had not been applying himself to his studies. His father had hoped that the new schoolmaster of St. Giles's might inspire in his son the diligence the schoolmaster of St. Lorenz's had not. Passing as lightly as possible over the trouble the boy was then having, Lorenz retrospectively admitted that he knew even then that the fault lay not in the teacher, but in the pupil. St. Giles's, he wrote in a later entry, was a place

> . . . where Lorenz Jr. could readily have learned something, if only he had wanted to, and had God granted the schoolmaster [Nentwich] a longer life.[98]

The transfer from St. Lorenz's to St. Giles's was thus intended to shore up the boy's slipping education and salvage an academic career. After Nentwich died unexpectedly in the spring of 1572, Lorenz Jr. was sent back to St. Lorenz's, as his father deemed Nentwich's successor at St. Giles's (Andreas Taucher) markedly inferior to his predecessor in skill, diligence, and reputation.[99] At the same time, Lorenz again acknowledged that instruction was not the problem, describing Lorenz Jr. during these critical years as having "studied as much with the one [master] as with the other,"[100] by which he meant, as little with the one as with the other.

That Lorenz could not at the time write more frankly about Lorenz Jr.'s academic shortcomings indicates how painful their recognition and recollection were for a sixteenth-century father. To discover then that one's eldest child and only son, in whom so much was invested emotionally and materially, simply lacked the aptitude and/or self-discipline to follow in a father's footsteps was a traumatic parental experience, second only to a child's death. If all the children in the past did not get the parents they deserved, there were also parents denied the children they were worthy of. As Lorenz now discovered, in the history of the family neither side has an umblemished record.

In these same days when Lorenz was despairing of Lorenz Jr.'s future prospects, Katharina was preparing to give her husband another, very different son. On December 4, 1571, at the end of a draining year in which her mother and two brothers had died, she gave birth to twin boys, Wolfgang (called "Wolfie") and Leonhard, their third and fourth offspring. Wolfie died within a week, while to everyone's surprise and delight, Leonhard, who had appeared to be every bit as frail, grew stronger with each passing day. Although his father could not know it at the time, here was a boy who would become the scholar his half brother could not be. Already at his birth, the newborn's fighting spirit impressed the father, who cheered him on:

> May he continue to live as God wills, and may God give him not only physical health and strength, but His Holy Spirit as well, so that he may grow up a devout, god-fearing, and learned man, one able to serve God and man, be of use to himself and to others, and find his journey through life a blessed one.[101]

Saddened at first, and in the end embittered, Lorenz watched as Lorenz Jr. failed repeatedly at school and then, for over a decade thereafter, squandered his every other vocational opportunity. In an attempt to give him a fresh start, Lorenz outfitted the now sixteen-year-old with new clothes, books, and other necessities of student life, and sent him off in September 1573 with the merchants' convoy for schooling in Strasbourg, a venture he recalled with the comment: "Whether and to what extent he applied himself there, he knows best."[102] Two years would pass before Lorenz Jr. returned, a homecoming his father noted on the day of his arrival (August 20, 1575) not with thanksgiving but with sarcasm: "My son Lorenz Jr. returned from Strasbourg today knowing no more than he did when he left."[103] Still, two months later (October 25), he sent the boy off again, this time to the University of Geneva in the company of the son of Lorenz's own godfather,[104] a local youth Lorenz apparently hoped would be a steadying influence on Lorenz Jr.

After a year and a half in Geneva, Lorenz Jr., now almost nineteen, returned home in January 1577 to another joyless welcome at his father's house. Lorenz remembered the day (January 20) with the measured words:

> After having wasted money enough, [Lorenz Jr.] came home again as he had done from Strasbourg, now explaining to me that he did not want to go to school anymore.[105]

As tempted by this point as his father might conceivably have been simply to leave his son to his own devices, and as deserving of such a fate as Lorenz Jr. then arguably may have been, in sixteenth-century burgher society, families did not abandon children, least of all the eldest son.[106] Although sights were now lowered, parental efforts to find Lorenz Jr. a congenial alternative career redoubled. In May 1577, two months after his nineteenth birthday, again fully provisioned by his father, Lorenz Jr. was sent to Austria to work as a nobleman's stable groom.[107]

While the failings of sisters Anna and Margaretha may have distressed their father just as deeply and their successes pleased him just as much, measured purely by retrospective chronicle commentary, the fortunes of the girls preoccupied their father far less than those of their brothers. In November 1577, Margaretha, at fifteen, left home for the first time to enter domestic service in a local merchant's household.[108] She later (May 1586) married very well, especially in her father's eyes, as her husband was Philip Dietrich, chaplain of St. Lorenz's Church and the son of the late, locally renowned Lutheran reformer Veit Dietrich. And she further increased her father's pleasure by giving him four grandchildren before his death in 1594.[109] By contrast, eldest daughter Anna, apparently a sickly and unaccomplished girl who never married, goes completely unmentioned in the chronicle between 1570, when she was placed, at ten, with a new tutor, and 1593, when her death from dropsy is perfunctorily recorded.[110]

Lorenz Dürnhofer at forty-five, 1577. (Germanisches Nationalmuseum, Graphische Sammlung, Nr., Mp. 5940.)

Almost a year to the date of his departure for Austria (April 1578), Lorenz Jr. came home again to a now openly disparaging father:

My thoroughly spoiled junker, having had his fill of service and the horseman's life, as he had earlier tired of school, came home from Austria with no idea of what he wanted to do.[111]

Here the term "junker" is sarcastically used, suggesting behavior and character traits Lorenz associated with decadent court life and the idle rich—not the high compliment Christoph Scheurl intended when he bestowed the title on his toddling sons.[112] Lorenz was, however, more determined than ever to see Lorenz Jr. gainfully employed. While keeping his expectations realistically low, Lorenz sent him now to math and script master Adam Strobel, who a decade earlier had tutored his sisters. There, Lorenz Jr. acquired skills he needed not for an academic career but for decorative writing and bookkeeping, the work of a copyist or scribe. While perhaps a step down socially from his last venture—he was not now to be in the company of noblemen, albeit grooming their horses—the work of a scribe was a noble calling, and also one in which a diligent Lorenz Jr. could rise.

At the same time that Lorenz was swallowing this bitter pill, he was also finding new delight in the development of his eleventh child and second surviving son, the now six-and-a-half-year-old Leonhard, who had caught his father's eye at birth and continued to rekindle his pride in male progeny. On May 12, 1578, shortly after Lorenz Jr.'s unhappy return from Austria, Lorenz, with Leonhard in tow, had attended the marriage of his godfather's daughter (Magdalena Lantzinger). In recording the event, what stood out most in the father's mind was not the bridal pair, but "my little Leonhard, all dressed up for the occasion and walking behind the bridegroom,"[113] the most endearing comment on a child in the entire chronicle.

After Lorenz Jr. had acquired the skills of a scribe, his father, as loath as ever to permit a child's failing to suppress parental hope, sought aggressively to place him in the best possible circumstances. In September 1578, he traveled to Speyer "to search for a master for my eldest son," a search that ended at the doors of two officials on the imperial supreme court (*Kammergericht*), whom Lorenz Jr. began to serve successively in November,[114] a most promising clerkship for a disciplined and ambitious youth.

Five years would pass before Lorenz Jr. appeared again in the
family chronicle. In December 1583, Lorenz recorded his return
home and brought the chronicle up to date on his activities during
the five silent years. "As was his custom," the new entry began,
Lorenz Jr. had been unable to stay long in one place and so had soon
left Speyer for nearby Heidelberg, where he found work as a secretary to Count Christoph von Barby, apparently a position arranged
by his godparents, who had a connection with the count.[115] That
position, too, however, proved tedious for him, and, being homesick
as well, he began writing persistently to Nürnberg's city clerk
(Matthias Schiller) in search of a position in local city government. It
was in active pursuit of that goal that he now, at twenty-five, returned home[116] on the eve of the new year (December 30, 1583) to
beg his father's assistance.

Perhaps sensing a last chance to salvage his son's career and life,
Lorenz's response went beyond what even an endearing and successful son might at this point have expected. On New Year's Eve, the
day after Lorenz Jr.'s return, his father spent the entire day running
about the city in rain and snow, visiting the homes of all seven patricians on Nürnberg's all-powerful executive council (the *Septemvir*),
imploring each on his son's behalf.[117] Those efforts resulted in an
immediate traineeship for Lorenz Jr., [118] after which he was installed
in the corrector's office[119]—a lowly beginning, but also one from
which he could expect promotion to a higher position if he performed well. His father's concluding comment on the episode suggests that Lorenz Jr. neither appreciated the efforts made on his
behalf nor made the most of his new opportunity.

> How he thereafter rewarded me for this sincere fatherly advance-
> ment [of his career] and conducted himself in the office entrusted
> to him, he may answer in his own conscience.[120]

Confessional Games

The decade between 1573 and 1584 saw not only Lorenz's great-est parental challenge, but his rise and fall in ecclesiastical and city politics as well. As a member of the planning board for the new re-gional high school (Landeschule, collegium) in neighboring Altdorf, he had become a part of its administration as well. In 1573, he ac-companied the bürgermeister to the site, took part the following year in the hiring of the school's rector, and sat among the digni-taries on opening day (June 29, 1575), noting at the time in the pri-vacy of his chronicle that the rector's inaugural address was "nothing special."[121] Three years later, Emperor Rudolf II licensed the school as an "academy," thereby transforming it into a hybrid of gymnasium and junior university, now having the power to confer both bache-lor's and some master of philosophy degrees.[122]

In these years, educators, churchmen, and rulers throughout the German Lutheran world sought Lorenz's counsel. In August 1576, traveling with then Nürnberg church supervisor Hieronymus Paum-gartner, he attended the imperial diet in Regensburg. During the first two weeks of March 1579, he conferred with the authors of the Formula of Concord, under negotiation since 1577. Signed in 1580 by two-thirds of German Lutheran lands and cities (twenty-three princes, three of them electors; twenty-four counts; four barons; thirty-five imperial cities, and over eight thousand clerics), this landmark settlement of intra-Lutheran disputes was a moderate-conservative victory that left purists on both sides unhappy. How-ever, eleven principalities, including most of the south German imperial cities—Nürnberg standing out among them—did not sign.

The Formula tediously defined a middle Lutheran way and sharply distinguished Lutheran teaching from Calvinist. It rejected the extreme Flacian view that humankind was "utterly corrupted and dead toward good," while recognizing a certain natural orienta-tion to God and capacity for civil righteousness in all people—a po-sition congenial to Lorenz's faction. However, while disagreeing with those who compared humans to "logs or stones" in their dealings with God, the Formula still saw them playing a "merely passive" role in their conversion, turning to God only by the direct inspiration of the Holy Spirit—an emphasis Lorenz and other Philippists, eager to motivate laity, would have muted. From this it followed that good works did not aid and abet justification and salvation, which resulted solely from the imputation of "Christ's whole person, both as God and man" to the believer. The phrase "whole person" also targeted Calvinist Christological and Eucharistic teaching, which had attempted to protect Christ's divinity and majesty. According to that teaching, the risen Christ now sat at the hand of God in heaven, and thus could not be present in the Eucharist as the same person He was when He walked the earth in the first decades of the first Christian century.

This argument was ridiculed by the Genesio-Lutherans as the *extra-Calvinisticum* ("Calvin's little extra"), on the grounds that it portrayed Christ as now being permanently "outside" (*extra*) the world and the Sacrament—faith now able to welcome Him only partially, in a new spiritual, commemorative mode different from what He was when he appeared in the Incarnation. By contrast, the Formula of Concord had Christ miraculously appearing in the Eucharist just as He had been in the Incarnation, "the body and blood . . . truly and substantially present . . . together with bread and wine."[123]

With the Formula in place, Lorenz and the minority liberal faction he represented became more vulnerable than ever, even though Nürnberg sided at this time with the minority of Lutheran lands and cities refusing to sign the Formula. When, in 1583, Lorenz proposed to simplify the decor of the city churches by eliminating certain traditional paintings, icons, and sculptures, he ran afoul of both Lutheran tradition and the new orthodoxy, which was now more influential in the city. Majority Lutheran practice had long treated such decorations as benign and allowed them to remain in the churches, condemning the iconoclasm of spiritualists, Anabaptists, and Zwinglians. And the Formula also declared traditional images to be nonessential matters (*adiaphora*), over which Lutherans, unlike the sectarians and their Reformed Protestant rivals, need no longer quarrel and fight.[124]

To all appearances, Lorenz had conducted a quiet, successful campaign among his own parishioners and now wanted to preach

FATHERS AND SONS   253

publicly on the issue "images and idols" in the churches. The city council pulled him up short by asking that he first prepare a sermon on the subject for its own instruction, using the book of Ezekiel as his text. After reading that sermon and expressing no objections, the magistrates ruled that "now was not the time" to preach against images in the churches, evidently fearing open dissension among the city's rival clergy and congregations should Lorenz proceed. The decision angered Lorenz, who believed the council had acted both in error and against him personally.

> I asked them when the time to remove images *would* come, and Hans Welser [the council's spokesman] answered back that I had heard clearly what I had been told. And that was the end of a terribly important matter.[125]

In the same year (1583), the council instructed the city's pastors to resolve another divisive issue amicably and without public controversy—namely, the rite of exorcism. The majority of Lutherans, again following traditional practice, had kept the rite in the sacrament of baptism. The exorcism rite expressed an ancient Christian belief that infants, having been born into original sin and thus children of the devil, were as much in need of exorcism as they were of baptism—the former to release them from the grasp of the devil, the latter to annul the eternal penalty due them for the corporate sin of Adam and Eve. In his *Small Catechism* (1529), Martin Luther magnified baptism as an all-sufficient sacrament, "effecting forgiveness of sins, delivering from death and the devil, and granting eternal salvation to all who believe."[126] Reformed Protestants, by contrast, were more inclined to leave deliverance from sin, death, and the devil to eternal predestination, and did not attach it so strongly to the sacrament of baptism. Accordingly, they rejected the exorcism rite as unbiblical and papist, a point of view Nürnberg's Philippists shared.

Just how seriously this issue might be taken was illustrated when Elector Christian of Saxony (1586–1591) attempted to abolish the rite. In 1591, he had all reference to exorcism removed from the baptismal service of his newborn daughter, and a few months later banned it throughout his lands. His decision upset many, both theologians and laity alike, who feared its absence could jeopardize a newborn's salvation and might also spark iconoclasm among Lutherans. In the year of the elector's prohibition, a Dresden pastor reported a butcher's threat to split his head with a meat cleaver if he omitted the formula of exorcism from the baptism of his daughter at the court church[127]—an episode reminiscent, at the other end of the social and confessional spectrum, of Duke Georg of Saxony's refusal to be present in Nürnberg at the baptism of his godson because the new Lutheran rite eliminated the traditional chrism from the ceremony.[128]

Fortunately for the Lutheran majority in Saxony, Elector Christian died in September 1591, a few months after condemning the exorcism rite. His successor, Elector Christian II, not only restored it but banned all "crypto-Calvinism" from his realm as well. As for Nürnberg, the "amicable discussion" of the exorcism rite among the city's clergy, ordered by the council in 1583, must have been just that. Lorenz gives no indication that the issue ever involved the laity, and he blames "several hypocrites and mutineers [Genesio-Lutherans] (God forgive them)" for successfully obstructing a public debate.[129] Allowing the rite to remain an *adiaphorum*, something each congregation might or might not practice as sentiment dictated, was for the council the best possible resolution. However, for Lorenz, who had already lost on the issue of images, it was his second defeat of the year.

Leonhard and Wolf

In the 1570s and 1580s, Pastor Dürnhofer's second family continued to grow at the rate of one child every two years, making increasingly large demands on his time and support. Eight additional children arrived after 1573: Ursula (1573), Magdalena (1575), Wolfgang (1577), Paul (1579), Katharina (1580), Hans Martin (1582),

Maria (1584), and Georg Eberhardt (1586). However, only five of these survived beyond age twelve to join Leonhard, plague claiming Ursula at twelve and Hans Martin dying in the same year at three, while Georg Eberhardt, the last of Lorenz's twenty-three children, survived a mere three weeks.[130]

Of the six who beat death, it was the surviving twin and second son Leonhard who brought his father his greatest joy as a parent. After schooling at St. Giles's, where he received private instruction as well, Leonhard enrolled in the Altdorf Academy in October 1585, where, at eighteen, he took his bachelor's degree (December 1589), and three years later his master's (June 1592). Following a year of advanced study at Heidelberg, he returned to Altdorf to continue in his father's footsteps.[131] Not only did he succeed as a scholar where his elder half brother had failed, his hand, not Lorenz Jr.'s, would continue the family chronicle after their father became too weak to write.[132]

Lorenz's relationship to his third surviving son, the second Wolfgang, appears to have suffered from a shadow cast over them both by Lorenz's continuing painful memory of Lorenz Jr.'s poor academic performance. Placed on the same career track as his brothers, Wolfgang, at eight, joined Leonhard, at fourteen, in taking the entrance exam at Altdorf in September 1585[133]—Wolf for admission into his first year of Latin school at the gymnasium, Leonhard for his first year of higher education at the Academy. Two and a half years later (June 1588), while continuing his Latin studies, Wolf, like Lorenz Jr. before him, studied German script and math two hours a day with Adam Strobel.[134] That step had proven to be the end of Lorenz Jr.'s academic career, as it would eventually prove to be for Wolf's as well. Apparently his father suspected that Wolf was also not cut out for the scholar's life and decided to prepare him for an alternative career.

Lorenz's actions three years later confirm that to have been the case. In June 1591, he abruptly pulled Wolf out of Latin school and sent him to the French schoolmaster, explaining that Wolf "did not want to study."[135] Four months later, the chronicle announced the boy's beginning apprenticeship with one Eberhard Erdinger, apparently a Nürnberg merchant trading in France, to whom Wolf was contractually bound for four years with only room and board.[136] The suggestion is that Wolf, at thirteen, had been consigned to a practical vocation and would not get another chance at university study. His father's painful experience with his elder half brother may have shortened his patience with academic dawdling and poor progress, although Lorenz cannot be said to have acted precipitously in Wolf's case. While placed on a short leash much earlier than Lorenz Jr., Wolf was still allowed to continue a Latin education for almost three years before finally being apprenticed out.

Last Years

Virtually no information about Lorenz's professional life appears in the family chronicle after 1583. Beyond that date, announcements of births, marriages, and deaths within the family compete only with reports of failing health, as Lorenz's entries confine themselves to great physical pains and small family pleasures. Among the latter were the ten grandchildren Lorenz Jr. and Margaretha gave him before his death in 1594. Six of those grandchildren were Lorenz Jr.'s and four Margaretha's, and seven of them would outlive their grandfather, who recorded all of their births.[137]

Although Lorenz Jr. failed to rise as high as his father had hoped, he also did not fall as low as his father had feared. Not only did he remain gainfully employed at the city court, in January 1586, at the end of his first year on the job, he married the orphaned daughter of a deceased apothecary (Albrecht Pfister), a respectable match which, at this point, should have pleased his father.[138]

If there was a degree of reconciliation between father and son during these years, a wall still remained. That is made evident by Lorenz Jr.'s waiting until his second son (his fourth child) before bestowing the most esteemed family name—that borne by himself and his father—on a new generation. He named his first son Hans Hieronymus, two names not at all prominent in the family tree (there was only a half brother, Hans Martin, who died at three, and no Hieronymus in recent generations). Not only was the name "Lorenz" not given to Lorenz Jr.'s first son, but when he later did give that name to a second, it was as a middle, not a first name: "Wilibald Lorenz"—Wilibald being, like Hieryonymus, another distant family name.[139] Clearly, not all the wounds father and son inflicted on one another over many years could heal.

The maladies of middle age struck early in the sixteenth century, and Lorenz began recording his at age forty-three. Over the remaining nineteen years of his life, he was annually bedridden by gout, sciatica, tertian fever, St. Anthony's fire (erysipelas, a streptococcal infection), and/or kidney stones. In only three of the years between 1576 and 1594 did gout not afflict his feet, knees, and fingers for periods up to six weeks, on two occasions causing "pain so unholy" that he resigned his life.[140] After 1590, also the year of a great, damaging earthquake, kidney stones brought him still more exquisite pain. His one recorded public outing of that year—the annual school ceremonies at Altdorf in June—was completely overshadowed by a kidney stone attack on the return trip home, which he describes as leaving his bladder obstructed for a full thirty-six hours "until a very large stone suddenly shot forth."[141] His last full year of chronicle entries (1593) reported what was by then a typical large spectrum of annual ailments, interspersed with equally typical notices of children and grandchildren:

After lying near death with dropsy for four months, my eldest daughter from my first marriage, Anna, calmly and blessedly departed this world in the Lord Christ on the first day of March an hour after midday and was buried the following Sunday, March 4.

Since April 2, I have lain ill for five weeks with stone, sciatica, and gout.

Since June 8, I have for two weeks suffered unspeakable pain from gout in my right hand.

On August 4, my son Leonhard returned to Altdorf.

Since October 21, I have been laid low for two weeks with great pain in my back.

On November 14, around midnight, my daughter Margaretha

gave birth to her fourth child, this time a son, who was named
Leonhard.

From Advent to Christmas, I have lain ill with gout and every
other kind of inflammation.[142]

From the first Sunday after Easter 1594, Lorenz was permanently
bedridden. His last entry in the chronicle, on May 17, noted the
death of a brother-in-law. On July 18, nine days after blessing all his
children, he died. Two months later, Leonhard, henceforth the
keeper of the family record, made his first entry in the chronicle,
eleven concise lines describing his father's last acts and death throes
and noting that he had lived sixty-two years, five months, two
weeks, five days, and two hours.[143]

Family as Touchstone

Few fathers in the sixteenth century saw more of their children
live and die and succeed and fail than Lorenz Dürnhofer. Yet
throughout his long parenthood, this Lutheran father recorded none
of the morbid self-preoccupation and doubt in bad times that one
can find among contemporary Calvinist and Puritan divines, much
less the "anger at God" that Martin Luther expressed at the death of
his thirteen-year-old daughter.[144] Lorenz never interpreted the misfortune of his children as a divine judgment on them or himself.
Traumatic events within and outside the household triggered no
recorded grave suspicions about his own worthiness or God's good-
ness. When illness or death struck a wife or a child, he dwelt on the
circumstances of the victim and did not allow his own grief to take
center stage. Lorenz Jr.'s failure at school and subsequent squander-
ing of the opportunities his father painstakingly arranged for him
did not shake Lorenz's faith in God, salvation, or life's ultimate purpose. The boy's failings simply broke his heart and redoubled his efforts to help him succeed.

The result is a remarkably nonintrospective and nonjudgmental family history by a major cleric and theologian living in a tumultuous confessional age. Fifty years earlier Lorenz's compatriot Christoph Scheurl,[145] a still-believing Catholic, had also been whipped by family tragedy and Nürnberg's shifting religious currents. As the city's leading "liberal" Protestant, Lorenz was swept up in a conservative Lutheran tide that rolled over some of his cherished beliefs as uncaringly as the Reformation had earlier done to those of Scheurl. For both men, it was the strength and solace they derived from their family life, not the disputed doctrines of official religion in surrounding public institutions, that rescued them from their uncomfortable ecclesio-political worlds. Neither Scheurl the moderate Catholic nor Dürnhofer the liberal Lutheran questioned the righteousness of God or lost his personal faith when a family member died, a plague or an accident struck from the blue, a child failed to become all he or she might, or his professional career was disrupted or curtailed by higher authority.

Both men embraced reigning public institutions where those institutions strengthened their families' own regimens for protecting, socializing, and training their children. Lorenz patronized the city's gymnasium and academy in Altdorf all his life. After ministering midwives, priests, wet nurses, nannies, and physicians, the most frequent visitors to the Dürnhofer and Scheurl households were local tutors, and the institutions outside the home most often visited by their children were church schools. Otherwise, the church's creeds and the city council's decrees were not the final rules by which they lived.

CONCLUSION

I N PREMODERN SOCIETIES, THE YOUNG WERE REARED ON PRIN-ciples more modest and pragmatic than the high ideals of individualism and egalitarianism that grip much of the modern world today. Before 1700, such ideals were looked on as threats to what security a household might possess and to any lasting moral or political progress a society might make. Historically, the family has been at the core of the discipline that holds societies together; there, in home and household, civilization has made its stand against everything man and nature might devise against it. In that task, two overriding concerns have preoccupied parents: the physical safety of their children and their preparation for a vocation that might assure them an independent life. When offspring have remained healthy and become self-supporting, parents and society have counted themselves blessed, for therein lay both the continuance of their world and the promise of a new one.

To such seemingly humble ends, parents in preindustrial societies infused the years of childhood and adolescence with what was deemed to be the received wisdom of the ages: cooperate with and respect others, heed manifest authority, patiently acquire work habits early in life, and rely on skills and deeds rather than ideals and words to get ahead. That advice was also delivered to the young with rare contradiction by reigning political, educational, and religious institutions, which shared it uncritically with the family.

Compared to the high personal and civic goals often urged upon youths departing home in late twentieth-century America, such advice not only seems self-evident and unchallenging, it is also filled with disturbing talk about restraint and self-effacement: knowing one's place, not rocking the boat, playing the cards life has dealt one, turning the other cheek, going the extra mile—all clichés that suggest docility and subservience rather than heroic self-affirmation and the righting of social ills and injustice. However, like the preindustrial family we have found to be richly complex beyond its seeming simplicity, such advice upon closer examination also reveals itself to be wise beyond its modesty.

Consider the following formula for true manhood, written in 1539, and reputedly the most detailed surviving instruction of its kind in sixteenth-century Germany.[1] Although intended for a son, the virtues here portrayed were deemed no less appropriate for daughters, nor were they any less often conveyed to them by contemporary fathers.[2] The advice offered here is that of an Augsburg merchant to his fourteen-year-old son on the occasion of the latter's departure from home to begin a merchant apprenticeship three hundred miles away in Lyons, an outpost of his father's business. The father's first counsel was obedience and loyalty to God and parents.

> Dear son Christoph, may almighty God grant you good fortune and grace . . . so that you may live according to His will and remain true to the favor and love of your father and mother. . . . Attend the religious services in the land where you will be, as other devout and honorable people there do. Argue neither a little nor a lot over any matter of faith, for that will only put you at a disadvantage and may also endanger your life. . . .

Although a Lutheran, young Christoph was expected to join in the religious services of then-Catholic Lyons, and in all other respects follow the example of devout people there. No suggestion is made that he ignore or challenge the religion of the new society; ac-

commodation to the host culture was both a courtesy appropriate to
the boy's age and essential to his safety and success. Internally he
might believe and think otherwise, but he was not in Lyons to teach
the natives the error of their ways, much less to invite a martyr's
death by extolling the superiority of his own beliefs.[3] Local Catholic
services also provided an opportunity to improve his French and
Latin while making new acquaintances who might contribute to his
comfort and assist his progress. In a word, he was to do in Lyons as
the Lyonnaise.

His father arranged in advance for business associates there to
act in loco parentis. They were to place him with an appropriate master, who would prepare him for his father's business. Meanwhile,
Christoph was expected to show them the same respect and obedience as that due his parents. "Try your best to do what you are told,"
the father urges, "and when you are at last with your master, do
what he and his wife tell you, and do so with the utmost diligence,
always willingly and obediently."

Maintaining the appearance of honesty and good character was
the father's second admonition, again recommended as much for its
prophylactic qualities as for its intrinsic value.

> Above all else, take care not to lie or steal. Should you find your-
> self alone with the merchants' money or have their wares at hand,
> do not take anything. Often money or something else is intention-
> ally left lying about as a test for one in your position. So as dear to
> you as your life and my favor are . . . be false to no one about any-
> thing. . . . And do not let your lord's other servants or maids . . .
> entice you to steal from his house, be it food, drink, or anything
> else . . . for this may bring you great misfortune. They will tempt
> one [such as you] to see if he will let himself be led astray.
>   Be always ready and willing with others and not argumenta-
> tive. And do not give up too soon when someone [in authority]
> reproaches you, for it is done for your own good.

The father's third counsel was the use of common sense in matters of physical safety, reveling, and hygiene. Among the elective

vices of the age, alcoholism, then endemic in Germany[4] and comparable to present-day substance abuse, worried this father most.

> When bathing or swimming, avoid the great, threatening waters
> of the Soane and the Rhone [which meet in Lyons] . . . for many a
> good fellow has drowned there. . . . Avoid strong drink by mixing
> a lot of water in with your wine. Resolve not to get drunk either
> during your journey or after your arrival. . . . Keep yourself and
> your clothes clean and . . . your feet warm and dry; the world is
> an unholy bath and dry feet make you less vulnerable to diseases
> of the foot. And do not go about the streets at night unless your
> master sends you out, for he will then arrange that you may go in
> safety. . . .

The father wanted his son's maturation to be steady and uninter-
rupted, his eyes on the future, so that he might acquire the discipline
and vocational skills needed for not yet contemplated challenges
and responsibilities.

> Concentrate on your needs . . . and do not spend money need-
> lessly, for when you are grown and older, you will want and need
> it. . . . Great expenditures are now being made on your behalf,
> and they will also be made on behalf of your siblings, so that after
> my death, you will have all the less. Therefore . . . plan now to be
> self-supporting, and consider also how you might put yourself in a
> position to help the children of your brothers and sisters as well.[5]

The father provided a laundry list of temptations and bad habits
known to corrupt the young and divert them from carefully laid career paths.

> Avoid gambling, whoring, partying, cursing, and other bad asso-
> ciations and vices. Put yourself in the company of honest people
> whom you know to be good and accomplished and from whom
> you can learn good and useful things. When there is time, be sure

to practice your writing and math, so that . . . you learn both all
the better.

The father's fifth counsel expressed a concern that his son not fall
in love and marry rashly, also that he beware of sexual temptation
and the terrible diseases that can afflict those who succumb to it.

Take care in your innocence that you do not let yourself be talked
into a marriage on your own, or become entrapped [by some
woman]. Also, stay away from dishonest women, so that you do
not get the pox [syphilis] and the other maladies that flow from
such women.[6]

Behind these words was a father's fear that his son, now only fourteen, might incautiously enter, or be tricked into, a promise of marriage without benefit of prior parental advice and consent, thereby
derailing his career, wrecking his life, and shaming his family. Enter-
prisingly extending its authority over the enormous world of youthful sexuality and family morality, the Church had recognized the
validity of private vows between youths of canonical age (twelve for
women, fourteen for men) since the twelfth century. Not a few
youths took advantage of this option to escape premodern society's
rigid sexual rules, resulting often in lawsuits by pregnant women
against men who had no recollection of having promised marriage.
Sometimes the evidence was sufficient to enforce a marriage, which
was apparently this father's fear should his son be too casual or
headstrong in matters of the heart. And no more than he wanted
him to become trapped in an immature marriage did he want him to
fall prey to the new, barely treatable venereal disease of syphilis, then
reaching epidemic proportions in parts of western Europe.[7]

The father's final counsel to his son was also one a modern parent
can relate to: Don't forget us!

Write often to me and your mother, and let me know what kind
of master you have, what his name is, what he does, how many
servants he has, and how he treats you.

Sixteenth-century parents deemed such counsel realistic, not di-
dactic. Faith and prayer, loyalty and obedience, honesty and good
character, vigilance and common sense, clear life goals, self-reliance,
mature marriages, and remembrance of one's origins—those were
the eternal cornerstones of personal maturation and societal success.
Parents and others who stood *in loco parentis* also recognized the
dangers posed to the young by their own carefully cultivated consciences, observing with fright the symbiotic relationship between
the power of false prophets and the naïveté of their followers. The
same inner resources that helped the young maintain their self-
esteem and get ahead in life also made them vulnerable to the charms
and deceits of the gurus and hucksters operating early modern
Europe's great midway. For that reason, parents and educators urged
the young to heed as earnestly the lessons of their shortcomings and
failings as they did those of their successes and victories.

In the annals of advice to the young, the adult world has dwelled
historically on the infrastructure of life. The seemingly quaint and
obvious Old World instructions on diet and hygiene, discipline
and obedience, frugality and moderation, deference and discretion,
and devotion and gratitude have been viewed down to the present
day as part of the necessary maintenance of viable, reliable human
beings. Here was the commonsense wisdom of the ages, the enduring rules of human nature and nurture, a true description of the way
human life has been and must always be conducted if people are to
be of use to themselves and to others, and societies to survive and
succeed.

If families in the past appear to have remained intact better than
they do today—surviving high mortality rates more successfully
than modern families do high divorce rates, and managing to have
and to keep their children within the family at a time when most
children lived at home for much shorter periods—several factors
may explain why they were able to do so.

There was, first, the greater cohesion of family members in a
world without social security insurance, mutual funds, and elec-
tronic media. Until recent times, parents depended on successful
children for their support and well-being in old age. Widowed
mothers and younger siblings invested heavily in the careers of elder

males, in whom a sense of responsibility to family was drilled early and deeply.[8] Inheritance laws also assisted by protecting new generations from the self-indulgence of older ones.[9]

A second factor was the comparative absence of a viable, alternative true culture of youth for which the young might defy the parental world and flee to one of their own. For all the early departures from home, the haunts where the young might briefly unfurl their own banners, the protests against lapses in the culture and faith of their parents, and the covert sex and clandestine marriages, teenagers in the past grew up self-consciously in their parents' world and knew early that they were destined for it.

Thirdly, save for not infrequent periods of war and plague, families in the past were not so easily bullied by an official outside world. Not only was there comparatively scant competition from an independent culture of youth, but the state, the Church, and mass culture also could not undermine the life of the family. As intrusive as each might from time to time be, families managed to make their peace with them, often on favorable terms.[10] More so than today, familial experience and activity were the stuff of everyday life and the internal rule and logic of the household profoundly formative forces in a person's life until ten or twelve years of age. Before a child became a self-conscious political, social, and religious creature, he or she was first a carefully molded familial being, shaped by parents and a household that were peculiarly one's own. Subsequent integration into the outside world also occurred with continuing family influence and oversight. Parents viewed and monitored their children's service, apprenticeship, and schooling in the homes, shops, and institutions of new masters and mistresses as consistent, if different, extensions of the original familial experience.

Finally, more so than today, the family was a major player in the larger world around it. For most of its history, it supported, educated, blessed, and entertained itself with minimal external instruction and coercion. Whatever obeisance it gave to the state, the Church, and society at large, it did not do so as a docile "farm team" for any one of them, despite the efforts of larger bodies and institutions to render it such.[11] The family pursued its own organizational, moral, and spiritual regimens, willingly interacting with and integrating itself into the polities, societies, and cultures that surrounded it, as the latter aided and abetted the fulfillment of its own needs and the realization of its own goals. In this respect, the family was both a conformist and its own boss.

In the Nürnberg this book has visited, magistrates and clergy came readily to an obliging, yet independent home. When a couple became formally engaged, a city official might as often as not notarize the marriage contract in one or the other family's house.[12] When a child was baptized, the priest or a steward performed the sacrament ideally on the day of the birth in the delivery room at home. City hall and parish church were often the last places to be visited by both newlyweds and newborns, although those visits were sincerely desired and most dutifully made.

Also, all sides acknowledged something that is still true today where families remain together and in control of their own lives: no matter how united and wholesome—or divided and dysfunctional— a family may be, a person is first and foremost the product of it, regardless of how deeply state, Church, and mass society may subsequently penetrate his or her life. Past generations have recognized a second truism about the family: when parents neglect or lose control of their children, denying them the familial support they need in their formative years, the alternative higher institutions are poor substitutes. The problem with being raised by a village, local or global, is that there are a lot more idiots there than in the average family household.

A final advantage families in the past arguably had over their modern counterparts is one that might more easily be replicated today: a realistic consensus on the imperatives and goals of child rearing. If by some magical means of time travel, the parents, guardians, and educators who have spoken in the pages of this book could attend a commencement address at a modern American college or university, most would likely find the missions assigned the young in late twentieth-century America grandiose beyond youth's ability and decry those who tantalize our children with pipe dreams. As the history of medieval religious crusades, early modern colonial missions, and twentieth-century nationalist movements make clear, a fine line separates presumptuous idealism from holocaust in every age and culture.[13] For every generation, the greater challenge is not to teach what is abstractly good and right, but to grasp the historically possible, to recognize and pursue ideals that are achievable at a particular point in time.[14]

Historically, parents and societies have frowned on unrealistic expectations of the young and the alternately permissive and overbearing child-rearing practices that accompany them. The fear has been that the young would not be properly equipped to tackle life's less glamorous but more essential tasks, or to fulfill society's more modest yet realistic dreams, both of which are vital to individual souls and the body politic. When the eyes are on a prize that is clearly unattainable, the steadier the gaze the deeper the dejection, embitterment, and incivility when one's reach, as it must, proves to exceed its grasp.

However, what would most disturb visiting parents from the past is the folly of exhorting the young to right a world before they have first discovered and mastered themselves. Unlike a projected, large-scale remodeling of human nature and society, plain mastery of useful work skills and the sound building of individual character are the really achievable parental tasks and the ones most essential to society as well. Devotion to such finite goals gives the young a clear and present role in the fulfillment of society's immediate needs and the realization of its possible dreams, while at the same time sparing them a gratuitous experience of abject defeat.

Societies, like children, develop and renew themselves in small, steady, practical steps, and they are only as smart and foresightful, disciplined and productive, secure and charitable as their individual members prove to be to themselves and to others. To this end, the family has historically subjected its offspring to high physical, educational, moral, and spiritual demands, sparing them neither swift punishment nor stubborn love. It has introduced its children as honestly to the dark side of human nature as to its bright, while at the same time making clear society's limited ability to achieve all that is good and right. By such rude awakenings, the family of the past did not intend to deny the young their dreams, only to save them from nightmares.

NOTES

INTRODUCTION

1. See the discussion of Michael Anderson, *Approaches to the History of the Western Family, 1500–1914* (Cambridge, 1994), especially chapter 3, which discusses the "sentiments approach" represented by Philippe Ariès, Edward Shorter, Jean-Louis Flandrin, and Laurence Stone; Michael Mitteraurer and Reinhard Sieder, *The European Family: Patriarchy to Partnership from the Middle Ages to the Present*, trans. K. Oosterven and M. Hörzinger (Chicago, 1983; German, 1970). Many of these arguments trace themselves back to Ariès's famous, and more cautious, study of family and childhood under the Old Regime: *L'enfant et la vie familiale sous l'ancien regime* (1960); English: *Centuries of Childhood: A Social History of Family Life,* trans. Robert Baldick (New York, 1962).

2. Especially, Georg Steinhausen, *Geschichte des deutschen Briefes*, vols. 1 and 2 (1898, 1891); Erich Maschke, *Die Familie in der deutschen Stadt des späten Mittelalters* (Heidelberg, 1980); Klaus Arnold, *Kind und Gesellschaft in Mittelalter und Renaissance* (Paderborn, 1980); Mathias Beer, *Eltern und Kinder des späten Mittelalters in ihren Briefen. Familienleben in der Stadt des Spätmittelalters und der frühen Neuzeit mit bes. Berücksichtigung Nürnbergs* (1400–1550) (Nürnberg, 1990); Theodore Brüggermann, *Handbuch zur Kinder- und Jugendliteratur: Von Beginn des Buchdrucks bis 1570* (Stuttgart, 1986); and Ulrich Herrmann, et al.,

Bibliographie zur Geschichte der Kindheit, Jugend und Familie (Munich, 1980).

3. Gerhard Pfeiffer, et al., eds., *Geschichte Nürnbergs in Bilddokumenten* (Munich, 1970), p. 24.

4. Ibid., pp. 58, 62; Gerald Strauss, *Nuremberg in the Sixteenth Century* (New York, 1966), pp. 130–131.

5. Eugen Kusch, *Nürnberg. Lebensbild einer Stadt* (Nürnberg, 1951), pp. 280–81 passim.

6. See chapter 2; Lewis W. Spitz, *The Religious Renaissance of the German Humanists* (Cambridge, Mass., 1963), pp. 156, 177–178.

7. Ibid., p. 156.

8. That school would later move to neighboring Altdorf and quickly evolve into an academy and eventually a university.

9. J. Kamann, "Zwei Gastmähler bei Dr. Christoph Scheurl, 1525 u. 1528," *Anzeiger für Kunde der deutschen Vorzeit* 29 (1882), pp. 333–336.

10. Kusch, *Nürnberg*, p. 364; William Smith, "A Description of the cittie of Noremberg . . . 1594 [English-German]," trans. William Roach, *Mitteilungen des Vereins für die Geschichte der Stadt Nürnberg* [henceforth, *MVGN*] 48 (1958), pp. 214, 222.

11. See the examples in Steven Ozment, *Three Behaim Boys: Growing Up in Early Modern Germany* (New Haven, 1990).

CHAPTER 1

1. Paul Behaim II's teenage years as a student in Italy is the subject of chapter 3.

2. Johann Gottfried Biedermann, *Geschlechtsregister des Hochadelichen Patriciats zu Nürnberg* (Nürnberg, 1982), Table 9. In addition to Biedermann, my summary of Lucas's life draws on Anton Ernstberger's introduction to his edition of Lucas's letters: "Liebesbriefe Lukas Friedrich Behaims an seine Braut Anna Maria Pfinzing 1612–1613," *MVGN* 44 (1953), pp. 317–326.

3. Rudolf Endres, "Zur Einwohnerzahl und Bevölkerungsstruktur Nürnberg im 15./16. Jahrhundert," *MVGN* 57 (1970): pp. 256–257, 259; Steven Ozment, ed., *Three Behaim Boys*, pp. 2–6; Strauss, *Nuremberg in the Sixteenth Century*, pp. 147–149.

4. Endres, "Zur Einwohnerzahl," pp. 257–259; Johann F. Roth, *Lebensbeschreibungen und Nachrichten von merkwürdigen Nürnbergern und Nürnbergerinnen aus allen Standen*, vol. 2 (Nürnberg, 1796), pp. 267–283.

5. Endres, "Zur Einwohnerzahl," p. 263; Gustav Aubin, "Bartholomäus

Viatis. Ein Nürnberger Grosskaufmann vor dem Dreissigjährigen Kriege," *Vierteljahrschrift für Sozial- und Wirtschaftsgeschichte* 33 (1940), pp. 145–157.

6. *Streit und Vergleich wegen der Vormundschaft über den Anteil des Lucas Friedrich Behaim an der Ursula Sitzingerischen Erbschaft* (mines in Tyrol and Steiermark), 1591, 1601–1608), described in *Archiv Abt. B, Hist. Archiv: Familien Behaim v. Schwarzbach*, Teil 2 (Stadtarchiv Nürnberg), p. 81.

7. Compare the clauses for reversion of maternal property and wealth to the family of the deceased spouse in the late fifteenth-century marriage contract of Anna Büschler's parents. Steven Ozment, *The Bürgermeister's Daughter: Scandal in a Sixteenth Century German Town* (New York, 1996), pp. 131–133.

8. *Eigenhändige Aufzeichungen des Lucas Friederich Behaim . . . (1587–1622)*, (Stadtarchiv Nürnberg E 11/2, 710), p. 4b.

9. On his role as guardian to Stephan Carl (1612–1638), the eldest child of Paul Behaim II's third marriage, see Ozment, *Three Behaim Boys*, pp. 162–163 passim.

10. On the school's founding and development into an academy and a university, see pp. 248–249.

11. Ernstberger, "Liebesbriefe," pp. 321–22; Biedermann, *Geschlechtsregister*, Table 9. Compare his uncle Friedrich's experience at Altdorf between 1578 and 1581 in Ozment, *Three Behaim Boys*, pp. 93–160. On Lucas's patronage of music at the academy: Heinz Zimtauer, "Lukas Friedrich Behaim, der Nürnberger Musikherr des Frühbarok," *MVGN* 50 (1960): pp. 330–351.

12. Anton Ernstberger, "Nürnberger Patrizier- und Geschlectersöhne auf ihrer Bildungsreise durch Frankreich 1608–1610," *MVGN* 43 (1952), note 8.

13. Maria Magdalena Baier's mother was a Paumgartner from Holenstein, as was Paul Behaim's second wife Rosina. See Biedermann, *Geschlechtsregister*, Table 9. Given their relationship, one might ask if the deceased wife had recommended the new wife, something not unheard of in sixteenth-century Nürnberg. When Nürnberg *Schreiber* Hieronymus Köler married his second wife (Birgida Waldstromer) within two months of the death of his first (Barbara Münsterer, Philip Melanchthon's sister-in-law) after a three-year marriage, he did so not only with the latter's blessing, but at her explicit, persistent request. See Hannah S.M. Amburger, ed., "Die Familiengeschichte der Köler. Ein Beitrag zu Autobiographie des 16. Jahrhunderts, *MVGN* 30 (1931), pp. 204–272, 259–260.

14. Ernstberger, "Liebesbriefe," pp. 323–25.
15. Hajo Holborn, *A History of Germany: The Reformation* (New York, 1961), pp. 240, 243, 284–285.
16. Ibid., pp. 284, 288–291.
17. Ibid., pp. 292–296, 302, 304, 313.
18. Ludwig Rötel, *Alt Nürnberg. Geschichte einer deutschen Stadt* (Nürnberg, 1895), p. 596.
19. Ernstberger, "Liebesbriefe," pp. 324–325. See cover illustration. The knighting is reproduced and discussed by Andreas Tacke, *Die Gemälde des 17. Jahrhunderts in Germanischen Nationalmuseum. Bestandskatalog* (Mainz, 1995), pp. 378–379.
20. Rötel, *Alt Nürnberg*, p. 596.
21. "Durch Wohlverhalten in Kriegswesen oder durch gute und glückliche Heirat." Theodor Hampe, "Die Reise des jungen Nürnberger Patriziersohnes Georg Hieronymus Behaim an den Hof des Fürsten Bethlen Gabor von Siebenbürgen (1614)," *MVGN* 31 (1933), pp. 143, 153.
22. Maria Magdalena, 16, married in June, and Rosina, 18, in October. Biedermann, *Geschlechtsregister*, Table 9.
23. Hampe, "Die Reise . . . George Hieronymus Behaim," (Dec. 1, 1614), p. 157.
24. Ibid. (Dec. 2 and 6, 1614), pp. 157–158.
25. Ibid. (Feb. 11, 1615), p. 159.
26. Ibid. (Mar. 18, 1615), p. 161.
27. Ibid.; also Biedermann, *Geschlechtsregister*, Table 9.
28. Ernst Gagel, *Der Kartograph der Reichsstadt Nürnberg (1554–1599)* (Hersbruck, 1957), pp. 1–4; F. Schnelbögl, "Paul Pfinzing als Kaufmann," *MVGN* 45 (1954), p. 378; Biedermann, *Geschlechtsregister*, Table 405.
29. Katharina (1585–1637), Maria (1589–1563), Paul Jr. (1588–1631), and Helena (1590–1660). A fifth sibling, Esther (1599–1622), the only surviving child from Paul Pfinzing's three-year second marriage to Anna Pömer, would have remained with her mother.
30. Ernstberger, "Liebesbriefe," p. 327.
31. The comment appears in a postscript to a letter written to Lucas at the conclusion of the latter's apprenticeship in Kitzbühl (May 1613). In a brief summary of recent events at home involving relatives and friends, the senior Behaim states matter-of-factly: "Your old match (*heirat*) Judith Finold today celebrated her marriage (*handschlag*) to Sigmund Bonifacius Ebner, the junior supervisor in Gostenhof." Paul Behaim to Lucas, May 2, 1613 (Behaim-Archiv, Fasz. 154). Bride-

groom Ebner was the grandson of Hieronymus and Helena Ebner, Christoph Scheurl's foster parents at his marriage, suggesting that his bride (Judith) was of sufficient substance not to have been merely one of Lucas's "flings." On the Ebners, see Biedermann, *Geschlechtsregister*, Table 27.

32. See pp. 23–25.
33. The extensive litigation occasioned by such vows makes it clear that unprincipled men used false promises of marriage to have their way with women. On Lucas's and Anna Maria's private vows, see Ernstberger, "Liebesbriefe," p. 327.
34. "Wohl nicht immer nur platonisch erlebt hatte," according to editor Ernstberger, in "Liebesbriefe," p. 327, n. 17. See below, pp. 22–23.
35. See n. 61.
36. See n. 141.
37. The family also imported lard from the Tyrol and exported grain to it. Ernstberger, "Liebesbriefe," p. 328.
38. *Eigenhändige Aufzeichnungen*, p. 2b.
39. Biedermann, *Geschlechtsregister*, Table 327.
40. *Eigenhändige Aufzeichnungen*, p. 4a.
41. This is Ernstberger's judgment, which attributes Lucas's talent for writing love letters to a credible combination of "faith and longing." "Liebesbriefe," pp. 328–329.
42. In letter of Jan. 14, 1613, below, n. 74.
43. *Factor*, his father's agent in Kitzbühl.
44. "Ehliche Verlöbnis."
45. "Mürlein," Anna Maria's younger sister Helena, who married Johann Hieronymus Mürr in September 1608. Biedermann, *Geschlechtsregister*, Table 412; Ernstberger, "Liebesbriefe," p. 369, n. 27.
46. Suspecting a romance and possible intimacy, her siblings had evidently teased Anna Maria about her relationship with Lucas even before secret vows had been exchanged. Now having done so, she could more easily take such teasing in stride.
47. Ernstberger, "Liebesbriefe" (Dec. 1, 1612), p. 330–333.
48. Ibid. (Dec. 17, 1612), p. 333.
49. The personal prayer was not recorded in his draft book. The second Lutheran prayer is identified as "no. 12" in the Lutheran *Eh[e]büchlein*, described below, n. 110.
50. "Zu zeiten gar zu geschämig und gewissenhaft." Ernstberger, "Liebesbriefe" (Dec. 17, 1612), p. 334. As a general rule in this and subsequent chapters, I cite the original German from an available modern edition only when a passage or turn of phrase is of particular interest

or difficulty, or when the quotation significantly supplements the text.
However, in most instances when I cite an unedited manuscript, I
preserve the original text in the notes.

51. "Gestalt." Ibid.
52. Ibid.
53. Katharina (née Pfinzing) Imhof (1585–1637), then married to Jakob
    Imhof, the first of her three husbands.
54. Johannes Schröder was pastor of St. Lorenz's from 1611–1621. See
    Ernstberger, "Liebesbriefe" (Apr. 12, 1613), pp. 366, 370, n. 52.
    "Knebelspiess" (cudgel) can also mean a stick of wood used to wind a
    person's hair in punishment or torture; also a stick suspended on a
    rope, on which criminals sat as they were lowered into their prison
    cells. See *Matthias Lexers Mittelhochdeutsches Taschenwörterbuch*, 23rd
    ed. (Stuttgart, 1966), p. 111.
55. Ernstberger, "Liebesbriefe" (Apr. 12, 1613), p. 366; cf. ibid. (Dec. 17,
    1612), p. 335.
56. Ibid. (Dec. 31, 1612), pp. 335–336.
57. That is, clandestinely; not yet by law. Ibid., p. 336.
58. "Jfrgesell." *Eigenhändige Aufzeichnungen*, p. 4a.
59. Albrecht to Lucas, Jan. 29, 1613 (Behaim Archiv, Fasz. 154); see Bie-
    dermann, Table 8.
60. The reference is to Lucas's and Anna Maria's private vows.
61. ". . . Darauss ich . . . die garn guete Bewilligung deinem lieben An-
    nelein das feüer auss dem arsch zublasen/vernomen/welches ich
    auch warlich hertzlich gern thun wolte wofern ich dessen erlaubnus
    von meiner lieben jungenfrauen haben könte/dan ich vermeint
    solches nicht füglicher geschehen könte als so ich ihr mein selbst
    gewachenes Rohr am bauch vorn hienein steckete und darmit dapfer
    hienein bliese so wirden alsodan die Kolen und übrige hitz zum hin-
    dern hienauss fahren/so dir nun solches mein Rath gefellig kanstu
    leichtlich durch ein schreiben solches bei meiner jungenfrauen auss-
    bitten/dan wofarn [?] ich solches ohne ihr vorwissen thete würdt war-
    lich die suppen sauer und die gueten wort gar theuer werden. Hab
    auch gern gehoert das dir dein pimp [pimmel] so sehr steht und alle
    tag dein erster Wecker seie/welche fröliche zeitung ich dan den sohn-
    tag capis casarij/solches deinem liebsten Annelein zuverkünden und
    sie darmit zutrösten und zu einer gernigen gedult zuwisen. . . ." Al-
    brecht to Lucas, Jan. 29, 1613 (Behaim Archiv, Fasz. 154).
62. Ernstberger, "Liebesbriefe" (Dec. 31, 1612), pp. 336–337.
63. Biedermann, *Geschlechtsregister*, Table 245.
64. Ernstberger, "Liebesbriefe" (Dec. 31, 1612), p. 337.

65. Ibid., p. 337.
66. Ibid. (Jan. 23/24, 1613), p. 343; on dating this letter, see ibid., p. 370, nn. 39, 40.
67. "Weiln ich aber allzeit an ihme vermerket, dass er sowohl Euren Herrn Vettern Jörg Pfintzing, wegen Eurer und Eurer Geschwistert, als auch, doch in Vertrauen, Euer Schwester Sebastian Imhoff wegen ihrer Stiefkinder und vielleicht auch, dass sie ihn hat durch den Korb fallen lassen, niemals aufs beste gewogen gewest, wunderts mich so sehr nicht, dass er sich dieser Zeit, noch vor unserer Zusagung, ihrer äussert, weil ers auch sonderlich in seinem Sinn so gar heimblich halten will, dass es auch der Zehent nicht vermerken soll." Ibid. (Jan. 23/24, 1613), p. 343.
68. Ibid. p. 370, n. 41; see also Biedermann, *Geschlechtsregister*, Table 9.
69. Katharina married Sebastian in November 1612, eighteen months after Paul Behaim married Maria Magdalena Baier.
70. Ernstberger, "Liebesbriefe" (Jan. 23/24, 1613), p. 344.
71. Ibid. He apparently meant in his adult life.
72. Biedermann, *Geschlechtsregister*, Table 412.
73. Ernstberger, "Liebesbriefe" (Dec. 31, 1612), p. 338.
74. Ibid. (Jan. 14, 1613), p. 339.
75. Ibid., p. 340.
76. "Beständig bis in unser Ruhebettlein sollten beisammen sein, wohnen und bleiben können . . . in unsern züchtigen Ehebett." Ibid., 341. This is an apparent allusion to the Lutheran description of marriage as "the only chastity," the marriage bed being the one place where sexual relations are purposeful and righteous—a traditional point of view that Luther heightened by making it the "only" chastity. On Lutheran marriage, see Ozment, *When Fathers Ruled*, pp. 2–49.
77. Ernstberger, "Liebesbriefe" (Jan. 14, 1613), pp. 341–342.
78. Ibid., p. 344.
79. iIbid., p. 345.
80. Ibid.
81. On the dramatis personae of the Pühlersee gathering, see Lucas's account in the preserved drafts of letters to Aunt Löffelholz. Lucas to Frau Wolf (Maria) Löffelholz, Feb. 1, 1613, pp. 1a–5a; Mar. 15, 1613, pp. 3a–5a (Behaim Archiv, Fasz. 151).
82. Ernstberger, "Liebesbriefe" (Jan. 23/24, 1613), p. 345.
83. "Das Jungfrau-Probieren von ihme zu lernen." Ibid.
84. Ibid.
85. In early February, Lucas wrote two letters five days apart, which Ernstberger describes as versions of the same letter. Skeptical that it

could be known which was finally mailed, or whether both were sent on the different dates indicated (February 1 and 5), he let both stand in his edition. Ibid., p. 370, n. 45. Because the second ("alio modo") conveys new information obtained by Lucas since having written the first, I discuss the two letters together as if they were one.

86. Ibid. (Feb. 1, 1613), p. 346.

87. Ibid. (Feb. 15, 1613), p. 355.

88. This assurance is repeated in the second letter. Ibid. (Feb. 1, Feb. 5, 1613), pp. 346, 350.

89. "Dass Ihr solche Eure schöne Haar auf meinen platteten Peterskopf hättet setzen und machen können, als eine solche Hatschnur, die an ihr selbst schön ist, damit zu zieren." Ibid. (Feb. 1, 1613), p. 347.

90. Ibid.

91. Ibid.

92. Lucas to Wolf Löffelholz, March 15, 1613. (Behaim Archiv, Fasz. 151), pp. 6a–b: "Diese vergangene Charwoche vest die Sehnsucht so hart ist ankommen/und laider von tag zu tag also zu und uber handt nimbt also das ich nit weiss/was ich darfür brauchen soll. Wie man mir aber räth/soll auf St. Annaberg ein Krautlein sehn so Annalein genandt/welches mir meines doctors mainung nach/gar wolfügn solte/und weil mir so starckg darzu gerathen wirdt will ich wills Gott künfftige Pfingsten ein raiss dahin thun/dasselbig nach gebür zugebrauchen und zu sehen wie es mir bekommen mag . . . Ferners so dankhe ich auch/Gott von hertzen das er mich seidher vor einen Tyrolischen kropf so gnediglich behutet hat/unangesehen das ich allerlei nudl und nackhn gessn/alss schmaltz nudl/dempf nudl/geschnitten nudl/aijr nudl, schabnplatl und sotz kuchlein/hab aber niemals kein wasser drein getrunkhen/sondern dasselb allezeit geflohen wie den Teufel/weil mir . . . so grosse gefahr drauf gestandten/das man mir den kauf mit dem Annelein wider wolle aufsagen wo ich einen kropf mit hieauss bringe/derwegen ich wol billich auf meinen halss hab zu sehen gehabt/das mir nichts drumb oder drein komme." Lucas to Frau Sebastian Imhof, April 8, 1613 (Behaim Archiv, Fasz. 151), pp. 8a–b.

93. Ernstberger, "Liebesbriefe" (Feb. 1, 1613), p. 348.

94. Ibid.

95. Ibid., pp. 348–349.

96. "Dass er sich aber ein Zeitlang vor seiner Bewilligung [unserer Ehe] also gesperret, ists Mehr aus Anreizen seiner Geschwistert als mit seinem Willen geschehen." Ibid. (Feb. 5), p. 351; see also Biedermann, *Geschlechtsregister*, Table 8.

97. Ernstberger, "Liebesbriefe" (Feb. 5, 1613), p. 351.

98. "Das sie ihm gar eine liebe Schwieger und Ihr, liebster Schatz, seine liebste Tochter und Schnur seyd." Ibid. (Feb. 1), p. 349.

99. Ibid., p. 351.

100. Ibid. (Feb. 1, 1613), p. 349; (Feb. 15, 1613), p. 354.

101. Ibid. (Feb. 15, 1613), p. 354.

102. The eldest of the nine was Paul III, now twenty-one; the youngest was Stephan Carl. Biedermann, *Geschlechtsregister*, Table 9. On Stephan Carl, see Ozment, *Three Behaim Boys*, pp. 161–282.

103. "Im fall mir ie die nutzung der ahnfraulichen erbschafft solte abgesprochen werden/das er mir aufs wenigst etwas gewisses alle iahr/ seinen versprech nach darvon/aussagte/es were am end gleich viel oder wenig/wenn es nur gewiss were; dann ob er sich wol vorhin erbeüt auf mein wolverhalten mir iährlich darvon etwas zu kommen zulassen/ist es doch misslich/weiln ihme mein andere geschwistret auch täglich auf den halss wachssen/und er von tag zu tag auch mehr auf sie werden muss/also besorge ich/wann er on end so hart von ihnen solte gedrungen werden/er würde viel mehr ihnen helfen und mich lassen hinach sehen. Bitt also nachmal die Fr Bass wolle unbeschwert ein Calendar nachsehen/wann gut wetter und wol mit ihme zu reden ist/und doch sehen das ietz was gewisses von ihme mochte herauss gebracht werden/und wann es müglich were/das man auch mein hochzeit verlag von ihm erlangen könte." Lucas to Frau Wolf Löffelholz, Feb. 15, 1613, pp. 3b–4b (Behaim Archiv, Fasz. 151).

104. Ibid., pp. 5a–b.

105. Paul Behaim to Lucas, March 16, 1613 (Behaim Archiv, Fasz. 154).

106. Ernstberger, "Liebesbriefe" (Feb. 15, 1613), p. 354.

107. In the later marriage contract between Georg Pfinzing and Paul Behaim (September 1, 1613), witnessed by Martin Pfinzing and Christoph Behaim, Anna Maria's paternal guardian (Georg Pfinzing) promised an 800-gulden dowry as her portion of her parents' estate, which she shared equally with her five siblings: "Und ime [Lucas] zum heiratgut versprechen soll 800 gulden in gold/sie auch kleiden und fertigen nach Ehren und die hochzeit/sambt was derselbigen anhengig/verlegen/alles von iren der Jungfrauen Vatter und Mütterlichen Erbe." *Heiratsabrede zwischen Lukas Friedrich Behaim ... [und] Anna Maria Pfintzing* (Stadtarchiv Nürnberg, E 11/II Fa Behaim Nr. 706).

108. "Will ich hertzlich gern mit allen so wol der Cost alss der wohnung verlieb nehmen/wann ich nur alle nacht beim Annelein schlafen darf." Lucas to Frau Löffelholz, Feb. 15, 1613, pp. 4b–5a (Behaim Archiv, Fasz. 151).

109. Biedermann, *Geschlechtsregister*, Table 245. Katharina's first husband, Jakob, and Sebastian, son of Wilhelm Imhof I (1558–1630), were cousins, Andreas Imhof I (1491–1579) being Jakob's grandfather and Sebastian's great-grandfather. Ibid., Table 244, 245, 247, 249.

110. "Weiss ich nicht, so er Gott zu seinem vorhabenden Werk ernstlich umb Hilf angerufen und umb Verzeihung all seiner Sünden von Herzen gebeten, warumb ihn Gott also sollte heimbsuchen und ein so schwere Verhängnus über ihn ergehen lassen." Ernstberger, "Liebesbriefe" (Feb. 5, 1613), p. 350. Lucas cites the Lutheran *Ehebuchlein*, a popular guide and devotional book for marriageable youth: *Christliches Ehebuchlein/Für Mannbare Gesellen und Jungfrawen/Unnd in gemein/Für alle Christliche Eheleute. Mit allerley darzu gehorenden Christlichen Ehegebeten. Auffs new zugericht/Durch D. Casp. Melissandrum/Superintendenten zu Aldenburg in Meissen* (Leipzig, 1587).

111. "Die gäntzliche Vermutung seiner kranckheit ist nichts anders als das er seines membri virilis durch eine lose Vettel solle beraubt worden sein/welches ihme anjetzo so hefftig zusetzt/und stetig eine zimliche auch übernatürliche Anzahl harms (reverenter) von ihm treibt." Letter to Lucas, January 29, 1613 (Behaim Archiv, Fasz. 154). The ability to take away a man's penis, or to make a man think it was no longer there, was among the powers attributed to witches in the great pornographic classic of the late Middle Ages, the *Malleus Malificarum* (1486). See Alan C. Kors and Edward Peters, *Witchcraft in Europe, 1100–1700: A Documentary History* (Philadelphia, 1978), pp. 105–192.

112. Ernstberger, "Liebesbriefe" (Feb. 5, 1613), p. 350–351.

113. Ibid. (Feb. 15), p. 352–353; (Feb. 27, 1613), p. 356.

114. Ibid. (Mar. 5), p. 357; cf. ibid. (Feb. 5, 1613), p. 356.

115. Ibid., (Mar. 5), p. 358. The diet occurred in early July/late August with Lucas present, and a description of its proceedings was sent to his father from Regensburg on August 4. Ibid. (Aug. 4, 1613), pp. 368, 370, n. 56.

116. Ibid. (Mar. 12, 1613), p. 358.

117. Ibid., p. 359.

118. Ibid. (Mar. 5, 1613), p. 358; see also Biedermann, *Geschlechtsregister*, p. 322.

119. Ernstberger, "Liebesbriefe" (Mar. 19, 1613), p. 359.

120. Ibid., p. 360.

121. Ibid., p. 361.

122. "Ein billich costgelt." Paul Behaim to Lucas, March 16, 1613 (Behaim Archiv, Fasz. 154).

123. This was apparently rental property, then occupied, into which the newlyweds could expect to move once it had been vacated and renovated.

124. Maria Wolff Löffelholz to Lucas, April 13, 1613 (Behaim-Archiv, Fasz. 154).

125. Paul Behaim to Lucas, Apr. 15, 1613 (Behaim Archiv, Fasz. 154).

126. Paul Behaim to Lucas, Apr. 24, 1613 (Behaim Archiv, Fasz. 154).

127. *Eigenhändige Aufzeichnungen*, p. 4b.

128. "Das du doch beim Herr P. Pfintzing/oder Murren und der f[rau]. Sebast[ian] Imhof antriebst/in iren sachen bei herr Jorg Pfintzing/ vormundschafft/richtigkeit zumachen dan [niemands der katzen die schellen will anhencken/aber] ich dich/ausserdessen/nichts anfangen lasse/oder beförderung darzu thue. Magst derwegen auch neben inen dem herrn Wolf Löffelholz zu schreiben [damit er kei (sic) der Linderin/und irem sohn dem Gabriel auch vormundt/und andern treibe]." Bracketed text is written in the margin, with indications to insert where they appear. Paul Behaim to Lucas, Mar. 23, 1614 (Behaim Archiv, 154).

129. From his father's letter of March 23, 1613. Ibid.

130. Ernstberger, "Liebesbriefe" (Apr. 12, 1613), p. 365; "Heiratsabrede zwischen Lucas Friedrich Behaim und Anna Maria Pfinzing" (Stadtarchiv Nürnberg, E11/II-706).

131. Variously called *Handfestung, Handschlag,* or *Lautmerung.* In the case of Christoph Scheurl and Katharina Fütterer, both the contract between the families and its notarization by the principals occurred at city hall, both apparently officiated by his uncle.

132. August Jegel, "Altnürnberger Hochzeitsbrauch und Eherecht besonders bis zum Ausgang des 16. Jahrhunderts," *MVGN* 44 (1953), pp. 238–274.

133. Beer, *Eltern und Kindern,* pp. 81–112; "Ehealltag in Mittelalter. Eine Fallstudie zur Rekonstruction historischen Erfahrungen und Lebensweisen anhand privater Briefe," *Zeitschrift für Württembergischen Landesgeschichte* 53 (1994), pp. 101–123. On emotion and romance in these early centuries, see the selections in Maria E. Müller, *Eheglück und Liebesjoch. Bilder von Liebe, Ehe und Familie in der Literatur des 15. und. Jahrhunderts* (Weinheim, 1988).

134. Steven Ozment, *When Fathers Ruled: Family Life in Reformation Europe* (Cambridge, Mass., 1983), pp. 25–44; Thomas Max, *The Control of Marriage in the German Southwest* (Kirksville, Mo., 1984); Safley, *Let No Man Put Asunder,* pp. 152–154, 176–177.

135. Beatrice Gottlieb, "The Meaning of Clandestine Marriage," in *Family and Sexuality in French History,* ed. Robert Wheaton and Tamara K. Hareven (Philadelphia, 1980), pp. 57–65.

136. Jegel, "Altnürnberger Hochzeitsbrauch," pp. 245–247. On Nürnberg's sumptuary laws: Julia Lehner, *Die Mode im alten Nürnberg. Modische Entwicklung und sozialer Wandel in Nürnberg aufgezeigt an den Nürnberger Kleiderordnungen* (Nürnberg, 1984); Kent R. Greenfield, *Sumptuary Law in Nürnberg: A Study in Paternal Government* (Baltimore, 1918).

137. Jegel, "Altnürnberger Hochzeitsbrauch," pp. 250–251; on Catholic and Protestant impediments to marriage, see Ozment, *When Fathers Ruled*, pp. 10–12, 47–48, 73–74; and John Witte, Jr., "The Transformation of Marriage Law in the Lutheran Reformation," in John Witte, Jr., et al., eds., *The Weightier Matters of Law* (Atlanta, 1988), p. 57. On banns and feast days *(Feiertagen)*, see *KirchenOrdnung, In/meiner gnedigen herrn der margrauen zu Brandenburg Und eins/Erhern Rats der Stat Nürmberg Oberkeyt und gepieten, wie/man sich bayde mit der/Leer und Ceremo/nien halten/solle*, in Emil Sehling, ed., *Die evangelischen Kirchenordnungen des XVI. Jahrhunderts* (Tübingen: 1961), pp. 200, 204.

138. Jegel, "Altnürnberger Hochzeitsbrauch," pp. 252–255.

139. A ceremony Protestants moved inside to the church altar in the late 1520s.

140. Jegel, "Altnürnberger Hochzeitsbrauch," pp. 252–253.

141. In the seventeenth century, these penalties were reduced to simple shaming: Guilty artisans were required to exchange their vows before the "black table" in St. Sebald's choir gallery instead of at the altar, while the upper classes could find themselves exchanging theirs in the tower or city prison. Ibid., pp. 253–254.

142. Ibid., pp. 255–256, 261.

143. "Hochzeitskraut."

144. Jegel, "Altnürnberger Hochzeitsbrauch," pp. 256–257.

145. Ibid. pp. 259–260.

146. *Heimladungen* or *Höfe.*

147. Ernstberger, "Liebesbriefe" (May 1613), p. 367.

148. On Friedrich Behaim's boyhood, see Ozment, *Three Behaim Boys*, pp. 93–160.

149. Paul Behaim to Lucas, Apr. 24, 1613 (Behaim Archiv, Fasz. 154).

150. Paul Behaim to Lucas, May 13, 1613 (Behaim Archiv, Fasz. 154).

151. Ernstberger, "Liebesbriefe," p. 367. Biedermann misdates Martin's death (in January instead of June), *Geschlechtsregister*, p. 9.

152. The following chronology is taken from Lucas's own biographical summary of his life to 1622, *Eigenhändige Aufzeichnungen*, p. 4b.

153. *Heriatsabrede zwischen Lucas Friederich Behaim . . . und Anna M. Pfintzing* (Stadtarchiv Nürnberg, E11/II-706).

154. Ernstberger, "Liebesbriefe," pp. 367-368.

155. *KirchenOrdnung* (1533), pp. 200–202.

156. "Die haimladung . . . mit 2 tisch gasten/gang umb 3 gen tag." *Eigenhändige Aufzeichnungen*, p. 4b.

157. Albrecht Behaim to Lucas, Sept. 6, 1613 (Behaim Archiv, Fasz. 154).

158. "Ritter zu Jerusalem unnd schlosshaubtman zu Nürmberg."

159. "S'il sera á present la brunette, il vous prie de me faire la courtesie, que la faire mes tres humbles services, et baiser les mains et tanser avec elle pour l'amour de moi." Paul Pfinzing to Lucas, Sept. 6, 1613 (Behaim Archiv, Fasz. 154).

160. Georg Hieronymus Behaim to Lucas, Oct. 13, 1613 (Behaim Archiv, Fasz. 154).

161. "50 g zu ein gulden bareth verehrt." *Eigenhändige Aufziechnungen*, p. 4b.

162. "Sein 1/7 selbst zuverwalten." Ibid.

163. "Sein 1/2 mütterliche Erbschafft gar eingeraumbt." Ibid., p. 4b.

164. This was the inheritance his mother's brother had contested Paul Behaim for in the year of Ursula Sitzinger's death (1591) and intermittently again a decade later. See above, n. 6.

165. "Mein aigen haushalten angefangen auf der Vesten." *Eigenhändige Aufzeichungen*, p. 4b.

166. Ibid., p. 6a.

167. "Bin ich von der Vesten in mein hauss gezogen." Ibid.

168. Thirteen-year-old Magdalena from the second marriage, and ten-year-old Stephan Carl, five-year-old Maria, and two-year-old Barbara from the third. See Biedermann, *Geschlechtsregister*, Table 9, 10.

169. Ibid., Table 10.

CHAPTER 2

1. Heinrich Heerwagen, "Bilder aus dem Kinderleben in den Dreissiger Jahren des Sechzehnten Jahrhunderts," *Anzeiger des Germanischen Nationalmuseums (Mitteilungen aus dem germanischen Nationalmuseum)*, vol. 1 (1906) (henceforth, Heerwagen), pp. 97–98 (fol. 10a). Heerwagen drew excerpts about the Scheurl children from what he described as the *Scheurlbuch* (Scheurl Archiv, Codex Ab 274/284), a

formal family chronicle written over generations by the heads of Scheurl households, one sizable section of which is Christoph Scheurl II's description of his life and times. The source excerpted by Heerwagen was actually a different work—a running account of Christoph's daily household expenditures in which he also occasionally reported the human events of the day. This source survives today, not as part of the *Scheurlbuch,* but within a three-generation account book, catalogued in the family archive under the title *Tagebücher dreier Generation der Familie Scheurl, 1531–1603* (Scheurl Archiv, MS Bd. 275/337)—henceforth referenced as *Tagebücher,* or when cited from Heerwagen's version, *Tagebücher*/Heerwagen, and referred to in the text as "the account book." When Heerwagen worked on these materials at the turn of the century, they were among the patrician letter collections of Nürnberg's German National Musuem. Today, they exist in a private family archive in the Nürnberg suburb of Langwasser.

2. In addition to the "hintern haus . . . gegm rosnpad," Christoph's parents added a second structure to the main house: the "back rooms," which faced the Dominican cloister (*die hintere Stuben gegen den Predigern).* It was to these rooms that the family retreated when royalty or special guests visited, and they also served as a tutor's residence during Christoph's childhood. See Franz Frhr. von Soden, *Christoph Scheurl der Zweite und sein Wohnhaus in Nürnberg. Ein biographisch-historisch Beitrag zu den Sitten des Sechszehnten Jahrhunderts* (Nürnberg, 1837), p. 112. In 1491, tutor Lienhard Vogel lived there with his wife (he gave Christoph and his brother Albrecht their first lessons in grammar, Latin, and math). See *Scheurlbuch* (Scheurl Archiv, Handschriften Codex Ab 274/284), fol. 147v. In 1535, Georg's brother (Christoph III) was born there. On Nürnberg's Jews, see Eugen Kusch, *Nürnberg. Lebensbild einer Stadt* (Nürnberg, 1951), pp. 71–79, and below, n. 224.

3. "Homo pius et probus . . . hat stark nach Mailand gehandelt." *Genealogia Fütterer, ca. 1400–1586* (Stadtarchiv Nürnberg E1/340 Fütterer 2).

4. Biedermann, *Geschlechtsregister,* Table 5, 6/A. Ulrich Fütterer headed the third of six lines of Fütterers living during the fifteenth and sixteenth centuries. See *Genealogia Fütterer.* On Martin Behaim's famous map, which underestimated the distance between the Canaries and Japan by 8,200 nautical miles, see Samuel Eliot Morison, *Admiral of the Ocean Sea: A Life of Christopher Columbus I* (New York, 1942), pp. 88–89.

5. See below, pp. 70–71.

6. "Gasse unter der Veste," or Burgstrasse 10. Cf. Jeffrey Chipps Smith, *Nuremberg: A Renaissance City, 1500–1618* (Austin, 1983), pp. 6, 12.

7. The family-owned lucrative silver mines, purchased from Counts Hieronymus and Lorenz Schlick. See Soden, *Christoph Scheurl der Zweite*, p. 69, n. 1. Their lucrative holdings are described in the *Scheurlbuch:* "Scheurls und seiner shün Jorgen und Christofen perckwergk . . . bis auf 1541," fols. 182r–184v.

8. Soden, *Christoph Scheurl der Zweite*, p. 76. On brother Albrecht's tragic life, see pp. 80–81. On Annaberg, C.F. von Posern-Klett, *Münzstätten . . . Sachsens im Mittelalter* (N.P. 1846), p. 15.

9. Gerald Strauss, *Nuremberg in the 16th Century*, pp. 154–159; Bernd Hamm, *Bürgertum und Glaube. Konturen der städtischen Reformation* (Göttingen, 1996).

10. In addition to Luther's *Disputation Against Scholastic Theology* and *95 Theses* (1517), Christoph would have been aware of such popular works as Erasmus's *Praise of Folly* (1511) and the anonymous *Letters of Obscure Men* (1515), the former an earnest theological critique, the latter a violent caricature. On *Folly* and its influence, see Clarence H. Miller, ed. and trans., *The Praise of Folly*, (New Haven, 1979), pp. x–xxv. For others, see Ericka Rummel, ed. and trans., *Scheming Papists and Lutheran Fools: Five Reformation Satires* (New York, 1993); Lewis W. Spitz, *The Religious Renaissance of the German Humanists*, pp. 18, 208; Steven Ozment, *Protestants: The Birth of a Revolution*, (New York, 1992), pp. 43–86.

11. In 1517, Christoph stepped directly into the contemporary theological debates by translating into German Staupitz's Latin treatise on predestination. See Wilhelm Graf, *Doktor Christoph Scheurl von Nürnberg* (Leipzig, 1930), pp. 54–56; Soden, *Christoph Scheurl der Zweite*, p. 10. On Staupitz's teaching, see David Steinmetz, *Luther and Staupitz: An Essay on the Intellectual Origins of the Protestant Reformation* (Durham, 1980).

12. In these transitional decades, there were many so-called "Nicodemites" and "politiques"—that is, men and women willing to behave differently in public than they believed in their hearts. On this problem, see Carlos M.N. Eire, *War Against the Idols: The Reformation of Worship from Erasmus to Calvin* (New York, 1986); and Brad Gregory, "The Anathema of Compromise: Christian Martyrdom in Early Modern Europe," (Dissertation: Princeton University, 1996), pp. 511–540.

13. Soden, *Christoph Scheurl der Zweite*, p. 42, n. 1. Ibid., p. 50, n. 2. Three days after writing, Christoph sent the same request to Georg

Spalatin, Elector Frederick the Wise's secretary and Luther's influential friend.

14. On Christoph and Wittenberg's "Gnadengüter," see Graf, *Doktor Christoph Scheurl*, pp. 75–76; on the contents of the collection, see Julius Köstlin, *Friedrich der Weise und die Schlosskirche zu Wittenberg* (Wittenberg, 1982), pp. 13–26, especially p. 17.

15. Graf, *Doktor Christoph Scheurl*, pp. 75–81, 84, 88, 91–92, 97; Spitz, *The Religious Renaissance of the German Humanists*, p. 178.

16. Cited by Graf, *Doktor Christoph Scheurl*, p. 101; "Bericht Christoph Scheurls über das Nürnberger Religionsgespräch 1525," in *Caritas Pirckheimer 1467–1532. Eine Ausstellung der Katholischen Stadtkirche Nürnberg 26. Juni–8. August 1982* (Munich), no. 157, p. 149. On the changes wrought by the Reformation: Gottfried Seebass, "The Reformation in Nürnberg," in *The Social History of the Reformation*, ed. L. P. Buck and J. W. Zophy (Columbus, 1972), pp. 29–34; and Strauss, *Nuremberg in the 16th Century*, pp. 170–175, both of whom describe these deliberations as "rigged" (Strauss) to placate majority popular sentiment: "The result was admittedly to be foreseen, as the agenda for the day contained chiefly points of Protestant dogma" (Seebass).

17. Günter Zimmermann, "Das Nürnberger Religionsgespräch," *MVGN* 71 (1984): pp. 129–148.

18. The son of Sigmund Fürer II and Christoph's aunt Anna Tucher. Biedermann, *Geschlechtsregister*, p. 377. Soden, *Christoph Scheurl der Zweite*, p. 32.

19. See Hans-Jürgen Bachorski, ed., *Ordnung und Lust. Bilder von Liebe, Ehe und Sexualität in Spatmittelalter und Früher Neuzeit* (Trier, 1990); Müller, *Eheglück und Liebesjoch;* and chapter 1, pp. 22–23.

20. *Scheurlbuch*, fol. 195a–b.

21. Eugen Frhr. Löffelholz von Kolberg, ed., "Dr. Christoph II. Scheurls Hochzeit mit Katharina Füttererin am 29 August, 1519," *MVGN* 3 (1881), pp. 155–68. Christoph's mother was Helena Tucher (1462–1516), daughter of Herdegen Tucher and his second wife, Elisabeth Pfinzing, two long-standing and powerful families. Biedermann, *Geschlechtsregister*, Table 441, 495. Christoph began the Tucher family chronicle and wrote the Pfinzing-Löffelholz genealogy as well, among other genealogical exercises. Helmut Frhr. Haller v. Hallerstein, "Nürnberger Geschlechterbücher," *MVGN* 65 (1978), p. 212–235.

22. *Scheurlbuch*, fol. 166r.

23. "Junckhfrau ring."

24. The *Verlobung, Handfestung/schlagen*, or *Vermehlung*—for the making of a contemporary marriage, the most important part.
25. Löffelholz, "Hochzeit," 158; *Scheurlbuch*, fols. 107v ff. Well over a hundred invited guests appear in the *Scheurlbuch*, fols. 197a–198b.
26. Löffelholz, "Hochzeit," pp. 159–162.
27. H. A. Oberman, *Luther: Man Between God and the Devil*, trans. Eileen Walliser Schwarzbart (New Haven, 1989), pp. 144–145.
28. Löffelholz, "Hochzeit," p. 166.
29. Spitz, *The Religious Renaissance of the German Humanists*, pp. 178–179.
30. Hajo Holborn, *A History of Modern Germany: The Reformation* (New York, 1961), pp. 144–145; Graf, *Doktor Christoph Scheurl*, pp. 72–73; Strauss, *Nuremberg in the Sixteenth Century*, p. 163; Seebass, "The Reformation in Nürnberg," pp. 17–40; Steven Ozment, *The Reformation in the Cities: The Appeal of Protestantism in Sixteenth Century Germany and Switzerland* (New Haven, 1975), pp. 74–79. Pirckheimer and Spengler were later absolved. See also Harold J. Grimm, *Lazarus Spengler: A Lay Leader of the Reformation* (Columbus, 1978).
31. Graf, *Doktor Christoph Scheurl*, p. 7; Soden, *Christoph Scheurl der Zweite*, p. 68.
32. *Caritas Pirckheimer 1467–1532*, pp. 98–99; Biedermann, *Geschlechtsregister*, Table 495.
33. Cited by Graf, *Doktor Christoph Scheurl*, p. 9.
34. They departed Nürnberg in March 1496 and matriculated at the university in September 1497 after a year of private tutoring at the city's Dominican school. See *Scheurlbuch*, fol. 147r; Graf, *Doktor Christoph Scheurl*, p. 9–12. Soden has the boys going to Heidelberg at ages ten and nine: *Christoph Scheurl der Zweite*, p. 7. On the Tucher genealogy, see Ludwig Grote, *Die Tucher: Bildnis einer Patrizierfamilie* (Munich, 1961), pp. 89–94.
35. Graf, *Doktor Christoph Scheurl*, p. 6.
36. Soden, *Christoph Scheurl der Zweite*, p. 112.
37. Graf, *Doktor Christoph Scheurl*, p. 9; Biedermann, *Geschlechtsregister*, Table 496.
38. Son of Anton, brother of Herdegen Tucher; see Biedermann, *Geschlechtsregister*, Table 498; Graf, *Doktor Christoph Scheurl*, pp. 10–11, 13.
39. "Nullum unquam offendere consuevi." Cited by Graf, *Doktor Christoph Scheurl*, p. 17–18.
40. "Erste Weich [Weih]." *Scheurlbuch*, fol. 149r.
41. Graf, *Doktor Christoph Scheurl*, pp. 16–17, 19, 121, n. 118.
42. *Scheurlbuch*, fols. 155v ff.

43. Biedermann, *Geschlechtsregister*, Table 275. On the priors of St. Lorenz's and St. Sebald's, see Karl Schlemmer, *Frömmigkeit und Gottesdienst in der Reichsstadt Nürnberg am Vorabend der Reformation* (Würzburg, 1980).

44. Biedermann, *Geschlechtsregister*, Table 498.

45. Compare the similar complaints of extravagance and family sacrifice in the case of student Paul Behaim II, below, chapter 3.

46. Graf, *Doktor Christoph Scheurl*, pp. 21–22.

47. Ibid., pp. 26, 30, 32–33.

48. Ibid., pp. 27–28; Pamela S. Datsko Barker, "Charitas Pirckheimer: A Female Humanist Confronts the Reformation," *Sixteenth Century Journal* 26 (1995), pp. 259–272.

49. "Unachtbar Fleckh." Cited by Graf, *Doktor Christoph Scheurl*, p. 36.

50. Claus Grimm, et al., *Lucas Cranach. Ein Maler-Unternehmer aus Franken* (Augsburg, 1994).

51. On their relationship, see Graf, *Doktor Christoph Scheurl*, pp. 35–40, 42, 53; Soden, *Christoph Scheurl der Zweite*, p. 14.

52. Professor and bishop in Civitá Ducale under Pope Paul III. See Soden, *Christoph Scheurl der Zweite*, p. 75.

53. G.A. Will, *Nürnbergisches Gelehrter-Lexicon* (Nürnberg, 1758), pp. 37–38; C. G. Jöcher, *Allgemeines Gelehrter-Lexicon*, vols. 1–4 (Leipzig, 1750–1751; reprint, Hildesheim; 1960–1961) vol. 4: p. 1230.

54. Graf, *Doktor Christoph Scheurl*, pp. 50–53, 55–56.

55. "Erlied solich gros unnd schwer ungefel/als kein ander weib zur selbenn Zeit in der gantzen statt heth/mit schuldiger gedult. . . . Einn behennde gutte kindthaberin . . . die zeit aber stundt nit bei ir/sonnder beim herren got." *Scheurlbuch*, fols. 193b, 195a.

56. "Ja" or "Jachtaufft."

57. *Scheurlbuch*, fols. 165r–170v. A brief summary of these failed pregnancies was made on August 29, 1535, his sixteenth wedding anniversary. In the entry, Christoph mentioned only three miscarriages (not four) and did not name the misbegotten children: "Warn gerade vor 16. jar das ich hochzeit gehabt. Und hat mein weib in disen 16 jaren jarn [sic] gehabt 3 pruch. ein abgangen kint. 3 tochter. 3 shun unzeitig und baid mein lieb shun jorgn und Christofn." *Albrecht III. Scheurl register darin er . . . seine kinder und hawshalten geschriben hat . . . Christoph II Scheurl . . . mein haushalten und ander mein zufallent sachen vhon tag zu tag;* henceforth, *Albrecht III/Christoph II Scheurl Haushalten* (Scheurl Archiv, MS Bd. 596/492), fol. 173v. Like the *Tagebücher dreien Generation*, this work is also a daily record, but is focused on the human stories of the day rather than household ex-

penses, although here, too, Christoph rarely misses an opportunity to tell the reader how much something costs. I refer to it in the text as "the diary" or "family diary" to distinguish it from the "account book" and the "chronicle" or "family chronicle"—the three sources of information about his marriage and family. The name of Christoph's grandfather (Albrecht III) appears in the title because it was the latter's diary that Christoph here transformed into his own. Having discovered his grandfather's partly filled notebook in 1534 during a journey to Breslau, Christoph turned it over, reversed it, and made its unused back pages his own for the next eight years, folios 1v–100r ("von vorne") containing Albrecht's entries, and folios 173r–38v ("von Rückwärts/rückwärtiger Spiegel") Christoph's. Mathias Beer is preparing an edition of the former: "Forschungsprojekt Albrecht Scheurl," in *Forschungen zur schlesischen Geschichte*, ed. N. Conrads (Stuttgart, 1990), pp. 26–32.

58. So Frankfurt am Main physician Eucharius Rösslin, author of *Der Rosengarten* (1513), then the authoritative German guide to gynecology and obstetrics. In *Alte Mesiter der Medizin und Naturkunde*, ed. Josef Stein (Munich, 1910), fol. H1b/p. 57.

59. Opitz, "Zwischen Fluch und Heiligkeit," pp. 78–122; Klaus Arnold, "Kindheit im Europäischen Mittelalter," in *Zur Sozialgeschichte der Kindheit*, eds. Joaichen Martin and August Nitschke (Munich, 1986), pp. 458–461. The causes and prevention of miscarriage and stillbirth were described for contemporaries by Rösslin. See Ozment, *When Fathers Ruled*, pp. 103–107.

60. P. P. A. Biller, "Birth-Control in the West in the 13th and 14th Centuries," *Past and Present* 94 (1982), pp. 3–26.

61. Boesch, *Kinderleben in der deutschen Vergangenheit*, pp. 6–7; Beer, *Eltern und Kinder*, pp. 205–214.

62. Johannes Coler, *Oeconomia ruralis et domestica. Darinn das gantz Ampt aller trewen Hauss-Vätter und Hauss-Mütter/bestandiges und allgemeines Hauss-Buch* (Frankfurt, 1680), part 2, book 4, chapter 5, p. 344. The first edition appeared in 1592.

63. Boesch, *Kinderleben*, pp. 6–7.

64. *Tagebücher*/Heerwagen, p. 96 (fol. 5a).

65. "Die saget mir schrepfen het ir geholfen." *Tagebücher*/Heerwagen, p. 96 (fol. 5a). There is no indication of when in the course of her pregnancies she did so.

66. For Nürnberg examples, see Steven Ozment, *Magdalena and Balthasar: An Intimate Portrait of Life in Sixteenth Century Europe* (New Haven, 1989), pp. 114–121; *Three Behaim Boys*, p. 113, 116.

67. For a possible episode of bleeding to induce an abortion, cf. Ozment, *The Bürgermeister's Daughter*, pp. 61–62.

68. *Tagebücher*/Heerwagen, p. 96 (fol. 5a).

69. On Duke Georg, see pp. 81–83 below.

70. "Geborn . . . am . . . mithwoch 15 Marchij . . . 1522/wie der Christennlich furst hertzog Jorg von Sachssen etc. am Regiment hie was und beij ir [Katharina] herbrigkt/ein achtizehen woching todts kneblein/ oder ehe mit wenig lebenns . . . die hertzogischenn beschuldigten das aderlassen als in Meithssenn ungewönlich/wo nit verderblich/dagegen aber het sich die mutter/des vorgeendenn abents/ainer verdechtigen maidt halbenn/zu viel hart erzurnt bewegt unnd damit diese unzeitige gepurt verursagt." *Scheurlbuch*, fol. 193a. Christoph comments on the early birth of Christoph III (see p. 106): *"ethlich wochen vor der rechungl vieleicht vorgeendts zorns halben."* Ibid., fol. 1946.

71. Boesch, *Kinderleben*, pp. 8–9; Beer, *Eltern und Kinder*, p. 220. On Nürnberg midwives, see Friedrich Baruch, *Das Hebammenwesen im reichsstädtischen Nürnberg* (Erlangen, 1955); and more generally on the subject in early modern Europe: Hilary Mailand, ed., *The Art of Midwifery: Early Modern Midwives in Europe and America* (London; 1993); and Beryl Rowland, ed. and trans., *Medieval Woman's Guide to Health: The First English Gynecological Handbook* (Kent, Ohio, 1981), that of Tortula.

72. "Ich ward verjagt vom aufschlohn des pets." Cf. Merry Wiesner, "Early Modern Midwifery: A Case Study," *International Journal of Women Studies*, 6 (1983), pp. 26–43; and, more to the point, Beer, *Eltern und Kinder*, pp. 218, 220. On places that required a father's presence, see ibid., pp. 216–219.

73. *Tagebücher*/Heerwagen, p. 98 (fol. 11b), p. 100 (fol. 13).

74. "Anna di hebamm" is distinction from "Anna seugammen," who would not arrive in the household until May 1. Ibid., p. 98 (fols. 10a, 11b). The same Anna (midwife) would assist at the birth of Georg's brother Christoph three years later.

75. The second wife and widow of Andreas (1453–1521) and Christoph's second cousin by marriage, Biedermann, *Geschlechtsregister*, p. 508.

76. As the widow of Friedrich Tetzel and sister of Lutheran patricians Sigmund and Christoph Fürer, she was Christoph's first cousin (her mother was Christoph's great-aunt Anna Tucher [d. 1487]). Ibid., Table 369, 370.

77. The widow of junior bürgermeister, Hans Mugenhofer. Löffelholz, "Hochzeit."

78. Katharina was the daughter of Hans Imhof and married to Christoph Fürer (d. 1537). Biedermann, *Geschlechtsregister*, Table 370.

79. Margaretha Tucher's deceased husband's great-uncle Hans Tucher (d. 1449) was Christoph's maternal grandfather—Hans, the father of Herdegen (d. 1462), who was in turn the father of Christoph's mother Helena (1462–1516). Ibid., pp. 494, 495, 507.

80. See p. 62.

81. Josef Pfanner, ed., *Die "Denkwürdigkeiten" der Caritas Pirckheimer*, (Landshut, 1961), chs. 6–12; on the three girls' entry into St. Clara's, see *Caritas Pirckheimer, 1467–1532*, p. 114.

82. *Die "Denkwürdigkeiten,"* chs. 6 and 34; Kusch, *Nürnberg*, pp. 305–306. This was reported to the confessor's successor in Bamberg by a former servant in the Nürnberg cloister, who had witnessed the visits: "etlich mahl im Jahr in weltlichen Kleidern nach Nürnberg zu den Clarisser Jungfrawen hienüber geraist, doch seinen Habit verborgen mit sich gebracht und in dem Closter denselbigen angezogen, die Closter Jungfrawen beicht gehört, mess gelesen und gespeist. . . ." "Bericht über die letzten Jahre des Klaraklosters," in *Caritas Pirckheimer, 1467–1532*, p. 88.

83. See n. 58 above.

84. Ozment, *When Fathers Ruled*, pp. 116–118; Boesch, *Kinderleben*, pp. 15–16.

85. Apparently, these fruits were perceived to reflect in some way male and female physiques or temperaments. Boesch, *Kinderleben*, p. 23.

86. Ibid., pp. 19–21.

87. As in the case of Paul Behaim's sisters. See chapter 3.

88. "Tres femellas et totidem inde liberos melioris sexus, sed omnes immaturo partu." Cited by Graf, *Doktor Christoph Scheurl*, p. 112. Beer cites a March 5, 1532, letter in which Christoph asks Apollonia Tucher and her convent, a month and a half before Georg's birth, to pray for a boy. *Kinder und Eltern*, pp. 230–231.

89. Graf, *Dr. Christoph Scheurl der Zweite*, p. 73; *Tagebücher*/Heerwagen, p. 96 (fol. 4b).

90. On popular superstitions about the fate of infants who died unbaptized, Boesch, *Kinderleben*, p. 25.

91. Ibid., pp. 25–26, 28; the traditional elements are described by Luther, below, n. 92.

92. As late as his *Small Catechism* (1529), Luther deemphasized, but did not absolutely forbid, the human additions to the service. "So gedenke nu, dass in dem Täufen diese äusserliche Stücke das geringste sind,

als da ist: unter Augen blasen, Kreuze anstreichen, Speichel und Kot in die Ohren und Nasen tun, mit Oele auf der Brust und Schuldern salben und mit Cresem die Scheitel bestreichen, Westerhembd anziehen und brennend Kerzen in die Händ geben, und das mehr ist, das von Menschen, die Taufe zu zieren, hinzugetan ist; denn auch wohl ahn solchs alles die Taufe geschehen mag und nicht die rechte Griffe sind, die der Teufel scheuet oder fleucht." Martin Luther, *Kleiner Katechismus*, in *Die Bekenntnisschriften der evangelisch-lutherischer Kirche*, 6th ed. (Gottingen, 1967), pp. 536–537. Liberal Nürnberg, however, excluded most of these elements and later also contested the exorcism rite.

93. *Die brandenburgisch-nürnbergische Kirchenordnung von 1528*, in Sehling, *Die Kirchenordnungen des XVI. Jahrhunderts, XI*, p. 135; *Kirchen-Ordnung* (1533) in ibid., p. 174: "Man soll dise ding diser zeit unterwegen lassen."

94. Ibid., pp. 135 (1528), 177 (1533).

95. Although a priest is not directly mentioned, I infer this from the fact that godfather Pistoris is described as taking him from the baptismal fount (evidently from the hands of a priest), and later, at second son Hieronymus's birth, a church steward was summoned to the house to baptize him within hours of his birth.

96. When the pastor of St. Lorenz's baptized his newborn daughter at church in 1698, it raised eyebrows. Boesch, *Kinderleben in der deutschen Vergangenheit*, p. 29.

97. Soden, *Christoph Scheurl der Zweite*, p. 76; Biedermann, *Geschlechtsregister*, Table 442; *Tagebücher*/Heerwagen, pp. 98–99 (fol. 11a–b). On Absberg, see Joseph Baader, *Fehde Hanns Thomas von Absberg wider den Schwäbischen Bund* (Munich, 1880).

98. "Ir in eurm schreiben . . . meldet das man fursichtig sey und nit zu hart eill damit die enthelter die schatzung des weniger hochspannen/darauf ist mein von herzen hochtes und fleissigs pit an euch ir wollet umb gotzwillen darob sein als vil euch moglich ist das man die schatzung oder das gelt nit zu hart bedenck dan ir ie meins herzliben hauswirts schwachhait und kranckhait wol wist das mir got seis klagt/am hertesten zu herzen get solt man dan vons gelts wegen des weniger eillen und die sach zu lang verziehen damit kem mitler zeit umb sein leib und leben." Oct. 11, 1530 (Scheurl Archiv. Familienakten aus dem 16 Jh. II, 35b/1); Beer, *Eltern und Kinder*, pp. 147–149.

99. Christian G. Jöcher, ed., *Allgemeines Gelehrten-Lexicon, darinne die Gelehrten aller Stände sowohl männ-als bweiblichen Geschlechts, welche*

vom Anfange der Welt bis auf jetzige Zeit gelebt (Leipzig, 1750–1751; reprint, Hildesheim, 1960–61), pp. 1597–1598.

100. For this and other examples of corporate godparentage, see Boesch, *Kinderleben*, pp. 27–28.

101. Pistoris's wife later sent Georg presents as a godparent. On Pastor Dürnhofer's practice, see pp. 226–228.

102. Ozment, *Magdalena and Balthasar*, p. 138.

103. Mark Edwards, *Printing, Propaganda, and Martin Luther* (Stanford, 1995), pp. 36–37; Oberman, *Luther*, pp. 18–20.

104. "Item mein g. herr herzog Jorg zu Sachsen beschwert sich die gevatterschaft zu ratificirn. Het solchs dem lantgrafen und andern abgeschlagen, mangl halben des Chrisma. Schrib mir doch am pfingstabent mit aigner Hand, und erzaigt sich vast mein gnedigen Herrn sein." *Tagebücher/* Heerwagen, p. 100 (fol. 12b).

105. Karl Ulrich, *Die Nürnberger Deutschordenskommende in ihrer Bedeutung für den Katholizismus seit der Glaubensspaltung* (Kallmünz, 1935), pp. 16–21.

106. Ibid. See Christoph Imhof's arrest, with others, pp. 155, 200.

107. *Tagebücher/*Heerwagen, p. 99 (fol. 12a).

108. Biedermann, *Geschlechtsregister*, p. 444.

109. The *Wester* was also called a "Westerlein" and "Chrismhemd." See J. A. Schmeller, *Bayerisches Wörterbuch*, 3rd ed., vol. 2, G. Karl Frommann, ed. (Aalen, 1973), pp. 1043–1044. According to Jakob and Wilhelm Grimm, it disappeared among Protestants during the sixteenth century. See *Deutsches Wörterbuch*, vol. 14 (Leipzig, 1960), p. 634, 637–638. Luther, however, permitted it to be worn at the service of baptism and the *Westerbad* to occur three days later, while urging his followers against thinking that the clothing of the Sacrament, rather than one's faith in it, saved the child. He also warned parents and priests against binding the newborn too tightly in such celebratory attire and forcing it to endure a long and tedious service. The "true baptismal shirt of eternal life" would be donned by all only in heaven. Hans-Ulrich Delius, ed., "Von den Konziliis und Kirchen," in *Martin Luther: Studienausgabe*, 5 (Berlin, 1992), pp. 614–615; "Ein Sermon von dem heiligen hochwürdigen Sakrament der Taufe," ibid., 1, p. 261.

110. "Margaret kindtpethwarterin Suntag den 21 Aprilis das erst mall/aus der wester padet." *Scheurlbuch*, fol. 196a.

111. Boesch, *Kinderleben*, pp. 29–31.

112. The *Nürnberg Kindbettordnung* of November 22, 1578, permitted

patricians (*erbare Geschlechter*) eighteen to twenty guests at a *Wester-bad* meal. See J. Kamann, "Aus Nürnberger Haushaltungs- und Rech-nungsbüchern des 15. und 16. Jahrhunderts," *MVSN* 7 (1888). Paul's teen years are the subject of chapter 3.

113. *Tagebücher*/Heerwagen, p. 98 (fol. 11a).
114. Ibid., p. 98 (fol. 11a).
115. Ibid., p. 100 (fol. 12b).
116. Twenty-eight and a half Eln (Eln = 60–80 cm = 24–32 in.), here cal-culated at 70 cm or 28 in. per Eln.
117. *Tagebücher*/Heerwagen, p. 96 (fol. 4a–4b).
118. Ibid., pp. 96 (fol. 4b), 111–112 (fol. 124a). "[Anna Erhart] hat mir meinen shun Jorgen geseugt vhom Wallburgis [May 1] 1532 bis auf halben October 1533." *Albrecht III/Christoph II Scheurl Haushalten*, fol. 172r.
119. *Tagebücher*/Heerwagen, p. 96 (fol. 4b).
120. Ibid., p. 101, (fol. 14a).
121. Beer, *Eltern und Kinder*, pp. 250–251, 256–257.
122. *Ammen* can mean "Pflegemutter" as well as "Seugammen."
123. *Tagebücher*/Heerwagen, pp. 96–97 (fol. 6a).
124. Steven Ozment, *Protestants: The Birth of a Revolution*, p. 174; *Shu-lamith Shahar, Childhood in the Middle Ages* (London: 1992), pp. 53–54.
125. "So kundt sie auch aus mangel der milch nit seugen so wenig als ir schwiger selige." *Scheurlbuch*, fol. 195a. Evidently, Christoph's mother had been unable to nurse him and his brother.
126. Ibid.
127. Beer, *Eltern und Kinder*, p. 249.
128. See below, pp. 88–89.
129. Beer, *Eltern und Kinder*, pp. 244–258. The seventeenth-century wife of Puritan Ralph Josselin (1613–1638) weaned her ten children at be-tween twelve and nineteen months, nursing some up to a year after their teeth appeared, in an effort to space her pregnancies. Alan Mac-Farlane, *The Family Life of Ralph Josselin: A Seventeenth Century Clergy-man* (Cambridge, Mass., 1970), pp. 83, 90.
130. *Tagebücher*/Heerwagen, p. 98 (fol. 10a).
131. "Er wurd mild werden." *Tagebücher*/Heerwagen, p. 98 (fol. 11a).
132. *Tagebücher*/Heerwagen, p. 101 (fol. 14a).
133. Ibid., p. 98 (fol. 11b).
134. Ibid., p. 100 (fol. 13a).
135. Christoph identifies Wagner as a lining maker (*futermacher*), prog-nostication apparently being a sideline. Ibid., p. 100 (fol. 12b).

136. Ibid., p. 99 (fol. 12a), p. 101 (fol. 13b), p. 102 (fol. 36b).
137. From Georg Neusesser, a twenty-gulden share in the lower twelve veins of the Abertham (or Abertamy) mine near the royal mining town of St. Joachimsthal, near modern Neideck and Brzesnitz; and from Hans Lienhart, Hans Bucher, and Wolf Lochmayer, four shares in Mt. St. Anna (St. Anneberg, south of Chemnitz, in Saxony). Wolf Lochmayer sold Christoph two additional shares in unidentified mines operated by Emperor Charles V. See ibid., pp. 100–101 (fols. 13a, 14b, 35b). On the location of these mines, see J. G. Sommer, *Das Königreich Böhmen statisch-topographisch dargestellt*, vol. 15 (1846), pp. 106–119; Ludmila Kubátová, et al., *Lazarus Ercker. Probierer, Berg-und Münzmeister in Sachsen, Braunschweig und Böhmen* (Leipzig, 1994), p. 45.
138. "In 8 wochen ein funtgrubner ist worden." *Tagebücher*/Heerwagen, p. 102 (fol. 37a).
139. Ibid., p. 103 (fol. 52b).
140. Ibid., pp. 100–101 (fols. 13a, 35a).
141. "Das erst mals ins pad hinüber trug." Ibid., p. 102 (fol. 36b).
142. Ibid., p. 99 (fol. 12a).
143. Ibid., P. 100 (fol. 12b).
144. "Dinest zu der memori und anderm mer." Ibid., p. 100 (fol. 12b).
145. Laura Ackerman Smoller, *History, Prophecy, and the Stars: The Christian Astrology of Pierre d'Ailly, 1350–1420* (Princeton, 1994), pp. 128–130. The Church deemed astrology a competitor, and Nürnberg catechetical instruction emphatically warned the young not to place their trust in it. Ozment, *Protestants*, p. 106.
146. According to Christoph III's 1591 retrospective on his father: "Er betet vil, auch die horas canonicas, unnd fastet die hohen unnd die vier fron fest ein jahr biss in sein gruben . . ." *Herrn Christoff Scheurls . . . Ankhunfft, Wandel undt Leben undt Sterben durch seinen Sohn Christoffen Scheurl Statrichtern zu Nurimberg zusammen getragen undt beschrieben Anno 1591* (Scheurl Archiv II, 42), p. 7.
147. "Ein ueberaus gross man." *Tagebücher*/Heerwagen, p. 114 (fol. 166a). See below, p. 123. The family chronicle elaborates on the judgment of a Mirandolan Jew, who prophesied a son who would be "ein gros man," go to school in Bologna, be poor in his youth but rich in his old age, and have a son of his own who would bring honor to an entire land. *Scheurlbuch*, fol. 200a–b. Another Jewish seer (Raphael Ferreser) predicted two sons, both of whom would become "gros leuthen wurdenn werden." Ibid.

148. *Tagebücher*/Heerwagen, pp. 100–101 (fols. 126, 13a, 35a).
149. "Annala Jorgen wiergerin." *Tagebücher*/Heerwagen, pp. 102–103, 111 (fols. 37a, 46a, 121a).
150. "Desselben tags hat linhart [Scheurl] seinen shun Mathesn inn funften jar seins alters auch herbracht den mir mein gnadigen herr pischof Christof vhon Augspurg von der leibaigenschaft gefreiet hat und ich Maister Hannsen balbirer im Vischpach in di kost verlasn hab dises jar um 6 gulden den 15 Oct. 1532 und als er gen haus zoch/leh ich im fhur ainen zinen zunachst 13 gulden/doran ghin ab 2 gulden artztlon/ains armen erbgrindigen [grindig = scabby, also inheritance poor] knabns/den knaben hab ich vhon im [sc. maister Hannsen] genomen sterbens halben und dem Heftlamacher heimgestelt am tag Jacob [July 25] 1533." *Tagebücher dreier Generation*, fol. 46a.
151. In one entry, Christoph dates Ketter's arrival in the household on January 8, 1534 (*Tagebücher*/Heerwagen, p. 111 [fol. 121a]), while in a later one, she arrives on January 13, 1535. "Mathes Scheurl siben jare alt/Juncker Jorgn Scheurls liber knecht"; *Albrecht III/Christoph II Scheurl Haushalten,* fol. 152r.
152. "In unserm hinterhauss . . . iss mein weib, unser liber shun Jorg/sein knecht Mathes Scheurl . . . sein maidtn Annala Scheurl, etc." Ibid., fols. 152r, 173r. "Junker" became a routine description of Georg and later his brother Christoph III.
153. "Matthes Scheurl, den er ser liebet, nachreiten, und auf ine warten, als ein knecht auf seinen herrn, das den vater nit wenig freuet." *Tagebücher*/Heerwagen, p. 107 (fol. 71a).
154. Beer, *Eltern und Kinder*, p. 295.
155. *Tagebücher*/Heerwagen, p. 103 (fol. 38a).
156. "Er hielt fur gewies mein weib trueg ainen sun, das verleih der hr. got." Ibid., p. 103 (fol. 52af). Erasmus was the son of Hieronymus and Helena, who had stood as Christoph's "father" and "mother" at his marriage. Biedermann, *Geschlechtsregister*, Table 28; *Allegemeine Deutsche Biographie* (Leipzig, 1874–1912/Berlin, 1967–1971), 5, p. 591f; *Neue Deutsche Biographie* (Berlin, 1953), 4, p. 263–264.
157. "Das kind regt sich zimlich fluchs dorauf." *Tagebücher*/Heerwagen, p. 103 (fol. 48a).
158. Ibid., p. 103 (fol. 48a).
159. Day now ran from ca. 5:45 A.M. to ca. 6:45 P.M., and night from ca. 6:45 P.M. to ca. 5:45 A.M., so the birth occurred ca. 2:45 A.M. Ibid., p. 103 (fol. 53a).
160. Ibid., p. 104 (fol. 53a).
161. This was Georg Mann, the church's first officer.

NOTES 295

162. This is the second structure behind the Scheurl house, not the "back house" in which Georg was born. See note 2.

163. *Tagebücher*/Heerwagen, p. 103 (fol. 53a), n. 64.

164. Ibid., p. 104 (fol. 53a).

165. Ibid., p. 104 (fol. 53a–53b).

166. *Albrecht III/Christoph II Scheurl Haushalten*, fol. 174v; *Tagebücher/* Heerwagen, p. 104 (fol. 54a–b). On Kreutzer (d. 1540), see G. A. Will, *Nürnbergisches Gelehrter-Lexicon*, vol. 2 (1756), p. 370.

167. Rösslin associated such cramps and convulsions (*gegicht oder krampff/ Spasmus*) with poor digestion, poor circulation, and the appearance of teeth and recommended oil rubs and bathing in mullein to improve circulation. *Rosengarten*, pp. 87–88. His English counterpart, Thomas Phaire, described "Crampe or Spasmus" as a "debilitie of the nerues and cordes, or els of grosse humours, that suffocate the same," and recommended numerous herbal ointments and plasters. Thomas Phaire, *The Boke of Chyldren* (Edinburgh, 1951), pp. 30–31.

168. He adds reassuringly in the margin: "Raptus est ne malitia mutaret intellectum. Sap[ientia]. 4."

169. "Des wol widerumb ergetzn."

170. *Tagebücher*/Heerwagen, p. 104 (fol. 53b). Compare Martin Luther's similar fumbling efforts to praise God after the death of his thirteen-year-old daughter. Ozment, *When Fathers Ruled*, p. 168.

171. On parental observation of the development of children at this time, cf. Beer, *Eltern und Kinder*, pp. 268–273.

172. Apparently meaning "da, da."

173. "Wi im auch der kopf noch offen stet ains gulden prait."

174. "Mach ein boslein."

175. "Verstund und zaiget datla." Christoph is aware of the imitative nature of young children.

176. "Verweist sich im jar mit rullen und seinen geberden, als ob er beherzigt und fraidig werden wolt."

177. *Tagebücher*/Heerwagen, p. 105 (fol. 55b).

178. This is apparently Eberhart Khun, Jr., son of Christoph's uncle Eberhart Sr., who earlier rode Georg's horse to Joachimsthal. Young Eberhart appears to have been more Albrecht's age and a playmate.

179. *Tagebücher*/Heerwagen, p. 105 (fol. 62b).

180. "So vil ungeschicks und boses pronosticirt." Ibid., p. 106 (fol. 65b).

181. He was to travel there with brother-in-law Hans Johann Fütterer, and, among other planned official business, help the latter's father, Lorenzo Johann, collect a debt of 3,700 gulden from the latter's brother-in-law (Conrad Sauerman).

182. *Tagebücher*/Heerwagen, pp. 106–107 (fol. 70a–70b). On Meuschel, see Kusch, *Nürnberg*, p. 189.

183. In Amberg, the Scheurls lodged in the home of Margareta Gerstner.

184. He identifies Pfinzing (evidently Seifried) and Sigmund and Christoph Fürer.

185. The Counts Schlick began selling shares in Joachimsthal's mines to Nürnbergers in 1518. See Karl Siegl, "Zur Geschichte der 'Thalergroschen.' Ein Beitrag zur Historiographie des St. Joachimstaler Bergwerks und Münzwesens," *Mitteilungen des Vereins für Geschichte der Deutschen in Böhmen*, 50 (1911), pp. 198–219. Johannes Mathesius, Wittenberg graduate, pastor in Joachimsthal, and author of the city's Lutheran *Kirchen- Schul- und Spitalordnung*, describes Neusesser as a devout businessman/engineer (*Mercatorem/Macenatem*), who gave the church silk coverings for its altar and pulpit, and furnished the city's hospice with medicinal herbs and spices. Letter to Paul Eber (Dec. 1, 1547), in *Johannes Mathesius Ausgewahlte Werke*, vol. 4, ed. Georg Loesche (Prague, 1904), p. 510; Georg Loesche, *Johannes Mathesius: Ein Lebens- und Sitten-Bild aus der Reformationszeit*, vol. 1 (Nieuwkoop, 1971), p. 108; and Mathesius, *Chronica der keyserlichen freven Berkstadt Sanct Joachimsthal* (1563), entry for year 1539. Mathesius would later become Martin Luther's first Protestant biographer. That Neusesser could be close friends of both Mathesius and Scheurl is further commentary on the ability of blood and friendship to survive religious division at their social level.

186. *Tagebücher*/Heerwagen, p. 107 (fol. 70b). It was during this trip that he discovered his grandfather's diary. See note 57.

187. "Geschelten" = *scheln* = *schälen*.

188. *Tagebücher*/Heerwagen, p. 107 (fol. 71a).

189. Ibid., p. 105 (fol. 62b).

190. Ibid., p. 107 (fol. 73b).

191. Ibid., p. 108 (fol. 74a).

192. Ibid., p. 108–109 (fol. 90b).

193. Christoph estimated the household's ("meine leut") travel expenses during the fourteen weeks in Amberg at seventy-eight gulden, which included the ten paid Frau Gerstner for rent and firewood, but not the cost of the wine and their board. Ibid., p. 108 (fol. 74b).

194. *Albrecht III/Christoph II Scheurl Haushalten*, fols. 170r–169v, 168v–r, 160v, 159v.

195. Ibid. fols 166v, 163v, 154r.

196. "Kauft ich meinem shun Jorgn ein schons neues petlein mit laufen dann dass andere was ers im got lob zu klain . . . und leget in des

abends selbst dorein und das erst mal auf federn/got verleiche das er dorauf in seinen gnaden gotfurchtig ersterb." Ibid., fol. 163r–v; Beer, *Eltern und Kindern*, p. 264.

197. Or *Moriske*. Heerwagen, *Bilder aus dem Kinderleben*, p. 108, n. 84.

198. "Hat all sein freud zu reiten und zun pferden." *Tagebücher*/Heerwagen, p. 108 (fol. 83a).

199. Ibid.

200. Georg as *"Erben"* and Albrecht as *"Aftererben."*

201. Of the four (Christoph Gugel, Gothert König/Kunig, Lienhart Thomas, and Georg Neusesser), only Neusesser had actually agreed to do so at the time of this entry. On April 2, 1535, Katharina stood as godmother to the Königs' daughter Barbara. See *Tagebücher*/Heerwagen, p. 109 (fol. 95b); *Albrecht III/Christoph II Scheurl Haushalten*, fol. 145v. None of the above in fact served as a guardian after Christoph's death. In 1543, Martin Pfinzing and Mathias Löffelholz became the guardians of Christoph's nephew and nieces, while Jobst Tetzel and Balthasar Dörrer assumed that responsibility for Georg and Christoph III. See Soden, *Christoph Scheurl der Zweite*, p. 89.

202. *Tagebücher*/Heerwagen, p. 109 (fol. 104a).

203. *Albrecht III/Christoph II Scheurl Haushalten*, fol. 166v. See Beer's detailed account of schooling in *Eltern und Kinder*, pp. 314–342.

204. "Er [Christoph] thett seinen freundten vill guts/auch den armen zu Dilligen/denen samblet er von seinem und seines brudern kindern pergkwerck gefellen [Einkünfte] 500 g barschafft, das doch wenig ersprosen/und ubel angelegt wardt." *Herrn Christoff Scheurls . . . Ankunfft . . . 1591*, pp. 6–7.

205. "Ganz keinen aufstoss gehabt, ist gar nichzit gefallen." *Tagebücher*/Heerwagen, p. 109 (fol. 103a).

206. Beer, *Eltern und Kinder*, pp. 314–315 passim. On the seeming universality of this approach to child rearing, see Brian Jackson, *Fatherhood* (London, 1983); and David Gilmore, *Manhood in the Making: Cultural Concepts of Masculinity* (New Haven, 1990).

207. *Tagebücher*/Heerwagen, p. 109 (fol. 103a).

208. Ibid.

209. "Furcht di ruten über aus ser; vermaint etwan dem vater und der ruten zu entloufen." Ibid., p. 109 (fol. 103a).

210. On moral development and corporal punishment, see Beer, *Eltern und Kinder*, pp. 333–337.

211. Helena was the childless widow of Christoph Kress (1484–1535), who had shared with Christoph the lion's share of the city's diplomatic chores, making over sixty-five missions during his lifetime. See

Biedermann, *Geschlechtsregister*, Table 275, 496; Jonathan W. Zophy, *Patriarchal Politics and Christoph Kress (1484–1535) of Nuremberg* (Lewiston, N.Y., 1992).

212. "Gen Pillenreut gefaren/zu singen und fruemal und zu nachts haben wir mit inen im closter collecht [Kolleckte, Altargebet] und sein auf meins liebstn shuns Jorgn fest frolich und gutter dingk gewesen." *Albrecht III/Christoph II Haushalten*, fol. 141r. A similar *presentz/fest* had been held earlier for Georg at Gnadenberg.

213. *Tagebücher*/Heerwagen, p. 109 (fol. 105b).

214. *Albrecht III/Christoph II Scheurl Haushalten*, fol. 130r; *Tagebücher*/Heerwagen, p. 109 (fol. 105b). Biedermann, *Geschlechtsregister*, Table 499.

215. *Albrecht III/Christoph II Scheurl Haushalten*, fols. 138r, 137r.

216. *Tagebücher*/Heerwagen, pp. 109–110 (fol. 105b).

217. "Sunabent, 7. Augusti, gegn abent, als mein ander lieber sun Christof elter dan vir tag alt worden, derhalbn ich nie reicher wass, kam potschaft, das unser aller herr, di Romisch kayserlich Mt die bevestigung La Goleta sambt dem geschloss und stat Tunis gewaltiglich erobert, das ich acht meinem neu gebornen sun und der ganzn christnhait ein gluckliche zeitung sein . . . Das ist aber war und verfolgt statlich: den 14 Julii hat unser herr kaiser Goleta gewonnen, den dritn Augusti ist mein liber sun Christof von gots gnadn geborn, den 21 Julii hat kaiserlich Mt gschloss und stat Tunisy gewunnen . . ." Ibid., p. 110 (fol. 106b). Bonney, *The European Dynastic States*, p. 137.

218. "Ein juditium . . . das ich hab einpinden lasn zu den zeitung vhon Tunis." *Albrecht III/Christoph II Scheurl Haushalten*, fol. 135v.

219. Ibid., fol. 137v.

220. Ibid., fol. 135v–r.

221. "Kindsplatern."

222. Ibid., fol. 133v; *Tagebücher*/Heerwagen, p. 110 (fol. 108a–b). On childhood diseases, see Beer, *Eltern und Kinder*, pp. 285–290; Rösslin and Coler, in Ozment, *When Fathers Ruled*, pp. 121–126.

223. Ibid., p. 110 (fol. 108b). Cf. *Scheurlbuch*, p. 199b.

224. Also referred to as "die Füssin," her married name. It would make our story even more interesting if Katharina were related to Nathan Aaron Stafelsteiner, a converted Jew who took the name of Paul after his baptism and lived just around the corner from the Scheurls on the Judengasse. See G. H. Will, *Gelehrten-Lexicon*, vol. 3 (Nürnberg, 1757), p. 762; Andreas Würfel, *Historische Nachrichten von der Juden-Gemeinde welche ehehin in der Reichsstadt Nürnberg angericht gewesen aber Ao. 1495 ausgeschaffet worden* (Nürnberg, 1755), pp. 108–109.

Katharina appears to have been a native of Staffelstein in the vicinity of Reinsweinsdorf and Fischbach before her marriage to Nürnberger Füss.

225. *Scheurlbuch,* fol. 199b; Graf, *Doktor Christoph Scheurl von Nürnberg,* p. 7.

226. *Tagebucher*/Heerwagen, p. 110 (fol. 108b).

227. *Tagebücher*/Heerwagen pp. 110–111 (fol. 108b). On the boy's chronic inability to substitute wine and beer for milk, see p. 114 and n. 265. Cf. *Scheurlbuch,* fol. 199b.

228. "Ainen eingevesten rechten Wolffzahn." *Albrecht III/Christoph II Scheurl Haushalten,* fol. 128.

229. "Mein shun Jorg hat di flecken gewonnen dan 13 und mein shun Christof den 26 dess 1535." Ibid., fol. 128v. Since one cannot have measles twice, one or the other episode of "flecken" must have been something else, perhaps chicken pox, rubella, or some other measle-like rash.

230. Appears as Rempersdorf in text.

231. "Diweil herr Sebastian von Rotenhan . . . mein liber und guter freund gewesen ist . . . hab ich seins brudern Hansn von Rotenhan zu Rentweinsdorf sun Jorgen, seins alters 6 Jar und 8 tag, den 23 Augusti 1535 in mein behausung angnomen . . ." See *Tagebücher*/Heerwagen, p. 111 (fol. 122b); "Gern angenomen treulich zuerzihen und lernen zulassen," *Albrecht III/Christoph II Scheurl Haushalten,* fol. 138r. Georg's birthdate is based on the information here supplied, as there is no listing in the Rotenhan genealogy; see Gottfried Frhr. v. Rotenhan, *Die Rotenhan. Genealogie einer fränkischen Familie von 1229 bis zum Dreissigjährigen Krieg* (Neustadt a.d. Aisch, 1985), p. 291. He remained with Christoph until at least age nine. In September, 1541, he matriculated at the University of Tübingen. Ibid., p. 292.

232. On Sebastian von Rotenhan, see ibid., pp. 224–233; Graf, *Dr. Christoph Scheurl von Nürnberg,* pp. 93, 96; Karl Bosl, ed., *Handbuch der Historischen Stätten Deutschlands: Bayern* (Stuttgart, 1961), pp. 586–587.

233. "Domit auch mein liber sun Jorg Scheurl, mit erlicher geselschaft erzogen wurd." *Tagebücher*/Heerwagen, p. 111 (fol. 122b).

234. Soden, *Christoph Scheurl der Zweite,* p. 81.

235. "Den . . . auszuzihen und lernen zu lasn, im auch zucht er und veterliche guthait zu beweisen." *Tagebücher*/Heerwagen, p. 111 (fol. 122b). Christoph mentions as boarding at the same time Georg Miltz, Jr., and two months earlier, (September) copyist (*schreiber*) Michael Albrecht. *Albrecht III/Christoph II Scheurl Haushalten,* fols. 135r, 132v.

236. See n. 280 below.

237. "Aller posselarbeit."

238. *Tagebücher*/Heerwagen, p. 116 (fol. 217a).

239. "Meinen liben sun Jorgn gemuttert und 4 1/4 kar treulich erzogn hat." Ibid., pp. 111–112 (fols. 124a, 134a).

240. I infer this from her marriage fourteen months after her hire; see n. 242 below.

241. *Tagebücher*/Heerwagen, p. 112 (fol. 134a).

242. "Suntag 24 verlobet ich meinem schreiner Petern meins shuns Christofn seugamen in unserm gartn." *Albrecht III/Christoph II Scheurl Haushalten*, fol. 117v. Peter Weishamer (Weishand?) was from Hall in Inthal, near Innsbruck.

243. An unidentified Gugel, Sebastian Groes, and Franz von Imhof are mentioned.

244. "Peters tanz was zu mittag bei der voitin [Vogtin, wife of the Vogt = Vormund] zu ga[s]thof und juncker Jorg Scheurl het den ersten vorreien [vortanz] mit der braut." *Albrecht III/Christoph II Scheurl Haushalten*, fol. 115r.

245. "Montag hilten maister Mathes Dhener striglmacher und Anna meins shuns Jorgen seugam hochzeit. gingen in unserm haus aus zur fruemess 50 mannern und weibern/warn Bartl Haller und ich vetter. hiltn das mittagmal zur Weisn Kron/zu 3 tischen/do warn d. Ch. Zugl. herr Georgori Krautzer. Conrat Haller Herr Jorg Hartman. Hanns Khun. Johan Neudorfer. Johan Petreius . . . Des nachts assen braut und preutigam [Anna and Mathes Striglmacher]/auch Maxen und Peters Weiber mit mir/denen und den schreinern [Katharina und Peter Schreiner Weishamer] hilt ich Mertens nacht einen tantz dornach/und si lagen bei/also das in kurtz Jorg Gotz. Max. Peter. di schreiner[in] und diser Mathes in unsern haus auf dem obern gang/auf der ab seiten beigelgn sein/nemlich in 13 monatn." Ibid., fol. 114v. Although Anna is not mentioned among the guests laying over, it is difficult to imagine her departing the household on her wedding day and leaving her new husband behind.

246. Ibid., fols. 99v, 90r, 75v.

247. *Tagebücher*/Heerwagen p. 116 (fol. 247a).

248. Katharina Weishamer did not live long after the child's birth, for on August 22, 1541, her husband celebrated a new marriage at St. Sebald's Church. See *Albrecht III/Christoph II Scheurl Haushalten*, fols. 80r–79v; *Ehebuch der Pfarrei St. Sebald* (1524–1543), fol. 174.

249. "Hat seer spat angefanngen zu reden/und erst nach sechs jarn vatter gesagt." *Scheurlbuch*, fol. 199a.

250. "Pet gern, kan noch nit r sprechen, aber zu tisch peten, lateinisch, pa-

ter noster, ave maria, simbolum, decem precepta, Benedicite, Ego sum dominus deus tuus, summa legis und der gelichn mer, hat lust zun pferden, kurzweilt gern ... trinkt aus der masn gern wein, ist gern wol, und hat freud zu gulden hembden und seiden claidern." *Tagebücher*/Heerwagen, p. 113 (fol. 159b).

251. "Ein pferdla." *Albrecht III/Christoph II Scheurl*, fol. 107r.

252. "Wolt er des vattern gepeu/auch die schonnen grossen stuben/ umbkeren/eitell pferstallung daraus machen und nur viell pferd haltenn." *Scheurlbuch*, fol. 199a. No clear date for this episode is given.

253. *Tagebücher*/Heerwagen, p. 113 (fol. 159b); cf. *Scheurlbuch*, fol. 198b. Fischbach was a Scheurl homestead outside the city.

254. Ibid., fol. 198b. Some modern theories hold that late talking by otherwise understanding children is more biological than cultural and would thus view the boys as intelligent "absorbers" in these early years. See Thomas Sowell, *Late-Talking Children* (Boston, 1997).

255. "Ist ein schoner, frolicher holtseliger pueb, der den vater ser liebet, und mit ofnem weiten maul an ine felt und kust, und widerumb von im herzlich geliebet wirdet, in masen er auch sein mutter überaus ser libet, und grose naigung zu pferden hat, erzaigt sich auch, als ob er gern peten wolt." *Tagebücher*/Heerwagen, p. 113 (fol. 159b).

256. See n. 299.

257. "[Schickt ich] ... 13 Mai frauen Katharina Prickhamerin ... auf ir krbei [kirbe = kirchweih] ... zu einer saur milch mein lieb 2 shun Jorgn und Christofen/die ir wolgefhelen/und si het einem hivhor in der vhastn geschenckt eins klains veslein pirs." *Albrecht III/Christoph II Scheurl Haushalten*, fol. 180v.

258. Ibid., fols. 104, 94r–93, 92v.

259. "Ainen silbren schau groschn dorauf stet rechts recht ist wogrecht. und weiber list ubertri[f]t/Leben starck." Ibid., fol. 102v. A contemporary catalogue description of the medallion reads: "Rechts.Recht. Ist.Wag.Recht;Weiber.List.Ueber.Trift. Lebn. Sterck." Josef Neumann, *Beschreibung der bekanntesten Kupfer Münzen* (Prague, 1868; reprint, New York, 1966), p. 58 (no. 28799–800).

260. *Albrecht III/Christoph II Scheurl Haushalten*, fol. 91r.

261. Heide Wunder, "Wie wird man ein Mann? Befunde am Beginn der Neuzeit (15.–17. Jahrhundert)," in *Was sind Frauen? Was sind Männer? Geschlechterkonstruktionen im historischen Wandel*, ed. Christiane Eifert, et al. N.F. 735 (Frankfurt/M, 1996), pp. 127–130; Ozment, *When Fathers Ruled*, pp. 144–147.

262. Christoph cites eleven biblical passages, most from the New Testament, that Georg could recite by heart.

263. That is, he knows his Maker.
264. *Tagebücher*/Heerwagen, p. 114 (fol. 171b).
265. Repeatedly commented on: ibid., pp. 115–116 (fols. 174b, 181 [Feb. 9, 1538]; fol. 189b [July 1538]; fol. 202b [late 1538]; fol. 211a [Feb. 1, 1539]; fol. 215a [August 1, 1539]; fol. 221a [October 31, 1539].
266. Ibid., p. 115 (fol. 172a).
267. *Albrecht III/Christoph II Scheurl Haushalten*, fol. 94v.
268. Among those in attendance were the patrician and noble playmates and surrogate "big brothers" of Georg's childhood: Eberhard Kurn, Jr.; Gabriel (12), Sixt (10), and Daniel (8) Tucher, now his most frequent playmates; Paul Volckamer (8); nephew Albrecht (13); ward Georg von Rotenhan (9); Georg Neusesser, Jr. (15); and brothers Caspar and Fabian Multze, the latter, with Georg von Rotenhan, soon to become Georg's new schoolmates in Master Handen's Latin School at St. Sebald's. Also seated at the table were Master Lamprecht and the not-yet-exposed predatory preceptor Michael Schmidt.
269. *Albrecht III/Christoph II Scheurl Haushalten*, fol. 91v–r.
270. Ibid., fol. 92r.
271. *Tagebücher*/Heerwagen, p. 216 (fols. 221a, 224b).
272. *Albrecht III/Christoph II Scheurl Haushalten*, fol. 65v.
273. Ibid., fols. 55r, 54v, 53v.
274. "Gab . . . glait." Ibid., fols. 81v, 75r. On Mathias, see Rotenhan, *Die Rotenhan*, pp. 285–291.
275. "Fhur das erstmal aufm wasser." *Albrecht III/Christoph II Scheurl Haushalten*, fol. 82r.
276. Ibid., fol. 70v.
277. Ibid., fol. 60v.
278. "Ainen forrheien/mit der ainen tischjunckfrauen, margreten pettermans tochter." Ibid., fol. 49r. Christoph had stood as godfather to Melchior Taig, Jr., on November 4, 1540. Ibid., fol. 61v.
279. "Mein shun Jorg schrib fur sich und brudern Christofen seinen ersten prief. Jorgen Neusessor juniorn. Vil vereret in an dise dingk zu neuen jar/das den vatter vol erfreuet darumb er got danck saget." Ibid., fol. 45v.
280. Madlena Kress, Martha Tucher, and Madlena Fütterer. Ibid., fol. 43v.
281. Ibid., fol. 38v.
282. Ibid., fol. 38r; Biedermann, *Geschlechtsregister*, Table 370, 3701b.
283. "Ehrrock."
284. *Albrecht III/Christoph II Scheurl Haushalten*, fols. 72r–71v.
285. Ibid., fol. 67r.

286. "Filii magni—quo ad staturam—verum dixit." *Tagebücher*/Heerwagen, p. 114 (fol. 171b). See n. 147.
287. "Verwundrit meinen shun Christofen/das man nit mher zu essen geben solt/dann ein stuck flaisch." *Albrecht III/Christoph II Scheurl Haushalten*, fol. 59v.
288. Graf, *Dr. Christoph Scheurl*, p. 72, n. 3.
289. "3 kunstpucher der perspectiva ires schwagers Albrecht Dürers." *Albrecht III/Christoph II Scheurl Haushalten*, fol. 71v.
290. Ibid., fol. 50.
291. "Peichtvatter." Ibid., fol. 67v. With the exception of the Commandery of the Teutonic Knights *(der Deutsche Orden)*, all city cloisters were under orders to observe the new Evangelical Mass and confess their sins only to Evangelical clergy. Although it lay outside the city, Pillenreut, where three Scheurl relatives lived, was also subject to such an order, and an Evangelical confessor visited the cloister for that very purpose. In neither cloister, however, were the sisters forced to comply. Like St. Clara's, Pillenreut may have had surreptitious visits from friars who dispensed the traditional sacraments. See Kusch, *Nürnberg*, pp. 306–308 (on the German Order). The Scheurls give every appearance of having participated in both Evangelical and Catholic services during the late 1520s and 1530s. On the larger issue of confession, see Ronald Rittgers, "The Lutheran Practice of Confession: Authority, Discipline, and Freedom in the German Reformation" (Dissertation, Harvard University, 1998).
292. "Gut clarer zu sein." *Albrecht III/Christoph II Scheurl Haushalten*, fol. 82v.
293. "Diweil mein bruderlicher freundt doctor Johann Eck itzo Letare/auf der fursten pundtstag zu Ingelstat gestorben wirdt. und meinen shun Jorgen mit hossen und wammes veert/hat/im derselb mein shun den 10 Marti in obgemelter groser forhen eine und darzu 20 gangvisch geschenckt und geschriben." Ibid., fol. 83f. While it is unknown whether the fish can be credited for it, the famous Dominican recovered to live another four years.
294. Ibid., fols. 61v, 60r.
295. Ibid., fols. 56r, 52r–51v.
296. "Meine herrn die eltern begrusten mich durch Herrn Seb. Pfintzing burgermaistern/meinen g. herrn Lantgrafen Philipen vhon Hessen etc. als den sie gern wol bewirten und vhor andern ehren solten/zu herb[e]rgen/das wolten si in gutem widerumb erkennen/also kam sein f.g. in unser haus mitwoch nach oculi. 23 Marchi und zoch

widerumb weg am tag annuntiationis 25 Marchi/ass ich 2 mal und erkennet mich mit seinen f.g. eben wol. fing an zimliche gnad zu uberkomen. sein g. und alles hofgesint lobet das haus. schancket mir ir dritte verantwortung. g. Braunschweig. der doctorin ein garnetn ringk. kostet 6 gulden/jr und meiner geschwigen 20 gulden patzn zur letz. Und verhies mir ainen pecher mit ir g. wappen. erzaiget sich gnug gnedig und speiset furstlich und wol/was frolich und gutter dingk." Ibid., fol. 55r.

297. "Machet sich gern bei vill grossen jenken und fremben leuten bekant unnd zu freundt/bei denen er durch schreibung zeittung unnd genealogias gnadt unnd gutt gunst fandt/Er war ein guter kaiser/könig/österreicher/gutt kirchisch/ein priester freundt/ein guter tucher/erbarer unnd geschlechter/ ein böser Lutheraner/wie er von ihme selbst schreibt odivi ecclesiam malignantiam als den des lestern/schelten unnd verdammen/und sich selbst gerecht zu sprechen/höchlich missfiel/obwol die handlung mit enderung der religion zwischen einem Erbare Rhat geistlicheit unnd Closterleben alhie 1521 durch ihne allein tractirt/furtrag unnd antwort gethon wardt." *Herrn Christoff Scheurls . . . Ankhunfft . . . 1591*, pp. 5–6.

298. Cf. Graf, *Doktor Christoph Scheurl*, pp. 5–7. Losing his own father at five and his mother at nine was perhaps a factor in Christoph Scheurl I's angry temperament.

299. ". . . Seinen zweien sohnen die er uber die masen liebet/das er auch geduldet/ihme der jungst auf den achsseln riet/unnd die ketten in mundt leget/uberwandt seine widerwertigkeit/anstöss und verfolgung/mit gedult/unnd obsieget." *Herrn Christoff Scheurls . . . Ankhunfft . . . 1591*, p. 6.

300. In March 1531, he estimated that wealth at 16,000 gulden, "do vhon geburn sich zugebn 16 rock thun 16 gulden." *Scheurlbuch*, fol. 1–b.

301. Soden, *Christoph Scheurl der Zweite*, p. 67.

302. *Albrecht III/Christoph II Scheurl Haushalten*, fol. 134r.

303. "Macht ich die heyrat zwischen unsern schreiner Casparn Rosdorfern von Wafingen/maister und burgern und junckfrauen Katherina Kreftin von Schweinau meiner geschweien kochin." Ibid., fol. 66v.

304. "Nam ich in mein behausung und kost/junckfrauen Felitzn Jorgen Pfanmüsn und Anna Tucherin tochter am geding gutter hofnung si wol zuverheiretten." Ibid., fols. 76v, 70v. Anna Tucher (1494–1574) appears to be the daughter of Stephan Tucher and Anna Reiz. Cloistered in Engenthal in 1519. (Biedermann, *Geschlechtsregister*, Table 507), she would have to have left the cloister before 1540.

305. *Albrecht III/Christoph II Scheurl Haushalten*, fol. 49r. Johannes Petrius and his wife stood with them.
306. Soden, *Christoph Scheurl der Zweite*, p. 88.
307. *Albrecht III/Christoph II Scheurl Haushalten*, fols. 117v, 65r, 54v.
308. "Leben wol waren frolich"; "wir waren frohlich und gutter dingk"; "lebten wol und frolich"; "tanzet flugs . . . tanzet man frolich"; "tanzten zu abents/mit baiden meinen shunen." Ibid., fols. 77r, 76v–r, 67v, 59r.
309. On the marriage, see n. 304. On the Peter von Watts family, see Bosl, *Bayern*, p. 171.
310. Biedermann, *Geschlechtsregister*, Table 508.A.
311. Apparently Elsbeth Hofmann, later cook and future Frau Hubschman.
312. *Albrecht III/Christoph II Scheurl Haushalten*, fol. 79r. Although Christoph here describes Katherina (Ketterla) as "Christoph the carpenter's wife," that marriage was still a year in the future at this time; the entry is evidently a later, retrospective addition.
313. Ibid., fol. 76v.
314. Soden, *Christoph Scheurl der Zweite*, p. 89.
315. "Des heiligen Romischen Reichs Stadt- Blut- und Bannrichter."
316. G. A. Will, *Der Nürnbergischen Münz-Belustigen* 4 (1767), pp. 219–222; Biedermann, *Geschlechtsregister*, Table 444, 610.

CHAPTER 3

1. A. Flegler, "Die Beziehungen Nürnbergs zu Venedig," *Anzeiger für Kunde der deutschen Vorzeit*, N.F. 10 (1867), pp. 289–300, 329–338; August Jegel, "Altnürnberger Hochzeitsbrauch und Eherecht, bes. bis zum Ausgang des 16. Jahrhunderts," *MVGN* 44 (1953), pp. 231.
2. He is the father of Lucas Friedrich Behaim, chapter 1.
3. Paul I's father (Friedrich Behaim) married Klara Imhof (d. 1548), Andreas's sister, in 1516. See J. Kamann, "Aus Paulus Behaim I. Briefwechsel," *MVGN* 3 (1881), pp. 74–75; "Aus dem Briefwechsel eines jungen Nürnberger Kaufmanns im 16. Jahrhundert," *Mitteilungen aus dem germanischen Nationalmuseum* II (1894), p. 12; Gerhard Seibold, "Die Imhoffsche Handelsgesellschaft in den Jahren 1579–1635," *MVGN* 64 (1977), pp. 201–214. Biedermann, *Geschlechtsregister*, Table 235, 244.
4. Wilhelm Loose, "Deutsches Studentenleben in Padua 1575 bis 1578," in *Beilage zur Schul- und Universitätsgeschichte* (Meissen, 1879), pp. 12, 40, n. 11; Biedermann, *Geschlechtsregister*, Table 237.

5. The Tetzels apparently died out in Nürnberg in the eighteenth century. See G. A. Will, *Nürnbergisches Gelehrter-Lexicon*, 4 (1758): p. 15.

6. Heide Wunder, " 'Er ist die Sonn, sie ist der Mond.' " *Frauen in der Frühen Neuzeit* (Munich, 1992), pp. 178–179; cf. Ilana Krausman Ben-Amos, *Adolescence and Youth in Early Modern England* (New Haven, 1994), pp. 135–136.

7. Richard von Dülman, *Kultur und Alltag in der Frühen Neuzeit, I: Das Haus und seine Menschen 16.–18. Jahrhundert* (Munich, 1990), pp. 43–47; Olwen Hufton, *The Prospect Before Her: A History of Women in Western Europe*, vol. 1 (New York, 1996). ch. 2.

8. Spitz, *The Religious Renaissance of the German Humanists*, p. 159; Ernst W. Zeeden, *Deutsche Kultur in der frühen Neuzeit* (Frankfurt am Main, 1968), pp. 214–216.

9. Wunder, " 'Gewirkte Geschichte,': Gedenken und 'Handarbeit:' Ueberlegungen zum Tradieren von Geschichte im Mittelalter und zu seinem Wandel am Beginn der Neuzeit," in Joachim Heinzle, ed., *Modernes Mittelalter. Neue Bilder einer populären Epoche* (Frankfurt/M, 1994), pp. 324–354.

10. Wilhelm Loose, ed., "Briefe eines Leipziger Studenten aus den Jahren 1572–1574," in *Beigabe zum Jahres-Bericht der Realschule zu Meissen* (Meissen, 1880), pp. 1–23.

11. Jane C. Hutchison, *Albrecht Dürer: A Biography* (Princeton, 1990), p. 27.

12. Biedermann, *Geschlechtsregister*, Table 7. Paul II was the second Paul II; the firstborn of his father's first marriage, also named Paul II, died three months after his first birthday (Dec. 10, 1549–Mar. 12, 1551). No children survived from this first marriage.

13. Biedermann, *Geschlechtsregister*, p. 564. Her mother, also named Magdalena (1505–1582), would outlive her daughter by a year. Paul sent greetings to her when he wrote his mother, suggesting that his grandmother was living with the family by the 1570s.

14. "Wen man nor vom pendlein zert und kein gewinets ist." Magdalena to Christoph (Nov. 16, 1582). Germanisches Nationalmuseum (Behaim File 80), reproduced in Ozment, *Magdalena and Balthasar*, p. 34.

15. Paula S. Fichtner, *Protestantism and Primogeniture* (New Haven, 1989), pp. 8–9, 20. cf. Judith J. Hurwich, "Inheritance Practices in Early Modern Germany," *Journal of Interdisciplinary History* 23 (1993), pp. 669–718.

16. Cf. Frank J. Sulloway's controversial correlation of higher and lower

birth order with conservatism and rebelliousness: *Born to Rebel: Birth Order, Family Dynamics, and Creative Lives* (New York, 1996).

17. For a German example of forced equity, see the legal dispute of the Büschler family of Schwäbisch Hall. See Ozment, *The Bürgermeister's Daughter*, pp. 125–184, with reference to relevant legal codes.

18. On Gienger's family, see Loose, "Deutsches Studentenleben," p. 41, n. 52.

19. Ibid., pp. 12–13. Loose's edition both excludes and excerpts numerous letters from Paul's correspondence. Because we have different goals and approaches in dealing with the correspondence, I draw on many of those deleted or excerpted letters. On the latter's identification and our different interests, see n. 48 below.

20. Ibid., pp. 13–14.

21. "Fur mich zupuss behalten."

22. A fabric whose warp is linen and whose woof is wool. Apparently a form of barchent. Loose, "Deutsches Studentenleben," p. 40, n. 19.

23. "Geselschaft."

24. "Uns auch mitt eim himelreich versehen."

25. Apparently an early experience of betrayal by a presumed fellow student, whose identity is unclear.

26. Loose, "Deutsches Studentenleben," pp. 14–15.

27. *Grobgrün* (French: *grosgrain*), a lower quality woolen material. See Jakob and Wilhelm Grimm, *Deutsches Wörterbuch* (Leipzig, 1854–1919), 4: col. 412.

28. "Strimpffen an den hosen . . . den allein gestrickte von faden."

29. "Dieweil man mitt unseren preceptor dis jar durch die finger muss sehen."

30. Loose, "Deutsches Studentenleben," p. 15.

31. "Einen bestelten doctor."

32. Emperor Justinian I's (r. 527–565) codification of Roman law, published in 529.

33. Dr. jur. Bartholomäus Flick, a "Gennanter" or member of Nürnberg's large council (*Grösser Rat*) between 1566 and 1594 and close Behaim relative (his first marriage was to a Römer), was informally overseeing Paul's studies abroad. See p. 168 below. Loose, "Deutsches Studentenleben," p. 22, n. 45.

34. "Damitt er auff den herbst nicht solches bussen möge"; that is, succumb to serious illness, due to weakened immunity, when cold weather strikes.

35. "Paul II Briefe," To Magdalena (Aug. 4, 1575), no. 5 (Behaim Archiv,

Germanisches Nationalmuseum [GNM], Hist. Archiv, Fasz. I, 1572–1576 [105]). Paul Imhof's mother was Paul's Aunt Katharina, but no direct relation of Carl Imhof. Caspar Reh was a long-standing family friend and a recent Wittenberg graduate, whose theological education Paul's mother had earlier assisted. See Paul's letter of August 5, 1575, in Loose, "Deutsches Studentenleben," pp. 16, 40, n. 39.

36. Martin Brecht, *Martin Luther: Shaping and Defining the Reformation, 1521–1532*, trans. James L. Schaaf (Minneapolis, 1990), p. 201.

37. The youth in question, Sebastian Hölzschuher, is reported in his family's genealogy later to have fought with the Spanish in the Netherlands and to have died in battle at Maastricht in 1579. Loose, "Deutsches Studentenleben," p. 41, n. 5.

38. Ibid., pp. 16–17.

39. "Einfeltigkeit."

40. Veit Hölzschuher (1515–1580) directed the Hölzschuher charities: "Senior Familiae und Pfleger der Holzschuherischen Stiftungen." Biedermann, *Geschlechtsregister*, Table 200.B. On Sebastian, see Loose, "Deutsches Studentenleben," p. 41, n. 54; and Biedermann, *Geschlechtsregister*, Table 176A.

41. Loose, "Deutsches Studentenleben," pp. 17–18.

42. On dating, see Loose, "Deutsches Studentenleben," p. 41, n. 57.

43. In a witch trial, the confession that convicted an accused person had to be made, or remade, voluntarily by that person as well. See the tortured reasoning on this point in the *Mallus Malificarum*. Alan C. Kors and Edward Peters, *Witchcraft in Europe, 1100–1700. A Documentary History* (Philadelphia, 1978), pp. 161–162. On Italian practice: Thomas Kuehn, *Law, Family, and Women: Toward a Legal Anthropology of Renaissance Italy* (Chicago, 1991).

44. Loose, "Deutsches Studentenleben," pp. 18–19.

45. "Geschlagene leuth." Apparently so described because of their economic straits.

46. Excusing them if illness or lack of news prevented their writing, he asked them "aber forthin/ir wollet mitt dem wenigsten allezeit mit der mutterlichen brieff ein schreiben von euch lassen herein khomen/ schreibett eine unter euch nicht/so schreibe doch die ander/kondt ir nicht ein gantze seitten herab schreiben/schreibett doch ein halbe oder ein zeil nur/den es alles mir eins ist." "Paul II Briefe," Paul to Magdalena and Sabina (Aug. 25, 1575), no. 10.

47. Loose, "Deutsches Studentenleben," p. 19.

48. "Paul II Briefe," no. 13. This portion of Paul's letter of October 19 is among those deleted by Loose on the grounds that they express only

"local interest," the latter being a secondary goal of his edition, but a primary goal of the present study. To this point I have drawn on Loose's edition and followed his numbering of the letters. Henceforth, the MS numbers of the letters, as they appear in the Behaim Archive of the German National Museum, are given in the notes when additional letters not in Loose, or parts of letters deleted by him, are cited or presented. In those cases where I reintegrate deleted portions with Loose's excerpts, both the original MS number and that of the letter in Loose's edition are given, as in (n. 52 below).

49. Loose, "Deutsches Studentenleben," no. 11, p. 20.

50. Georg Fütterer was apparently the son of Nürnberg councilman Jakob Fütterer and probable distant relation of Katharina Scheurl (see chapter 2), whose family was one of six lines of Fütterers. See *Genealogia Fütterer, ca. 1400–1586* (Stadtarchiv Nürnberg, E1/340, Fütterer 2); Loose, "Deutsches Studentenleben," p. 41, n. 73. Loose describes the Fütterers as "third class *Ehrbaren*," who traded in Milan and Genoa and died out as a family in 1586.

51. It is unclear whether this foundation (*Stifftung*) is a family-run charity like the Imhofs'—or is even that of the Imhofs'—or a public charity in the city.

52. "Paul II Briefe," no. 18; Loose, "Deutsches Studentenleben," no. 12, p. 21.

53. "Auff dem rathaus," where litigation occurred.

54. At sixteen pfennigs, one *batzen* was about one-sixteenth of a gulden (252 pfennigs) and two-thirds of an Italian crown. Over two years, the rented five books of the *Corpus Civile*—at seven *batzen* a month—would have cost Paul 168 *batzen*, or 2,568 pfennigs, or ten gulden, or about seven crowns. Despite the accuracy of his figures and the logic of his argument, he was told to borrow the books he needed, perhaps because his mother hoped to have him out of Italy and productively employed at home before two years passed.

55. John Edwards, *The Jews in Christian Europe, 1400–1700* (London, 1988), pp. 67–70, 80. On Erasmus, see Marcella and Paul Grendler, "The Survival of Erasmus in Italy," in *Erasmus in English* 8 (1976), pp. 2–12.

56. Edwards, *The Jews in Christian Europe*, pp. 81–82.

57. The "little edition by Neuber" is mentioned. "Paul II Briefe," (Fasz. 1 [106], 1576), no. 1. With the new year came a new collection of letters; hence, the archive's new MS numberings. See Sebald Welser's use of this same Lutheran material in chapter 4.

58. "Dieweil aber mein Register etwas viel ist/wollestu darnoch

gedencken/dass ichs an wahr widerumb hab/als am pelz und am Instrument, etc." "Paul II Briefe," To Mother (Jan. 13, 1576), no. 2.

59. "Paul II Briefe," no. 3.

60. Paul identifies Starschedel as having earlier attended the wedding of
Wilibald Imhof's daughter's in Nürnberg, implying that Frau Behaim
had met him there. Evidently, he and Paul had been students together
in Leipzig sometime between 1572 and 1575.

61. "Das grausame gelt."

62. "Sich selbst zu regiren lehrnet."

63. Loose, "Deutsches Studentenleben," no. 14, pp. 22–23.

64. "Paul II Briefe," no. 5.

65. The agent in the Imhof office from whom Paul got his quarterly
stipend.

66. A Nürnberg merchant with offices in Bologna.

67. Welser is the subject of chapter 4.

68. Magdalena wrote Paul of the family's concern on April 3, six weeks
before he mentioned it to them. See "Paul II Briefe," Magdalena to
Paul (Apr. 3, 1576), no. 6.

69. Loose, "Deutsches Studentenleben," no. 16, p. 24.

70. "Es wer dan/das ich solt ein gans hinaus komen wie ich bin herein
khomen." "Paul II Briefe," no. 10.

71. "Paul II Briefe," To Mother (June 21, 1576), no. 11.

72. Ibid., no. 13.

73. I have been unable to identify this safe haven, frequented by Germans, apparently in northern Venetia.

74. See p. 168.

75. "Montarton" is the word Paul uses. One Italian mile in Lombardy was
a little longer than one English mile: 1,785 meters to 1,609, while the
German mile was 7,449 meters. See *Brockhaus Enzyklopadie* 14
(Mannheim, 1986–1996), p. 213; *Enciclopedia Italiana di scienze, let-
tere ed arti* 23 (Rome, 1929–1939), p. 246. Another possibility is
"Montagnon," about eight Italian miles southwest of Padua.

76. Loose, "Deutsches Studentenleben," no. 17, pp. 22–23.

77. "Still legen."

78. Otto von Starschedel and Schweikhard Wanibold, the latter later
[1577] counsel to the Elector Palatine. Loose, "Deutsches Studentenleben," p. 42, n. 96.

79. "Den medicis."

80. "Paul II Briefe," no. 16.

81. This Greck was Isaac's brother Jacob, and Otto was a merchant who

exchanged money for students. Loose, "Deutsches Studentenleben," p. 42, n. 87.

82. Ibid., no. 18, pp. 25–26.
83. "Damitt sie nicht gleicher weis ein bösenlufft von mir empfiengen."
84. To Mother (Jan. 17, 1577); Loose, "Deutsches Studentenleben," no. 19, p. 26.
85. Loose, "Deutsches Studentenleben," no. 20, pp. 26–27.
86. "Allerlei zu besehen."
87. "Paul II Briefe," To Mother (Feb. 14, 1577), no. 21 (Behaim Archiv, GNM, Fasz. II, 1577–1580 [106]).
88. On parental suspicion that sons were not writing their own Latin letters, see the examples in Mathias Beer, " 'Et sciatis nos fortiter studere' Die Stellung des Junglichen in der Familie des späten Mittelalters und der frühen Neuzeit," in Martin Kintzinger, et al., eds., *Das andere Wahrnehmen. Beiträge zur europäischen Geschichte. August Nitschke zum 65. Geburtstag gewidmet* (Cologne, 1991), pp. 394–395; also that of Stephan Carl Behaim, who got another to write a proper Latin letter to his guardian and half brother Lucas Friedrich in 1630. See Ozment, *Three Behaim Boys*, pp. 181, 201–203 (his dictated German version).
89. "Paul II Briefe," To Mother (Mar. 13, 1577), no. 8; To Mother (Apr., 5, 1577); Loose, "Deutsches Studentenleben," no. 23, p. 29.
90. Loose, "Deutsches Studentenleben," no. 22, pp. 28–29. The translation from the Latin is by Bruce Venarde, with touches by James Hankins and myself.
91. François Hotman (1524–1590), a leading authority on Roman and French law and author of the Huguenot tract *Francogallia* (1573), documenting legal precedents for the right of lower magistrates to resist tyrants. See Donald R. Kelley, *François Hotman: A Revolutionary's Ordeal* (Princeton, 1973).
92. Actually Paduan professor Laurentius Castellanus. Loose, "Deutsches Studentenleben," p. 43, n. 111.
93. Lagus was a Wittenberg professor of law. Ibid.
94. The "digest" of Roman laws compiled by a team of Roman lawyers during the reign of Emperor Justinian.
95. The first part of the *Corpus Iuris civilis.*
96. He died during the plague.
97. To Mother (April 5), in Loose, "Deutsches Studentenleben," no. 23, p. 29.
98. "Der zerrissneste lumpenman."

99. "Edelleuten . . . oder . . . [andere], so eines erbarn wandels sein."

100. Loose, "Deutsches Studentenleben," April 20, 1577, no. 24, pp. 29–31.

101. Loose, "Deutsches Studentenleben," no. 25, p. 31.

102. Christoph Imhof's deceased stepmother, the second wife of his father, Sebastian II (1511–1572), was Paul's and Magdalena's Aunt Katharina (1530–1574). Biedermann, *Geschlechtsregister*, Table 224.

103. "Paul II Briefe," no. 17.

104. "Heimlatung."

105. "Ein klein ablass Brieflein." Christoph appears to have been in Verona at the time Magdalena wrote, but perhaps was soon to depart for Rome. It is possible that an allusion to his Catholicism, rather than a geographical location, is here intended. On this indulgence, see chapter 4, pp. 211–212.

106. "In gar mit dem gespet [spettel, spetlein = Fetzen] aus der wiegen [Waage] werfen"; literally, "throw it away with the fat from the scales."

107. In a letter to Paul dated April 3, 1576, Magdalena mentions having asked Christoph to deliver a letter to Paul in Padua, but as his departure was delayed, it was given to someone else to deliver. ("Paul II Briefe," Fasz. 1 [1576], no. 6.) Christoph evidently had been among Magdalena's trusted couriers. From her point of view, the conflict had more to do with the surreptitious reading of her letter than any deep insult she had subjected him to in it. However, she does acknowledge the hurtfulness of her remarks. Apparently, she had criticized him for haughtiness, as she also does at the conclusion of the letter of April 3. Her later critical remarks about Christoph, made directly to his older brother Paul, who in turn reported them back to Christoph, also heightened the original conflict.

108. See below, chapter 4.

109. Loose, "Deutsches Studentenleben," no. 26, p. 32.

110. Contemporary funeral sermons indicated that stepmothers were not generally viewed as real mothers, that they treated stepchildren more harshly than they did their own, and, where possible, that aunts and uncles were preferred over stepmothers in the rearing of children who lost their birth mothers. On the other hand, rearing at the hand of a stepmother was believed to inculcate greater self-discipline that served well those who survived it. Elisabeth Ines Kloke, "Das Kind in der Leichenpredigten," in Rudolf Lenz, ed., *Leichenpredigten als Quelle historischer Wissenschaften*, 3 (Marburg a/d Lahn, 1984), pp. 112–114. See the case of Sebald Welser in chapter 4.

111. Loose, "Deutsches Studentenleben," no. 28, p. 33.

112. No biblical reference is given.

113. That would be after the third quarter, ending in September.
114. "Deiner rechnung nach."
115. Loose, "Deutsches Studentenleben," no. 29, pp. 33–34.
116. "Wie hoch du mich solt aussmachen."
117. "Wo mir [wir] . . . in getheilten guttern weren"—so that Paul then could only have drawn on his own reduced share. Frau Behaim evidently pointed this out to him in her letter.
118. ". . . Ehe das hauptgutt selbst angreiffen."
119. "Einen Strich . . . thun."
120. "Paul II Briefe," no. 38.
121. Apparently since August 7.
122. "Hat solgs auf wog geschriben."
123. "Du habst den zu vor etwas gesehen zu nutz und fiterung deiner und unser ehr."
124. "So unpruderlich."
125. "Paul II Briefe," no. 41; Loose, "Deutsches Studentenleben," no. 30, pp. 34–35.
126. Loose's excerpt begins here. "Deutsches Studentenleben," no. 30, p. 34.
127. Actually, he did so at least twice.
128. December 7, 1577; Loose, "Deutsches Studentenleben," no. 31, p. 35; Jan. 16, 1578: ibid., no. 32, pp. 35–36.
129. Ibid., no. 32, pp. 35–36.
130. Ibid., no. 33, p. 36.
131. "Andern leüthen auch nutz köndt sein."
132. Loose, "Deutsches Studentenleben," no. 35, p. 37. In response to hers of March 18.
133. Christoph Behaim (1562–1624) was apparently then a merchant's apprentice in Augsburg.
134. To Mother (April 16, 1578); Loose, "Deutsches Studentenleben," no. 36, p. 38.
135. For imperial Hofrath, Dr. Andreas Gail. Loose, "Deutsches Studentenleben," p. 12.
136. "Des aeltern geheimen Raths vorderster Losungs Herr und Reichs Schultheiss." Biedermann, *Geschlechtsregister*, Table 9.
137. Especially with Lucas Friedrich, Georg Hieronymus, Friedrich VIII, and Paul III. "Paul II Briefwechsel" (1596–1621) (Behaim Archiv, Fasz. VII [111]–XI [113]); Biedermann, *Geschlechtsregister*, Table 7–10.

CHAPTER 4

1. An early version of this chapter appeared under the title, "The Private Life of an Early Modern Teenager: A Nuremberg Lutheran Visits Catholic Louvain (1577)," *Journal of Family History*, 21 (1996), pp. 22–43.

2. "Vitae suae moderator, iuventutis suae praesidium et decor." See Ludwig Krauss, ed., *Die Altdorfer Gedächtnisrede auf Sebald Welser (d. 1589). Der lateinische Text mit Uebersetzung, Einleitung und Erläuterungen* (Nürnberg, 1976), p. 13. On dating, I follow Biedermann, *Geschlechtsregister*, p. 567.

3. *Die Altdorfer Gedächtnisrede*, p. 30.

4. Lewis W. Spitz and Barbara Sher Tinsley, *Johann Sturm on Education: The Reformation and Humanist Learning* (St. Louis, 1995); Rudolf Endres, "Nürnberger Bildungswesen zur Zeit der Reformation," *MVGN* 71 (1984), pp. 109–128.

5. *Die Altdorfer Gedächtnisrede*, p. 33. For contemporary criticism of lawyers and Roman law, see Gerald Strauss, *Law, Resistance, and the State: The Opposition to Roman Law in Reformation Germany* (Princeton, 1986).

6. See Paul Behaim II's comments on his condition in Italy, chapter 3 pp. 148–154.

7. Ursula Koenigs-Erffa, ed., "Das Tagebuch des Sebald Welser aus dem Jahre 1577," *MVGN* 46 (1957) [henceforth, *Tagebuch*], p. 268, n. 13; entry for May 16 (5/16), p. 298; 6/1, p. 302. On the Harstörffers, see Biedermann, *Geschlechtsregister*, Table, 149; on the Imhofs, see Table 237.

8. My summary of these events is taken from J. H. Elliott, *Europe Divided, 1559–1598* (New York, 1975).

9. Richard Bonney, *The European Dynastic States, 1494–1660* (Oxford, 1991), pp. 146, 154.

10. *Tagebuch*, p. 262; *Allgemeine Deutsche Biographie*, 26, pp. 519–520. Throughout the essay, I rely on editor Koenigs-Erffa's excellent apparatus for basic historical information about the people, proceedings, and events on which Sebald comments, supplementing it modestly where I can.

11. Although Louvain remained a Catholic stronghold, it harbored within its university a Catholic reform movement known as Baianism, after the Louvain theologian, Michael Baius (d. 1589), which shared with mainstream Lutheranism and Calvinism a belief in the bondage of the will in salvation. Modern scholars view it as a forerunner of the Catholic heresy of Jansenism, after another Louvain theologian, Cor-

nelis Jansen (d. 1638), who made St. Augustine's views on predestination the center of his theology. Elliott, *Europe Divided*, p. 74.

12. *Tagebuch*, 7/13, pp. 332–333.
13. Ibid., p. 332, n. 503.
14. Bonney, *The European Dynastic States*, pp. 154–159. On Netherland's religious history in this period, see Benjamin J. Kaplan, *Calvinists and Libertines: Confession and Community in Utrecht, 1578–1620* (Oxford, 1995).
15. *Tagebuch*, 7/13–14, p. 333, n. 506.
16. "Hab ich die Procession gesehen und das Gauckelwerk geküst." Ibid., 7/14, p. 333.
17. "Ablass zu S. Michael geholt." Ibid., 7/21, p. 336. The editor describes the act as "surprising at least for a Protestant from Nürnberg" (n. 525).
18. "Ordnung im gebet und lesen." Ibid., 6/25, p. 623.
19. Ibid., entries for 1/1, 2/3, 2/9–20, 6/24–25, 7/2, 7/25, 7/27, 8/5, 9/14, 9/18, 10/1, 10/11, 10/17–18, 10/25.
20. Ibid., 1/22, p. 274; 2/1, p. 276; 3/9, p. 283. On Musculus, excerpted at his dreariest, see Strauss, *Luther's House of Learning*, pp. 47, 145–146, 206, 215, 219–220.
21. After the Old Testament, the *Institutes* of Emperor Justinian, a basic legal manual for young scholars, was his priority reading for the year, the first book of which he set out to memorize "A.S.T." (*Auxilio Sanctae Trinitatis*—"with the aid of the Holy Trinity"). See *Tagebuch*, 2/11, p. 277. He looked forward to finishing the book of Tobias and beginning that of Judith "A.S.T." (*Annuente Sanctissima Trinitate*—"with the concurrence of the most Holy Trinity"). Ibid., 10/4, p. 277. He hopes that the next time he poses for his portrait it will also be his last, "G.G.G." (*Gott geb Glück*—"if God gives luck"). Ibid., 11/4, p. 368. On one occasion, he invokes God's help with a novel expression, pledging to memorize the second book of Justinian's *Institutes*, as he had already done with the first, *Deus Fax*—"if God sends the torch (or guidance)." Ibid., 2/11, pp. 177–78.
22. Johann Michael von Welser, *Die Welser. Des Freiherr Johann Michael v. Welser Nachrichten über die Familie*, vol. 1 (Nürnberg, 1917), pp. 436, 483, 468–487.
23. *Tagebuch*, p. 279, n. 98.
24. Cf. Ozment, *When Fathers Ruled*, pp. 9–25.
25. *Tagebuch*, p. 279, n. 98.
26. See above, chapter 2.
27. *Tagebuch*, 5/1, p. 295.

28. Ibid., 5/9, p. 297; 5/17, p. 299; 5/31, p. 301.

29. Ibid., 7/18, p. 335; 11/5, p. 366.

30. "Et vidimus quondam a vanis hominibus S. Mariae adferre donandi gratia." Ibid., 3/25, pp. 286–87.

31. "Haben die Jesuiter das gauckelspiel bey der monstranzen gemacht an der gassen, mit dem himelbrott und Aronis schaubroth." Ibid., 6/6, p. 306. Here, "showbread" ("bread of divine presence") refers to the twelve loaves of unleavened bread placed in the tabernacle by Hebrew priests, according to Exodus 25:33.

32. Ibid., 6/10, p. 311; ed. n. 361.

33. Ibid., 6/10, p. 312.

34. Ibid., 6/10, p. 314.

35. Ibid., 6/12, pp. 315–16; 7/8, pp. 328 ff.

36. Ibid., 6/24, p. 323.

37. Ibid., p. 275, n. 74; cf. chapter 3.

38. Ibid., 7/5, p. 327.

39. Ibid., 8/1, p. 339.

40. Ibid., 8/19, pp. 345–346.

41. On such practice, see Beer, *Eltern und Kinder*, p. 225.

42. *Tagebuch*, 9/22, p. 357.

43. The student's name was Johannes Berswort (Bersbrot). Ibid., 8/26, p. 347.

44. Ibid., 8/29, p. 348.

45. "Lernen stricken." Ibid., 9/13, p. 354. Apparently how to patch clothing is meant.

46. "Welcher . . . 16 wochen gelegen und fast melancolisirt glaubenssachen hatte." Ibid., 3/13, pp. 284–85.

47. Ibid., 8/4, p. 340.

48. Ibid., 9/11, pp. 353–54.

49. Ibid., 7/28, p. 337.

50. Bonney, *The European Dynastic States*, p. 157. Orange, however, treated Aerschot magnanimously, as an ally of the new Calvinist republic of Brabant.

51. *Tagebuch*, 4/7, p. 291; 5/25, p. 300; 6/23, p. 322: "Haben wir die predig versaumbt und in der herberg die kuchen gezehret."

52. Ibid., 6/27, p. 324–325, n. 460.

53. See editor Koenigs-Erffa's discussion of possible political and economic reasons for Sebald's apparent "tolerance." Ibid., pp. 324–25, n. 460; p. 341, n. 556.

54. As happened in the 1590s, after Catholic authorities in Lucca put

Nürnberg merchants trading there under surveillance and pressured them to observe local religious celebrations, evidently suspecting that visitors from so Protestant a city might transport and disseminate Lutheran propaganda with their wares. Nürnberg merchants protested to both Luccan and Nürnberg authorities. See Ozment, *Magdalena and Balthasar*, p. 187, n. 142.

55. Cf. Leo Ravenburg's advice to his fourteen-year-old, as the latter departed Augsburg for Lyons. See p. 259 below.

56. *Tagebuch*, p. 325, n. 460, and n. 53 above.

57. Ibid., 8/13, p. 343; 9/8, p. 352; 9/19, p. 355.

58. Ibid., 7/15, pp. 334–35; 9/25–26, pp. 357–358. Peter Ernst, count of Mansfeld, a former governor of Luxembourg, is cited by the editor among Brussels' noble critics of the Spanish occupation. Ibid., p. 334, n. 513.

59. Ibid., 9/25–26, pp. 357–358; "Summo belli duce," 10/3, p. 359.

60. Ibid., 8/29, p. 348.

61. Ibid., 10/3, p. 360.

62. Gerald Strauss, "Protestant Dogma and City Government: The Case of Nuremberg," *Past & Present* 36 (1967): pp. 38–58; Lyndal Roper, *The Holy Household: Women and Morals in Reformation Augsburg* (Cambridge, 1989).

63. Ozment, *Protestants*, pp. 105–116; cf. Strauss, *Luther's House of Learning*, ch. 10.

64. Hans Medick, "Village Spinning Bees in Early Modern Germany," in *Interest and Emotion: Essays on the Study of Family and Kinship*, ed. Hans Medick and David W. Sabean (Cambridge, 1984), p. 324.

65. "Bin ich zum Philip Römer geladen worden, hat mans aber für mich abgeschlagen, dieweil er einen jungfrauenhoff gehabt." *Tagebuch*, 1/7, p. 270.

66. Ibid., 1/8, p. 170.

67. Ibid., 2/24, p. 281.

68. Ibid., 5/7–8, p. 297.

69. See Albrecht Behaim's near pornographic discussion of the sex life he would like to have with the fiancée of cousin Lucas Behaim. Chapter 1, p. 22–23; also, Erasmus of Limpurg's and Anna Büschler's love letters, referenced in n. 70.

70. Cf. Lucas Behaim's sublimation of lustful thoughts and desires, chapter 1, pp. 19–21, 26–29. Cf. also Magdalena Paumgartner's oblique description of her pregnancy (Ozment, *Magdalena and Balthasar*, pp. 38–39) and discussions of infidelity, pregnancy, apparent abor-

tion, and syphilis between a Schwäbisch Hall couple (Ozment, *The Bürgermeister's Daughter*, pp. 35–102). On syphilis and the baths, see Ozment, *Three Behaim Boys*, p. 136.

71. *Tagebuch*, 2/14, p. 278.

72. "Indusium cum corona." *Tagebuch*, 8/20, p. 346. Koenigs-Erffa reads "indusium" as "Hemd" (shirt or vest for either man or woman), apparently understanding it to apply to Sebald. However, the Latin indicates the layer of clothing closest to a woman's body, or an undergarment.

73. Ozment, *Protestants*, pp. 144–145.

74. *Tagebuch*, 3/26, p. 287.

75. Ibid., 8/9, p. 342.

76. Ibid., 9/21, p. 356.

77. "Egregie." Ibid., 9/28, p. 358.

78. Ibid., 10/13, p. 363; 9/27, p. 358.

79. "War ich zu nacht sehr [word missing], also das ich nit wuste, was ich getan hatte." I read the missing word to be "betrunken." Ibid., 10/20–21, 10/28, p. 365.

80. Ibid., 1/20, p. 276; ed. n. 79.

81. The pieces from Sachs were *Princess Gismonda*, adapted from a Boccacio novella, *The Tragedy of Lucretia*, and a *Fastnachtspiel* about bad wives—the one to which Sebald apparently contributed. *Tagebuch*, 2/3, pp. 276–77, ed. n. 79; 2/10, p. 277; 2/21, pp. 280–281, ed. n. 108; 3/1, p. 282, ed. n. 122; 3/4, p. 283.

82. Compare the friendship of Stephan Carl Behaim and Georg Wilhelm Pömer; Ozment, *Three Behaim Boys*, pp. 196–99 passim.

83. "Donavi Carlo Imhof das lemblein und hirschen von butter gemacht." *Tagebuch*, 5/16–5/18, p. 299. Sebald was ill and purging at the time. Wax lambs, symbolic of "the lamb of God," were common devotional items.

84. "Nolui ut Harstorffer amplius videret apud meum lumen." Ibid., 9/19, p. 356; 11/3, p. 366.

85. I am baffled by the editor's comment that Sebald does not express feelings: "Gefühle werden nicht geäussert—der Sprache der Zeit fehlt noch die Ausdrucksmöglichkeit." Ibid., p. 263.

86. Ibid., 2/12, p. 278.

87. Ibid., 5/3, p. 296.

88. Ibid., 3/12, p. 284; 3/30, p. 289. On Pastor Dürnhofer, see chapter 5.

89. He died on October 26, 1578. Ibid., 4/4, 4/6, p. 290.

90. Ibid., 8/4, p. 340.

91. Ibid., 5/13, p. 297; Loose, no. 15, p. 23.

92. "Nassenwasser." Ibid., 4/3–6, p. 290; on Dr. Ayrer, see p. 271, n. 44.
93. Ibid., 4/25, p. 293; on "Pisamknopff," ed. n. 217.
94. Ibid., 5/17, 5/30, pp. 299, 301.
95. Ibid., 6/18, p. 322.
96. "Das Gebet von meiner krankheit gemacht." Ibid., 7/5–6, pp. 327–328.
97. Ibid., p. 328; ed. n. 482.
98. Ibid., 6/21, p. 322; 7/20, p. 335.
99. "Stehent zu betten." Ibid., 8/23, p. 346.
100. Ibid., 9/11, p. 353, n. 653.
101. "Was fürs gift."
102. Both are cited in Welser, *Die Welser*, pp. 476–477.
103. The episode, briefly summarized here, is described at length in Magdalena's letter of July 24, 1577, to brother Paul. See chapter 3, p. 174.
104. Among Sebald's Nürnberg peers and inferiors, apprenticeship began as early as age twelve and university study at fourteen. See the examples of Michael Behaim (1510–1569) and Friederich Behaim (1563–1613) in Ozment, *Three Behaim Boys*, pp. 1–10. In contemporary England, rural youth as a rule did not live and work away from home until age thirteen, while their urban counterparts began apprenticeships at fourteen and university study at sixteen. An appreciable number of urban youths, however, did "board out" at younger ages for periods up to several years before departing home for apprenticeships or schooling. In Ben-Amos's sample, one quarter of urban youth had done so for a few days or weeks and up to several years. *Adolescence and Youth in Early Modern England,* pp. 54, 62.
105. On both continuity and discord, see ibid., pp. 101, 165; Ozment, *Three Behaim Boys*, pp. 21–38.

CHAPTER 5

1. For background on the city's transformation by the Reformation in the first half of the century, see chapter 2.
2. "Dürnhofer MS," p. 45b (1586), (Germansches Nationalmuseum, Reichsstadt Nürnberg XVIII Dürnhofer 1). On the surviving manuscript, see Karl Schornbaum, "Die Chronik der Dürnhofer," *MVGN* 42 (1951), pp. 171–197. Schornbaum misdates the birth of Dürnhofer's twenty-third child—1596 instead of 1586, clearly a typographical error, as he knows Lorenz died in 1594. Ibid., p. 175. He offers a succinct summary of the contents of the MS in the context of other

family contributors. There also exists a two-page genealogy of Lorenz's and Lorenz Jr.'s children, with modest elaboration, both apparently in the former's hand: "Dürnhofer Genealogy" (Stadtarchiv Nürnberg, E1/230, nr. 1).

3. Only three survived from the first marriage. Five of the eleven were born prematurely, three of them early miscarriages ("vor der geburtszeit abgangen"), while the remaining two (one reached three months) could be identified as males. Like Christoph Scheurl, Lorenz counted miscarriages in the first trimester among his children, but did not give them names. Three other children arrived closer to term, but no more successfully: one stillborn, a second dying within days of birth, and the third within weeks. Unlike the previous five, each of these received a Christian name. Six of the twelve from the second marriage survived into their teens—four of their siblings dying within days or weeks of their birth, a fifth at three years old, and the sixth at twelve. "Dürnhofer Genealogy;" "Dürnhofer MS," p. 32a (1532). On Scheurl, see chapter 2.

4. According to the leading authority on the Dürnhofer chronicle, Lorenz talked "only about what was important for the family" and not much else, as this first entry also suggests. See Schornbaum, "Die Chronik der Dürnhofer," p. 181. As Lorenz mentions all his children in the first entry, it could only have been written after 1586, when his last child was born. However, among the records drawn on during the last eight years of his life, when the chronicle was composed, were very likely his own saved contemporary accounts of earlier experiences, so that at certain junctures chronicle descriptions arguably convey a "live" report.

5. Reinhold Seeberg, *Textbook of the History of Doctrines*, trans. C. E. Hay, vol. 2 (Grand Rapids, 1964) pp. 362–378.

6. "Dürnhofer MS," p. 32a (1544); Schornbaum, "Die Chronik der Dürnhofer," pp. 174, 181.

7. "Dürnhofer MS," p. 32a (1544). On Culman, see Strauss, *Luther's House of Learning*, pp. 143, 188, 190, 203. The major factors behind a burgher son's choice of a particular vocational preparation were family tradition, parental/paternal wishes, and, as in Lorenz's case, the pursuit of one's own individual desire and aptitude. See Beer, "Et sciatis nos fortiter studere," pp. 388–392, 406.

8. See chapter 2, p. 127.

9. Beer, *Eltern und Kinder*, pp. 329–330. Neudörfer is also known for his history of contemporary artists and architects, a work that brought him posthumous fame. Eugen Kusch, *Nürnberg. Lebensbild einer Stadt*

(Nürnberg: 1951), pp. 182–183; *Allgemeine Deutsche Biographie*, 23: pp. 481–83.

10. "Dürnhofer MS," p. 32a (1545).

11. Seeberg, *Text-book of the History of Doctrines*, vol. 2, pp. 349–362; and Spitz, *The Religious Renaissance of the German Humanists*, p. 76 passim; cf. Wilhelm Mauer, *Der junge Melanchthon*, vols. 1–2 (Göttingen, 1967, 1969).

12. "Dürnhofer MS," p. 35b (1559); *Allgemeine Deutsche Biographie*, 5: pp. 529–531.

13. "M. Paulus Eberus/vor der zeitt mein preceptor/unnd nachmals mein lieber gevatter/als er zum Pastore der kirchen zu Wittenberg erwehlet/ist Doctor Theologie promovirt worden den 7 decembris. Hatt mir hernach auff mein widerkunfft noch zum gedechtnis verehrtt munera doctoralia ein par handtschuch and barrett." Ibid.

14. "Depoinert," Ibid., p. 32b (1550).

15. "Dürnhofer MS," p. 33a (1551).

16. Ibid., p. 33a (1551).

17. Ibid.

18. "Eine geschwinde hauptkranckheitt/daran vil leutte kranckh lagen/vil ihrer sinn beraubt wurden/der mainste thail stürben." Ibid., p. 33a (1552).

19. "Ohne zweifel durch gottes sonderbare schickhung." Ibid.

20. Ibid.

21. "Ein sendtbrief ahn meine mutter," ibid.; reproduced in Schornbaum, "Die Chronik der Familie Dürnhofer," pp. 190–191. A second saved writing of Melanchthon is the *Carmen de oppido Torgau*, Melanchthon's epithalamium on the occasion of their wedding. "Dürnhofer MS," p. 33b (1553); Schornbaum, "Die Chronik der Familie Dürnhofer," pp. 191–192, discussed below.

22. "Auff mein ahnkunfft bin ich erstlich mitt solchem schreiben von meiner mutter ubel empfangen worden/als sie lieber gesehen/das ich mich zu Nürnberg mitt einer burgers tochter verheirattet hette." "Dürnhofer MS," p. 33b (1552).

23. "Unnd nach dem ich sie sambt den beiden vormunde/wegen meines väterlichen and anfrewlichen arbtheils für gericht quittirt/hatt sie mir ettliche geschenckh gegeben/welche ich von ihret wegen meines künfftigen Brawt uberantwortten soltt." Ibid.

24. Cf. Schornbaum, "die Chronik der Familie Dürnhofer," p. 174.

25. "Als ich widerumb gen Torga kommen/unnd meiner mutter consens unnd verwilligung mittgebracht/hatt obgedachter jungfrau Elisabeth ihre mutter unnd vormunde/sie mir ehlichen zuvertrauen zugesagt." "Dürnhofer MS," p. 33b (1553).

26. Ibid., p. 33b (1553)

27. Ibid.

28. "Schuldienst." Ibid.

29. "Den 22 Augusti bin ich nach nürmberg verraisst/und hab mein väterlich erbthail vollend eingenohmmen." Ibid., p. 33b (1553).

30. Ibid., p. 33b (1553).

31. Ibid., p. 34a (1553).

32. "Hab . . . gehling und unverhoffter ding urlaub genommen." Ibid.

33. Ibid., p. 34a (1554).

34. "Ahm fraissle," Ibid., p. 34a (1555).

35. Ibid.

36. Ibid.

37. Between October 1555 and June 1556, there is an unexplained eight-month break in the chronicle.

38. "Dürnhofer MS," p. 34b (1556, 1557).

39. Unexplainably, only one item of information—Lorenz's ordination at the hands of Georg Major on the Sunday after Trinity—is reported for the year 1557. On Major, see Will, *Nürnbergisches Gelehrten-Lexicon*, 1, p. 90.

40. "Dürnhofer MS," pp. 34b–35a (1558). On the countess, see *Allgemeine Deutsche Biographie*, 39, pp. 308–310.

41. "Als ein expectant umb gepürliche besoldung ihn bestallung sein sollt/so lang biss ihn den Kirchen etwas ledig würde." "Dürnhofer MS," p. 35a (1558).

42. Kusch, *Nürnberg*, pp. 321–323. On Paumgartner, see J. Haniel, "Kirchenhoheit und Kircheregiment des Nürnberger Rates," *MVGN* 51 (1962), pp. 378–383.

43. "Dürnhofer MS," p. 35a (1558, 1559).

44. Ibid., p. 35a–b (1559).

45. Ibid., p. 35b (1559).

46. Ibid., p. 36a (1560).

47. "Dürnhofer MS," p. 36a (1560).

48. "Das sie [the Wittenberg theologians] sich mitt einer ausfürlichen schrifft/das Abendmal dess Herren belangend/gefasst machtten/ damitt wann sie etwa gen der Naumburg erfoddert wurden/sie dieselbe in bereitschafft hetten." "Dürnhofer MS," p. 36b (1561).

49. Flacius and former Luther associate Nicolaus von Amsdorf (1483–1556) had earlier led the Protestant opposition to the Interim, the thinly veiled Catholic religious settlement imposed on Protestants by Emperor Charles V after his defeat of the elector of Saxony and the

landgrave of Hesse in 1547. Hajo Holborn, *A History of Modern Germany* (New Haven, 1959), pp. 229–235.

50. A summary of the intraconfessional and interconfessional controversies from John Calvin's death (1564) to the Formula of Concord (1580) is provided by Seeberg, *Textbook of the History of Doctrines*, vol. 2, pp. 362–378.

51. *On the Freedom of a Christian*, in Lewis W. Spitz, ed., *Luther's Works*, 31 (Philadelphia, 1960), pp. 333–371; Ozment, *The Age of Reform*, pp. 372–380.

52. Ibid., pp. 334–337; Werner Elert, *The Structure of Lutheranism*, I (St. Louis, 1962), pp. 307–313. The Formula of Concord drove many liberal Lutherans into Calvinism, which after 1580 made even greater inroads into Germany, especially in the Palatinate. See Williston Walker, *A History of the Christian Church* (New York, 1959), p. 391. On Lorenz's role in the drafting of the Formula, see p. 249 below.

53. G. R. Potter, *Zwingli* (Cambridge, Mass., 1976), pp. 328–330; Seeberg, *Text-book of the History of Doctrines*, vol. 2, pp. 318–331, 336, 382 (Nürnberg), pp. 386–387 *(manducatio oralis)*, pp. 412–419; Theodore Tappert, *Book of Concord* (Philadelphia, 1959), p. 590; Hans Leube, "Die alte lutheranische Orthodoxie, ein Forschungsbericht," in *Orthodoxie und Pietismus*, ed. Martin Schmidt, et al. (Bielefeld, 1975).

54. Duke John Friedrich II, head of the Ernestine branch of the Wettin family, remained the emperor's prisoner until his death in Vienna in 1595. See Holborn, *A History of Modern Germany*, pp. 230, 261.

55. Walker, *A History of the Christian Church*, pp. 390–91; Holborn, *A History of Modern Germany*, pp. 261–262. Only in the universities of Wittenberg and Leipzig, and in two of Nürnberg's three churches (St. Sebald's and St. Giles's) did the Philippists hold sway during the decades of conflict leading up to the Formula of Concord (1580).

56. "Dürnhofer MS," pp. 36b–37a (1561).

57. Ibid., pp. 36a–37b (1561).

58. Schornbaum, "Die Chronik," p. 184. An apparent typographical error falsely dates this event in March 1561.

59. Holborn, *A History of Modern Germany*, pp. 231, 237. On Küstrin, see Gerd Heinrich, ed., *Berlin und Brandenburg, Handbuch der Historischen Stätten Deutschland*, vol. 10 (Stuttgart, 1973), pp. 442–443.

60. "Dieweil ich aber allezeit ein abscheu für dem hoffleben." "Dürnhofer MS," p. 37a (1562).

61. "Allerley accidentia und zugeng." Ibid.

62. Ibid., p. 37b (1562).
63. "Decanus collegii Philosophii." Ibid., p. 38a (1564); p. 38b (1566).
64. "Privatas repetitiones" with Frederick Balduin. Ibid., p. 38a (1565).
65. Ibid.
66. Ibid., p. 38a (1564).
67. Ibid., p. 38b (1566).
68. Ibid., p. 38b (1566), p. 39a (1567).
69. Ibid., p. 38a (1566).
70. Ibid., p. 38b (1566).
71. "Einbedeuttung unnd vorpott." Ibid., (1567), p. 39a.
72. "Ueber die massen hefftig erschrocken." Ibid., p. 39b (1567).
73. Ibid., p. 39a (1567).
74. "Ein catharrus suffocativus . . . zween paroxismi epileptici." Ibid., p. 39b (1567).
75. "Wol christlich/unnd einig/in stetter lieb unnd trew im ehestandt." Ibid.
76. "Der andern tag hernach/das ist/den 21 Juli/hab ich sie nach gebreuchlicher gewonheitt unnd gelegenheitt dess ortts/ehrlich unnd meinem stand gemess zur erden bestatten lassen/auff dem kirchhoff ausserhalb der statt/wie sie solches bei ihrem leben zu öfftermaln von mir begert/unnd ich auch ihr versprochen gehabt/darumb das ettliche unser kindlein daselbs begraben worden. Sonst pflegt man/wan etwas ahnsehenliche unnd fürnehme leütte sindt/dieselben ihn der statt auff den pfarrkirchhoff zubegraben/dafür sie aber umb ettlicher ursachen willen ein sonderlich abschewen gehabt/also das ich ihr gewissens halben wilfahren müssen." Ibid.
77. Ibid.
78. "Ein gewelbtes obdoch drüber bawen lassen/auch eine tafel/darauff die historia heimsuchung Maria gemahlet/in die pfarrkirchen zu Wittenberg auffgemacht." Ibid. On Lorenz's iconoclasm, see p. 250 below.
79. "Dahin ich dann umb viler ursachen willen gutten lust unnd willen gehabt/dieweil ich aber noch ihn trawrtagen/unnd dermassen betrübt war/das ich nicht gedenckhen oder schliessen kundt/wie forthin ihn meinem widtwenstandt meine hausshaultung unnd andere sachen fürsichtiglich unnd fruchtbarlich ahnzustellen/hab ich auch wider meinen willen diesen ehrlichen standt abschlagen müssen." Ibid., p. 40a (1567).
80. "Mich als ihren ahngeerbten Burger." Ibid.
81. Ibid., p. 40b (1567). The MS is falsely numbered after p. 40a, going from p. 40 to p. 42, an apparent lapse in attention by a busy archivist.

I have ignored the misnumbered pages and numbered the pages in sequence throughout.

82. The Heyner siblings had by this time apparently been placed either with other relatives or in domestic service or apprenticeships. No mention was made of their age when they joined Lorenz's household, nor any further mention made of them afterward.

83. "Dürnhofer MS," p. 40b (1567).

84. Karl Schornbaum, "Nürnberg im Geistesleben des 16. Jahrhunderts. Ein Beitrag zur Geschichte der Konkordienformel," *MVGN* 40 (1949), pp. 1–96.

85. "Ist bald ihm ahnfang dises ihars sehr beschwerlicher unnd verdriesslicher handlung mitt den Flacianern gepflogen worden/welche 3 gantzer monat gewehret/unnd endtlich durch ein Colloquium auff dem pfarrhoff bei S. Sebald/ihn beisein dreier herren/Joachim Hallers/ Geörgen Volckhamers/unnd Thomas Löffelholtes/verrichttet unnd beigelegt. Darnach aber die Flaccianer nichts bescheidener noch frömmer/sonndern nhur erger unnd bosshafftiger worden/unnd unruhige practicierende meütmacher gebliben einen weg als den andern." Ibid., p. 40b (1568).

86. "Den 17 Septembris/als meine liebe mutter fast bei einem halben jhar ahm krebs/ahn der linckhen brust sehr schwerlich kranckh gelegen/ unnd grossen schmertzen erlidten/ist sie sehliglich ihm herren entschlaffen." Ibid., pp. 40b–41a (1568).

87. Ibid., p. 40b (1568). Chandler was evidently her legal guardian.

88. The three were Lorenz Spengler, Andreas Mehlfürer, and Michael Schmid, the latter the second husband of one of Lorenz's aunts. Ibid., p. 40b (1568).

89. Ibid. pp. 40b (1568), 41a (1569). The buyer was Sigmund Richter.

90. Ibid., p. 41a (1569).

91. Ibid., p. 41a (1570).

92. See above, n. 39.

93. Ibid., p. 40b (1568), p. 41a (1569, 1570). Hans Heyden may have been a relation of Sebald Heyden, primary schoolteacher and author of textbooks for the Nürnberg schools. Strauss, *Luther's House of Learning*, pp. 190, 226, 232. Hausslaub was evidently a tutor of some repute.

94. "Dürnhofer MS," p. 41a (1570).

95. Ibid.

96. Ibid., p. 41b (1572).

97. "Erstlich an den flecken/ darnach ahn den blattern." Ibid., p. 41a (1570).

98. "Den 29 Januarii [anno 1571] . . . hab ich meinen Lorentzen . . . von M. Endres Beham ihn die Schul gen St. Egidien transferirt/ da er dann wol etwas studirn hett können/wann er selbst gewolt/unnd Gott dem schulmeister lengers leben gegönnet hette." Ibid. p. 41b (1571). Nentwich died on March 12, 1572.
99. Ibid. p. 41b (1572).
100. "Den 12 Martii/ nach dem mein schulmeister Caspar Nentwich mitt tod abgangen/unnd Endres Taucher ahn seine statt erwehlet/welcher ihm aber ahn geschickligkeitt/fleiss/unnd ansehen/bei weittem nicht zuvergleichen/als bin ich gezwungen worden meinen Lorentzen abermals zutransferin/habe ihn derwegen widerumb zu M. Andreas Beham gen S. Lorentzen ihn die Schul gethan/hatt doch bei einem sovil studiert als bei dem andern." Ibid., p. 41b (1572).
101. The oft-repeated parental goal of rearing a child who is of use to himself and to others jumps out of the larger passage: "Der Gott unnd menschen/ihm selbs unnd ander leütten zu nutz . . . dienen möge." Ibid., p. 41b (1571).
102. "Dasselbige [studirn] ob unnd wie ers gethen/weiss er ahm besten." Ibid., p. 42a (1573).
103. "Eben so gelehrt/als da er hinzog." Ibid., p. 42b (1575). Compare Paul Behaim and his mother's fear that he will return home from Italy "the same goose he was when he left." See chapter 2.
104. The youth was Wolf Lantzinger, Jr. Ibid.
105. Ibid., p. 42b (1577).
106. See the parallel case of Stephan Carl Behaim, an even more flagrant ne'er-do-well and youngest son of a family that patiently tolerated his abuse of its trust in a futile effort to salvage his life, which ended tragically, at twenty-six years, in Brazil. See Ozment, *Three Behaim Boys*, pp. 161 ff.
107. "Sich bey einem Herren für einen Stallbuben zu verdingen." "Dürnhofer MS," p. 42b (1577).
108. "Beide ihm kram unnd haushalttung etwas zulernen." Her employer was Martin Khun (d. 1585). Ibid.
109. Ibid., p. 44a (1586); see p. 254.
110. Ibid., p. 45a (1593).
111. "Ist mein wolgerattner junckher Lorentz/nach dem er dess dienens unnd reütterlebens/gleich wie dess studirns/auch genug gehabt/abermals wider auss österreich ahnheims kommen/unnd nicht gewüsst wo auss oder ein." Ibid., p. 42b (1578).
112. See chapter 2, pp. 93, 110, 114.
113. Ibid., p. 42b (1578).

114. Ibid., pp. 42b.-43a (1578). These were Dr. Nicholas Cisnerus and Dr. Christoph Reifstock.

115. Count Christoph was apparently a relation of Countess Magdalena, wife of Lorenz Jr.'s godfather, Hans von Ungnad.

116. Ibid., p. 43b (1583).

117. "Ahm newen ihars abend/bin ich den gantzen tag ihn regen unnd schne herumb geloffen zu den sieben altten herren/zu einem iedlichen ihn sonderheitt ihn seine behausung/unnd für meinen Lorentzen gepetten." Ibid., p. 43b (1584).

118. "Syndicat."

119. "Lochschreiberampt."

120. "Wie er nhun mir für dise trewe väterliche befürderung hernacher gelohnet/unnd wie er sich ihn seinem bevolhenem ampt verhaltten/mag er sein eigen gewissen drumb fragen." "Dürnhofer MS," p. 43b (1584).

121. Ibid., pp. 42a–42b (1575).

122. In 1622, Altdorf became a proper university, offering a full array of higher degrees. See Georg Mertz, *Das Schulwesen der deutschen Reformation im 16. Jahrhundert* (Heidelberg, 1902), p. 190; Ozment, *Three Behaim Boys*, pp. 93–96, Appendix 3 (the school ordinance), p. 287.

123. Heinrich R. Schmidt, *Konfessionalisierung im 16. Jahrhundert* (Munich, 1992), p. 13; Walker, *History of the Christian Church*, p. 391; Seeberg, *Text-book*, vol. 2, pp. 383–387.

124. Ozment, *The Age of Reform, 1250–1550*, pp. 324–328, 341–343. On English Puritans and iconoclasm, see Patrick Collinson, *The Elizabethan Puritan Movement* (Oxford, 1990), pp. 34–35.

125. "Meine herren . . . achtteten aber dafür/das es ietz die zeit nicht were von den Bildern zupredigen/fragt ich/wann dann dieselbe zeit kommen würde? antworttet mir herr Hans Welser/ich hörtte wol was man mir sagtte. Unnd dabei blib es. Ein grausamer wichtiger handel, etc." "Dürnhofer MS," p. 43b (1583).

126. Cited by Bodo Nischan, "The Exorcism Controversy and Baptism in the Late Reformation," *Sixteenth Century Journal* 18 (1987), p. 48.

127. Fear of a "domino effect" was clear when the issue first became a major point of contention between Lutherans and Calvinists. In 1551, Gothan theologian and church superintendent Justus Menius wrote a treatise on the subject, warning: "[The Calvinists] are now eliminating exorcism from baptism, [next] the altars will have to go, thereafter pictures and paintings, and finally all organs and singing." Cited by Nischen, "The Exorcism Controversy," p. 42; see also pp. 36–37, 39.

128. See p. 82, chapter 2.

129. "Den 5 Augusti/ haben wir predicanten semptlich/auff bevelh meiner herren/deliberirn müessen/von abschaffung dess exorcismi oder Teüfelsbeschweerung bei der kindertäuf/ist aber durch ettliche heüchler unnd meüttmacher unter uns (Gott verzeihe es ihnen) verhindert/ nichts draus worden." "Dürnhofer MS," p. 43b (1583).

130. Ibid., pp. 41a (1569, 1570); 41b (1571); 42a (1573, 1575); 42b (1577); 43a (1579, 1580, 1582); 43b-44a (1584); 44a (1586).

131. Ibid., pp. 44a (1585); 44b (1589); 45a (1592, 1593).

132. Lorenz's last entry, noting the death of his brother-in-law, was on May 17, 1594, and Leonhard's first entry, describing his father's death, appeared on June 28. Ibid., p. 45a (1593, 1594).

133. "Den 28 Septembris/hab ich meine zween söne/Lenhartten unnd Wolffen/zu Adtorff deponirn lassen." Ibid., p. 44a (1585).

134. "Den 3 Juni/hab ich meinen Wolffen zu Adam Strobel des tags zwo stünd ihn die schul gehn lassen/dammitt er neben dem latein teüsch schreiben unnd rechnen lernet." Ibid., p. 44b (1588).

135. "Den 2 Juni/hab ich meinen Wolffen (dieweil er nicht studirn wöllen) auss der Latinischen schul genhommen/und zu Levino dem Frantzöschen Schulmeister gehen lassen/die sprach zulernen." Ibid., p. 44b (1591).

136. "Den 21 Octobris/hab ich meinen Wolffen verdingt zu Eberhartt Erdinger/unnd 4 ihar zu ihm versprochen/gibt ihm keinen lohn." Ibid., p. 44b (1591).

137. Lorenz Jr.'s six were born in 1586, 1588, 1590, 1591, 1594 (twins), the latter dying within a week; Margaretha's four were born in 1587, 1588, 1590, 1593, the first (Veit) dying on the day of his birth. Ibid. p. 44a–45a.

138. Ibid., p. 44a (1586).

139. Ibid., p. 45a (1591).

140. Ibid., p. 44b–45a (1591, 1592). Compare Hermann von Weinsberg's description of his aging: Robert Jütte, "Aging and Body Image in the 16th Century: Hermann Weinsberg's (1518–1597) Perception of the Aging Body," *European History Quarterly* 18 (1988): pp. 259–290.

141. Ibid., p. 44b (1590). He likely could not have been obstructed for so long without permanent distension of his bladder.

142. Ibid., p. 45a (1593).

143. Ibid., p. 45a (1594).

144. See Ralph Houlbrooke, ed., *English Family Life, 1576–1716* (Oxford, 1989), pp. 10–11, 116, 128, 142; Paul Seaver, *Wallington's World: A Puritan Artisan in Seventeenth Century London* (Stanford, 1985), pp. 1–2, 6, 8–9, 87, 89, 93; Ozment, *The Age of Reform*, pp. 378–380,

and *When Fathers Ruled*, pp. 167–168. Cf. Theodore Beza, *Life of Calvin*, trans. Francis Gibson (Philadelphia, 1836), passim; Margo Todd, "Puritan Self-Fashioning: The Diary of Samuel Ward," *Journal of British Studies* 31 (1992): pp. 236–264.
145. See chapter 2.

CONCLUSION

1. Friedrich Beyschlag, ed., "Ein Vater an seinen Sohn (1539)," *Archiv für Kulturgeschichte* 4 (1906): pp. 296–302. Cf. my "Premodern Advice for the Postmodern Young," The Public Interest, 119 (1995), pp. 54–67.
2. For examples, see Erika Hoffmann, ed., *Briefe Grosser Deutscher an Kinder. Deutsche Männer schreiben an Kinder* (Berlin, 1943), no. 7 (Oct. 28, 1621; Sept. 13, 1623; Feb. 17, 1625), pp. 19–21; no. 20 (Nov. 4, 1823; Feb. 24, 1825), pp. 41–43. Cornelia N. Moore, *The Maiden's Mirror: Reading Material for German Girls in the Sixteenth and Seventeenth Centuries* (Wiesbaden, 1987), pp. 105–106. "Dr. Gregory: A Father's Legacy to His Daughters," in *The Young Lady's Pocket Library, or Parental Monitor* (1790), in Linda Pollock, ed., *A Lasting Relationship: Parents and Children Over Three Centuries* (London, 1987), p. 256.
3. On martyrdom's appeal and role in the religious culture of the sixteenth century, see Brad Gregory, "The Anathema of Compromise: Christian Martyrdom in Early Modern Europe" (Dissertation: Princeton University, 1996).
4. See, among others, the contemporary tracts against alcoholism by Sebastian Franck, *Vonn dem grewlichen laster der trunckenheit* (1528), and the Elector of Saxony, *Vormanung/unsers gnedigsten herren des Chürfursten zu Sachssen befehl/gestellt/durch die prediger ... widder Gotslesterung und füllerey* (Wittenberg, 1831), discussed in Steven Ozment, *Mysticism and Dissent: Religious Ideology and Social Protest in the Sixteenth Century* (New Haven, 1973), pp. 137–138, and *Protestants*, pp. 144–145.
5. Whose godfather, and hence benefactor, Christoph was someday likely to become.
6. While apprenticing in Antwerp, the then twenty-one-year-old Paul Behaim I (1519–1568)—the father of the protagonist of chapter 2— had been advised by his paternal aunt, Lucia (Mrs. Albrecht) Letscher to "protect yourself from the women [prostitutes], who can quickly rob one of both his possessions and his health (*gut ... und ... gesunt*)." See J. Kamann, ed., "Aus dem Briefwechsel eines jungen Nürnberger

Kaufmanns im 16. Jahrhundert," *Mitteilungen aus dem Germanischen Nationalmuseum* [unnumbered] (1894), pp. 13–14. On parental warnings to sons about the dangers of whores, see also Beer, *Eltern und Kinder*, pp. 74–75.

7. Far more than the alleged sexism and puritanical morality of the Reformation, it was this new plague from the New World that led to the closing of many of Germany's brothels. See Bruce Boehner, "Early Modern Syphilis," *Journal of the History of Sexuality*, I (1990), pp. 197–214; Robert Munger "Guaiacum: the Holy Wood from the New World," *Journal of the History of Medicine and Allied Sciences* 4 (1949), pp. 196–229. On feminist efforts to blame the closing of brothels on heightened sexism in the wake of the Protestant Reformation, see Roper, *The Holy Household*, pp. 114–115, and "Discipline and Respectability, Prostitution and Reformation in Augsburg," *History Workshop*, 19 (1985), pp. 3–28; and Hufton, *The Prospect Before Her*, pp. 309–315, who contrasts the kinder, if ephemeral, Catholic approach to prostitution. On the latter subject, cf. Lance Lazar, "Bringing God to the People: Jesuit Confraternities in Sixteenth Century Italy" (Dissertation: Harvard University, 1997).

8. On the universality of the male sense of duty and sacrifice, cf. Gilmore, *Manhood in the Making*, pp. 222–229; for the Reformation period, see Hendrix, "Masculinity and Patriarchy in Reformation Germany," *Journal of the History of Ideas*, 56 (1995), pp. 177–193; Wunder, "Wie wird man ein Mann?"

9. Ozment, *The Bürgermeister's Daughter*, pp. 147–152; Scott H. Hendrix, "Loyalty, Piety, or Opportunism: German Princes and the Reformation," *Journal of Interdisciplinary History*, 25 (1994), pp. 211–224; Fichtner, *Protestantism and Primogeniture*.

10. In addition to the stories of the five families presented in this book, see Govind Sreenivasan's study of the survival and material progress of German peasant families throughout the disasters of the sixteenth century and the Thirty Years' War: "Land, Money, and Power at Ottobeuren, 1525–1710" (Dissertation: Harvard University, 1995).

11. Envisioning an ascending divine hierarchy of family, city (government), and Church ("God's home and city"), even as well-meaning a friend of the family as Martin Luther viewed the home, which he placed beneath the state and the Church, as a handmaiden to the gospel and the Church's mission of saving souls: The *paterfamilias* was to receive instruction from the *paterpoliticus* and the *patertheologicus*, as magistrates, teachers, and pastors, in turn, protected, enlightened, and guided parents and children toward eternity. See John Witte, Jr.,

"The Civic Seminary: Sources of Modern Public Education in the Lutheran Reformation of Germany," *Journal of Law and Religion*, vol. 12 (1995–1996), pp. 188, n. 71.

12. "Die öffentliche-rechtliche Verbriefung des Heiratsvertrages, 'Lautmerung' genannt, fand für das Patriziat auf dem Rathaus oder im eigenen Hause unter Beisein von je zwölf Personen von beiden Seiten statt." Ludwig Grote, *Die Tucher. Bildnis einer Patrizierfamilie* (Munich, 1961), p. 11. In the exceptional case of city counsel Christoph Scheurl, who notarized both his marriage contract and exchanged his marriage vows in the chambers of the city council, the ceremonies were presided over by his uncle.

13. Hans Eberhart Mayer, *The Crusades*, trans. by John Gilligham (London, 1972); D. C. Munro, "The Children's Crusade," *American Historical Review* 19 (1914), pp. 516–524; Bernard Queenan, "The Evolution of the Pied Piper," *Children's Literature*, 7 (1978), pp. 104–114; Norman Cohn, *The Pursuit of the Millennium: Revolutionary Messianism in Medieval and Reformation Europe and Its Bearing on Modern Totalitarian Movements* (New York, 1961); Walter Laqueur, *Young Germany: A History of the German Youth Movement* (New York, 1962). J. H. Parry's description of the religious zeal of European explorers and conquistadors to the New World may be applied to all of these disparate movements. The first goal was to convert unbelievers by using preaching, reasoning, and force of example; the second was to ensure the safety, independence, and superiority of the believer by killing, humiliating, or subduing the unbeliever. *The Age of Reconnaissance* (New York, 1963), pp. 35–36.

14. Realistic utopias also have a well-documented history. See Miriam Eliav-Feldon, *Realistic Utopias: The Ideal Imaginary Societies of the Renaissance, 1516–1630* (Oxford, 1982), pp. 109, 119, 121–133.

INDEX

Page numbers in *italics* refer to illustrations.

abandonment, 149, 181–82, 247, 267
Absberg, Thomas, 80–81
accidents, 87, 103, 105, 114–15, 119, 122, 211, 236–39
account books, xii, 53, 94, 113–14, 146–47, 157
    as diary, 53, 94, 113, 124
Adam, Hans, Baron of Wolfstein, 81
Adam, Tobias, 8
Adam and Eve, 253
Adelphoi (Terence), 210
adiaphora (nonessential matters), 240, 252, 254
adolescence, xvi–xvii, 11, 117–18, 121, *123*, 135, 167, 179, 185–87, 192, 207, 260–68
Advent, 45
Aershot, Duchess of, 204
aging, xv–xvi, 121–22, 257–58
Ahab and Jezebel (drama), 210
Alba, Duke of, 196, 206
Albertus Magnus, 202
Albrecht, Cardinal of Brandenburg, 83–84, 97, 126
alcoholism, 207, 209, 262–63
almanacs, 196–97

Altdorf, 7–8, 194, 199, 215, 255, 257, 259
Amberg, 100–101
ambivalence, spiritual, xvi, 193, 197–98, 200–206, 210–11, 214–16
America, xiv, 54, 261, 267–68
Ammen, Hans, 122
amulets, 91–92, 110, 114–15
Anabaptists, 252
Ancona, 158
anger, 73–74, 76, 178–79, 181, 185–86, 203
Annelein (herb), 32
Anne of Saxony, 195
Annunciation festival, 201
anti-Semitism, 157–58
Antwerp, 143, 196, 200, 206
apprenticeship, 6, 11, 15, 16, 21, 30, 32, 112, 128, 149, 216
Aquinas, Saint Thomas, 202
architecture, 201–2
art and artists, xiii–xiv, 10, 103, 121, 124–26, *137*
    religious function of, 90, 135, 201, 240, 252–53

artisans, xiii, xiv, 5, 91
assault, 81, 155–56, 178–79, 201–2, 211
astrology, 69, 73, 90, 92, 94, 95, 108, 110, 114
Augsburg, 188–90
Augsburg, Diet of (1530), 58
Augsburg, Peace of (1555), 8
Augsburg Confession (1530), 58, 232
August I, Elector of Saxony, 232–35, 238
Augustinian order, 57
Ayrer, Melchior, 204, 212–13

"bachelor journeys," xvi, 3, 11, 64–65, 135, 138–40, 158–59, 162, 170, 179–90
Baier, Conrad, 21
Baier, Maria, 7, 8, 25, 34
Balsmann, Benedict, 239
Balsmann, Elisabeth, *see* Dürnhofer, Elisabeth Balsmann
Balsmann, Margaretha, 224–26, 239
Bamberg, bishopric of, 82
banking, 138, 194, 205
banns, 44
banquets, 85–86, 107, 120, 176, 238
    nuptial, 46, 48–49, 61–62, 113–14
baptism, 77–85, 86, 107, 228, 253–54, 267
    emergency, 70–71, 78, 79, 202–3, 237
barber-surgeons, 122, 128
Barby, Christoph von, 250
Barby, Magdalena von, 230
Barcelona, 70, 77
bathing, 76, 85–86, 91, 105, 263
Beckmann, Otto, 58, 77
beds, 87, 103
beer, 89, 115, 124, 165
Behaim, Albrecht, 21–22, 36, 49
Behaim, Anna, 52
Behaim, Anna Maria, *see* Pfinzing, Anna Maria
Behaim, Apollonia, 8

Behaim, Christoph, 47–48, 162, 188, 190
Behaim, Friedrich, 47
Behaim, Georg (half-brother of Lucas Behaim), 11–12, 49
Behaim, Georg (son of Lucas Behaim), 52
Behaim, Georg (son of Paul Behaim I), 49, 138
Behaim, Hans Sebald, 5
Behaim, Johann, 52
Behaim, Lucas Friedrich, xv, 3–52, 54
    father's behavior excused by, 24–26, 32–33
    formal engagement of, 24, 33, 38–39, 42–44
    health of, 32, 37, 39–40
    lodging sought by, 24, 34–35, 40–41, 51
    mining apprenticeship of, 11, 15, 16, 21, 30, 32
    passion expressed by, 19–21, 26–32
    patrimony of, 6–7, 34, 49–50
    piety of, 18–19, 21, 27–30, 34–36
    secret engagement of, 14–15, 16, 18, 21–25, 43, 46
    travels of, 3, 8–11, 14
    wedding of, 42–52
Behaim, Magdalena (daughter of Magdalena Römer Behaim), 138–40, 143–44, 147, 153–54, 174–77, *175*, 179–84, 214
Behaim, Magdalena (half-sister of Lucas Behaim), 8
Behaim, Magdalena Römer, xvi, 138–91, 214
    son advised by, 158–61, 167–70
    son's expenses paid by, 143–50, 155–59, 173–74, 181, 183–90
    son's quarrels with, 179–88
Behaim, Maria, 8, 23
Behaim, Martin, 47
Behaim, Martin, II, 54
Behaim, Michael, Jr., 122
Behaim, Paul, I, 4, 135–36, 138

Behaim, Paul, II, 3, 47–52, 54, 85–86,
    135–91, 212
  bad debts of, 139, 143, 177–78, 188
  courtship of, 24–25, 36
  education of, 135–39, 146–47, 159,
    170–74, 184–85, 187
  family quarrels of, 14, 23–26,
    176–88, 214
  health of, 161–73, 179, 180, 186,
    190
  marriages of, 3, 6–7, 191
  money spent by, 139–48, 155–61,
    165, 167, 170, 173–74, 181,
    183–90
  money stolen from, 150–56, 179
  in son's marriage negotiations,
    11–12, 14, 16, 23–26, 32–35,
    39–42
  travels of, xvi, 135–43, 159–61
Behaim, Rosina, 8
Behaim, Sabina, 139–40, 143–44,
    153–54, 174, 175, 182
Behaim, Stephan Carl, 7, 49
Behaim, Susanna (daughter of Lucas
    Behaim), 52
Behaim, Susanna (half-sister of Lucas
    Behaim), 8
Behaim, Ursula, 54
Beham, Andreas, 243
Belgium, xvi, 192, 195–98, 203–7, 213
  see also Netherlands
betrothal, 24, 33, 38–39, 42–44,
    47–48, 226, 242
Betterman, Margaret, 122
Beur, Anna, see Dürnhofer, Anna Beur
Beyl, Johannes, 243
Bible, 48, 59–60, 72, 91, 94, 100, 108,
    117–18, 157, 198, 203, 221
birthdays, 103, 105, 107–8, 114,
    118–20, 122, 228
birth trees, 76
bleedings, 73–74, 95, 121, 231
Blochinger, Matthias, 222
Bologna, 141, 145, 160–64, 170
Bologna, University of, 65–67, 111,
    205

bonding, parental, 105, 115, 118–19
Bonomen, Constantine, 108
books, 147, 157–58, 188
  religious, 198–99, 204, 206, 215
  see also account books
Bosch, Hieronymus, 208
Botenbrot ("good news money"), 74–75,
    107
Braun, Stephan, 160–61
brigands, 80–81, 211, 230
Brussels, 197, 205–7, 215
Brussels, Union of (1577), 195, 196
Buchenbach bei Erlangen, 82
Bünau, Rudolf von, 8
Burghley, William Cecil, Lord, xiv
burial, 239–40

calendars, 73
Calvinism, 194–97, 219–20, 232–35,
    251–54, 258
Candlemas, 45
canon law, 65, 66, 136
carpenters, xiv
cartography, 54
Castellanus, Stephan, 172
Catholicism, 56–60, 62–65, 125–27,
    136, 200–203, 219
  ceremonies of, 197–98, 200–201
  clandestine, 76, 82–85, 198, 202
  geopolitics of, xvi, 8–10, 83–84,
    195–98, 200, 202, 204
  Jews under, 157–58
Celtis, Conrad, xiii
charity, 46, 90, 93, 97, 100, 103, 107,
    114, 122, 128, 149, 155–56, 199
Charlemagne, 202
Charles V, Holy Roman Emperor, 83,
    84, 107–8, 126, 200
charms, 91–92, 110, 114–15
childbirth, xv–xvi, 53, 70–77, 87,
    95–96, 106–7
  announcement of, 74–77, 107
  premature, 70–73, 95, 106, 202–3,
    237
chrism, 78, 79, 83, 254
  see also baptism

Christian, Elector of Saxony, 253–54
Christian II, Elector of Saxony, 254
Cistercian order, 83
citizenship, 5, 220, 240
City Council, Nürnberg, 56–57, 60, 74, 79, 126, 136, 194, 253–54, 259
city hall, Nürnberg, 44, 61, 267
clergy, 44, 45, 48, 56, 63–64, 79, 87, 125, 192, 209, 251, 259, 267
cloisters, 61, 63, 67, 89–91, 99–100, 106, 117, 120, 125–26, 202
  charitable gifts to, 90, 97, 100, 103, 107, 122
  Protestant abolition of, 75–76, 83, 199–200, 203
clothing, 34, 78–79, 85, 90, 114, 120, 123–24, 128, 165–66, 175, 176, 184, 221, 263
  academic, 141, 222
  cost of, 141–45, 157, 160, 174, 188–89
  gendered, 118
  heraldic, 103, 121–22
coats of arms, 54–55, 80, 111, 116, 121–22, 129
Cochlaeus, Johannes, 62
coins, xiii, 76
Coler, Johannes, 76
Cologne, 201–2
Cologne, Diet of (1505), 66
Columbus, Christopher, 54
Commandery of the Teutonic Knights, Nürnberg, 83
Committee of Ten, Nürnberg, 24
Commonplaces (Melanchthon), 221
conception, xv–xvi, 70–72
confession, 60, 76, 125, 152
Constantinople, 12
consubstantiality, doctrine of, 234
contraception, 71, 89
Corpus Civile (law text), 157, 172
Council of Seven, Nürnberg, 15, 39, 40, 194, 250
  see also City Council, Nürnberg
Counter Reformation, 232–33
courtship, xv, 4–5, 47–48, 224–26

  see also betrothal
Cranach, Lucas, 67–68, 116, 240
Cranach, Lucas, the Younger, 223
crime, xiv, 150–56, 178–79, 201–2, 211, 230, 262
Culman, Leonhard, 220
Cum Nimis Absurdum (papal bull), 157–58

damnation, 202–3, 234
dancing, 45, 46, 49, 62, 103–4, 113–14, 122, 176, 208
Decet Pontificem Romanum (papal bull), 62
deposition (academic ritual), 222
Devil, 36, 77–78, 149, 154, 186, 253
Dhener, Christoph, 114
Dhener, Mathias, 113–14
diaries, xii, 5, 74–75, 88, 94, 103, 105–6, 108, 113–14, 122–24, 196–99, 204, 208–11
Dietrich, Philip, 247
Dietrich, Veit, 247
diets, imperial, xiv, 37, 58, 66, 77, 87, 230, 251
diplomas, xii
discipline, 105–6, 127, 137, 215–16, 260–65
diseases, 8, 93, 99–101, 154, 161–70, 180, 186, 213, 222–24, 230–32, 235–38
  childhood, 97, 109–10, 244
  of middle age, 258–59
  spiritual interpretation of, 167–68, 229–30, 258
  treatment of, 32, 91, 109, 121, 165, 169, 211–12, 231
  venereal, 208, 264
Dominican order, 62, 64, 83, 87, 202, 219
Don John of Austria, 206–7
Dormitz, Catholic festival at, 201
Dörrer, Balthasar, 130
Dörrer, Sybilla, 130
dowries, 13, 35, 41–42, 140

dreams, 211, 236
Dresden, Protestant conference at
    (1561), 235
drunkenness, xiv, 155, 209, 262–63
Dürer, Agnes Frey, 125
Dürer, Albrecht, xiii, 55, 56, 62, 68,
    124–25, 135, 136, 138
Dürnhofer, Anna, 232, 237–38, 240,
    243–44, 247, 257
Dürnhofer, Anna Beur, 220–21,
    224–28, 241–42
Dürnhofer, Elisabeth Balsmann,
    224–31, 235–39
Dürnhofer, Georg, 228
Dürnhofer, Hans Hieronymus, 256–57
Dürnhofer, Katharina, 242
Dürnhofer, Katharina Lebender,
    242–43, 246
Dürnhofer, Leonhard (brother of
    Lorenz Dürnhofer), 226, 227–30
Dürnhofer, Leonhard (father of Lorenz
    Dürnhofer), 218, 220, 228
Dürnhofer, Leonhard (son of Lorenz
    Dürnhofer), 218, 246, 249,
    255–57
Dürnhofer, Lorenz, xvi–xvii, 81,
    217–59, 218, 248
  children fathered by, 217, 228, 229,
    232, 236, 254–56
  education of, 220–24, 226, 231
  health of, 223–24, 231, 256
  marriages of, 217, 224–27, 238–43
  as preacher, 229, 232, 235–37, 244,
    253
  in Reformation politics, 219–20,
    233–35, 241, 244, 251–54
  on sons' failures, 244–50, 255–56
Dürnhofer, Lorenz, Jr., 229–30, 232,
    236–38, 240, 241, 243–50,
    255–58
Dürnhofer, Margaretha, 236, 240,
    243–44, 247, 256, 257–58
Dürnhofer, Maria Magdalena, 242
Dürnhofer, Wilibald Lorenz, 257
Dürnhofer, Wolfgang, 246
Dürnhofer, Wolfgang, II, 255–56

Easter, 204
Eber, Paul, 222, 223, 224–25, 229,
    232–33, 235, 240
Ebner, Erasmus, 94, 99–100
Ebner, Helena, 62, 75, 88
Ebner, Hieronymus, 62
Ebner, Katharina, 75
Ecclesiasticus (Apocrypha), 108
Eck, Johannes, xiii, 58, 59, 62. 126
"Eck Hewed" (Pirckheimer), 59
education, 7, 56, 63–65, 104, 118–20,
    192, 220–22
  cost of, 139, 159, 186–88
  of girls, 63, 136, 137, 232, 237,
    243–47
  goals of, 138–39, 172, 174, 187–88,
    243–44, 247, 263–64
  Humanistic, xiv, 60, 136, 194,
    221–22, 232, 237
  legal, 64–67, 136, 138, 147,
    170–74, 188, 194–95
  religious, 63, 106, 199, 215–16
  travel as, 3, 135, 160, 162,
    182–84
egalitarianism, 260
Egmont, Count of, 195–96, 206
emergency baptism, 70–71, 78, 79,
    202–3, 237
Engelthal, cloister at, 63
England, xiv, 21, 139, 196, 200
Erasmus, Desiderius, 57, 136, 157
Erdinger, Eberhard, 255–56
Erhart, Anna, 87–89, 90, 98–101, 106,
    112–14, 128
Eucharist, 197–98, 211, 220, 232–35,
    252
exorcism, 77–78, 253–54
Exsurge Domine (papal bull), 62

fabric, 74–75, 87, 107, 141, 142,
    144–46, 160, 189–90
failure, academic, 244–50, 255–56
faith, salvation by, 202–3, 233,
    251–52
falls, childhood, 103, 105, 114–15,
    119, 122, 236–37

family:
  affection in, 26, 48, 61, 63, 105,
    115–17, 118–19, 127–29,
    149–50, 194, 240, 242–43
  authority and discipline in, 105–6,
    127, 137, 215–16, 260–65, 268
  biblical models for, 48, 72, 91, 94,
    108, 117–18
  celebrations within, 42–49, 61–62,
    79–80, 85–86, 106–7, 113–14,
    127–30
  early modern vs. modern, 261,
    265–68
  failure in, 244–50, 255–56, 258,
    268
  organization of, ix–x, xiv–xv, 106,
    111–12, 128–29, 228–29, 265
  pragmatism in, 58–59, 125–27,
    204–5, 260–65, 267–68
  privacy in, xi–xii, xv, 57, 60, 84–85,
    127–28, 207–8, 210–11, 259,
    265–66
  quarrels within, 14, 23–26, 117,
    176–91, 214, 256–57
  spirituality in, 84–85, 106, 114–15,
    215–16, 259
family chronicles, 217–20, 237, 242,
    255, 256–57
fasting, 92
fatherhood, 11–12, 26, 63, 66, 98–99,
    101–2, 194, 219, 244–50, 261–64
  joys of, 105, 115, 118–19, 255
feast days, see holidays
fencing, 119–20
Ferdinand I, King of Rome, 80, 83, 84,
    111
Ferdinand II, Holy Roman Emperor,
    9–10
Ferrara, 141–42, 162–63, 170
fevers, 166, 169, 180, 186, 222–24,
    231, 257
Flacians, 241, 244, 251
Flacius Illyricus, Matthias, 233, 241
Flick, Bartholomäus, 147, 163, 170–74
Florence, 182
food and drink, xiv, 32, 89, 105, 110,

    115, 118–19, 121, 122, 126, 130,
      186–87, 210
  celebratory, 44, 46, 63, 80, 85–86,
      97, 107, 117, 120, 124, 238
  preservation of, 147, 165
  price of, 33–34, 86, 158, 165, 170
Formula of Concord (1580), 233–35,
      251–52
foundling home, Nürnberg, 34, 46
Franciscan order, 76, 83, 219
Frank, Johann, 100–101
Frankfurt am Main, 10
Frederick, Count Palatine, 122, 130
Frederick III, Holy Roman Emperor,
      xiii
Frederick the Wise, Elector of Saxony,
      66–67, 82, 84, 126
fumigation (against plague), 213
funerals, 47, 194, 239–40
Fürer, Carl, 122
Fürer, Christoph, 60
Fürer, Moritz, 122
furniture, 87, 103
Fütterer, Erasmus, 108, 120
Fütterer, Gabriel, 60–62
Fütterer, Georg, 155–56
Fütterer, Katharina, see Scheurl,
      Katharina
Fütterer, Magdalena, 61, 99
Fütterer, Ulrich, 54

Gandelfinger, Ursula, 130
Gauricus, Lucas, 69, 92, 94, 97, 114
Gebel, Matthes, 96
gender, 71–72, 76–77, 118, 137, 138,
      202, 247, 261
Genesio-Lutherans, 233–35, 241, 254
  see also Reformation
Geneva, University of, 246–47
Genoa, 143
Georg, Duke of Saxony, 73, 81–84,
      101, 254
German House, Venice, 135, 140–41
Gerstmann, Martin, 244
Geuder, Julius, 194–95, 204–5, 213
Geuder, Sabina, 131

Ghent, Pacification of (1576), 195, 196
ghettos, Jewish, 157–58
Gienger, Gabriel, 140–42, 145,
    147–53, 156–58, 179
gifts, 26, 49, 63, 100–103, 106–7, 110,
    122, 126, 210, 231
  birth and birthday, 84, 97, 103,
    107–8, 114, 128, 129, 228
  symbolic, 71–72, 86, 89–91, 102,
    108, 117–18, 129, 222
  wedding, 49, 61, 62, 209, 226
glaziers, xiv
Glöss, Cardinal Christoph, 80
Gnadenberg, cloister at, 100, 103
God, nature of, 203, 252
godparents, 81–84, 88, 106, 122, 129,
    136, 228–30, 232, 250
  gifts from, 78, 84, 96–97, 108, 114,
    117–18, 124
goiter, 32
Goletta, fall of, 108
Good Samaritan, 117
gossip, 21–22, 24, 25, 33, 181
Götz, Georg, 129
gout, 121, 257–58
Granvella, Cardinal, see Perrenot,
    Antoine
Greck, Isaac, 160, 165
Greck, Jacob, 167
grief, 71, 97–98, 240
guardians, xv, 80–81, 111–12, 130,
    220–21, 234–35
  financial authority of, 104, 136, 140,
    144, 145, 148, 182–86, 225–26
  in marriage negotiations, 23–25, 35,
    41–42, 128, 224, 225
Gundelsingen, 128
gymnasia, xiv, 7, 171, 194, 251

hair, xii, 31, 72, 91–92
Haller, Bartel, 113
Haller, Joachim, 240–41
Haller, Johann Jacob, 131
Haller, Katharina, 131
Haller, Maria, see Welser, Maria Haller
Haller, Sebald, 194, 199, 211–13

Harstörffer, Wolfgang, 195, 210
Hausslaub, Erhard, 243–44
Hebraeorum Gens (papal bull), 158
Heidelberg, University of, 63, 64, 69,
    255
Heiner, Susanna, 231
Heiner, Wolf, 231
herbs, 32, 91, 109
heresy, xiii, 83
Heuren, cloister at, 202
Heyen, Hans, 243
Heyner, Benedict, 238
Heyreddin Barbarossa, 107–8
hobbyhorses, 93–94, 101, 104
Hofmann, Elspeth, 128, 130
holidays, 26, 45, 60, 63, 79, 87, 90,
    92, 94–95, 170, 200–201, 204
Holy Roman Empire, xii–xiv, 9–10, 108
Hölzschuher, Caspar, 149
Hölzschuher, Sebastian, 149, 155
Hölzschuher, Veit, 149
Hölzschuher Foundation, 149, 156
honor, 11–12, 178–80, 182, 186, 264
horoscopes, 69, 73, 92, 108, 110
horses, 99, 101, 104, 105, 120, 121,
    141–42, 189
hospices, Nürnberg, 34, 200
Hotman, François, 172
Hubschman, Blasius, 128
Humanism, xiii–xiv, 56, 59, 60, 62, 67,
    136, 194, 221–22, 232, 237
Hungary, 235–36
Hus, Jan, 235

iconoclasm, 58, 200, 240, 252–54
idealism, 267–68
illegitimacy, 79, 264
images, attitudes toward, 58, 200–201,
    240, 252–53
Imhof, Andreas, 107, 136, 176
Imhof, Carl, 136, 141–42, 144, 148,
    155, 158, 177, 195, 202, 208,
    210
Imhof, Christoph, 162, 176–81, 214
Imhof, Felicity, 107
Imhof, Jakob, 23

Imhof, Katharina, 75
Imhof, Katharina Pfinzing, 20, 23–25,
    29, 33, 35–36
Imhof, Paul, 147, 176, 179, 214
Imhof, Sebastian, 24, 25–26, 35–36
Imhof, Wilibald, 136, 140, 144, 145,
    148, 182–84, 122
Imhof Trading Company, 135–36,
    140–41, 149, 156, 160–61, 167
impotence, 36
Index of Forbidden Books, papal, 157
individualism, 260
indulgences, 56, 58, 65, 83–84, 198,
    205, 213, 214–15
infant mortality, 70–71, 86, 97–98,
    106, 202–3, 217, 229, 237, 242
infants, care of, 76, 87–92
infertility, xv–xvi, 70–73
inheritance, 39, 49–50, 104, 125, 129,
    199, 222, 225–28, 265–66
    maternal, 6–7, 49–50
    partible, 34, 77, 139–40, 176,
        181–82, 263
Institutiones Juris (law text), 147
Italy, 4, 135–36, 140–90
    bachelor travel in, xvi, 3, 64–65, 135,
        138–40, 158–59, 162, 170, 179
    crime in, 150–56, 178–79
    Jews in, 157–58
    plague in, 160–73

Jerusalem, 8, 12, 19
Jesuits, 201, 232–33
Jesus Christ, nature of, 233–34, 252
Jews, 53, 92, 143, 145, 157–58, 197
Joachimthal, mines at, 101, 102, 106
Johann, Margrave of Küstrin, 236
John, Elector of Saxony, 84
John Frederick, Elector of Saxony, 84
jokes, 208–9
journeymen, 5, 41
Judengasse, Nürnberg, 53
"junker" identity, 93–94, 249

Kaiper, Frau, 110
Kamerer, Leonhard, 220

kidnapping, 80–81, 230
kidney stones, 231–32, 235–37, 257
Kitzbühl, mine at, 11, 15, 16–17, 21,
    32
knights, 49, 80, 111, 230
Koniglohn, 163, 166
Kornberg, cloister at, 120
Krafft, Endlein, 90
Kreft, Katharina, 128–30
Krell, Wolf, 113
Kress, Anton, 66, 69
Kress, Helena, 106
Kress, Katharina, 91
Kreutzer, Gregory, 97
Külin, Frau, 118
Küstrin (Kostrzyn), court at, 236

Lagus, Conrad, 172
Lambert, Francis, 244
Lamprecht, Fencing Master, 119–20
Lantzinger, Magdalena, 249
Latin, 7, 63, 114, 118, 120, 147, 170,
    173, 197, 220, 222, 232, 256–57
lawyers, 5, 65–69, 136, 194, 205
    Italian, 151–56
    training of, 64–67, 136, 138, 147,
        170–74, 188, 194–95
Lebender, Katharina, *see* Dürnhofer,
    Katharina Lebender
Lebkuchen (honeycakes), 44, 63, 85,
    91
Leimbach, Georg, 69
Leipzig, 62, 138, 143, 188, 227, 230,
    234–35
Lent, 37, 45
Lepanto, battle of (1571), 206–7
letters, xii, xv, 15–22, 27–39, 90, 122,
    214, 225
    delivery of, 146, 166–68, 208, 213
    desire for, 18, 153–54, 174–76, *175,*
        264
    sex discussed in, 22, 208
Leuschner, Christopher, 224
"liberal" Protestants, 233–35, 241,
    252–53, 259
Lindner, Gabriel, 13, 38, 42

Lindner, Sabina, *see* Pfinzing, Sabina
   Lindner
Lisbon, 143
liturgy, 58, 59, 77–78, 82–83
Loci communes (Melanchthon), 221
lodging, 24, 34–35, 40–41, 51, 55–56,
   135, 140–44, 159, 164–65,
   229–32, 241–42
Löffelholz, Maria Sitzinger, 15, 18,
   26–27, 34–35, 38–41
Löffelholz, Wolf, 15, 38–39, 41, 42,
   47–48
Lord's Supper, 233–34
   see also Eucharist
Loreto, shrine at, 64
Louvain, xvi, 192, 195–207, 210–13
   student life in, 202–3, 207, 208–10
Louvain, University of, 195, 204–5,
   213
Ludwig, King of Bavaria, 102
Luther, Martin, xiii, xvi, 57–58, 62, 66,
   67, 148, 158, 221, 230, 236, 240,
   258
   Catholic practices attacked by, 78,
   82–84
   on Eucharist, 220, 232–34
Lutheranism, *see* Reformation
Lyons, 261–64

Magdeburg, University of, 233
"maidens' courts," 207–8
mail delivery, 146, 166–68, 208, 213
Mainz, 201
Major, Georg, 232–33, 243
majority, age of, 225–26
manners, 117, 153, 160, 171, 263–64
Mansfeld, Count of, 206
Margareta (Scheurl family servant), 85,
   90, 100–101, 107, 128, 130
Maria, Queen of Bavaria, 102
Market Square, Nürnberg, xiii,
marriage, xv, 4, 11–12, 14–15, 23–25,
   42–43, 61–62, 192, 232–43, 256
   age at, 55, 224, 264
   childbirth expected in, 26, 34, 48,
   70–72

clandestine, 43, 264, 266
   economics of, 13–14, 42, 138–40
   of servants, 113–14, 128
marriage contracts, 29, 33–35, 38–39,
   42–43, 61, 267
martyrdom, 215, 262
Mary, Queen of Scots, 200
Mary, veneration of, 201, 213, 240
Mass, 58, 60, 61, 63, 76, 83, 106, 202
Mathias, Holy Roman Emperor, 9–10,
   37
Mathias, Sebastian, 229
Maurice, Elector of Saxony, 195, 224
Maurice, Saint, 55
Maximilian I, Holy Roman Emperor, 64
Maximilian II, Holy Roman Emperor, 9,
   13, 200, 244
measles, 109–10, 244
Mecheln, plague at, 213
medallions, *96*, 102, 108, 117–18
medicine, 71–74, 91, 103, 121, 122,
   165, 169, 211–13
   herbal, 32, 109, 212
   for plague, 165, 169, 170
Meilendörfer, Hans, 220
Melanchthon, Philip, xiii–xiv, 58,
   221–22, 224–27, 229–33, 240,
   241
Menander, 93
Meuschel, Hans, 100–101
Michel, Wolf, 227
midwives, 74–76, 79, 87, 107, 259
milk, 89, 119, 124
   mother's, 87–89, 105, 109, 115
mining, 11, 15, 16, 21, 30, 32, 50,
   90–91, 101, 104, 129
miracles, 197
miscarriages, 70–73, 217, 239
money, xiii, 5–6, 67, 140–49, 156–61,
   165, 167, 170, 173–74, 209
   attitudes towards, 102–3, 108, 165
   gifts of, 76, 104, 227, 231
   marriage and, 13–14, 34, 42,
   138–40
   quarrels over, 177–90
   theft of, 150–56, 179

money (*cont.*)
  transfer of, 140–41, 160–61, 164, 167
  see also inheritance; salaries
moneylending, 64, 139, 157–58
monks, 56, 57, 59, 62, 75–76, 83
monstrances, kissing of, 197–98, 205–6, 214–15
Monte Ortone, 164–67
More, Thomas, daughters of, 136
Moses, 108, 117–18, 203
motherhood, 6–7, 61, 70–74, 88–89, 105, 115, 119, 149–50, 180, 185–86
  anxieties of, 159–61, 167, 173–74, 179–80
  single, xv–xvi, 138
  as social norm, 26, 34, 48, 70–72
  symbols of, 71–72, 76, 86–87, 89–90
mourning, 47, 71, 97–98, 240
Mugenhofer, Anna, 97
Mugenhofer, Christa, 97
Mugenhofer, Magdalena, 75, 97
Mulino, Johann (Stromius), 221
Multz, Gaspar, 218
Murascha (dance), 103–4
murder, 81, 155–56, 178–79, 201–2, 211
Mürr, Helena Pfinzing, 26, 39
Mürr, Johann Hieronymus, 26, 41–42
Musculus, Andreas, 198–99, 204, 215
music, 7, 44, 48, 61, 80, 143, 158

name days, 90
names, 230, 256–57
Nassau, William of, *see* William of Nassau, Prince of Orange
Naumburg, Protestant council at (1561), 232–34
Nentwich, Caspar, 245
Netherlands, 11, 192, 195–98, 201–7
  religious practices in, 197–98, 201–2, 205–6, 215–16
  religious struggle in, xvi, 126, 192, 195–97, 204–6

Neudörfer, Johannes, 56, 101, 102, 106, 129, 221
Neudörfer, Magdalena, 121
Neusesser, Georg, 101, 102, 104, 106–8, 111–12, 122, 124, 130
Neusesser, Georg, Jr., 111–12, 122
New Testament, translations of, 157
New Year's holiday, 26, 63, 87, 106–7, 110, 117, 122–24, 211, 250
Ninety-five Theses (Luther), 57–58, 83–84
nobility, 49, 80, 93–94, 111
nuns, 61, 63–64, 75–76, 83, 87, 106–7, 117, 200
Nürnberg, xii–xiv, xviii–xix, 3–6, 23, 81, 120, 201, 216
  Catholic-Protestant relations in, 9–10, 56–60, 62, 75–76, 82–85, 125–27, 136, 199–200, 202
  charitable institutions in, 34, 46, 128, 149, 156, 199–200, 220
  crime in, xiv, 211
  ecclesiastical establishment in, 230–35, 240–41, 244, 251–54
  government of, 15, 39, 40, 56–57, 60, 74, 85, 191, 194, 209–10, 252–54, 267
  Humanist culture in, xiii–xiv, 56, 59, 60, 62, 67, 136, 221
  imperial visits to, xiii, 9–10, 64, 244
  in intra-Protestant disputes, 234, 241, 244, 251–54
  Jews in, 53
  marriage in, 14–15, 42–46, 60–62
  mercantile establishment in, xiv, 3–4, 54, 135–36, 138, 149, 160–61, 194, 205, 220, 255–56
  plague in, 99–101, 154
  "Protestantized" institutions of, 78–79, 82–83, 199–200
  sexual mores in, 14–15, 24, 45–46, 207–8
nursing, 87–89, 105, 109, 115
Nützel, Caspar, 61, 75

oaths, see vows
Obernitz, Hans von, 62
Oelsnitz, school at, 227–28, 231
Oertel, Sigmund, 209
omens, belief in, 211–12, 238–39
Orange, Prince of, see William of
    Nassau, Prince of Orange
ordination, 65
organs, 10, 143
original sin, 202–3, 219–20, 251–53
Otto, David, 167
Ottoman Empire, 107–8

Pacification of Ghent (1576), 195, 196
Padua, 141–88, 201, 212, 230
    cost of living in, 141–45, 157–60,
        165, 167, 170, 174, 181
    crime in, 150–56, 179
    plague in, 161–73, 179
Padua, University of, 64, 136, 139,
    171, 195, 215
palm readers, 124
Pandect (law text), 172–73
Paneltier (fabled animal), 54–55
papal bulls, xiii, 62, 157–58
papal states, 157–58, 162
paper, xiii
parenting, xv–xvi, 260–68
    see also fatherhood; motherhood
Paumgartner, Hieronymus, 230, 251
Paumgartner, Rosina, 6–7, 25
Perger, Mathias, 100
Perrenot, Antoine, 126, 195
Perrenot, Nicolas, 126
Peter (barber-surgeon), 122
Petreius, Johann, 220–22, 230
Petz, Father, 125
Pfanmüsin, Felicitas, 128, 130
Pfinzing, Anna Maria, xv, 13–52
    dowry of, 13, 35, 42
    formal engagement of, 24, 33,
        38–39, 42–44
    guardians of, 23, 25, 41–42, 47–48
    health of, 39–40
    in marriage negotiations, 29, 33–35,
        38–39

portrait of, 19–20, 28–29
secret engagement of, 14–15, 16, 18,
    21–25, 43, 46
wedding of, 42–52
Pfinzing, Georg, 13, 25, 38, 47–48
Pfinzing, Helena, see Mürr, Helena
    Pfinzing
Pfinzing, Katharina, see Imhof,
    Katharina Pfinzing
Pfinzing, Martin, 48
Pfinzing, Melchior, 13
Pfinzing, Paul, 13, 20–21, 29, 37, 41,
    49
Pfinzing, Sabina Lindner, 13, 23–24,
    26–29, 33–35, 38–42
Pfinzing, Seifried, 91, 102
Pfister, Albrecht, 256
Philip, Landgrave of Hesse, 126, 195
Philip II, King of Spain, 126, 196, 205
Philippists, 233–35, 241, 252–53, 259
    see also Reformation
physicians, 5, 165–69, 187, 190,
    211–13, 224, 231, 259
Piccart, Michael, 50–51
Piccolomini, Enea Silvio, xiii
piety, 18–19, 27–29, 77–78, 90–92,
    106, 108, 115, 125–26, 203–5,
    214–16, 258–59, 261–62
    rewards of, 19, 21, 28, 35–36,
        71–72, 97–98, 102–3
    spectacles of, 197–98, 200–202
    survivors', 167–68
pilgrimages, 19, 65, 71–72
Pilgrim Hospice, Nürnberg, 200, 210
Pillenreut, cloister at, 91, 99, 103, 106,
    107, 120, 122
Pirckheimer, Charitas, 67, 75, 90,
    136
Pirckheimer, Katharina, 117
Pirckheimer, Wilibald, xiii, 59, 60, 62,
    67, 136
Pistoris, Simon, 81, 103
plague, 8, 93, 99–101, 154, 160–73,
    179, 197, 213, 224, 226, 238
plays, 209–10
poetry, 227

police, 59
poorhouse, Nürnberg, 220
portraits, 19–20, 28–29, 67–68, *68,*
    116, 121, 126, *218*
poverty, 33–34, 35, 186–87
pragmatism, 58–59, 125–27, 204–5,
    260–62
Prague, 8, 191
prayer, 48, 77–78, 90, 97, 100, 106,
    114, 156
    private, 19, 31, 72, 98, 102, 103,
    115, 199, 204, 213, 215
prayer books, 198–99, 204, 206, 215
Prayers From the Old Orthodox Doctors,
    the Hymns and Songs of the Church,
    and the Psalms of David
    (Musculus), 198–99, 204, 215
predestination, doctrine of, 253
pregnancy, xv–xvi, 45, 70–74, 94–95,
    208, 217, 235–36, 264
Pretorius, Johann, 196–97
primogeniture, 77, 139
printing, xiii
private life, xi–xii, xv, 60, 127–28,
    207–8, 210–11
    spirituality in, 19, 57, 84–85,
    198–99, 203–5, 214–16, 258–59,
    261–62
processions, 79–80, 197–98
propaganda, 67, 82, 244
prostitutes, 208–9, 264
Protestants, *see* Reformation
Protestants, Reformed, 252, 253
    see also Calvinism
"Protestant Scholasticism," 219–20
Protestant Union, 9
Pühler, Christoph, 122
Puritanism, 259

quarantine, 163–64, 238

Rabelais, François, 208
Rachel (biblical), 91, 94
Rasch (linen), 142, 144
Rathaus, Cologne, 201–2
Rathaus, Nürnberg, 44, 61, 267

real presence, doctrine of, 220,
    232–35, 252
Reformation, xiii–xiv, 44, 56–60, 62,
    75–76, 83–85, 125–27, 194–207
    educational efforts of, 60, 194, 199,
    221–22, 251
    factions within, 219–20, 232–35,
    241, 244, 251–54
    geopolitics of, xvi, 8–10, 83–84,
    195–98, 202, 204, 233–35,
    251–54
    inner life in, 57–58, 84–85, 214–16,
    258–59, 261–62
    practices altered by, 78–79, 82–83,
    199–200, 253
    propaganda of, 67
Regensburg, 84, 136
    imperial diets at, 37, 77, 87, 251
Reh, Caspar, 147
relics, xii, 30–31, 58, 91–92, 201–2
remarriage, xv, 6–7, 191, 194, 217,
    220, 222, 226, 241–42
Resch, Hieronymus, 227–28
Reuchlin, Johannes, xiii
Richter, David, 143
Rindfleisch, Daniel, 204–5, 213
Roman law, 65, 66, 136
Rome, 64–65, 160, 182–84, 186–87,
    190
Römer, Magdalena, *see* Behaim,
    Magdalena Römer
Rosdorfer, Caspar, 128, 129
Rosenbad (public bath), Nürnberg, 53
Rösslin, Eucharius, 71, 76
Rotenhan, Georg von, 111–12
Rotenhan, Hans von, 111
Rotenhan, Mathias von, 121
Rotenhan, Sebastian von, 111
Rudolf II, Holy Roman Emperor, 8–10,
    136, 251
Rügel, Elisabeth, 232

Sabbath, 203
Sachs, Hans, xiii, 210
sacraments, 78–79, 82–83, 253–54
    see also baptism; Eucharist; marriage

safe conduct, 121
Saint Anthony's fire, 109, 257
Saint Clara's Cloister, Nürnberg, 63, 67, 75–76, 83, 89–90, 97, 100, 117, 125–26
Saint Georg's Day, 90
Saint Giles's Church, Nürnberg, xvii, 104, 194, 199, 211, 217, 241, 245
Saint Katharina's Cloister, Nürnberg, 61, 83, 199–200
Saint Lorenz's Church, Nürnberg, 20, 45, 48, 64, 66, 230, 245
Saint Martin's Day, 94, 113
Saint Sebald's Church, Nürnberg, 45, 94, 96
salaries, 5, 41, 67, 87, 112, 118, 148, 230, 235–37, 241
salt, 78, 79
salvation, Protestant views on, 202–3, 233, 251–54
Salzburg, 221
Samson, 108, 117–18
Samuel, Book of, 72
Saragossa, 135
satire, 59, 62
Saxony, 66–69, 82–84, 195, 232–35, 253–54
sayings, xii, 64, 261
Schaffhausen, 76–77
Schedel, Hartmann, xiii
Scheurl, Albrecht, 56, 63, 80–81, 117, 125, 127
Scheurl, Albrecht, Jr., 86, 99, 100, 102, 104–6, 111, 121, 124–25, 129
Scheurl, Anna (of Dilligen), 93, 100–101, 104, 108, 129
Scheurl, Anna (wife of Albrecht Scheurl), 80–81, 84, 100, 107, 121, 122–24, 129–30
Scheurl, Christoph, I, 55, 63–66, 101, 109, 127
Scheurl, Christoph, II, xiv, xv–xvi, 53–131, 200, 220, 249
  astrologers consulted by, 69, 92, 94, 108, 110, 114
birthday journal of, 98–99, 103–5, 115, 118–21
Catholic patrons of, 62, 81–84, 126
charity of, 90, 93, 97, 100, 103, 107, 114, 128
as city counsel, 56, 59–60, 69–70, 100
diplomatic missions of, 69–70, 77, 84, 87, 100–101
on discipline, 105–6, 117, 127
education of, 63–67, 111
Lutheran patrons of, 62, 66–67, 84, 126–27
marriage of, 55, 59, 60–62, 70, 92, 125
marriages promoted by, 113–14, 128
portraits of, 67–68, *68, 116*
professorship held by, 67–69
relatives raised by, 80–81, 93–94, 104, 111–12, 124–25, 128
religious convictions of, 56–60, 63, 79, 84–85, 92, 97–98, 102–3, 111, 115, 125–26, 198, 259
social mixing enjoyed by, 93–94, 107, 113–14, 128–30
at sons' birth, 53, 74–77, 95, 107
sons' recollections of, 126–28
will of, 104, 129
writings of, 66–67, 102–3
Scheurl, Christoph, III, 106–31
father recalled by, 126–27
health of, 109–10, 115, 119, 124
portrait of, *116*
temper of, 109–10
Scheurl, Eberhart, 99
Scheurl, Georg, 72–131
baptism of, 77–85, 86, 87, 96, 106
birth of, 53, 55, 70, 72–77, 87, 95
companions of, 93–94, 111, 119–22
gifts for, 90–91, 101–3, 108
growth of, 93, 98–99, 101–6, 114–15, 118–22
health of, 91, 98–100, 103–4
horses loved by, 99, 101, 104, 105, 114–15, 121, 130

346 INDEX

Scheurl, Georg (cont.)
  language skills of, 98, 101, 104, 105, 109, 114, 115, 118
  portrait of, 116, 121
Scheurl, Hans Christoph, 131
Scheurl, Hieronymus, 94–98, 106, 109
Scheurl, Katharina, xv, 53–55, 70–77, 86, 88–89, 91, 104, 124–25, 128, 130
  children borne by, 53, 70–77, 81, 87, 95–98, 106–8
  marriage of, 55, 59, 60–62, 70, 92, 125
  pregnancies of, 70–74, 81, 89, 94–95
  sons' love for, 105, 115, 119
  travels of, 100–101
Scheurl, Ketter, 93, 106, 108, 112
Scheurl, Lienhart, 93, 104, 108
Scheurl, Mathias, 93–94, 100–101, 104, 106, 108, 111
Schiller, Conrad, 230
Schiller, Matthias, 250
Schlick, Hieronymus, 101, 104
Schlick, Lorenz, 102, 104
Schlick, Stephan, 102, 104
Schmalkaldic League, 84
Schmidt, Caspar, 104
Schmidt, Georg, 128, 130
Schmidt, Kechela, 130
Schmidt, Michael, 118
school, xiv, 7–8, 120, 122, 171, 194, 199, 215, 227–28, 231, 251, 255, 257, 259,
schoolmasters, 5, 227–28
Schröder, Johannes, 20
Schweitzer, Thomas, 222
scribes, 249
Septemvir, see Council of Seven, Nürnberg
servants, 4, 74–77, 84, 87–91, 107, 112–14, 118, 128, 143, 149, 216, 264
sexuality, 20–22, 27–28, 86, 117–18, 137, 208, 266
premarital, 14–15, 45–46, 60, 207–9, 264
sibling relations, 6, 34, 77, 108, 117, 127–28, 139, 174–76, 226, 263, 265–66
Siebenbürgen Protestants, 235–36
Siena, 145, 160, 164
Sitzinger, Helena, 30
Sitzinger, Lucas, Jr., 6
Sitzinger, Maria, see Löffelholz, Maria Sitzinger
Sitzinger, Ursula, 3, 6–7
Small Catechism (Luther), 253
smallpox, 109, 244
Smith, William, xiv
Soacia, Piso Guarinus, 172–73
social gatherings, xiv, 42–50, 61–62, 79–80, 85–86, 106–7, 113–14, 127–30, 207–8
Sodalitas Staupitziana, 57
soldiers, 11, 151–55, 196
solitude, 190–91
songbook, Lutheran, 158
Spain, xvi, 126, 192, 195–96, 206–7
"Spanish Fury" (1576), 196
spanking, 105–6, 127
Spengler, Juliana Tucher, 91, 117
Spengler, Lazarus, 62
Spengler, Lorenz, 220
Speyer, Imperial court at, 230, 244, 249
"spinning bees," 207–8
Spital (poorhouse), Nürnberg, 220
Staffelstein, Katharina von, 109, 113–14, 128
Starschedel, Otto von, 158–59
Staupitz, Johannes von, 57
stepparents, xv, 6–7, 34, 180–82, 194, 220–21
Stöckel, House of, 149
Stör, Johannes, 236
Strasbourg, 194–95, 215, 246–47
Strobel, Adam, 249, 255
Stromius (Johann Mulino), 221
Sturm, Johann, 194
sumptuary laws, 45, 85

Swabian League, 80
syphilis, 264

Taig, Helena, 122, 130
Taig, Melchior, Jr., 130
tailors, 121
Talmud, 157
Taucher, Andreas, 245
taxes and fees, 46
teasing, 21–23, 30, 49, 174
Tegler, Jacob, 121–21
Tehl, Engelbrecht, 122
Terence, 210
Tetzel, Jobst, 130, 140, 144–45,
    147–48, 183
Tetzel, Jobst Friedrich, 136, 140,
    144–45, 148, 157, 158
Tetzel, Johannes, 83–84
Tetzel, Ursula, 75
theater, 209–10
Thirty Years War, 10
Thuringia, 234–35
toasts, 72
Tockler, Conrad, 69
toddlers, 94, 99, 102–4, 119, 232
Torgau on the Elbe, 222–27, 232, 239
torture, 151–52, 154
trade, xiv, 3–4, 54, 135–36, 143, 194,
    205
translation, 63, 157, 173
transubstantiation, 197, 234
travel, 8, 10–12, 64–65, 69–70,
    100–101, 105, 138–40, 158–59,
    170, 179–90, 231
    cost of, xvi, 138–50, 158–61,
        183–90, 263
    cultural accommodation in, xvi, 193,
        197–98, 200–206, 210–11,
        214–16, 261–62
    dangers of, 80–81, 155–56, 211,
        213, 262–63
    hardships of, 186–87
    during plague, 8, 160–67, 213
    as rite of passage, 3, 11, 120, 121,
        135, 138, 160, 162, 182
    of women, 100–101, 136, 182

tuberculosis, 229–30
Tucher, Andreas, 130
Tucher, Anna, 128
Tucher, Anton, 61, 66, 107
Tucher, Apollonia, 63, 75, 89–91, 97,
    100
Tucher, Barbara, 63
Tucher, Daniel, 119–20
Tucher, Helena, 54–55, 66
Tucher, Juliana, see Spengler, Juliana
    Tucher
Tucher, Juliana (of Gnadenberg),
    100
Tucher, Juliana (wife of Albrecht
    Behaim), 21–22
Tucher, Lorenz, 122
Tucher, Margaretha, 75, 86, 87–90
Tucher, Martha, 91
Tucher, Sixt, 63, 64, 65, 66
Tucher, Stephen, 64
Tudor, Mary, 200
Tunis, 108
tutors, 56, 104, 118, 194–95, 232,
    237–38, 243–44, 259

ubiquity, doctrine of, 233–34
umbilical cords, xii, 92
Ungnad, Hans von, 230
Union of Brussels (1577), 195, 196
universities, 63–67, 136, 221–24, 226,
    231, 238, 251
    cost of, 139, 159
    religious politics at, 204–5, 221
Ursula (Scheurl family cook), 74–75,
    90
Ursula (Scheurl family maid), 118

venereal disease, 208, 264
Venice, 143, 157–58, 195, 201
    German institutions in, 135, 140–41,
        145, 149, 156, 160–61, 189
    plague in, 8, 161–65
Vento, Anthony, 96, 99
Verona, 162–64, 170–71, 177–79
Viatis, Bartholomäus, 6
vices, 207–10, 263–64

vows, 31, 42–43, 46, 48, 61, 94, 113,
    204–5
  private, xv, 14–15, 21–22, 264

Wagner, Sebastian, 90, 92, 110
Walpurgis Night, 95, 200
Wankel, Barthel, 222
Watt, Peter von, 129
weaning, 88, 101
wedding announcements, 50–51
weddings, 4, 14–15, 34–35, 42–49,
    61–62, 124, 176, 209, 222,
    226–27
  social mixing at, 79–80, 113–14,
    128–29
  stand-in "fathers" at, 113–14, 128, 242
Weishamer, Peter, 113–14
Welser, Hans, 194, 195, 213, 253
Welser, House of, 194, 204–5
Welser, Jacob, 138
Welser, Jakob, 194, 195
Welser, Maria Haller, 193–94, 213
Welser, Sebald, xvi, 6, 161, 177,
    192–216, 193
  fears of, 210–13
  health of, 193, 195, 212–13
  Lutheran upbringing of, 198–200,
    215–16
  religious ambivalence of, xvi, 193,
    197–98, 200–206, 210–11,
    214–16
  temptations of, 207–10
Welser, Sebastian (father of Sebald
    Welser), 193–94

Welser, Sebastian (grandfather of
    Sebald Welser), 6, 199, 200,
    204–7
Werbung, see courtship
Wester (baptismal shirt), 78–79, 85
Westerbad, see "white bath"
wet nurses, 87–89, 98–99, 109, 113,
    259
"What has she got, what can she do"
    (dance), 46
"white bath," 85–86, 96–97, 107
Widmann, Wolf, 81–82
widows, xv, xvi, 5, 25, 87, 113, 117,
    138, 194, 265–66
William of Nassau, Prince of Orange,
    195–97, 204, 206
wills and testaments, 23, 104, 129
  see also inheritance
wine, 80, 85–86, 89, 105, 114, 115,
    119, 124, 165, 263
witchcraft, 36
witch trials, 152
Wittenberg, 57–58, 65–69,
    236–41
Wittenberg, University of, 65–67,
    221–27, 229–31, 234–35,
    237–38, 243
Wolgemuth, Michael, 56
World Chronicle (Schedel), xiii

Zingel, Christoph, 121
Zinner, Katharina, 125
Zwingli, Ulrich, 232
Zwinglians, 252